Saints and Their Cults in the Atlantic World

The Carolina Lowcountry and the Atlantic World

Sponsored by the Carolina Lowcountry and Atlantic World Program of the College of Charleston

Money, Trade, and Power
Edited by Jack P. Greene, Rosemary Brana-Shute, and Randy J. Sparks

The Impact of the Haitian Revolution in the Atlantic World
Edited by David P. Geggus

London Booksellers and American Customers
James Raven

Memory and Identity
Edited by Bertrand Van Ruymbeke and Randy J. Sparks

This Remote Part of the World
Bradford J. Wood

The Final Victims
James A. McMillin

The Atlantic Economy during the Seventeenth and Eighteenth Centuries
Edited by Peter A. Coclanis

From New Babylon to Eden
Bertrand Van Ruymbeke

Saints and Their Cults in the Atlantic World
Edited by Margaret Cormack

Saints and Their Cults in the Atlantic World

Edited by Margaret Cormack

University of South Carolina Press

Published by the University of South Carolina Press
Columbia, South Carolina 29208

www.sc.edu/uscpress

23 22 21 20 19 6 5 4 3 2

Library of Congress Cataloging-in-Publication Data

Saints and their cults in the Atlantic world / edited by Margaret Cormack.
p. cm. — (The Carolina lowcountry and the Atlantic world)
Proceedings of a conference held Feb. 20–22, 2004 at the College of Charleston.
Includes bibliographical references and index.
ISBN-13: 978-1-57003-630-9 (cloth : alk. paper)
ISBN-10: 1-57003-630-6 (cloth : alk. paper)
1. Saints—Cult—Congresses. 2. North America—Religious life and customs—Congresses. 3. Central America—Religious life and customs—Congresses. 4. South America—Religious life and customs—Congresses. I. Cormack, Margaret (Margaret Jean) II. Series.
BX2333.S25 2006
235'.209—dc22

2006016886

Contents

Illustrations

Acknowledgments

First, the authors of this book would like to thank all participants in the conference on "Saints and Pilgrimage around the Atlantic," held at the College of Charleston on February 20–22, 2004. All of the research presented there stimulated interesting, energetic, and thought-provoking discussion. Next, the editor thanks all those who at various stages of the project read over, commented on, and gave advice concerning individual essays and other aspects of this book; they know who they are. In addition, we would like to thank Jane Aldrich and Jannette Finch for administrative and technological assistance, respectively. Thanks too to Flora Ward, who designed the posters and helped with mailing. All those departments and programs at the College of Charleston whose support made the conference possible, especially the Carolina Lowcountry and Atlantic World program, deserve our gratitude. We give thanks to the following institutions for permission to reproduce material from their collections: Archive of the Archdiocese of Boston, Massachusetts; Florida State Archives, Tallahassee; the National Museum of Ireland, Dublin; and the Museum of Fine Arts, Boston.

Introduction

To those unfamiliar with the history of their veneration, saints are often known only as symbols for an occupation, hobby, or problem or as exemplars of the human condition to be taken more or less seriously as role models. To devotees, however, saints are much more: they are sources of power, consolation, and hope, whose aid can be sought in any sort of difficulty or emergency. Recent works such as Robert Orsi's *Thank You, St. Jude* and Thomas Tweed's *Our Lady of the Exile* examine in detail the psychology and motivations of those who venerate saints. It was in 1971, however, that the publication of Peter Brown's article "The Rise and Function of the Holy Man in Late Antiquity" (*Journal of Roman Studies* 71) caused a revolution in the historical study of saints' cults by calling on scholars of saints to focus not on an unknowable historical or theological truth, but on the image of the saint produced by a given society, and to "analyze this image as a product of the society around the holy man" (Brown, 81; see Payne, this volume, 54).

As Brown reminds us, sanctity is a social construction, not the product of a solitary religious virtuoso; while it is often primarily associated with such individuals, objects and localities may also be essential to the larger expression of a devotion. Pilgrimage—whether to visit shrines, venerate relics, or bathe in holy waters—is but one action that reminds us that place as well as person helps to define attitudes toward sanctity. The essays in this volume were selected not only for the light they shed on the changing images of specific saints and on the societies that created those images to suit varying psychic and social needs, but also for the ways in which they illuminate the nature of the relationship between holy persons, holy objects, and holy places.

The scene for this volume is set by John Corrigan in "Saints and Pilgrims on Land and Water: French and Spanish Missionizing Strategies in Colonial North America." In this essay he examines the different approaches to religion, and to mission, of the Franciscans and Jesuits who were the major Catholic missionaries to the Americas. The results of these missionaries' work are illustrated by many of the other essays in this volume.

Several essays underline the importance to minority communities of having a saint who was a member of that community. This theme appears most explicitly in Giovanna Fiume's discussion of St. Benedict the Moor. It can also be seen in the resemblance of Our Lady of Guadalupe to an Aztec maiden (Robert Westerfelhaus), in St. Amico as a "dark man" whose ambiguous color reflected the status of his Italian devotees in the racially divided South (Rodger Payne), and in the reconfiguration of the Holy Child of Atocha from infant prince to peasant child (Juan Javier Pescador). Irish American Catholics (whose status as second-class citizens in Protestant New England in the early part of the twentieth century is often forgotten) felt that it was time for their own saint, Father Patrick Power (Patrick Hayes). Michael Pasquier describes an attempt by ecclesiastical authorities to counter such regionalism and promote Our Lady of Prompt Succor as a manifestation of the Virgin that would unite nationalistic factions in venerating a patron of all America. In this they were unsuccessful; the devotion lacked the groundswell of popular support necessary for its growth. Ironically, devotion to Patrick Power, in spite of such support, was discouraged by the authorities. One reason for the authorities' lack of enthusiasm was undoubtedly the undisciplined fervor of those who sought aid from the purported saint, which must have appeared to be running out of control. The attitudes of Protestant intellectuals toward the "superstition" and "commercialism" associated with Father Power probably rankled upwardly mobile, educated churchmen—indeed, they may have agreed with such assessments of the activity associated with the devotion.

One wonders what the Boston establishment would have thought of the activity outside the shrine at Mexico City described by Westerfelhaus. The "Catholic kitsch" he analyzes embodies precisely the sort of commercialism the Archdiocese of Boston deplored. As described by Westerfelhaus, objects physically associated with the shrine acquire some of its power ("indexicality") even though the portrayal of the saint herself ("iconicity") on these objects may vary. Contrary to the conventions of icon painting in the Orthodox Church, accurate reproduction of the precise features of Our Lady of Guadalupe is *not* required for the effective transmission of sacred power. Accurate knowledge of "the story" is not important either; few pilgrims knew it (though all said they believed in it). It is this sort of flexibility that allowed St. Amico to be adapted to the needs of various constituencies, or St. Benedict the Moor to be identified with African gods. It is doubtful whether devotees of Father Power knew much about his uneventful life. Hayes's study, like that of Westerfelhaus, emphasizes the importance of place, and of objects connected to that place, even when such belief comes in conflict with the official ecclesiastical position.

The function of religious objects as political symbols recognized by Catholics, Protestants, and others is treated by Nicholas Beasley, who discusses the way destruction of such objects served to define both religious and political affiliations in the early modern period. Beasley's essay also illustrates the tension between officially promulgated doctrine and activity of laymen.

The importance of a sacred place is, of course, a commonplace in studies of pilgrimage. Tessa Garton's essay discusses the earliest practice of Irish pilgrimage, its reflection in the art of medieval Ireland, and how that art in its turn served as a guide to pilgrims.

When a sacred place is associated with a natural phenomenon such as a spring, the stories told about it may change to reflect changing circumstances—and even changing religions. Many "holy wells" throughout Europe were once associated with indigenous gods and only later with Christian saints. Where such traditions did not already exist, they were supplied; Margaret Cormack argues that the activity of Guðmundur Arason in Iceland created such an association and allowed him to be identified with Iceland from the Middle Ages to the present. As Cormack's and Robert Scully's articles show, some of the associations of holy wells were capable of surviving the Protestant Reformation. Here experience may have helped; in premodern societies, where water came from the sky or the ground rather than from a tap, differences in the quality of water sources were evident—and important. Even if the explanation of saintly origin is rejected, the healing properties of the water may be accepted, as in the post-Reformation examples cited by Scully.

Ryan Smith's essay was chosen to conclude the volume because it puts an important question mark beside many of the assumptions that are usually made about the cult of saints. One of the topics that arises in several essays is that of pilgrimage vs. tourism; can they be distinguished, and if so, how? No one would seriously mistake the "Fountain of Youth" for a saint's shrine, nor is it billed as such—though it shares many features with the Catholic shrine of Our Lady of La Leche just across the street. What *really* distinguishes the "Catholic kitsch" objects from ordinary souvenirs? In what spirit were bits of the shrine of St. Winefride requested and delivered—as historical mementos or as treasured relics? St. Winefride's well is a case in point for the variety of ways in which a site can be interpreted. It is clear that the continuous flow of the stream has attracted visitors, the curious as well as the devout, for centuries. As this volume was in the process of compilation, the editor learned that dipping oneself in the icy waters of the well had been something of a ritual in the youth of a correspondent, on his family's annual trip from Liverpool to their summer holidays in Wales. However, other visitors are less frivolous. Even though the water no longer flows from its original source—mining activity in the early part of the century led to its diversion, and the well is now fed from the municipal water supply—the devotion to the saint it commemorates continues to the present day.

Saints and Their Cults in the Atlantic World

Saints and Pilgrims on Land and Water

French and Spanish Missionizing Strategies in Colonial North America

John Corrigan

Land and Water

Any glance at a map of the French mission enterprise in North America immediately reveals that missions in New France were located on waterways. The St. Lawrence, the Great Lakes, the Mississippi, and their many tributaries were the roads traveled by Jesuits, Seminarians, Sulpicians, and others who undertook the Christianization of Indians in New France. The Franciscan initiatives in Florida and the borderlands of the Southwest included missions located on rivers, and especially on the seacoast, but Spanish conversion of Native Americans also took place in missions located away from waterways. Franciscans established strings of missions—most noticeably across the Florida panhandle—that were joined one to the other by overland trails. Even the California missions, which were near the coast, were connected by El Camino Real, which stretched from San Diego to Sonoma. Other branches of the "King's Highway," El Camino Real de Tientra Adentro and El Camino Real de los Tejas, likewise linked the outposts in New Mexico, Texas, and greater Louisiana to the historic center of New Spain, Mexico City. In short, the French navigated water and the Spanish traveled by land, and the missionizing strategies of the French Jesuits and the Spanish Franciscans developed distinctive emphases in those respective contexts.[1]

The Historical Development of the Missions of Franciscans and Jesuits

The Franciscan order technically dates from 1209, when Francis obtained from Pope Innocent III approval for his rule of community. Stressing poverty, obedience, and penance, the order grew, splintered into various species or suborders, and made its initial reputation on its successes in preaching conversions, and in the moral reform of Europe. By 1300 it had spread to points eastward as far as the court of the Great Khan in China. The culture of missionizing—the coalesced superstructure of ideas and practices that shaped the mission activities of the friars—emerged out of a worldview that was profoundly flavored by apocalyptic.

The author of the medieval Franciscan *Catalogus sanctorum* explained, "Now in these last days when the end of the world approaches, Christ the sun has made Francis shine as a symbol of himself."[2] The medieval preacher of Crusades and Franciscan-watcher Cardinal Jacques de Vitry likewise commented in 1216 that in "the twilight of the world which is sinking towards the west," God had commissioned the friars minor to preach a renewal of primitive Christianity as a line of defense against the imminent appearance of the antichrist.[3] This outlook was common in the thirteenth century, when church authorities—even those who inhabited the splendid rooms of ecclesiastical headquarters in Rome, Paris, or other cities—viewed the world as corruption, as a dung heap, and looked forward morosely, through a lens ground by Augustinian eschatology, to the horrors of the end times. Francis was received as an agent of change, raised up from the putridity of the world to deliver the faithful and the striving into the purity of evangelical life. As the last judgment approached, Christians, through repentance and devotion to the gospel, would prepare themselves to meet the telos of history clean and worthy. Much of this thinking came to the nascent Franciscan movement by way of the twelfth-century Cistercian abbot Joachim of Fiore, whose influence was still felt in New Spain five hundred years later, in the friars' explicit references to his works and, above all, in their embrace of Joachim's claim that mendicant clergy would lead the church to an age of renewal.[4]

The means by which persons were to prepare for their resurrection was through penance. The call to penance meant, first of all, the *imitatio Christi,* the modeling of one's life on that of Jesus of Nazareth. What this meant, in practice, was in fact the *imitatio crucis,* the imitation of the suffering of Jesus, through poverty, physical ordeal, and steadfastness. Franciscan preaching was not doctrinal preaching, and inasmuch as there was a distinctively theological content of Franciscan preaching, it tended toward a generalized ethics, eschewing the lexicon of medieval Christian systematics, the hairsplitting enterprise criticized by contemporaries as an exercise in determining "how many angels could dance on the head of a pin." Theological books were not numbered among the most essential items in the field packs of missionary Franciscans. What some later religious writers called "plain language" was the meat and potatoes of the Franciscan approach, together with the premium that was placed on the penitential character of the preacher's life, for how could others be converted by a man whose life was not a living example of penitence? As St. Francis stated it in his rule: "All brothers, nevertheless, preach by their works."[5]

The Franciscan mission, shaped as it was during the period of the Crusades, developed some of its key features as a mission to the Muslims. It accordingly was imbued from the thirteenth century on with the flavor of profound risk. Friars were to live among the infidels as shining examples of devotion, righteousness, patience, and perseverance by enduring suffering, living as paupers, and embracing the shame and tribulation heaped on them by their prospective flocks. Martyrdom was, in this context, a possibility, and a welcome one for some. Martyrdom was, after all, a way out of the world, this place of corruption and decay. The imitation of Christ might lead Franciscans to die for their faith, but such an outcome meant heaven for them. The upshot of this was that the Franciscan approach to missionizing rested on the notion of example rather than on doctrinal argumentation. Franciscans, to put it simply, sought to convert the "outer person" into a habit of virtue, believing that the reformation of the "inner person" would follow. In the short time before the end of the world, this meant taking chances to convert the heathens. The reward for such speculation with one's life might be martyrdom.

The twist in the Franciscan approach, its ambiguity, was the same mixture of perspectives that were found in many groups that predicted the imminent end to the world in medieval and early modern Europe—and still in some cases today. The Franciscans looked forward to, that is, anticipated, the end of a compromised world at the same time that they invested themselves hopefully in an attempt to reform that world. Indeed, the collective effort of the Franciscans is, in the long view, testimony to their trust in the *reformability* of the world, a lived statement of belief in the possibility of bringing in a millennium characterized not by the bloody housecleaning of a vengeful God, but rather by a cosmic act of approval that would crown the project of evangelization in wondrous fashion. Martyrdom remained a possibility in this scheme of things, but less so as the fervency for escape from the world was replaced by exultation in the astonishing effects of the hand of God waved over the earthly landscape of sin. This sense of history lay side by side with the apocalyptic (more specifically, millenarian) orientation of the order. Depending on the circumstances, one or the other might become prominent.

If the Franciscan approach pulled together, albeit tensively, competing notions of history in its ongoing definition of its mission, the Jesuits, the other order well represented in North American colonial missions, had their own complicated matrix of ideas and practices. Knowing the earliest history of the order is crucial to an understanding of the Jesuit mission enterprise. The order arose from the spiritual meditations of a Basque soldier, Ignatius of Loyola, who, while recuperating from a wound suffered in battle, experienced a period of intense religiosity. His reflections on that, which he put down on paper as the *Spiritual Exercises,* were largely focused on the conversion of the heart to God. They took the thinking and feeling self, which might again in keeping with the *Exercises* be referred to as the "inner person," as the proper site for religious renewal or conversion. With the *Exercises* as the blueprint for a heightened spirituality, groups of men in the

1530s began to pursue their renewal through prayer and meditation. Tellingly, this nascent program of devotion unfolded in the context of a retreat. Men removed themselves from the affairs of everyday life in the world to a territory characterized by psychological work, by inward-looking mental exercise. The regimen as set forth in the *Exercises* stressed examination of conscience and meditation on, for example, one's sins, on humility, on prayer, on love, and on a wide-ranging catalog of the "mysteries of our Lord." Centuries later the Jesuits are still known by many for their "retreat houses," hundreds of which around the world are available to persons interested in engaging in spiritual exercise.[6]

The Jesuits, like the Franciscans, expanded after the mid–sixteenth century and took a particular interest in missionary work, which together with their focus on education came to define them as an order. It is no accident that those two enterprises—missionizing and education—are the most visible components of Jesuit missions. The two have been linked in Jesuit self-understanding almost from the beginning. Doctrine was of fundamental importance to the Jesuits, and education was the means by which doctrine was taught; or, put another way, with respect to the linkage of education to missionizing, education was the means by which men were taught to preach doctrine. The goal of conversion of persons to Christianity accordingly emerged in Jesuit practice largely as a matter of reaching the "minds and hearts"[7] of prospective converts. Jesuits set out to instruct persons in the foundations of Christian theology, to teach reflexivity and meditation (on the general model of the *Spiritual Exercises*), and to draw converts into a mood of patient trust in the formal means of the church to foster spiritual development. In a nutshell, Jesuits sought to persuade their subjects to think and feel as Christians —as Jesuit Christians, that is—and by degrees to engage the full apparatus of ritual deployed by the church for the salvation of sinners. That meant, of course, that language mattered enormously. For that reason, Jesuits immersed themselves with extraordinary energy into the construction of grammars, dictionaries, and teaching texts of languages throughout the world. If one's purpose were to convert by teaching theology, one would need the language to do so. It should not surprise then that the first dictionaries and grammars (for Europeans) of languages spoken by peoples in India, China, and the Americas were of Jesuit provenance.

The Jesuit focus on the "hearts and minds" of potential converts was reinforced by a pattern of diminished disinterest—vis-à-vis the Franciscans—in modeling behavior as a strategy for the conversion of those who observed it. In its earliest days the order had rejected the usual monastic pattern of penance and fasts, so that such practice, which was fundamental to the species of *imitatio Christi* practiced by the Franciscans, consequently was less important in Jesuit missionizing. As a result, in the mission field there was not an emphasis on drawing subjects into mimicry of the virtues modeled by missionaries specifically as a way of opening them up to a broader world of spiritual renewal.

Jesuit interest in the soul did not lead the order to discount the importance of community, however. The Society of Jesus, founded by a military man, was deeply tinctured by the military sensibility. Jesuits imagined themselves engaged in battle to uphold the church (a devotion so unyielding that it led, by way of the usual labyrinth of European aristocratic politics, to the suppression of the Jesuits as a religious order in the late eighteenth and early nineteenth centuries). That military sensibility was visible especially in the Jesuit conceptualization of community. Military communities, as Ignatius knew, are among the most closely knit and clearly ordered kinds of social organization. The type of communities Jesuits built in mission fields, and especially in North America, were rather different from those favored by Franciscans, to whom we will return shortly. It is important to keep in mind that Jesuits had their feet on the ground, as it were, and that they understood the importance of forming religious communities both among themselves and among those they converted. However, circumstances in the mission field always dictate the terms of engagement.

French and Spanish Missions in North America

Spain sent a force of five hundred soldiers to Mexico in 1518, reduced the Aztec empire by 1521, and by the 1560s had begun planting missions along what is today the Atlantic coast of Georgia and Florida. Franciscans began arriving in New Spain in the early 1520s, and from the beginning they did the heavy lifting in terms of the construction of the mission system, although Jesuits who accompanied the Spanish later in the sixteenth century made some contributions as well (notably in Baja California). The *Laws of the Indies,* particularly in the form given them by the Spanish monarchy in 1542, set forth the plans for these mission settlements inasmuch as they made clear the priority of establishing labor forces of Indian citizens in places where that labor (as a form of the tribute that was required by the *Laws*) could be expected to support the colony and enrich the state.[8] Church and state were to rule together—the church sharing the plaza with the offices of the civil authority in the larger missions—and trade with more distant tribes was to be encouraged with a view to expansion of the mission settlements in the direction of exploitable native populations. In all of this the Native Americans were to be converted to Christianity as well.

In Florida the initial settlements naturally were on the coast. St. Augustine (founded in 1565), which was a large settlement and included an impressive fort and port, served as a model for later coastal missions. However, relatively early in the Spanish exploration of Florida the soldiers and friars began to move inland. Less than fifty years after the founding of St. Augustine, they had established a string of missions across the north of Florida, in a more or less east-west line stretching eventually all the way to present-day Alabama. Archaeological evidence indicates that the Spanish favored bluffs—areas with elevations of one hundred to two hundred feet above sea level—as sites for missions. It appears also that they had relatively little interest in linking their missions by waterway, one to the other. In fact, what is striking about the north Florida missions—and over sixty of them were established after all was said and done—is that for the most part they were not connected to each other, or to the sea, by water.[9] They were truly inland settlements, built to sustain themselves—on the backs of Indian laborers, to be sure—as largely independent settlements. They were of course dependent on the supply caravans that came every two or three years, bringing them ritual artifacts, art, metal goods, ammunition, replacement soldiers and clergy, and other such things as were necessary for the defense of the missions and the administration of the sacraments. (Resistance to English encroachment was more important than response to Indian uprisings, and in fact, the north Florida missions came to an end in the early 1700s as a result of armed incursions by the English from Georgia.) Clergy and colonists kept in touch with nearby missions, but missions were designed largely to stand on their own feet and advance their projects under their own power.

In these missions, set deep in the mainland of Florida, the friars set about their work of converting the Indians. The missions mimicked, as much as possible, the way of life of Spaniards in Iberia. The Franciscans learned native tongues, but they did so with the expectation that this would hasten their teaching of Spanish to the Indians. The Spanish ruler Philip II had forbidden the translation of sacred texts into native languages, and the implied lesson—that theology did not translate well—was not lost on the friars. However, none of this crossed the purposes of the friars. The observation of Francis that "all brothers preach by their works" translated easily enough into missionizing native Floridians. Through example, through their tribulation and perseverance, their visible willingness to imitate the sufferings of Jesus, friars believed that they would reach a population with whom they shared few words and certainly no order of linguistic understanding capable of conveying complex theological ideas from one party to another.[10]

Crucial to this enterprise was the creation, in the mission, of a semblance of Spanish Catholic culture. Franciscans to a certain extent accepted Indian ways of life, but the mission ideally was to mirror as much as possible the order and habits and rhythms of life in a small Spanish town. People were to dress modestly. Inferiors and superiors were to engage in a dance of, respectively, deference and patronal sympathy for each other. Food was to be prepared along the lines of Spanish cuisine. Marriages and funerals and other ritual markings of the life cycle were to be decorated in Spanish custom. The settled life of agriculture was to be the backbone of the community. The Spanish language was privileged. A mission was a "little Spain," and the mission compound was built with an eye to the future—that is, it was built large and strong, and with some foresight concerning population increase and the enlargement of the industries carried on there. A rich material culture was reflected in the conglomeration of residences, a house of worship, government buildings, artisans' workshops, recreational areas, kitchens, a plaza, fortified walls and gates, educational resources, gardens, and rooms for the sick. The friars set up facilities for tailoring, shoe making, carpentry, and metal-working, among other activities. It may have been an outpost of Spanish culture, a distant mirror of Iberian life, but the mission was at the same time thought to be a plantation that one day would represent in full color the efflorescence of a triumphant global Christian culture of Spanish inflection.

The mission, then, was a place where friars expected, first of all, to draw the natives into the practice of Spanish-ness, to "civilize" them, to reform the "outer person" by acculturating that person to the Spanish way of life, religious culture and all. The crown's plan for the mission system—as a place to gather labor for focused, wealth-producing projects—set the friars up in an environment that elicited from Franciscan ideology a strong emphasis on the strand that stressed activity in the world as the core of the religious life, and that made example (the example of the friar) the central component in the friars' strategy of missionizing.[11]

As Franciscan activity in New Spain coalesced in this way, the eschatological perspective that framed it lost much of its apocalyptic flavor. The friars in New Spain reflected less on the imminent end of the world than on the future of a Christian North America. They remained strongly millennial; however, the form of millennialism that they embraced was not born of despair for the world as a corrupted site for human life, but rather sprang from their sense of the possibilities for bringing about in the New World the glorious culmination to Christian history. There was of course a background of fabulist historicizing of the Americas: Christopher Columbus's belief, sailing off the coast of South America, that he had discovered the edge of the Garden of Eden; rumors of the Fountain of Youth in Florida and elsewhere; El Dorado, the city of gold, which enticed explorers into the wildernesses of the Americas; the Seven Cities of Cibola; and other wonders, reports of which were recounted by the shipwrecked and miraculously rescued Spanish hero Cabeza de Vaca. These stories must have nurtured, in some measure, the hopes of friars that the New World was indeed to be a place of miracles.

In addition, as the friars looked over their successes in New Spain, they could not help but declare themselves hopeful that they were a sign of the coming millennial Christian era. There was a tone of hopeful expectancy in the writing of

Fray Alonso de Benavides when he commented on the piety of the mission Indians ("How Well They Take to Christian Practices") in 1630:

> Hardly do they hear the bell calling to mass before they hasten to the church with all the cleanliness and neatness they can. Before mass, they pray together as a group, with all devotion, the entire Christian doctrine in their own tongue. They attend mass and hear the sermon with great reverence. They are very scrupulous not to miss, on Saturdays, the mass of Our Lady, whom they venerate highly. . . . The boys and girls repair to catechism every morning and afternoon and are very careful not to be absent. The chanters, who take alternate weeks in the chapels, sing in the church every day at the hour of Prime, High Mass, and Vespers, and they are very punctual.[12]

If only the friars in Iberia could have said as much about their congregations, the worry about an awful coming judgment would have been much less. The friars' investment in the mission system, the pattern of conversion that required behavioral modification within the framework of a "little Spain," and the successes of that approach—especially, later, in California—were strands of the Franciscan experience that were interwoven in a worldview that shifted the apocalyptic eschatology of the order into a millennial vision of triumphant Christianity. The inland mission, built with an eye to a long future and decorated with as much material culture of Spanish life as the backs of mules could bear and the minds of the friars could imagine, materially grounded a hopeful view of the evangelical project—at least for as long as the English and the French would allow it.

The Jesuit undertakings in New France differed significantly from the pattern established by the Franciscans in New Spain. Jesuit missions, situated largely on waterways, likewise materially framed the practice of missionaries in ways that affected their style of missionizing. The French never had an equivalent of the tripartite Spanish goal of "God, Glory, and Gold" in their colonization of North America. New France evolved as a fur-trading enterprise, the French aristocracy of the time having developed a seemingly boundless affection for felt (especially in wide-brimmed hats), which could be made from the underbelly fur of the beaver, and, less surprisingly, for the beaver castoreum that served the perfuming industry in France well as a bearer of musk scent. From a base point—such places were established on rivers and lake shores throughout New France—individual traders would set out to visit the villages of Indians who wished to trade beaver pelts. They conducted business, in a particular region, until they had loaded their boats—for some, large canoes—with the cargos that they, with other traders, would then take to a place of brokerage where the goods would be bartered or sold for shipment to France. A celebration would ensue and last, by some accounts, throughout the winter, until the rivers unfroze and water traffic was once again possible. There was little interest in rounding up Indians to serve as a labor force for the production of other commodities—little interest, that is, compared to the priorities of the Spanish colonial order, by which missions built with a view to permanency were founded in the image of Spanish towns. In most of New France, what infrastructure there was—and there was not much—was in the form of waterway depots and simple shelters, where the population fluctuated widely depending on the season, where the military might garrison troops in between responding to Indian uprisings, and where the patterns of everyday life bore little resemblance to the way persons lived in France. Eventually, French traditions took root in Quebec and Montreal, but in most ways these settlements were exceptions to the pattern of French colonial life in the regions of the upper St. Lawrence, the Great Lakes and Mississippi, and the enormous territory of Louisiana.[13]

Missionaries came on the heels of the fur traders. From the start they labored diligently to keep French traders at a distance from the Indians they sought to convert, for it was generally agreed that the traders would bring sinful habits to the natives and make their conversion more difficult or even impossible. This meant not only that the missionaries discouraged contact with traders who visited Indian villages, but also that they sought, even more vigorously, to keep Indians from visiting the trading camps. This proved particularly hard in view of the fact that missionaries often found themselves posted at trading camps, and these camps became de facto missions. In addition, when missions were built, they had more the appearance of temporary stations than permanent investments in the region. Of course, as the history of Quebec and Montreal shows, it was impossible to separate the traders from the missionaries and their catechumens, so that when the flimsy upriver missions were built, those missions naturally attracted traders as mostly unwanted guests. In short, missions on waterways posed certain challenges to Jesuit missionizing, and Jesuits responded with a strategy that moved the pursuit of converts in another direction.

The problems posed by the siting and uses of missions brought an emphasis on the "inner person" to the forefront of Jesuits' thinking about their mission in the New World. Jesuits in Europe formed strong, close-knit communities—particularly in academic settings but not exclusively so—that were grounded in communal ideals embedded in the "military" side of Ignatius of Loyola's vision of the religious life. The several dozen successful *reducciones* in Brazil and Paraguay and the Baja California missions are examples of Jesuit pursuit of communities of the converted created from scratch in the New World. Some of the South American reductions, in fact, were miniature industrial states (with populations as high as twenty thousand persons) where the inhabitants produced not only handicrafts for local use but also sophisticated commodities such as watches and musical instruments. The Baja California missions likewise did not differ in significant ways from the Franciscan Alta California missions established in the second half of the eighteenth century. However, in New France the case was different. Jesuits responded to the colonial circumstances and settings there by deemphasizing ideas about the need for behavioral modification as a part of the conversion process and instead stressing inner renewal through an appeal to the "hearts and minds" of the natives. The missions, interestingly, came to function as "retreats" for the Jesuit missionaries—places where they could go to recuperate from their experiences in the field. Sainte-Marie, in fact, founded by French Jesuits in 1639 in Huron country, was planned as a retreat for itinerant missionaries.[14]

Unlike the Franciscans in New Spain, the Jesuits did not hope to convert Indians by acculturating them to a European way of life. Instead, they chose to learn the Indian way of life, from the language to dietary customs and habits of work. Jean de Brébeuf, author of a set of guidelines for the work of the Jesuits in New France, urged missionaries to come to terms with the native cultures and to mimic Indian lives, at least in certain ways. He wrote, "If you go naked and carry the load of a horse upon your back, as they do, then you would be wise according to their doctrine, and would be recognized as a great man, otherwise not."[15] The Jesuit plan also had the advantage of hindsight, in this case a view of the failures of the Recollet missionaries who preceded them, briefly, in the St. Lawrence. The French Recollets, or Recollect Franciscans, who arrived in Quebec in 1615 believed that only after Native Americans had settled among the French and learned their language, manners, and way of life would they be in a position to grasp the religious message of Christian salvation. Jesuit efforts were in the end shaped by the same forces that urged the French generally toward cultural hybridization in New France. As the historian Tanis C. Thorne has observed, "the administrators of New France bent to Indian protocol in order to win Indian trade and military alliances. Meanwhile the citizens of New France learned skills as hunters and trappers and learned Indian languages as well. Some men lived in Indian villages for part of the trading season and took native women as wives. As a result, these Frenchmen became quite Indianized in their habits and their dress." New France was, after all, profoundly "bicultural."[16]

The enormous energy of the Jesuits in learning native languages and producing the books that would teach other missionaries those languages signals especially well the emphasis on teaching doctrine that would lead to "inner renewal." The translation of concepts such as the Christian Trinity, and grace, into the Illinois or Huron tongue was of course a project fraught with difficulties, but the Jesuits remained steadfast in their trust that through their efforts at translation they could deliver to potential converts an understandable message—one that, with divine help, would lead to the Christianization of the Indians.[17] The Jesuit missionary Paul le Jeune wrote that language was the key to "interior consciousness" and that any missionary "who knew the language perfectly, so that he could crush their reasons and promptly refute their absurdities, would be very powerful among them." Father le Mercier, taking a slightly different tack, described the project in these words: "We gather up all the words from the mouths of the savages as so many precious stones, that we may use them afterwards to display before their eyes the beauty of our holy mysteries."[18] It is a sad fact that Jesuits seemed to reach natives most effectively immediately following a war or an outbreak of disease, when the social order and political order of the tribes were fractured. In any event, the missionaries believed that once the soul had been turned to God, the behavior of the convert would represent that change, like fruit maturing on a healthy tree, and this would lead to a Christian society of a higher order than the way of life invented by the aboriginal peoples.

Saints and Pilgrims

The ways in which certain elements in Franciscan and Jesuit ideology came to the forefront of their respective strategies of missionizing, and the roles of mission location and other material factors in eliciting those developments, are historical issues that deserve more analysis, as they have been painted only in broad strokes here. As long as I am painting in broad strokes, I will remark by way of conclusion on the ways in which thinking about sainthood and pilgrimage developed in New Spain and New France within the context already sketched.

Jesuits, from the beginning, counted pilgrimage as a fundamental part of their religious life. Ignatius of Loyola included "pilgrimage to Jerusalem" as one of the crucial elements of the religious life, and his followers made that pilgrimage during times when the Holy Land was in Christian hands. In fact, in many of his writings Ignatius referred to himself as "the pilgrim."[19] It should not surprise, then, that the Jesuit missionaries in New France typically thought of themselves as pilgrims. However, their sense of what kind of pilgrimage that was—why they were there, what was supposed to happen, and how it would end up—was different from what much of the rest of the order, stationed in Europe, imagined a pilgrimage to be. Typically, the reports of pilgrims to Jerusalem described them as "coming home" to the center of Christianity. For the North American missionaries, a visit to New France was a pilgrimage, but to a strange land, to a place that was as far from the center of Christianity as one could imagine, to a place of heathen savages and barely a sign of French culture, especially on the upcountry rivers and lakes, where there was nothing to remind missionaries of their French Christian culture except for their breviaries and bibles and the few ritual artifacts —chalices, crosses, relics—that they carried in their packs. For this reason, the pilgrimage to America—much different from a pilgrimage to the Holy Land—was an ordeal of such magnitude that it carried with it a premium of spiritual advantage. That advantage was compounded by the suffering that missionaries endured at the hands of Indians—the torture and killing of missionaries recounted dramatically in the Jesuit *Relations,* the chronicles of the Jesuit exploits in New France. Against this background many missionaries achieved noteworthy status, and none more so than a cohort of clergy known as the "North American Martyrs," eight men who suffered torture and death among the Indians in New France between 1642 and 1649. The hagiographies of these eight persons—among whom are figures such as Isaac Jogues and Jean de Brébeuf—stress their bravery in entering, and in some cases reentering, a strange world, a world as different from their own as could be imagined, a world without Christianity and without European culture. Jerome Nadal, a Jesuit contemporary of Ignatius, had made the connection explicit in arguing that pilgrimage was synonymous with "journeying for ministry."[20] In sixteenth- and seventeenth-century Jesuit self-understanding, pilgrimage increasingly became constructed as a test, as the story of Father Massé, in the *Relations,* makes clear: "As it is one of the tests which our Society makes of those who wish to be enrolled in it, to send them on certain pilgrimages, asking alms, the good Enemond Massé, as well as the others, was sent out thus, with desires for the contempt and the hardships which accompany that probation."[21] The stranger the land, the harder the mission. The harder the mission, the better the pilgrimage. The better the pilgrimage, the more likely was sainthood. By remaining strangers in a strange land, Jesuits set the stage for their mission in a way to ensure that the "test" would be hard and the rewards, in spiritual terms, great. The missions upriver from Quebec and Montreal remained waterway missions, in the sense that the colonists never built them into "little Frances."

No Franciscan missionary saints were from North America. One, St. Francis Solano, was from South America. Franciscans to a certain extent embraced the idea of pilgrimage, but never to the extent that the Jesuits did. The Franciscan idea of mission, moreover, was not cast as a species of test (although it is fair to say that in early Franciscanism, the desire for martyrdom played a limited role in the coalescence of the order's mission—until the fourteenth century, when some instances of overeagerness led Franciscan theologians to skeptically view cooperation in one's own martyrdom). In addition, Franciscans tended not to assess the value of their missionary fieldwork in terms of degree of difficulty—for example, obstacles overcome or suffering endured. Their primary assessment was made on the evidence of the founding of Christian congregations, and their successes were made in planting seedlings of European civilization deep in the North American soil. The better rooted that civilization, the greater the likelihood of the survival of native communities as Christian communities. Franciscans, certainly, thought themselves in a strange land, and occasionally that realization led to uncertainties about their role as Christian clergy. However, more often they imagined the strange land as ripe with possibilities for establishing Spanish Catholic culture, in all of its rich tradition. Although there were some exceptions, they experienced the strangeness of North America as an invitation to permanently settle the native inhabitants into a Spanish way of life and its familiar Catholicism. Franciscanism in the New World accordingly tended toward the notion of mission more as an outward-focused "example" to others than as a "test" or "probation" of the individual missionary. Such was in keeping with the observation of the early Franciscan mystic David of Augsburg, who had advised that only mature friars who had already proven their virtue be licensed as missionaries.[22] In the "little Spains" of the Spanish dominions in North America, Franciscans thus labored under a rather different set of expectations for their work, and they felt less need to seek out the dramas that Jesuits did as a course to sainthood.

The story of missions in New France and New Spain, then, has rich potential for our understanding of how material conditions and religious ideologies cooperated in setting the strategies of the Franciscans and the Jesuits. This approach also affords a path to understanding how in-group notions of sainthood and pilgrimage were contextualized by those factors. The land and water of the New World were no less influences on the missionizing strategies of Jesuits and Franciscans than were the founding visions of Francis and Ignatius.

Notes

1. An interactive electronic Internet Web site that displays as maps data queries about French and Spanish missions is John Corrigan and Tracy Leavelle, with Arthur Remillard, *French and Spanish Missions in Colonial America,* California Digital Library and University of California, http://www.ecai.org/na-missions/index.html (accessed August 3, 2006).

2. Quoted in E. Randolph Daniel, *The Franciscan Concept of Mission in the High Middle Ages* (Lexington: University Press of Kentucky, 1975), 28.

3. Ibid.

4. Stephen E. Wessley, *Joachim of Fiore and Monastic Reform* (New York: Peter Lang, 1990); Marjorie Reeves, *Joachim of Fiore and the Prophetic Future: A Medieval Study in Historical Thinking,* rev. ed. (Stroud, U.K.: Sutton, 1999).

5. Francis of Assisi, *Regula Prima,* chap. 17. See the *Rule and Life of the Brothers and Sisters of the Third Order Regular of St. Francis,* commentary by Margaret Carney and Thaddeus Horgan (Washington, D.C.: Franciscan Federation, 1982); Ignatius Brady, *The Marrow of the Gospel: A Study of the Rule of Saint Francis by the Franciscans of Germany* (Chicago: Franciscan Herald Press, 1958), 212–15, 268–72. For Jacques de Vitry's similar emphasis on example, see *The Exempla or Illustrative Stories from the Sermones vulgares of Jacques de Vitry,* ed. Thomas Frederick Crane (London: D. Nutt, for the Folk-Lore Society, 1890).

6. *Ignatius of Loyola: Spiritual Exercises and Selected Works,* ed. George E. Ganss (New York: Paulist Press, 1991), 113–214. An overview of the Ignatian focus on "interiority" is in W. W. Meissner, *The Psychology of a Saint: Ignatius of Loyola* (New Haven, Conn.: Yale University Press, 1992), 279–346.

7. Paul Le Jeune cited in Reuben Gold Thwaites, ed., *The Jesuit Relations and Allied Documents: Travels and Explorations of the Jesuit Missionaries in New France 1610–1791,* 73 vols. (Cleveland: Burrows Brothers Company, 1898), 28:65. The Jesuit emphasis on "intellectual" conversion is discussed in Daniel, *Franciscan Concept of Mission,* 37–75.

8. Labor was a form of "tribute" required by the laws. See *The New Laws for the Government of the Indies and for the Preservation of the Indians, 1542–1543* (Amsterdam: N. Israel, 1968).

9. Amy Turner Bushnell, *Situado and Saban: Spain's Support System for the Presidio and Mission Provinces of Florida,* Anthropological Papers of the American Museum of Natural History (Athens: University of Georgia Press, 1994); John E. Worth, *The Struggle for the Georgia Coast: An Eighteenth-Century Retrospective on Guale and Mocama,* Anthropological Papers of the American Museum of Natural History (Athens: University of Georgia Press, 1995); Wendy M. Nettles, "A New Mission Model? A Study of Long Term Research at Six Franciscan Missions in La Florida" (M.A. thesis, Florida State University, 1996); Jerald T. Milanich, *Florida Indians and the Invasion from Europe* (Gainesville: University Press of Florida, 1995); Christopher B. Ruff and Clark Spencer Larsen, "Reconstructing Behavior in Spanish Florida: The Biomechanical Evidence," in *Bioarchaelogy of Spanish Florida: The Impact of Colonialism,* ed. Clark Spencer Larsen, 113–45 (Gainesville: University Press of Florida, 2001); Mark F. Boyd, Hale G. Smith, and John W. Griffin, *Here They Once Stood: The Tragic End of the Apalachee Missions* (Gainesville: University Press of Florida, 1999).

10. A discussion of Franciscan failure to adequately learn the native languages in New Spain is in Jim Norris, *After "the Year Eighty": The Demise of Franciscan Power in Spanish New Mexico* (Albuquerque: University of New Mexico Press in cooperation with the Academy of American Franciscan History, 2000).

11. Robert H. Jackson, *Indians, Franciscans, and Spanish Colonization: The Impact of the Mission System on California Indians* (Albuquerque: University of New Mexico Press, 1995).

12. Fray Alonso de Benavides, *A Harvest of Reluctant Souls: The Memorial of Fray Alonso de Benavides, 1630,* trans. and ed. Baker H. Morrow (Niwot: University Press of Colorado, 1996), 42–43.

13. On the fur trade, see Susan Sleeper-Smith, *Indian Women and French Men: Rethinking Cultural Encounter in the Western Great Lakes* (Amherst: University of Massachusetts Press, 2001).

14. John F. Hayes, *Wilderness Mission: The Story of Sainte-Marie-among-the-Hurons* (Toronto: Ryerson Press, 1969).

15. Quoted in Angelyn Dries, *The Missionary Movement in American Catholic History* (Maryknoll, N.Y.: Orbis, 1998), 14. Ignatius of Loyola recommended adaptation to local

cultures as part of the strategy of missionizing (John W. O'Malley, *The First Jesuits* [Cambridge, Mass.: Harvard University Press, 1993], 255).

16. Tanis C. Thorne, *The Many Hands of My Relations: French and Indians on the Lower Missouri* (Columbia: University of Missouri Press, 1996), 64–65. See also W. J. Eccles, *Canadian Society during the French Regime* (Montreal: Harvest House, 1968), 75.

17. Tracy Neal Leavelle, "Religion, Encounter, and Community in French and Indian North America" (Ph.D. diss., Arizona State University, 2001).

18. Quoted in Carole Blackburn, *Harvest of Souls: The Jesuit Missions and Colonialism in North America, 1632–1650* (Montreal: McGill-Queen's University Press, 2000), 100–104. See also John Webster Grant, *Moon of Wintertime: Missionaries and the Indians of Canada in Encounter since 1534* (Toronto: University of Toronto Press, 1984), 26–39.

19. Ignatius of Loyola, *Autobiography,* in *Ignatius of Loyola,* 82–83, 86–88.

20. On Nadal's conceptualization of ministry, see William V. Bangert, *Jerome Nadal, S.J., 1507–1580: Tracking the First Generation of Jesuits,* ed. Thomas M. McCoog (Chicago: Loyola University Press, 1992).

21. Thwaites, *Jesuit Relations and Allied Documents,* 29:38–39. A view of Jesuit notions of suffering and martyrdom in Baja California is in Andrés Pérez de Ribas, *History of the Triumphs of Our Holy Faith amongst the Most Barbarous and Fierce Peoples of the New World,* trans. Daniel T. Reff, Maureen Ahern, and Richard K. Danford (Tucson: University of Arizona Press, 1999).

22. Quoted in Daniel, *Franciscan Concept of Mission,* 39.

St. Benedict the Moor

From Sicily to the New World

GIOVANNA FIUME

Devotion in the Americas

In Rome in 1716, at the Church of Santa Maria della Minerva, the canonization of the Franciscan monk Benedict of San Fratello reached a critical stage. The long process of canonization had been set in train immediately after his death in 1589 and had already gone through the most important phases: an ordinary process in 1595, two apostolic inquiries in 1620 (respectively in San Fratello, where St. Benedict was born in 1524, and in Palermo, where he lived for a long time and died), and two further processes in 1625. The devotion that Benedict had attracted during his lifetime and after his death had induced the local authorities, the Franciscan order and high-ranking devotees, to demand that an appropriate resting place should be found for his remains. These were transferred in 1591 from the common grave of the monks of the monastery of Santa Maria di Gesù to the sacristy of the church; then in 1611, perhaps with the consent of the Sacred Congregation of Rites, they were allowed into the church itself, in a position raised from the ground beneath one of the side altars.[1] It seems reasonable to view this last transfer[2] as a consequence of the desire for the beatification of Benedict; however, this was never officially promulgated, and the ecclesiastic authorities had to sanction it with an ad hoc proclamation that was not issued until 1743.

The 1716 process had the specific purpose of verifying the existence of a cult relating to the candidate for canonization, a cult that was openly practiced in the Spanish and Portuguese colonies, especially Peru, Mexico, and Brazil. Despite Pope Urban VIII's decrees between 1628 and 1634 stipulating that veneration and prayer should be accorded only to saints who had already been canonized and threatening severe penalties against anyone—ecclesiastics or lay devotees—infringing this stipulation, images of Benedict with rays shining from his head had been painted, printed, and carved and displayed in public places *ab antiquissimo tempore* (from time immemorial). Altars and votive chapels had been built in churches in his honor, and masses were celebrated in his name; the same images and statues were being carried in processions and publicly venerated by the faithful.

Thus, Benedict was being venerated in the Americas "by the assembled mass of the people with immense pomp and devotion,"[3] with a solemn Mass and a eulogy celebrating his virtues and his miracles; in addition, the appellations "blessed" and "saint" could be seen printed in books and documents and in epitaphs on monuments in his honor, both the old and the more recent. Many confraternities, with the authorization of the bishop of the diocese and the approval of the Holy See, had been placed under Benedict's title and patronage. Those who joined these confraternities "were predominantly Moors or Negroes who regard the aforementioned Benedict with such particularly ardent devotion that it would not be easy to prohibit their veneration of him without causing great damage and outrage."[4]

This "particularly ardent devotion" of black people of African origin whom the Atlantic slave trade brought to the New World reflects the ethnicity of Benedict. He was born to an African slave couple: Cristoforo, owned by the Manasseri family; and Diana, owned by the Larcan family. Although he was the son of slaves, he was freed at the time of his birth (if the first hagiographies can be trusted), but his brothers and sisters remained slaves. However, some doubt about whether or not he was freed is cast by the appellation "Santu Scavuzzu" ("St. Slave" in Sicilian dialect), by which he was sometimes identified by his Sicilian contemporaries who were witnesses in the first processes.

The small group of fourteen witnesses in the Rome process were, with one exception, all secular and regular religious persons. They had traveled to Rome from their far-flung sees in the Americas to testify at other processes. Some of them were petitioners for the cause of Martín de Porres; others were petitioners for Nicolò di Dio, Sebastián de la Aparición, or the martyr Giovanni del Prado. The New World was conducting a feverish search for its own local saints, often because of the racial intermingling that had already to a large extent taken place. The consequences of the transportation of the African masses to Mediterranean Europe, but more especially to the Americas, forced the church to seek a new model of black and mestizo sainthood. Among those who took their places in the new canon of saints was the mulatto Francisco Solano, who died in 1610 and was beatified in 1675. Also among them was the archbishop of Lima, Toribio Alfonso de Mongrovejo, who died in 1606 and was beatified in 1679 and canonized in 1726. Juan Macías (1585–1645) and the mulatto Dominican lay-brother Martín de Porres (1579–1639), son of a black African mother and a Spanish father, and a promoter of racial equality, were not beatified until 1837. Only the Dominican nun Rose of Lima (1586–1617), whose canonization process started days after her death, achieved sainthood rapidly: she was beatified in 1668 and in 1670 was proclaimed the main patron saint of America, the Philippines, and the West Indies. Pope Clement X canonized her on April 12, 1672, calling her the "first flower of the sainthood of the New World."[5]

The process of 1716 gave rise to a sort of census of the various forms of devotion to Benedict, starting with his iconography, which was characterized by halos, rays shining from his head, and inscriptions and epitaphs with the designation of "blessed" or "saint" on the statues and portraits. His statues were even found on the main altars of certain churches next to those of St. Francis and St. James or beside the blessed Virgin and St. Rose of Lima. One wooden statue showed him in Franciscan habit and holding "a piece of cloth or flax which is part of a bloodstained garment denoting the miracle which the saint performed in his lifetime" in one hand and the infant Jesus in the other.[6]

His cult was certainly not hidden from the authorities. In Cordoba (Spain) the statue of St. Benedict preceded that of St. Francis in the procession for the feast of Corpus Christi, in order that Benedict "should walk before the great standard-bearer of Christ who is St. Francis." On entering the cathedral the procession was received by the canons and by the whole chapter, and the statues were carried in procession and placed on the high altar during the sung Mass.[7] Processions in Mexico could not take place "without the knowledge and approval of the bishop of the diocese" since their route passed in front of the royal and archiepiscopal palaces.[8] Similarly, the collection of alms in Rio de Janeiro "had to be notified to the bishop of the Diocese, since no confraternity might go around requesting alms without a licence from the same."[9] Nor could the bishops have been unaware of "the huge crowd of people" that gathered on August 2 every year at the Porziuncola in the city of Pernambuco to earn plenary indulgences while a Dominican preacher delivered a panegyric "in the presence of a huge crowd who all acclaimed St. Benedict,"[10] or of the substantial procession of black devotees that took place in Mexico City on Monday and Tuesday of Holy Week, attracting further devotees from villages in the surrounding countryside.

Drawing Near to Paradise by Way of the Road of Suffering

Why did the veneration of this saint migrate so far from its place of origin?[11] What do places such as Cagnete de las Torres in the diocese of the Andalusian Cordoba or Cadiz, Madrid, and Lisbon have in common with the transatlantic cities of Lima, Bahia of All Saints, Recife of the Brazilian state of Pernambuco, Mexico City, Los Angeles, Rio de Janeiro, or Havana? The government at the time of a single very Catholic kingdom (from 1580 to 1640), a strong evangelical campaign by the Catholic Church, and the emphasis placed on missionary work by its orders did not always, or in all places, achieve such lasting success.

The devotion to Benedict was sustained in the above-mentioned places by the confraternities of "Mauri, vel Nigri, hispanice Pardos" (Moors or Negroes—in Spanish, Pardos), which bore his title and patronage. The thirty-two-year-old Paolino de Velasco was one of the witnesses at the process, having traveled to

Rome from the distant "City of the Kings" (present-day Lima) with the Jesuit procurator of the Peruvian province. His testimony brings us at once into the context of slavery and the effects of the slave trade: "My father's name was Diego de Figueroa, born in Ethiopia, from where he was taken to Peru[,] and my mother's name was Maria de la Cage, likewise born in Ethiopia from where she was taken to Peru [in slavery]." He continued: "Your Illustrious Lordships should not be surprised that I bear a name different from those of my father and my mother, since it was prescribed in those countries that anyone born of an Ethiopian slave at the time when he was in slavery should take the name of his master, not that of his father. Thus since I was born when my father and mother were slaves and servants, my father having been bought by the lady Giovanna Francesca Figueroa and my mother by Don Pietro de Velasco in the house where I was born when she was still serving him, I bear the surname Velasco."[12] Our witness was a captain of the "Ethiopian nation" and an official of the confraternity dedicated to St. Rose of Lima, but his veneration of Benedict goes back to his childhood, when he learned to kneel at his altar and pray to him: "As a small child I used to go willingly to that church to see the image of the said servant of God, whom I liked to see because he was black like me."[13] In Lima it was the black devotees, such as our witness, who made up the confraternity, which was authorized to collect alms to celebrate the festival in honor of the saint. As we shall see, nations and confraternities were two separate entities in colonial America—the one based on ethnic origin and the other on devotion, even if the confraternity in question welcomed only black devotees.

Juan Fernández y Zagudo, a sixty-year-old observer of the strict Franciscan rule, had come from Mexico to plead the cause of another servant of God. In his testimony to the process, he was to say: "There has never been any other formally professed black Ethiopian saint in my order . . . and the black Ethiopians glorify the Holy King (one of the three Magi) and St Benedict of Palermo, a black Ethiopian."[14] He accused the mulattoes of having no saint. Sainthood had thus become a racial emblem: a means of questioning the social hierarchy of the various ethnic groupings in Hispano-American society, where social stratification expressed itself in the language of the racial conflict between mestizos (born of part-European, racially mixed couples, usually Spanish and Amerindians), mulattoes (the offspring of black Africans and Amerindians), and *zambaigos* (the offspring of Europeans and black Africans). The witnesses revealed in Rome that the black saint had been unlawfully placed on altars in Latin American churches and that they could be obliged to remove them; they, the witnesses, were trying every possible means of persuasion to produce a rationale—the particular devotion that the saint inspired in the African slaves—to ward off this danger.

Our Franciscan witness adds: "They venerate this Saint [Benedict] so ardently that if this veneration were to be forbidden or repressed, this would cause widespread outrage and would arouse doubts about the other saints. The harm done [by removing his image from the altars] would outweigh the great goodness done by so many men who have preached and established the Catholic faith."[15] Then—fearing that he had not made himself sufficiently clear "concerning the uproar which would ensue among the peoples of the Americas"—he asked to be allowed, for the sake of the truth, to testify once more. This time, wanting to be more persuasive, he asked some crucial questions in an explicit manner: "They know all about Benedict's life, his saintliness, his miracles; if he is removed from the altars, what are they going to think about all the other saints and candidates for sainthood who have far less worthy claims than he has? What is more, the English and Dutch heretics who live in the neighbouring islands and carry out trade with the mainland and call all Catholics Papists, criticising them because they believe in Papal infallibility and in the canonizing of saints, are capable of corrupting more people than Luther corrupted in the whole of Catholic Europe." Furthermore, he said, the black believers who experienced "the suppression of their veneration of their compatriot would certainly become so confused and feel such a sense of shame that they could well fall into despair and lose their faith in the goodness of God." According to the Franciscan witness, the suppression of the veneration of Benedict

> would cause great damage to the encouragement of the widespread practice of Christian worship, which continues to spread among Ethiopians and mulattos: those two nations which comprise the confraternities of the Saint in question. . . . The practising of the said veneration has engendered a fair measure of respect for that race of God's servants, which has done much to mitigate the customary disdain with which they and the other two racial groupings (Indians and mulattos, most of them also slaves in that part of the world) are generally regarded. This is demonstrated by the fact that their masters treat them with more kindness and humanity; and the slaves for their part endure their harsh conditions more patiently, infused as they are with the honor which they bestow on their saint, in whose company they hope to draw near to Paradise by way of the road of suffering. . . . But any suppression of their form of devotion which in effect excluded them from Heaven, and thus condemned them to the same degree of contempt as in the past, could precipitate their grief and dismay and cause an uprising of these despairing but also bellicose people.[16]

Given that the veneration of Benedict was not suppressed after Urban VIII's decrees, any more than it was in the cases of Rose of Lima, the blessed Solano, and Sebastián de la Aparición, why should it be suppressed now when it had already taken root and was widely practiced? Father Alessio della Solitudine was to say, "The veneration of the Ethiopian Christians is at the highest level of piety because this saint is of their own nation and they therefore recognise that they too could become saints: fathers give the name Benedict to their sons, the better to inspire them to devotion."[17] If the veneration of Benedict were to be done away with, the Ethiopians would be horrified and would suppose that "the prohibition had been issued in order to bring the said Ethiopians into shame and contempt because they were black; or else they might be led to believe that no-one of the black nation could reach the rank of sainthood. . . . 'May God fashion you in the likeness of St. Benedict of Palermo,' they say in order to signify the highest concept of virtue and perfection which could be achieved." In short, these brothers in Christ would feel themselves deceived by any suppression of their devotion; at the same time, the perceived need to soften the effects of enslavement by means of the practicing of religion that inspired the masters to treat their slaves more humanely, and which in turn made the slaves endure their condition more patiently and made it easier for potentially unruly elements to be disciplined, all pointed to the advantages of recognizing Benedict as a saint. The abolition of the veneration of Benedict would be the equivalent of depriving the black congregation of any hope of reaching Paradise and of exposing them once again to disdain and contempt in their social relationships. The loss of hope could spearhead an uprising precisely because of their bellicose temperament. Thus, the exemplary image of the obedient, pious, industrious, and constantly smiling slave served to defuse this threat.

The Black Confraternities

The worship of Benedict accordingly took root thanks to the activity of the confraternities that brought slaves together; these confraternities were known by the appellations *negro* or *mulatto* in Spain and *preto* (black) in Portugal.[18] The confraternities, dedicated for the most part to the Madonna of the Rosary and to a lesser extent to St. Iphigenia, St. Antonio of Catagerona (or Noto), St. Elesbao, and St. Benedict, were among the first fruits of the evangelization of colonial America, where they assumed an importance even greater than in Europe. The veneration of the rosary, promoted especially by the Dominicans after the Battle of Lepanto (1571), gained ground in numerous groups in the Iberian Peninsula, such as the mariners of Oporto, and was considered to work miracles especially among the sailors. Miracles in the conversion of the Moors were attributed to an image of the Virgin of the Rosary that was ransomed in Algiers. The confraternity dedicated to her was originally made up of white devotees but gradually evolved into an association of black slaves, thanks to proselytizing by the

Dominicans among the slaves. The Christian rosary connected the devotee to the saint whose grace he was entreating[19] and bore a striking resemblance to the "rosary of Ifà" used in Africa as a divining instrument by African priests to interpret the messages sent by the gods to mankind:[20] this resemblance between the rosaries explains how the black believers came to adopt the rosary so readily. Similarly the confraternity as a form of organized worship was easily imposed on account of its resemblance to the existing African custom of celebrating the cult of ancestor and spirit worship, entrusting the conducting of worship to a priest, and engaging in processions with music and dancing.

Members of the confraternity in Lima would gather on Holy Thursday and parade publicly through the streets, their banner of taffeta with a small picture of the protecting saint carried by a standard-bearer with the help of two captains who bore the two side-ropes. From 1685 onward, Holy Week in the port of Vera Cruz (Mexico) was celebrated with an open procession in which the statue of St. Benedict was carried on the shoulders of black and mulatto devotees, followed by depictions of the Holy Mysteries of Christ's Passion. Furthermore:

> In Peru and in New Spain the Jesuit Fathers employ many of these black Christians in certain hamlets and households where there are sugar mills and plantations. [The homage paid to the saint consists] not only of building chapels and altars, taking part in processions, making music, celebrating Mass, ringing bells, festive lighting . . . but also in the performance of three styles of music, that is to say Spanish, Indian and Ethiopian. Thus the aforementioned Ethiopian Christians in those parts, even though they were far from their own country and could well have said what the Israelites said when they were enslaved in Babylon: "How shall we sing the Lord's song in a strange land?," nevertheless used to sing songs and make music in their own ethnic and national style with such joy that they might have been back in their native Ethiopia.[21]

The black faithful contributed to the costs of the festival by begging for alms and displaying, as in Rio de Janeiro, tablets two *palmi* (about ten inches) wide, "which by custom were carried by every one of the Christian Ethiopians of the confraternities established in honor of the saint . . . in order to request alms which would be used to maintain the devotion and the confraternity itself."[22] Confraternities of black devotees were associated in Bahia (Brazil) with the Virgin of the Rosary and in Mexico City with St. Iphigenia, while in Brazil confraternities dedicated to St. Anthony, St. Francis, or the Madonna of the Rosary, individually or together with St. Benedict, could have a racially mixed membership since "not only Ethiopian but also white Christians have come together in the confraternity for worship."[23] Expressions such as "Ethiopian nation" and "negro nation" do not accurately reflect African culture and were in fact terms used by colonizers in their attempts to create an identity for the slaves. The ethnic groups in colonial America were numerous, and this is reflected in their organization. In Minas Gerais (Brazil) at the end of the eighteenth century, there were the following "nations": Dagomé (Daomé), Tapa, Congo-Cabinda, Mozambique, Maqui, Sabará, Timbu, Cobu, Zamba, and Malé. In Rio de Janeiro in the middle of the nineteenth century, Mina, Cabinda, Congo, Angola (or Luanda), Cassanje, Benguela, and Mozambique could still be found. In the first instance they were all part of the same confraternity, "a true society of nations, . . . a mixture of different races,"[24] distinguishable solely by reason of their skin color. As a general rule, each African "nation" elected its own king and organized annual festivals (*congadas*) with songs, street processions, dancers, drummers, and drinks. We know that these festivals took place throughout the seventeenth century and more frequently in the eighteenth century in Colombia, Haiti, Martinique, Jamaica, Cuba, Venezuela, Uruguay, Argentina, Peru, and Brazil. They were supported by "Irmandades, Cabildos, Imperios and Confrarias" (Confraternities, Chapters, Empires and Brotherhoods) and can teach us something about the auxiliary organizations of the church in that large colonial area: confraternities of blacks, slaves or emancipated, assembled around their patron saint, an altar, a chapel, or other place of worship—a form of Catholicism based on the *irmandade* or confraternity rather than on the church.

The *irmandade* was "an auxiliary force which supplemented and sometimes took the place of the church" and was responsible for the building of the place of worship and the appointment of the priests.[25] Unlike the Indians in their Christian missions, the African slaves were converted to Christianity by "two means: baptism and the veneration of the saints which allowed a process of convergence and interaction with the African divinities. Their participation developed in rural chapels and in the urban confraternities."[26] This form of communal worship was an essential element in colonial religious observance, as it was in the Europe of the baroque era: a Europe characterized by the veneration of saints and by the devotional pomp of processions and festivals, which were marked by the grandiose outward and visible signs of a faith that inevitably combined the sacred and the profane. The confraternity was also entrusted with the task of solving important practical problems in the lives of its members, who were entitled by statute to receive part of the confraternity's revenues derived from dues, legacies, and alms. In addition to the celebration of the annual festival and of Mass, the confraternities would help members who were ill and above all would meet the cost of a Christian burial for deceased members; this was especially important for slaves, who would otherwise be buried without ceremony. The black confraternities that had already been founded in the sixteenth century multiplied and flourished in the eighteenth; at that time 165 were enumerated in Brazil alone (86 of them dedicated to the Madonna of the Rosary). Sixty-five of these fraternities mention the ethnic origin of their membership;[27] they shared the common surname "Angola." When confraternities had members of more than one ethnic origin, violent interracial quarrels sometimes exploded in their midst; this was testified in the regions of Minas Gerais[28] and Rio de Janeiro.

The functions carried out by the confraternities were many and varied. They served to integrate their black members into local society, representing above all an opportunity for social mobility; but in addition they created a physical and political space that gave their members a feeling of pride and identity. When the need arose, they were there as a center for cultural resistance and claims arising from racial prejudice. In this way they created and trained leaders and developed "black awareness." They offered a base of resistance in the face of the more extreme forms of slavery and sometimes a screen for illicit or subversive activities and plans for escape. They made a space for the cultural assimilation of the black community, a nucleus for self-help and support within the community. In addition, they offered a social meeting place. In Portugal the confraternities put forward petitions to find suitable buyers for the slaves and even acquired them. They lodged complaints against the agents of justice who burst into people's houses, presumably in search of stolen goods or of slaves who had run away, and who intimidated and bullied the occupants in an arbitrary fashion.[29] The attitude of the authorities toward these organizations and their gatherings for games and worship was inconsistent: some feared their autonomy and the risk that the festivals might provide occasions for uprisings; others saw them as indispensable means for preserving harmony between the social classes.

The King of the Festival

Antonio Andreoni, an Italian Jesuit who lived in Brazil from 1681 to 1716, wrote:

> One cannot deny the slaves the only consolation of their enslaved state and see them melancholy, unhappy and lacking in vigour and health. This is why their masters do not prevent them from electing their "kings of the festival," singing and dancing in a modest fashion for a few hours on a few days of the year and being cheerful until far into the night in anticipation of next day's festival in honor of the Madonna of the Rosary and of St. Benedict and the saint of the plantation chapel. These festivities cost the slaves nothing. Their master would see to the needs of the judges in as generous a fashion as possible, giving them a prize for their unstinting work.[30]

The term "judges" is explained in the *Compromisso,* the statute of the confraternity: they were the members who were charged with the task of organizing the festivities and acting as their custodians. To decline to contribute to the costs of the party, given that few of the judges had any means at their disposal, would be tantamount to stopping it from happening and would be interpreted as an insult to God and therefore cause massive problems. St. Benedict was still being celebrated together with the election of the king and the magistrates at the end of the seventeenth century, when Andreoni wrote the first volume of his book.

The election of the king provided a link between the slaves and their idealized vision of their past history and native land as an abstract concept. In many cases he was of the same ethnic origin as his fellow devotees in the confraternity (for example, the Irmandade do Rosário in the region of Minas Gerais requested the viceroy in 1767 to permit the Negroes of the "nation" of Benguela to elect a king of their own race). Many black confraternities were riven by rivalries and heated conflicts when their members came from different racial groupings. In the "empire" of St. Elesbao in Rio de Janeiro in the eighteenth century, there were seven kings of different ethnic groups,[31] which shows how complicated the ethnic inner workings of a confraternity could be.[32] The various ethnic groups could gather under the auspices of a single confraternity and remain under the authority of their own kings; each group would be distinguishable from the others during the processions, and its king would furthermore be marked out by the music being played, by his tattoos, and by the details of his clothes.

The slave masters made sure that the confraternity's funds were not the proceeds of theft and in some instances paid the confraternity dues for their own slaves. They also permitted their slaves to be absent from work if the slaves needed to fulfill the obligations imposed on them by the confraternity's lifestyle, and they lent the slaves clothes and ornamentation to enable them to cut a good figure in the processions. We should not underestimate "the prestige which joining a confraternity conferred upon its members (especially if they held responsible offices in it) and even upon the owners of the slaves in question."[33] The king had considerable authority at festival times: he could even exempt slaves from corporal punishment and yet retain the respect and regard of his community when the festivities were over. The membership records show opposite certain names the words "he was king," and a special burial place would be reserved for someone thus designated.[34] The contribution toward the festival owed by the king was often paid by his master, who thus enjoyed the prestige associated with his generous gesture. Those who held offices in the confraternity needed to have some funds available; therefore, a slave holding an office could be given additional paid work to do or might be allowed to cultivate a small plot of land. Further social subdivision was brought about by working conditions and by membership in a tradesmen's guild. Slaves and their freed black brothers, belonging to various racial groups and pursuing various occupations, formed diverse strata in the social hierarchies within the African element of the population.

Historical records show that in Lisbon, Portugal, in 1565 there was already a confraternity at the monastery of St. Dominic called the Irmandade de Nossa Senhora dos Homens Pretos (Black Men's Confraternity of Our Lady), perhaps the oldest black confraternity in Portuguese territory.[35] Its statutes provide that the holders of the offices of king, prince, count, judge, superintendent, treasurer, scribe, and administrator should be elected from among its members. The organization of black confraternities was therefore derived from the Portuguese model, as was the practice of collecting alms in the streets to an accompaniment of music and standard-bearing. The same devotional practices were widely attested in the Iberian Peninsula, including Cadiz, the diocese of Cordoba, and throughout Andalusia, another place where the black confraternities played leading roles in festivals. The archbishop Giuseppe Saporiti happened to be present at one; in 1716 he testified: "I was amazed to see St Benedict of Palermo for the first time, and it surprised and intrigued me to see a black Moorish saint, particularly considering the specific circumstances of the Moors. I noted that these Moors do not generally have long hair, but rather small bunches of hair in the style of the Moorish race."[36]

While the ethnic hairstyle struck Giuseppe Saporiti, there was an earlier emphasis on "three kinds of music." The styles of ethnic music in the processions of the black confraternities were attested as long ago as the mid–sixteenth century: "Is there any caste lower than the Negro slaves from Guinea?" an eyewitness wondered, "and yet there is no doubt that they are allowed to dance and sing, using their own musical instruments, their own songs and their own languages," while the Moorish community was not allowed to do this.[37] The typical dances of the black community, including the sarabande, the chaconne, the *guineo,* the *paracumbé,* the *ye ye,* and the *zarambeque* or *zumbé,* frequently aroused the suspicions or even the disgust of the churchmen. "Shameless dances" was what a Jesuit called them in the mid–sixteenth century, and Father Juan de Mariana reacted contemptuously, on account of its lascivious and unseemly movements, to the sarabande, which he saw being danced during the festival of Corpus Christi.[38] It seems that it was impossible to discipline the forms of worship practiced by the African slaves to the point of making them stop expressing themselves in their own typical rituals; they had imposed their own style on the form of homage that they paid to their saint.

The Congadas

There was by the sixteenth century a strong ethnic flavor in festivals organized by the black community, whose confraternities elected to honorary roles a king and a queen, who paraded richly adorned in the procession that bore the image of the saint. The *congadas* had a complicated ritual and formed a part of the festivities in honor of the black saints.[39] A Spanish Capuchin friar was present at a 1633 procession in Lisbon honoring the Madonna of Guadalupe (the Confraria da Virgem de Guadalupe e de San Benito had already been set up in the monastery of St. Francis in the first decade of the seventeenth century),[40] in which the black participants, who were dressed in accordance with their customs, were practically naked, with sashes tied around their heads, arms, and chests and colored cloths tied around their waists. They "thus adorned went off through the streets, dancing and accompanying themselves on African musical instruments as well as on viols, castanets, drums and flutes. Some of the men were carrying bows and arrows; the women had baskets on their heads containing offerings from their masters. And they entered the church of St. Francis singing and dancing, processing round two or three times and then when they participated in the Mass they deposited their offerings and ended up dancing."[41]

The officeholders of the Portuguese confraternities made their king's court into a theatrical spectacle. In Brazil, African tradition emphasized its identity in the symbolic figure of the king, who in Africa was governor over all. In the religious context of the festival the king had both a crown and a scepter, symbols of Portuguese power, and a baton, an African symbol—all these things being regarded as being on the same level as *nkisi* or fetishes. The *congada,* regarded as a festival par excellence in honor of King Congo and Queen Njinga,[42] was transformed into a religious festival in honor of black saints such as St. Benedict; this helped the worshipers celebrate the "myths of the origins" of the black community.[43] The image of the saint carved in wood was the *nkisi,* a sacred object that was imbued with the qualities of the divinity portrayed in effigy and represented the means of contacting the divinity. A French traveler who was present at a procession bearing the statues of St. John, St. Peter, St. Benedict, St. Lucia, and a black Virgin Mary described them as "truly sacrilegious caricatures."[44] The inhabitants of the Pacoval region on the Curuá River venerated images of holy persons that were fetishes rather than Catholic saints; or rather, they were true amulets that put the devotees in contact with their own ancestral divinities, recently incorporated into their new religious universe. This is why it was deemed necessary that the festivals should take place under the aegis of the confraternity, in order to compensate to some extent for the lack of supervision by the church of devotional practices in the colonies—where the Holy Office launched campaigns that were as radical as they were ineffective against the pagan practices and the superstitions of the Africans, whether enslaved or free.

Foreign travelers wrote descriptions, similar to the one from the sixteenth century quoted above, bearing witness to the duration of the processions of black devotees at least up to the nineteenth century and highlighting their grotesque, strange, or superstitious nature. At the beginning of the nineteenth century, the procession of the Irmandade do Rosário that took place in the church of the convent of Salvador in Lisbon was accompanied by an orchestra of more than three hundred players, mostly percussionists, who produced "a weird cacophony."[45] Music of African origin in the sixteenth century formed a part of popular entertainment. At the same time, black musicians were renowned for their virtuosity, especially those who played the *trombeteiro* and the *timbaleiro;* they were recruited also into royal music groups, where they played the *charanela* and the *sacabuxa.* The Spaniards and the Portuguese enjoyed seeing the slaves dancing with each other and applauded their musical spectacles,[46] and music and dance played an important role in the popularity of the plays and sacred performances inspired by the lives of the saints. In the course of the nineteenth century the election of the king started to lose its significance; it became more associated with folklore, and the *congada* became a festival for the populace, which had no appeal for the foreign travelers who witnessed it and described it as "ceremony without meaning," "a bizarre spectacle which makes one feel as if one were watching a group of monkeys," "a peculiar carnival," a "chaotic and indescribable din," and "picturesque spectacles which are starting to fall into disuse."[47] As slavery gradually became illegal and the number of slaves dwindled, their overlords lost interest in the festivals, the confraternities withered away, and the *congada,* that dramatic Afro-Brazilian dance, passed into the annals of folklore.

"He prayed for the conversion of the black peoples of the Indies"

How did Benedict's fame spread as far as the Iberian Peninsula? Then, his fame having traveled thus far, how did he become known in the Americas? There is no doubt that it was the Palermo merchant Giovan Domenico Rubbiano who took the first steps in bringing this about. His personal acquaintance with and particular devotion to Benedict while the saint was still living caused him to spend time and money to bring about the recognition of the saintliness of the black friar. Then, soon after Benedict's death, he collected *con grandissima fatica et diligentia* (with the greatest effort and diligence) a volume of affidavits of miracles performed by the friar while he was still living and by his relics, tomb, and images after his death in order to bring this information to the attention of the archbishop of Palermo, Giannettino Doria, and to persuade him to initiate the process of canonization in his see. The information thus assembled turned out to be sufficient for the Sacred Congregation of Rites to start the apostolic inquiry in 1594: the *Inquisitio super virtutibus et miraculis.* In fact, the devout merchant Rubbiano had spread his net wide for the purpose of securing the canonization of Benedict and had reached the most important institutions in Sicily, the court in Madrid, and the Roman Curia.

We find the first mention of Benedict's role in converting the American Indians in a letter of June 1607 from Giovan Domenico Rubbiano to the king of Spain recording the virtues and the miracles of "the holy servant of God, carried out by means of his images in Spain and among the South American Indians. In that realm it is known that he converted a king who was blind and his son, who was gravely ill and practically at the point of death. This king heard about a certain image and statue of the said blessed Benedict and when he obtained them, Our Lord God in his infinite grace gave sight to his blind eyes and healed his son. They were accordingly both baptized into the Catholic faith with a lot of people and committed themselves to the Holy Roman Church."[48]

In 1608 Philip III ordered the body of the friar to be transferred from the sacristy to a more fitting resting place, drawing attention to the miracles that had happened not only in Palermo but also in all the places his relics had reached: "It has pleased the Lord to use this humble servant black of hue to assist the conversion of the Negro population of the Indies, which could not have happened except by divine decree, since this your servant while alive interceded constantly with the Lord for the conversion of those people; and what he did with fervour while alive is now being done by the Lord, working in his own way on account of the devotion which these people sustain for this your most humble servant."[49]

There is no mention in Rubbiano's 1591 *Life* of Benedict, nor in the records of the processes of 1594, 1620, and 1625, that he prayed for the people of the Indies. In the brief hagiography of the friar written by Antonio Daça in 1611, there is just one reference to the veneration of an image of him kept at the church of St. Francis in Los Angeles. Judging from contemporary records, it seems that the matter of his conversion of the Amerindians and of the African slaves transported to the "Indies" was grounded in Iberian rather than Sicilian hagiography and that this had two explanations: the widespread veneration of the saint from Palermo among all classes, not simply among the African slaves; and the limited extent of the phenomenon of slavery in Sicily.[50] However, this hagiographic theme took hold as early as 1608, when Philip III decided to endow the uncorrupted body of Benedict with a silver coffin in order to pay homage to his services and above all "for the conversion of the black peoples of the Indies." His relics arrived in Spain in 1606 together with information about his miracles, described at length in Rubbiano's memoir. The Spanish playwright Lope de Vega was not slow to find material in this memoir for his plays.[51] Furthermore, "In the year 1609 in the [church] of the monastery of St. Anne in Lisbon there was established a confraternity of St. Benedict, who a long time ago was celebrated with great solemnity. This is stated in a certificate from Padre António Madeira justifying the summary of indulgences which Pope Paul V was to grant to that confraternity."[52]

Andrea Ortolani, comrade-in-arms of the famous *condottiero* Ottavio of Aragon and conqueror of the Berbers in the battle of Cherchell in 1613,[53] and Luigi La Farina, Marquis of Madonia and also Baron of Aspromonte and Senator of Palermo, were both envoys in an official mission to the Viceroy of Sicily, the Count of Castro. They testified at the process of 1625 that they were present at a procession that had taken place in Lisbon in 1618 in the presence of Philip III, in which "the genuine devotion displayed was still more admirable than the respect conveyed by the pomp and ceremony. . . . Among other things what was particularly striking was a huge crowd of Negro men, whose black faces, as they venerated their patron saint, formed a contrast with the innocent whiteness of their souls. Finally we caught sight of the image of a black friar, an Observant Franciscan, whom they call the Blessed Benedict of Palermo. . . . The procession went round the greater part of the city and ended up at the church of our [Franciscan] Fathers."[54]

On August 5, 1620, the friar Gaspare della Concezione of the province of Portugal wrote to Brother Paolo da Vizzini, guardian of the monastery of Santa Maria di Gesù in Palermo, about the devotion to the black saint that "is flourishing in our Lusitania," insisting on the need to add him as soon as possible to the canon of saints. He asked him to assemble every detail of Benedict's life and miracles. Once these had been sent to him, he would be in a position to carry out additional investigations in his own province "so that everyone should know and praise a man so blessed as Benedict, whether because of his deeds or because his name has been inscribed in the Chronicles of the Catholic faith."[55] In short, someone must write a hagiography of the saint, and the Portuguese Franciscans pronounced themselves ready to do so, while acknowledging that their fellow monks of Palermo had a sort of preemptive right by virtue of his origin in that city.

The veneration of the black saint became widespread in the Iberian Peninsula predominantly among black slaves. It was promoted tirelessly in the first instance by Rubbiano and by the distribution of images and relics, and subsequently by Antonino da Randazzo, the procurator who argued the case for Benedict's canonization. The latter was to present a relic to the "Father Commissioner of the Indies . . . where altars have been established not only in the Eastern but in the Western parts, congregations having been founded."[56] Between 1595 and 1620 Benedict had already become the saint of the black Africans who had been transported to the Iberian Peninsula.

The Franciscan Strategies

The veneration of Benedict began possibly as early as 1593, when Bonaventura da Caltagirone,[57] minister-general of the Franciscan order and formerly custodian of the only Sicilian province, presided over the sixty-second chapter, which was held in Valladolid. A large group of Sicilian Franciscans took part, including Bartolomeo da Siracusa, Atanasio da Messina, Serafino da Trapani, and Agostino da Palermo. The sixty-third chapter was held in Rome in 1600, and the sixty-fourth opened in Toledo in 1606. On the latter occasion Arcangelo da Messina, minister of the Sicilian Province, became minister-general and many of the friars who attended came from Palermo monasteries.[58]

The Observant Franciscans, most of them Spanish and Portuguese, had joined in the rush to the New World at the same time as had the discoverers: the Franciscan presence in the Americas goes back to Columbus's first voyage with Father Juan Pérez and Antonio de Marchena of the monastery of La Rabida. A large group had accompanied Pérez on subsequent voyages between 1493 and 1502. South America soon became the largest area covered by Franciscan missionaries in the colonial era. In some parts they had been the first and, sometimes, the only missionaries, and the number of their missionaries compared well with those of other religious orders.[59]

Franciscan archives and numerous accounts of journeys, reports to superiors in the order, diaries, and memoirs—a great many of which are preserved in manuscript form in the archives of the Franciscan Curia generalitia in Rome—give vivid descriptions of the ambivalent attitude of the friars toward the local population with whom they came in contact. The difficulties they encountered in preaching Christianity can be summed up in the sometimes violent reaction of the Indians toward the exploitation to which they were subjected by the conquistadores and the Spanish authorities. Their agenda was the bringing of the Gospel to the Indians; these sources tell us nothing about the strategies used by the missionaries toward the Africans who had been transported to the Americas by the slave trade, since they were fewer in number than the local population and were perhaps left to the care of their masters.

Decrees relating to the provinces of the Indies (*Pro Indiarum provinciis*) were issued at the chapter of 1600. The chapter of 1606 added *Pro Indiis,* in the context of the evangelization of the Americas referred to by those friars who had come from the mission areas and who began to take part in the deliberations of the chapters and of the congregations that took place between one chapter and the next. In 1618 Benigno da Genova[60] was elected minister-general of the order at the Chapter of Salamanca. In his capacity as protector of the order, he entrusted Antonino da Randazzo with the task of representing him in the 1620 and 1625 processes of the canonization of Benedict. News had begun to come through of heroic deeds and of the first missionaries, who sometimes became martyrs of their faith. The Sicilian friars would certainly have related the influence exerted by Antonio da Noto (or da Catagerona) and Benedetto da San Fratello (Benedict), both of them black and both of them demonstrating the effectiveness of the Christian message toward black slaves.

An important name in this context is that of the Spaniard Antonio Daça (or Daza), who was present at the chapter of 1606 and soon afterward wrote a monumental work that is an indispensable source of information about the Franciscan missions. The fourth part of his *Chrónica general del nuestro seráfico padre San Francisco y su apostólica orden* was printed in 1611 in Valladolid. It was the perfect sequel to a work by Marcos de Lisboa, a bishop of Oporto (who died in 1580) who edited a *Chronica Ordinis Minorum tribus partibus distincta.* Antonio Daça continued this work up until 1600, arranging for it to be printed appropriately in Valladolid and dedicating it to Philip III. Daça, known as the *Difinidor* (religious governor) of the province of La Concepción and general chronicler of the Franciscan order, custodian and "illustrious guardian of the monastery of Valladolid, Commissioner-General of the Curia for the *Famiglia Cismontana* (Franciscans from Germany and the Holy Land) in the city under the rule of Gregory XV,"[61] wrote "the Lives of 943 saints produced in recent times by the Regular order of our Father St. Francis, of whom 742 shed their blood for having confessed their faith."[62] The author states that he drew in ample measure on first-hand memoirs, authentic reports, processes drawn from archives, sworn testimonies, reliable books of stories, and primary documentation available in Latin, Italian, Portuguese, Catalan, Japanese, and Castilian Spanish. This mass of information is divided into four volumes devoted respectively to the conversion of the eastern part of the Indies, that of the West Indies, the persecution of the Franciscan order, and apostasy in England. In the fourth volume is a collection of information about "twenty-six Ministers-General of the Order; the lives of some saints and monks, martyrs and confessors, with many miracles and various happenings etc.," among them Antonio da Noto and Benedetto da San Fratello (Benedict).

Benedict was thus known in Franciscan circles, his cult having been widely involved in the conversion of Indians and African slaves. The Franciscan order devised a devotional project in his name, which originated in the Iberian Peninsula and was based on the perceived need to spread the Gospel in the conquered territories. He was a black saint and therefore would be just the person to convert black people. In the chapters the delegates of the order were confronting the problems of converting the black population of the Americas and, at the same time, became more acquainted with this worthy servant of God who in Sicily, a borderland, had inspired the devotion of all kinds of people with his virtues and grace.

Daça dedicates only a few pages to Benedict, and despite what he alleges, there are no archival or bibliographical references in the margins. We must presume that he had only indirect knowledge of the case through having heard about the process and the testimonies that emerged from it. He emphasizes in an obsessive fashion the racial characteristics of Benedict: "being black," Benedict confirmed the old adage that "black land brings forth good bread"; "his mother was a black slave, owned by a gentleman of the Lança family: and so the son, in consequence of the condition of his mother, was born black and enslaved"; he was "pleasant and honest, although black"; having become a hermit, "although black, he was the white man of all the spiritual men of that era."[63] The fact that he was venerated in effigy and that a miracle-working image of him was placed in the monastery of St. Francis in Los Angeles is the earliest indication we have of the devotion to him in the Americas. Daça makes the specific point that the Sicilian Inquisition gave permission for Benedict to be depicted "with shining rays and a crown on his head."

Daça gave more space to Antonio da Catagerona (also da Noto), who died in 1549 and for whom the process of canonization had reached an advanced stage;[64] he also "was a negro, born in the mountains of Barca . . . he was not merely a negro like those of Guinea, Xalofe and Monicongo, but also a Moor, born and brought up in the law of Mahommed and son of Moorish and negro parents."[65] Benedict had been black and the son of slaves, but at least his parents had become Christians and had brought him up in accordance with the precepts of that religion. In the case of Antonio, the contrast was still greater: he was the most unworthy of men, on account of both his religion and his race; he could well represent the apotheosis of the Creator who, in turning the vilest and most contemptible material in the eyes of man into a perfect creature, demonstrates his omnipotence to a correspondingly greater degree. However, the two Moors were to be equally instrumental in helping missionaries spread the Gospel, and they can often be found on the same altars ranging from Lisbon to Ouro Preto (Brazil). By the beginning of the nineteenth century the holy manuals dedicated to men of African extraction put Antonio da Catagerona, "known as The Black, because of his color," side by side with "Benedict of Palermo, known as The Moor, because of his color."[66]

The pantheon of saints in the sixteenth and seventeenth centuries was notably lacking in Africans, if one excludes the mythical Queen of Sheba; Balthazar (one of the three Magi); the Holy Eunuch, treasurer of Queen Candace; the Nubian princess Iphigenia; and St. Elesbao, the Abyssinian emperor who conquered the kingdom of the Jewish king Dunáan and was portrayed in the act of piercing him with a long lance. For their part, the newly converted slaves preferred saints of their own color. St. Benedict, an "Ethiopian," a black African, and the son of slaves, could represent a valid alternative to St. Elesbao, a black emperor but a slayer of white people and a cruel instrument of divine wrath against the white enemies of Christianity. Benedict represented the ideal slave: illiterate (Daça called him the "holy idiot"), a docile and trustworthy worker, a cook, and a shepherd. Gentle and ascetic, Benedict could teach slaves how it was possible "to draw near to Paradise by way of the road of suffering" without subverting social norms. The images showing him holding the infant Jesus tenderly in his arms were seen as an allusion to the need, given the "demographic disproportion between whites and blacks"[67] that was commonplace on the plantations and in the mines in the colonies, for masters and slaves to love each other, just as the black friar loved the white infant at whom he gazed adoringly. St. Benedict of Palermo made it easier for missionaries to spread the Gospel of Christ since he pointed to a model of sainthood centered on humility, obedience, and love between different social classes and races.

African Religious Influence: The Drummers of San Benito

When we look at the penetration of South America by the Franciscan missions, it is clear from all the evidence that it must have been that order, primarily its members from the Iberian Peninsula, who brought the knowledge of Benedict to the African slaves. In Venezuela, for example, the monastery of St. Francis was founded in Caracas in 1575–76, there was a monastery in Trujillo in 1578, and a steady stream of Franciscan missionaries was recorded as coming from Spain (twelve in 1580, fourteen in 1590, twelve in 1601, twelve in 1605, twenty in 1613, and similar numbers in 1618, 1633, 1655, and following years). The friars from this area participated in the general chapters, undertaking long and dangerous sea journeys (for example, Juan de Gálvez went to the 1617 chapter in Salamanca, and Bonaventura López Generes went to the 1638 chapter). Monasteries for novices were organized in Barquisimeto, Guanare, and Maracaibo. Indeed there had been a Franciscan monastery at Maracaibo since 1608 and one in Valencia in the eighteenth century. At the beginning of the eighteenth century there were already Creole and Canary Islands friars in the Venezuelan monasteries of Trujillo, Maracaibo, and Puerto Rico.[68] An agreement drawn up in 1663 by two Italians, Domenico Grillo and Ambrogio Lomellino, on behalf of a Dutch company obliged them to supply thirty-five hundred slaves per year for seven years to work in the ports of Cartagena, Portobelo, and Vera Cruz. The price of each slave who was in good health and who complied with the specifications required in the coastal ports of Barlovento, Santa Marta, Cumaná, and Maracaibo was three hundred pesos.[69] In short, we find in this area the two main ingredients of our story: Franciscan missionaries and African slaves. In 1585 a Franciscan *custódia* was also established with its headquarters in Olinda, Pernambuco; from there the missionaries spread throughout the land.[70]

From 1607 there were indirect reports about the introduction of the verneration of Benedict by the Franciscans on Lake Maracaibo's shores.[71] Official sources testify that Archbishop Mariano Martí paid a pastoral visit on February 14, 1775, to the church of Our Lady of the Rosary in the Villa del Rosario of Perijá. He described the images of the saints: "In the said church there are the following altars: the main altar of Our Lady of the Immaculate Conception, the altar of St. John the Baptist, one dedicated to Jesus Christ and one to the Holy Mother of the Light, and St. Benedict of Palermo."[72] The focal point of the veneration of the African saint was on the lake's shores, with its epicenter at San Pedro, between San José and Santa Maria, where the church was sacked in 1669 by the pirate Morgan and where most of the African slaves of the area used to gather. The Villa del Rosario was founded by families from the Canary Islands and in 1722 by Juan de Chourio, the proprietor of various plantations who received permission in that year to bring six hundred slaves into the area. The white fishermen of the lake, descendants of the Canaries families, adopted the saint, who was venerated by the black slaves in the sugar and cocoa plantations; in order to venerate him, they stained their faces black with the crude oil that was to be found everywhere in the region. At the end of the eighteenth century, because of the unrest among slaves from the Mina and Carabali racial groups around the city of Caracas, the archbishop was concerned to "eradicate dancing in processions," especially "dances with drummers," which had transformed what was originally "devotion and reverence" into "lawlessness"[73]—a worry that has in some instances lasted until the present day.

Up to this point, festivities in honor of St. Benedict of Palermo are recorded to have taken place in villages and towns around Lake Maracaibo and more generally in the states of Zulia, Trujillo, and Mérida (and to a lesser degree also in Lara, Portuguesa, Falcón, Aragua, Carabobo, and Bolívar). Benedict was often also the patron saint of the municipality (together with Our Lady of Mt. Carmel at Bobures and El Batey, with St. Anthony of Padua in Gibraltar (Venezuela), and with St. Lucia in the main places on the shores of Lake Maracaibo). He was celebrated with music and dancing, and his statue was sprinkled with liquor, which his devotees for their part drank copiously. The musical instruments played at the festivities were mostly flutes, *maracás, sayas,* and conch shells, but the most important ones were the drums, or rather those drums known as *chimbangueles.*

The *chimbangueleros,* or players of the *chimbangueles,* were organized into a confraternity with its own rules. The principal functions were those of the *mayordomo* or supervisor, whose main responsibility—indeed held for life—was to carry the baton of command; the first captain, or *capitán del Santo,* who directed the steps of the dance, guided the procession along its route, and together with the *mayordomo* had civilian authority during the festival; the *capitán de lengua* or *de plaza* (another office held for life, often by the most senior member of the confraternity, who would know the formulas, litanies, and poems to be chanted during the rites and the precise places where they were to be chanted in the course of the procession); and the *capitán de brigada* (the head of the *mandadores* who bore the litter with the image of the saint, in support of the other captains). The *director de banda* (bandmaster) knew all about drumbeats and exactly where they should be played and demanded a perfect performance from his percussionists; the *abanderados* (standard-bearers), varying in numbers, carried the blue and white standards that preceded the procession; the *cargadores* (porters) supported the saint's litter on their shoulders, richly decorated with flowers and festoons; the *hachoneros* (torchbearers) lit the route of the procession with torches when it took place at night; the *tamboreros* or *chimbangueleros* were responsible for the drums and sometimes played to fulfill a promise made to the saint.[74] Participants in the festivities included *vasallos* (servants), who were part of the confraternity, and *devotos,* believers whose prayers had been answered and who were taking part in the festivities to fulfill their vows. The "slaves of the Saint" were those who were specially devoted to him and had kept a *santo chiquito* (tiny statue of Benedict) in their houses for the whole year, while *el santo grande,* the full-sized statue of Benedict, belonged in the church and came out only on his feast day.

The drums, depending on their shape and sound, were considered masculine or feminine. Modifications in the diameter or height of the drums were generally made by the drummers themselves. The drums were accompanied by the sound of the *maracás,* which the drummers all held in their left hands and which were probably of indigenous origin, just as the drums were of African origin. During the procession there would be a succession of different kinds of music played by the drums (*golpes de tambor,*[75] or drum strokes). Many words of African origin rang forth in the rhymed verses of the song-and-dance ritual known as the *gaita de tambora.*[76] On New Year's Day the festival started with Mass attended by all the inhabitants of the *pueblo* (town) and the heads of the confraternity, while the drummers waited silently outside the church. Once Mass was finished, the *mayordomo* would accompany the image of Benedict out of the church and would deliver it over to the captains. The *capitán de lengua* would intone the first chant in the saint's honor while the crowd was already dancing and singing frenziedly; he was the one who ritually, inside the church, "effected the transformation of Benedict into Ajé," with the invocation that was soon picked up by the multitude: "Ajé, Ajé, Ajé, Ajé, Benito Ajé," thus creating the saint's "double." The procession would start out, preceded by the flag wavers, while the statue of the saint was sprinkled with perfume and rum. "St. Benedict as a saint of the Church was abstemious and hermit-like. Benedict-Ajé drank rum, liked dancing and revelling and was pleased that women should dance; he is Benedict the great dancer, as his people call him."[77] By contrast, the religious festival that took place two days earlier on December 30 was a serious procession—sober, composed, and the antithesis of the one held on the first day of January, which at times reached paroxysms of euphoria.

Discussion of the drums leads us back to the issue of ethnicity. Musicologists examine their use in order to trace the ethnic origins of the settlements of African slaves ranging from the Yoruba (who came from present-day Nigeria, Benin, and part of Togo), to the Kongo Ntoleta (from the Congo, Zaire, and Angola), to the Bushongo and Luanda (Zaire and Angola), for the most part coming from the regions of sub-Saharan Africa. From their ethnic origin one can identify their gods: the Orishas.[78] We find ourselves in the heart of the area from which the slave trade originated.

At the festivities of St. Benedict at the southern end of Lake Maracaibo, the devotees would chant: "Ajé, Songorogomeyaya, Ajé and mercy." So who was Ajé? The difficulty in tracking down written source material about the devotion to Benedict-Ajé can be in part circumvented, thanks to oral accounts noted down at Bobures between 1954 and 1986 by a local scholar who questioned the old people of the village and heard sixty-five different legends from them. The tradition prevailing among the villagers made no reference to the missionary work of the church but held that the saint had arrived at the lake with one of the slaves who had been landed at Gibraltar (Venezuela)[79] and who, falling ill at the house of his new master there, had invoked St. Benedict of Palermo. The cook on the slave ship that had conveyed him to the port of Maracaibo had presented him with a small *estampita* (engraving) of the saint, which he had unfortunately lost during a storm. The image of the "Negrito de Palermo" had made a profound impression on him, and he was certain that it had depicted a saint to whom he must devote himself and, in exchange for being healed, offer a small wooden statue as well as his personal veneration. In a short time the devotees of Benedict were to increase in number, and the African worshipers of Ajé would also gather under his banner.

In oral tradition Ajé was the son of the king of Dahomey, who lived in the capital Abomey and was brought up as a prince to rule over his people. While he was searching for his mother—who had refused to share her husband with sixty other wives and had gone back to her father's house—he gave food to the hungry along the way, healed the sick, and cared for the neglected and forgotten, giving them love and trust. When he died, without finding his mother, he was included in the pantheon of the holy men of Dahomey on account of the saintly way in which he had served his people. They celebrated his memory in October at the time of the first rains in a cycle of festivities that lasted for three months up to the first week of January, when Ajé resumed his search each year for his mother.

The god Ajé reigned over the blue waters of the rivers, lagoons, and lakes of Africa. He would be carried in procession on a litter and shaken about by the *cargadores* (porters) in imitation of a canoe at the mercy of the waves. The litter, preceded by a blue and white flag (the colors of the sea), moved forward swaying in order to clear negative impulses from the path ahead of the saint and thus create a sacred space.[80] The saint would be wearing the cap and uniform of a sailor. In Brazil they sing during the dance ritual known as *Moçambique* that St. Benedict "was already a sailor and left *Congada* as our compatriot, of the lineage of the Congo of Mozambique."[81] At the festival in his honor in the region of Espírito Santo, the saint is presented as a black sea captain in a white uniform and sits at the stern of a huge ship called the *Palermo*.[82]

As we know, water has a particular significance in African culture: the Madonna of the Rosary is often venerated from the moment she appears above the waters of the sea or the river, fetched by the slaves and carried while they dance and sing to the place where they gather for worship. Her devotees in Sergipe (Brazil) ask her, the "Lady of the World," for "a sip of water to protect them from the fires of the earth and the ragings of the sea, otherwise they will sink to the bottom."[83] Also sent on water from another world were the Spirit of the Virgin and the simulacrum of St. John, which, it was believed, were found in a chest that was floating in the sea.[84] The Bantu system of beliefs[85] is centered on the world of their ancestors, which is separated from the world of the living by the water that reflects that world and encloses its elements in religious objects called *nkisi*—sometimes anthropomorphic statuettes of carved wood, renamed "fetishes" by the Portuguese. These were used for rites through which the priests communicated with the spirit world. Some representations of Benedict, carved in wood of various kinds or on roots, recall this provenance.[86]

The drummers, both male and female; the dancing; and the rum created a space of freedom in the lives of the slaves, with their masters' consent, and St. Benedict and Ajé became one and the same divinity. At the same time something similar was happening in other parts of Venezuela through the combinations St. Peter–Legba, Our Lady of Mt. Carmel–Damballa, the Madonna of the Candlestick–Dada, St. Barbara–Shangò, and St. Anthony–Chopkono;[87] all these represent specific forms of veneration and devotion that challenge the notion of syncretism as "colonization of the world of the imagination."[88]

The area round the Gulf of Guinea is notorious as the place from where the largest number of slaves was transported to Venezuela and Brazil; the "Slave Coast" (Nigeria and Dahomey) and the Gold Coast (Fanti-Ashanti) contributed fewer than the Congo and Muslim Sudan (Senegal). In the seventeenth century, when Central Dahomey dominated the other peoples of the African coast, there was a city called Ajudà or São João (Ouidah), a large commercial market for West African slaves. At that time there were even diplomatic relations between Dahomey (Benin) and Bahia (Brazil). The black slaves of Dahomey were called

Evés or Eués (Ewe in English and Géges in Portuguese). This was a coastal tribe that was oppressed by the conquerors of Central Dahomey, and it was through these slaves that the cultural practices of Dahomey reached the Americas.[89] It is reasonable to think that around Lake Maracaibo, where Benedict is Ajé, the slaves originally came from the kingdom of Dahomey, as the oral tradition concerning the mother of Ajé would have us believe.

The polygamous practices of Dahomeyan rulers, who resided in the palace in Abomey with hundreds of wives, slaves of the harem, and Amazons conscripted into a standing army, are well known to scholars.[90] Tradition also points to a rejection of polygamy, doubtless influenced by the spread of Christianity in the colonial area. However, there is another aspect that may help us to understand the ease with which Benedict was welcomed into the Dahomeyan pantheon of saints: this is dualism, a "pervasive feature" of that culture, the "predilection for twos" that left its mark on the semantics of family relationships and on the organization of the state and the pantheon of saints. "A veritable obsession with the perfection of duality prevailed from the earliest mythological notions of a metaphysical order down to the domestic predilection for twin births. . . . At the head of the Dahomeyan pantheon was [a] dual divinity . . . a pair of twins of opposite sex or, more rarely, of the same sex."[91] So Ajé was not Benedict's double, but his twin!

During the eighteenth century the devotion to St. Benedict declined and became more of a popular folklore festival for all social classes.[92] The abolition of slavery in the second half of the nineteenth century and the consequential changes seem to have attenuated the links between the saint and his faithful. However, these links strengthened again in the twentieth century and became a visible instrument in society of religious and cultural identity among the African element throughout Latin America. We are talking here about a considerable number of people. The official statistics for 1950 reveal that 32 percent of the population of Venezuela was black; by 1992 this figure had fallen to 10 percent (in a population of twenty million), the remainder being 2 percent Indian, 20 percent European, and 68 percent mestizo. The proportion of black people in Brazil was still higher. However, if we stay with Venezuela, where slavery was abolished in 1854, the study of tradition goes hand in hand with the invention of new entertainments (often condemned, as in the case of the masquerade of *Los Apaches* or *Los Marrones*).[93] These were genuine "inventions," the making of which involved the community and helped them to reclaim and update their own culture. This seems to have been the case in Chacopo, La Venta, Mucuchíes, Timotes, and the Andean region in general, where those not of African origin would blacken their faces to resemble their saint (see fig. 2), and devotees organize themselves into dozens of confraternities and *Sociedades de vassallos* in order to take

Fig. 1. St. Benedict of Palermo, Timotes, Venezuela.
© by Giovanna Fiume

Fig. 2. Devotees blacken their faces to resemble the saint, Timotes.
© by Giovanna Fiume

Fig. 3. Dance of the little rope, Timotes. © 2002 by Giovanna Fiume

Fig. 4. Binding and loosing in the dance of the little rope, Timotes. © 2002 by Giovanna Fiume

part in processions in honor of the saint. During these processions they honored the saint with extraordinary forms of choreography: the dancers each held a *maracá* in one hand and the end of a colored rope in the other. Each used the rope to tie up and untie a stake, a statue of the saint, and one of their number as part of the dance, elaborating on the theme of loosing and binding, of capture and liberation, and of slavery (see figs. 3 and 4). However, it was generally the African element[94]—in the racial melting pot that joined not only whites with blacks but also blacks with Indians and Indians with whites[95]—that restored and increased the devotion to and veneration of the black saint in the whole area, from Uruguay[96] to Argentina[97] but more especially in Brazil and Venezuela.

Notes

"San Benedetto il Moro: Dalla Sicilia al Nuovo Mondo," translation from the Italian by Jennifer Radice, 10 Middleton Road, London, England.

1. On that occasion the Sacred Congregation of Rites welcomed the request for a further transfer put forward by the king of Spain but recommended to the cardinal of Palermo, Giannettino Doria, that the transfer should be carried out "privately, without any sort of procession, very secretly and without any sort of public pomp or show," since there had been no official beatification on the part of the church (Antonino da Randazzo, *Vita e miracoli del Beato Benedetto da San Fradello,* seventeenth-century manuscript, in *San Benedetto il Moro: Santità, agiografie e primi processi di canonizzazione,* ed. Giovanna Fiume and Marilena Modica [Palermo: Biblioteca Comunale, 1998], 178). The letter is dated March 11, 1611.

2. This gives us a glimpse of the conflict between canonization by a bishop, which had long been a tradition, and the recent establishment of the Sacred Congregation of Rites, a papal tribunal established by Pope Sixtus V with the papal constitution *Immensa* in the framework of a more general reorganization of the Curia. The Sacred Congregation had been entrusted since 1588 with the *instructoria* (inquiry) into the canonization of saints. See Giuseppe Dalla Torre, "Processo di beatificazione e canonizzazione," in *Enciclopedia del diritto* (Milan: Giuffrè, 1987), 36:932–43. There is a detailed chronology in L. Hertling, "Materiali per la storia del processo di canonizzazione," *Gregorianum* 16 (1935): 170–95.

3. Archivio Segreto Vaticano (ASV), *Sacra Congregatio pro Causis Sanctorum* (SCCS), vol. 2179, *Articuli pro canonizatione* (hereafter referred to as *Articuli*), eighteenth-century manuscript, fol. 36v.

4. "Precipue adscribentur Mauri, vel Nigri, qui praedictum Beatum peculiari adeo devotione numerantur ut non facile, nec sine damno aut scandalo prohiberi illis posset cultus quem predicto Beato exhibent" (*Articuli,* fol. 36v).

5. She represented for the Americas what Catherine of Siena represented for Italy and Teresa of Avila represented for Spain. See N. Del Re, *Rosa da Lima,* Bibliotheca Sanctorum, vol. 11 (Vatican City: Città Nuova Editrice, 1968), cols. 396–400; J. Flores Araoz, R. Mujica Pinella, L. E. Wuffarden, and P. Guidovich Perez, eds., *Santa Rosa de Lima y su tiempo* (Lima: Banco de Crédito del Perú, 1995); Francesca Cantù, "Rosa da Lima e il 'mistico giardino' del Nuovo Mondo," in *Ordini religiosi, santità e culti: Prospettive di ricerca tra Europa e America latina,* ed. Gabriella Zarri, 87–108 (Lecce: Congedo, 2003).

6. Benedict is said to have urged members of the confraternity not to waste even a crumb of food since it represented the blood of the poor when given to them as alms, and when he wrung out the *estropajos* (a Spanish word denoting rags tied to a small stick and used for washing dishes), blood came out of them. This was testified by Antonio Maria Bonuccio at the process on August 26, 1716 (*Articuli,* fol. 402v).

7. Fra Baltasar de San Diego, August 13, 1716, *Articuli,* fol. 360r.

8. Fra Giovanni Fernandez e Zegudo, July 4, 1716, *Articuli,* fol. 236r.

9. Fra Francesco di Sant'Elena, August 5, 1716, *Articuli,* fol. 323r.

10. Fra Filippo del Portogallo, March 1, 1731, *Articuli,* fol. 470v.

11. Alessandro Dell'Aira, "La fortuna iberica di San Benedetto da Palermo," in *Atti dell'Accademia di Scienze Lettere e Arti* (Palermo: Accademia di Scienze, Lettere e Arti, 1992); Alessandro Dell'Aira, *La rotta di San Benedetto il Moro da Palermo a Bahia* (Trento: Magazzini dell'Arsenale, 1999); Vittorio Morabito, "San Benedetto il Moro da Palermo, protettore degli africani di Siviglia, della penisola iberica e d'America latina," in *Negros, mulatos y zambaigos: Derroteros africanos en los mundos ibéricos,* ed. Berta Ares Queija and Alessandro Stella, 223–73 (Seville: Escuela de estudios hispano-americanos, 2000).

12. *Articuli,* cited by Don Paolino de Velasco, September 28, 1715, fols. 67r and 67v.

13. Ibid., fol. 72r.

14. Fra Juan Fernández y Zagudo, July 4, 1716, ibid., fol. 193r.

15. Ibid., fols. 270r and v.

16. Quotes from ibid., fols. 238v–239v.

17. Padre Alessio della Solitudine, July 29, 1716, ibid., fols. 300r and 312r.

18. Bernard Vincent, "Les confréries de Noirs dans la Péninsule Ibérique (XVe–XVIIIe siècles)," in *Religiosidad y costumbres populares en Iberoamérica,* ed. D. Gonzáles Cruz (Huelva: Universidad de Huelva-CER, 1999).

19. A. C. de C. M. Saunders, *A Social History of Black Slaves and Freedmen in Portugal (1441–1555)* (Cambridge: Cambridge University Press, 1982), 152.

20. José Ramos Tinhorão, *Os pretos em Portugal, uma presença silenciosa* (Lisbon: Editorial Caminho, 1988), 126–27.

21. *Articuli,* fols. 217v–218r. "Ethiopian" and "black" are used here synonymously.

22. Fra Francesco di Sant'Elena, ibid., August 5, 1716, fol. 323r.

23. Ibid., fol. 332r.

24. "Uma verdadera sociedade de nações, . . . mistura de raças diversas" (Julita Scarano, *Devoção e escravidão: A Irmandade de Nossa Senhora do Rosário dos Pretos no Distrito Diamantino no século XVIII* [São Paulo: Companhia Editora Nacional, 1976], 108). The black confraternities in Portugal had the same multiethnic character, according to Didier Lahon in *Le confraternite nere in Portogallo dal Cinquecento al Settecento: Privilegi acquisiti, privilegi perduti,* quoted in Giovanna Fiume, ed., "Schiavi, corsari, rinnegati," *Nuove Effemeridi* 14, no. 54 (2001): 83–96.

25. Caio César Boschi, *Os leigos e o poder: Irmandades leigas e política colonizadora em Minas Gerais* (São Paulo: Editora Ática, 1986), 3.

26. Oscar José Beozzo, "Il culto dei santi e della Vergine nella prima evangelizzazione del Brasile," in *Ordini religiosi, santità e culti: Prospettive di ricerca tra Europa e America latina,* ed. G. Zarri, 131–52 (Lecce: Congedo, 2003), 48. The author notes the lack of influence of the slaves on the structure of the church, despite their being in a majority among the faithful: only one parish in the whole of Brazil to this day is dedicated to St. Benedict, their most popular saint.

27. Patricia Ann Mulvey, "The Black Lay Brotherhoods of Colonial Brazil: A History" (Ph.D. diss., City University of New York, 1976), cited in Marina de Mello e Souza, *Reis negros no Brasil escravista: História da Festa de Coroação de Rei Congo* (Belo Horizonte: Editora UFMG, 2002), 162ff.

28. Célia Borges, "Devoção branca de homens negros: As irmandades do Rosário em Minas Gerais no século XVIII" (doctoral thesis, Departamento de História da UFF, Niterói, 1998), cited in de Mello e Souza, *Reis negros,* 195.

29. Lahon, *Le confraternite nere.*

30. Cited in Antonio Andreoni (João Antonil), *Cultura e opulência do Brasil,* 2nd ed. (São Paulo: Companhia Editora Nacional, 1966), 164.

31. Mariza Soares de Carvalho, *Devotos de cor: Identidade étnica, religiosidade e escravidão no Rio de Janeiro, seculo XVIII* (Rio de Janeiro: Civilização Brasileira, 2000), 196.

32. On the conflicts that set blacks, whether slaves or free, against mestizos, mulattoes, and Creoles, see Scarano, *Devoção e escravidão.*

33. De Mello e Souza, *Reis negros,* 200.

34. Scarano, *Devoção e escravidão,* 113.

35. However, its *Compromisso,* approved in 1565, mentions the construction of a chapel in 1460 for black men coming from distant lands ("homens pretos vindos das longes terras"). In 1549 King João III is said to have agreed to the collection of alms on the streets of Lisbon (see Mulvey, "Black Lay Brotherhoods," 17, 23). In 1586 (or 1589 in other sources) the Jesuits organized the Fraternity of Our Lady of the Rosary with the purpose of promoting piety and religious instruction for the Indians and the Negroes ("con o fim de promover a piedade e a instrução religiosa de Indios e de Negros") (see Julio Santana Braga, *Sociedade protetora dos desvalidos: Uma irmandade de cor* [Salvador: Ianamá, 1987]). The impulse given by the Jesuits, as well as by the Dominicans, Augustinians, and Franciscans, to the organizing of religion for the African slaves should not be disregarded.

36. ASV, SCCS, vol. 2179, *Articuli,* fol. 646r.

37. The writer is Nuñez Muley, a champion of the Moorish community of Granada, who testifies to the persistence of the traditional cultural practices of the African groups (cited in Aurelia Martín Casares, *La esclavitud en Granada del Siglo XVI: Género, raza y religión* [Granada: Universidad de Granada, 2000], 423).

38. Cited in Baltasar Fra Molinero, *La imagen de los negros en el teatro del Siglo de Oro* (Madrid: Siglo XXI Editores, 1995), 38.

39. Carlos Rodrigues Brandão, in *A festa do Santo preto* (Goiânia: Fundação Nacional de Arte, Universidade Federal de Goiás Editora, 1985), describes and illustrates, for example, the complicated ritual of the feast of the rosary, the ordering of the groups who parade in procession, the placing of the actors, and the songs. Alfredo João Rabaçal, in *As Congadas no Brasil* (São Paulo: Conselho Estadual de Cultura, 1976), gives a review of all the different types of *congadas,* with a calendar of them for each city.

40. Didier Lahon, *O Negro no coração do Império: Uma memória a resgatar, séculos XV–XIX* (Lisbon: Ministério da Educação, 1999), 67. We know that there was a Cofradia (Confraternity) de Nuestra Señora de la Salud y San Benito de Palermo y Santa Ifigenia in Cadiz in 1664, according to Hipólito Sancho de Sopranis, *Las cofradías de morenos a Cadíz* (Tangier: Instituto General Franco, 1940).

41. See William Beckford, *Voyage au Portugal et en Espagne* (Lisbon: Biblioteca Nacional, 1988). He is describing the procession on June 13, 1787, cited in Lahon, *O Negro no coração do Império,* 72.

42. Njinga Bandi, born in 1582, was chief of the Ambundos-Jagas people from 1623 to 1633. The Jaga were warriors, lived in settlements called *quilombos,* and practiced ritual cannibalism. Since there had been no previous female rulers, Njinga ruled at first in the name of her brother's younger son, until she killed him and usurped the throne from him. Once she had become queen (Ngola) she led battles and dressed her male concubines as women. She was baptized in 1622 in Luanda with the name of Ana de Sousa. Other women were to ascend the throne of the realm Ndongo and Matamba after her for the next 104 years. She became famous in the context of the struggle against Portuguese domination. See Joseph Miller, "Queen Nzinga of Matamba in a New Perspective," *Journal of African History* 13 (1975): 201–16.

43. In the case of the *cordão de Marambiré,* this was a Catholic festival in a *quilombo* in the Amazon. See Eurípedes Antonio Funes, "'Nasci nas matas, nunca tive Senhor': História e memória dos mocambos do baixo Amazonas" (Ph.D. diss., University of São Paulo), cited in de Mello e Souza, *Reis negros,* 222.

44. O. Coudreau, *Voyage au Rio Curuá, 20 novembre 1900–7 mars 1901* (Paris: A. Lahure Imprimeur-Editeur, 1903), 19.

45. C. Israel Ruder, *Viagem em Portugal (1798–1802*) (1805; repr., Lisbon: Biblioteca Nacional, 1981), cited in Lahon, *O Negro no coração do Império,* 73.

46. Lahon, *O Negro no coraçao do Império,* 76.

47. "Formalidade sem significação," "bizarro espetáculo que se imaginava estar deante de un bando de macacos," "extravagante carnaval," "algazarra caótica e indescritível," and "espetáculos pitorescos que começam a cair em desuso." The quotations are taken from de Mello e Souza, *Reis negros,* 278, 283, 288, 298 respectively.

48. Archivo General de Simancas, *Estado,* box 1162, doc. 195.

49. The order, dated June 1, 1608, is in Biblioteca comunale di Palermo, ms. 3QqC36, no. 19, fol. 304v.

50. Antonino Giuffrida, "Schiavitù e mercato del lavoro nella Sicilia rinascimentale," *Nuove Effemeridi* 14, no. 54 (2001): 30–46.

51. On the *comedias de santos* (plays about saints) by Lope de Vega and other writers of the "Golden Century," see Giovanna Fiume, *Il santo moro: I processi di canonizzazione di Benedetto da Palermo (1594–1807)* (Milan: Franco Angeli, 2002), particularly 192ff.

52. "Na [igreja] do monasterio de Santa Anna, Lisboa, no anno de 1609 se tinha instituido uma irmandade de S. Benedicto, a quem havia muito tiempo se fazia festa com grande solemnidade. Assim o diz una certidão do Padre António Madeira, justificando o summario de indulgencias que o Pontifice Paulo V concederá á propria irmandade" (Fray Diogo do Rosário, *Flos sanctorum* [Lisbon, 1869–70], vol. 4, in the chap. on Benedict).

53. See Vincenzo Di Giovanni, *Palermo restaurato* (1614; repr., Palermo: Sellerio, 1989), 348–49, for the honors that were bestowed on him for the occasion.

54. Pietro Tognoletto, *Paradiso serafico del fertilissimo Regno di Sicilia overo Cronica ove si tratta della origine della Riforma de' Minori osservanti di questo Regno* (Palermo, 1667), 1:323.

55. "Ut, et Chronicis Sacrae Religionis mandentur, et ex acta omnia tam benedicti Benedicti agnoscantur et perlaudentur" (ibid., 324).

56. Ibid., 319.

57. On Bonaventura Secusio da Caltagirone, the first minister-general of the Observant Franciscan friars, see A. Spadaro, "Note sulla permanenza di Caravaggio in Sicilia," in *L'ultimo Caravaggio e la cultura artistica a Napoli, Sicilia e Malta,* ed. Maurizio Calvesi, 289–92 (Syracuse, It.: Ediprint, 1987).

58. This included Bonaventura da Polizzi, Angelo da Piazza, Bonaventura da Trapani, Clemente da Messina, Auditus da Palermo, and Cataldo da Catania.

59. In Brazil, on the other hand, "compared to the Jesuits the other Orders were less active at the beginning of the colonial era," according to Charles Verlinden, *Le origini della civiltà atlantica* (Bologna: Avanzini e Torraca, 1968), 259.

60. For information on Benigno da Genova, see Tognoletto, *Paradiso serafico,* 1:566–68.

61. See Lucas Waddingus, *Scriptores Ordinis Minorum* (Florence: Quaracchi, 1934), 24:§15, 399.

62. Antonio Daça, prologue to *Quarta parte de la Chrónica general del nuestro seráfico padre San Francisco y su apostólica orden. Las vidas de novecientos y quarenta y tres santos, que en estos ultimos tiempos ha producido la Regular Observancia de nuestro padre San Francisco, . . . de los quales setecientos y quarenta y dos . . . derramaron su sangre por la confesión Historia, vida y milagros . . . de . . . Santa Juana de la Cruz* (Valladolid, 1611); *Exercicios espirituales* (Rome, 1626); *Excelencias de la ciudad de Valladolid con la vida y milagros del Santo Fr. Pedro Regalado* (Valladolid, 1627); and *Libro de la purissima Concepcion de la Madre de Dios* (Madrid, 1624).

63. "Siendo negro . . . tierra negra buen pan lleva . . . su madre fue una negra esclava de un caballero de casa Lança: y asi el hijo siguiendo la condición de su madre, nació negro y esclavo . . . aunque negro agraciado y honesto . . . aunque negro, fue el blanco de todos los varones espirituales de aquel tiempo." All quotations are from Daça, *Quarta parte,* 66–68.

64. Ibid., 155–69.

65. "Negro, nacido en los montes de Barca . . . no solo fue negro como los de Guinea, Xalofe y Monicongo, sino también Moro, nacido y criado en la ley de Mahoma, y hijo de padres Moros y negros" (ibid., 156).

66. "Dit le Saint Noir, à cause de sa couleur. . . . Benoît de Palerme, dit le Maure, à cause de sa couleur" (M. Grégoire, *Manuel de piété à l'usage des hommes de couleur et des noirs* [Paris, 1818], 89–92 [on Antonio], 93–103 [on Benedict]). On Antonio da Noto, see Giovanna Fiume, "Antonio Etiope e Benedetto il Moro: Il santo Scavuzzo e il Nigro eremita," in *Francescanesimo e cultura a Noto,* ed. Diego Ciccarelli and Simona Sarzana, 67–100 (Palermo: Biblioteca francescana, 2005).

67. Enrique Martínez López, *Tablero de Ajedrez: Imágenes del negro heroico en la comedia española y en la literatura e iconografía sacra del Brasil esclavista* (Paris: Fundaçao Calouste Gulbenkian, 1998), 123–24.

68. Lino Gómez Carredo, *La provincia franciscana da Santa Cruz de Caracas, Cuerpo de documentos para su historia (1513–1837),* vol. 1 (Caracas: Academia Nacional de la Historia, 1974); *Las misiones de Píritu: Documentos para su historia,* vols. 1, 2 (Caracas: Academia Nacional de Historia, 1967). The author analyzes the proselytizing by the

Dominicans and the Franciscans in the area between the Orinoco River and the Rio Negro, where the city of New Barcelona was founded.

69. Cited in Jesus Chucho García, *Africanas, esclavas y cimarronas,* Collección Afroamérica (Caracas: Ediciones Los Heraldos Negros, 1996), 35–36.

70. In the seventeenth century the Franciscan missions managed to spread out widely in this area, extending their territory from the Amazon to São Paulo. They relied on an administrative office in Pará, two provinces, and various tertiary confraternities, these last being built not only near the monasteries but also in areas where there had been no missions, as in the instance of Minas Gerais and Ouro Preto. The Brazilian provinces also sent representatives to the chapters.

71. As recorded by A. E. Vaquero Rojo, *San Benito de Palermo: El primer negro canonizado* (Madrid: Atenas, 1985), 25. It is said to have reached Brazil around 1610, according to Apolinario da Conceiçao, *Flor peregrina por Preta, ou nova Maravilha da Graça descoberta na prodigiosa Vida do Beato Benedito da S. Philadelpho* (Lisbon, 1744), 238.

72. "En dicha iglesia hay los altares siguientes: el altar mayor de nuestra senora de la Immaculada Concepción, el altar de San Juan Bautista, el del Santísimo Christo y el de la madre Santísima de la Luz, digo San Benedicto de Palermo" (cited in Juan de Dios Martínez Suárez, *El culto de San Benito de Palermo en Venezuela* [Maracaibo: Editorial La Llama Violeta, 1999], 20). Veneration of Benedict in Maracaibo is amply documented from 1880.

73. "Extirpación de baile en las procesiones," "bailes de tambor," "desorden," and "devoción y reverencia." The governor had intervened at the insistence of the ecclesiastical tribunal in 1793 but with negligible success, despite exhortations, threats of punishment, and promises of prizes "afin de extirpar de raíz este desorden" (in order to eradicate this lawlessness). See *Real hacienda,* 1429, Libro de Cofradías, Archivo nacional Venezuela, cited in ibid., 87.

74. "San Benito de Palermo," *Revista Bigott* 10 (1987): 7–8.

75. *Chocho* before the saint left the church; *Ajé* to ask him to come out; *Chimbanguelero Vaja* when he was already on the way; then *Misericordia* and *Cantica;* and finally *Los saludos a los Capitanes.* All these chants were also danced by those taking part in the procession. The dance steps are described in Juan de Dios Martínez Suárez, *Como bailar Chimbangueles,* Colección danzas étnicas y tradicionales, no. 1 (Maracaibo, n.d.); Juan de Dios Martínez Suárez, *San Benito de Palermo y sus Chimbangueles,* vol. 2, *La cultura popular en la escuela* (Maracaibo: Editorial La Llama Violeta, 2000). The St. Benedict drums were 70–100 cm high and 20–40 cm in diameter (but narrower at the base) and were of African origin, according to Jesús García and Bartolomé Duysens, *Afrovenezuelan Reflections: The Drums of Liberation,* Fundación Afroamérica (Caracas: Heraldos Negros Edition, 1999).

76. Juan de Dios Martínez Suárez, *Gaita de tambora,* Colección danzas étnicas y tradicionales, no. 2 (Maracaibo: Consejo Nacional de la Cultura–Fundajé, n.d.).

77. "San Benito como santo de la Iglesia fue abstemio e ancoreta. Benito-Ajé bebe ron, gusta de bailar, parrandear y que bailen las mujeres; es Benito el bailón, como llama su gente" (Stalin Gamarra Durán, *La semiosis entre el mito, el rito y la fiesta,* http://w1.461.telia.com/html [accessed March 2004]).

78. Such as Shango, god of thunder; Ogun, god of war and of iron; Olukum, goddess of the sea; and Oko, god of agriculture.

79. Gibraltar (Venezuela) was founded in the sixteenth century and, owing to its location on the shores of Lake Maracaibo and the fact that it was a landing place for trade in the Andean area, played a crucial role in the geography of the slave trade. Slaves were sold there for the cocoa and tobacco plantations; the slaves were assembled and sent to Vera Cruz and other destinations. The port was set on fire seven times between 1600 and 1678, in 1669 by the pirate Morgan. In the area around the lake, everyone knew about the life and miracles of the Moorish saint "que para el negro del Sur del lago es su protector completo [Amando Soto, uno degli informatori], porque negro africano no creía en ninguna imagen blanca. Añade el señor Simón Arrieta que fue muy vivaz, muy comunicativo; que le quitó publicidad a San Antonio, que es un pratiquín que no sale de la iglesia, mientras que San Benito se mantiene por la calle; que Gibraltar sin San Benito es como Maracaibo sin la Chinita" (who was the complete protector of the black slave to the south of the lake [according to Armando Soto, one of the informants], because the black African does not believe in any white image. Señor Simón Arrieta adds that he was very lively and communicative; that he suppressed any publicity for San Antonio, . . . who did not emerge from the church, whilst St. Benedict stayed in the street (Luis Britto García, *La Pascua negra de San Benito,* http://www.ultimasnoticias.com.ve [accessed March 2004]).

80. A description of the festivities can also be found in Carlos Rafael Bellorin Carmona, *Los ojos del pueblo: Entre muertos, santos y vivos* (Merida: Universidad de Los Andes, 2001), 147–70. However, for the purposes of the Brazilian *candomblé,* Axé is "a sacred force linked to an Orisha," "a force or power against evil influences," and also "the magic foundation of a house of worship" or "consecrated objects endowed with a special strength." For Bastide, it equates to a vital force, a type of mana (Roger Bastide, *Les religions africaines au Brésil: Contribution à une sociologie des interprétations de civilisation* [Paris: Presses Universitaires de France, 1960]). Originating from the Yoruba word *àsè,* meaning "order, commandment, authority," it is an attribute of Exu, or Eshu, the god who is the mediator, messenger, and interpreter of the Orisha and who divides himself into numerous mythical and ritual figures. Exu, too, is of Yoruba origin. See Stefania Capone, *La quête de l'Afrique dans le candomblé: Pouvoir et tradition au Brésil* (Paris: Karthala, 1999), 234–35.

81. "Jà foi marinheiro e deixou Congada para nós congueiro na linha do Congo do moçambiqueiro" (Maria de Lourdes Borges Ribeiro, *A dança do Moçambique* [São Paulo, 1959], cited in Luís da Câmara Cascudo, *Made in Africa* [São Paulo: Global Editora, 2002], 31).

82. Hermógenes Lima de Fonseca and Rogério Medeiros, *Tradições populares no Espírito Santo: Folkways and Folk-plays of Espírito Santo* (Vitória, E.S., Brazil: Departamento Estadual de Cultura, 1991).

83. "Senhora do mundo . . . fogos em terras, e fogos de mar . . . un côco dagua/senão vão ao fondo" (Melo Morais Filho, *Festas e tradições populares do Brasil* [Rio de Janeiro: Briguet & Cia, 1946], 104–5).

84. Leda Maria Martins, *Afrografias da memória: O reinado do Rosário no Jatobá* (São Paulo: Editora Perspectiva; Belo Horizonte: Maza Edições, 1997), 32–45. The author has collected versions of the legend going back to the period following the abolition of slavery.

85. In Central and West Africa, the large Bantu region (a macrogroup with similar languages and culture, organized in families, small villages, clans, kingdoms, and confederations) was the ideal scenario for producing slaves owing to the rivalries and internal feuds of African society; these were exacerbated by the pressing need for slaves, who came from the ports of Loango (supervised by the British, the French, and the Dutch) and Luanda and Benguela (supervised by the Portuguese). We find the pan-Bantu culture in those regions of Brazil where there was a preponderance of slaves from West and Central Africa.

86. Indicated also by St. Anthony, carved on the root of a pine tree by the slaves of the state of São Paulo in the eighteenth and nineteenth centuries (from Francisco de Castro Ramos Neto, "'No de pinho': Imaginária católica afro-brasileira em São Paulo," in Emanuel Araùjo et al., *Os herdeiros da noite: Fragmentos do imaginário negro* [São Paulo: Pinacoteca do Estado de São Paulo, 1995]).

87. For Venezuela, see *Santos patronos,* in *Atlas de tradiciones Venezolanas,* no. 5 (Caracas: Fundación Bigott, n.d.). Similarly in Brazil, St. George was transformed into Odé, Oxòssi, and Ogum; St. Anthony into Exu; St. Jerome into Xangô; St. Barbara into Iansã; and Our Lady into Iemanjà. For the cult of St. Bartholomew in Brazil, see Vittorio Giustolisi, ed., *São Bartolomeo—Oshoumaré nella Bahia de todos os Santos* (Palermo: Centro di documentazione Paolo Orsi, 2002). In Brazil, Benedict is alleged to have had links to the spirit of smallpox, the Orisha called Omulu-Obaluayè in Yoruba (Bastide, *Les religions africaines au Brésil,* 366), or else to Ossâim, the proponent of plant medicine, a divinity who lived alone in the forest and knew all its secrets (Gérard Police, *La fête noir au Brésil* [Paris: L'Harmattan, 1996], 246–47).

88. The "colonization of the world of the imagination" is not a one-sided act and presupposes a strong dynamic force on the part of those colonized, which goes some way to explaining the success of the process (Serge Gruczinski, *La colonisation de l'imaginaire: Sociétés indigènes et occidentalisation dans le Mexique espagnol* [Paris: Gallimard, 1988]; Tzvetan Todorov, *La conquête de l'Amérique: La question de l'autre* [Paris: Éditions du Seuil, 1982]). Acceptance—adaptation—reaction: the Africans transported to the Americas were people with complex social, political, and religious systems that their state of slavery transferred to the New World, without destroying their way of thinking and feeling. The concept of syncretism does not fully take into account the effect of domination in contact between different cultures. See Melville Herskovits, *The Myth of the Negro Past* (1941; repr., Boston: Beacon Press, 1990).

89. However, in Brazil, on account of the preponderance of Yoruba slaves imported en masse from the Coast of Slaves in the seventeenth century (Lagos became the strategic center of the slave trade in the Gulf of Guinea), these cultural practices created a strong degree of syncretism—mainly of a religious nature in the Gege-Nagô culture. The voodoo rituals of Dahomey were absorbed into those of the Orisha of the Nagô, especially in Bahia.

90. Women were furthermore entrusted with sensitive posts in government and administration: each state official had a female counterpart or "mother," whose task was to supervise and check on his decisions and choices. In addition a group of eight women was always present at meetings with the king and his advisers and another similar group at the king's meetings with his ministers and priests. See Herskovits, *Myth of the Negro Past,* 84, 111ff. For the kingdom of Dahomey, see Paul Mercier, "The Fon of Dahomey," in *African Worlds,* ed. D. Forde, 210–34 (1954; repr., London: Oxford University Press, 1965).

91. Karl Polanyi, *Dahomey and the Slave Trade: An Analysis of an Archaic Economy* (Seattle and London: University of Washington Press, 1966), 56–57.

92. Filho, *Festas e tradiçıões,* 104–5.

93. "Demás está por decir que su baile, vestimenta, maquillaje y música es diametralmente opuesta al legado histórico de nuestros antepasados" (moreover, it should be said that their dancing, clothes, makeup, and music were the complete opposites of the historic legacy from our ancestors) (Hugo Gonzales, "Toribio Gutierrez: El último de los fundadores de la comparsa de San Benito en Timotes" [typescript in possession of G. Fiume]).

94. The African origin can be recognized in the dancing devils in St. Benedict–Ajé, St. John the Baptist–Congo, and St. Mary–Lionza in Venezuela; in the Brazilian *candomblé* and *macumba* and Haitian voodoo; and above all in the religions and pantheons of saints preserved on the island of Cuba. See Luis Joaquín Muñoz, "Las religiones afroamericanas: Los Cultos yoruba en Africa y America," *Africamerica* 3 (July–December 1996): 10–19.

95. This produced a true rainbow of racial combinations known by Spanish words such as, for example, *trigueños, mulatos, zambos, cholos, chinos, castizo cuatrialbo, coyote, coyote mestizo, chamizo, barnizo, puchuelo, tresalbo, zamabayo,* and *cambujo.*

96. In Uruguay the African element (for example, Angola, Congos, Mandingas, Mozambiques, with a preponderance of Bantu), originating from Senegal, Sierra Leone, Guinea, Mozambique, and above all from Angola and indirectly from Brazil, sustained the veneration of St. Benedict as an expression of "African-ness." See *Raíces Afro-Uruguays, Africanía en el Uruguay,* http://www.mundomatero.com (accessed March 2004).

97. Those who brought the black slaves to religion concentrated on the veneration of St. Balthazar, the Magi, and St. Benedict. "Este santo de la esclavatura es honrado y venerado en la Capilla de San Roque a Buenos Aires y para mediados del siglo XIX funcionava una sociedad de negros, que organizaba desfiles por las calles porteñas luciendo sus integrantes fastuosos y curiosos trajes. La misma sociedad, u otras, se presentaban en los carnavales, desfilando con imágenes alusivas y cantando letras donde el nombre del santo era al centro de la rimas. Esta devoción porteña se etendió al Paraguay y al Brasil. En este último país se lo considera como sanador de varias enfermedades, especialmente la viruela" (This saint of slavery is honored and venerated at the chapel of San Roque in Buenos Aires and in the mid–nineteenth century there was an active society of blacks, who organized processions through the streets of that city, their team members wearing strange flamboyant costumes. The same people and others were present at carnivals, processing with appropriate images and singing songs featuring the name of the saint in the

middle of the rhymes. This devotion in Buenos Aires extended to Paraguay and Brazil. In the latter country he was regarded as the healer of various illnesses, especially smallpox) (Juan Carlos Coria, *Pasado y presente de los Negros en Buenos Aires,* October 1997, http://www.geocities.com [accessed March 2004]).

Image and Imagination in the Cult of St. Amico

Rodger Payne

My first knowledge of St. Amico came one day at the conclusion of a class discussion on Catholic devotions, when a student asked if I was familiar with a procession in Donaldsonville, Louisiana, that honored "a saint who isn't really a saint." Intrigued by this description and just beginning to discover the variety of Catholic devotions that were peculiar to south Louisiana, I had the opportunity a few years later to attend the procession and have since returned on numerous occasions. While the student's comment about St. Amico's illegitimacy as a saint proved not to be entirely accurate, the question of Amico's canonicity has played a significant role in the history of the procession. The image of Amico, in the sense of the way in which he has been imagined by the community of the devout, has become a site of contested meanings between devotees and the clerical representatives of the institutional church; it raises questions about the nature of historical memory and public presentation, the symbolization of corporate self-identity, and the transmission and adoption of devotional activities in the transatlantic world.

Donaldsonville's devotion to St. Amico began in the early part of the twentieth century when, devotees believe, the saint appeared as a "dark man" on River Road south of town, in an area inhabited by recent immigrants from southern Italy who had been recruited to work on the area's sugar plantations. Presenting himself as a physician of sorts, the otherwise unknown figure was brought to the home of one of these immigrants, a truck farmer named Tony Musco, in hopes that the stranger could heal Musco's seriously ill son Lucien. After applying a series of folk remedies, the stranger predicted the child's rapid recovery, and almost instantaneously the child, who had not eaten for days, called out to his startled parents for food. When the parents turned to find the stranger and thank him for this miraculous cure, he had mysteriously disappeared. When the parents questioned their son as to whether the stranger had revealed his name, the child identified the man by pointing to a picture of St. Amico hanging on the wall. Believing that he had unsuspectingly entertained a saint in his home, Musco constructed a small private chapel to honor Amico and sent to Italy for an image of the saint to display there. When the image arrived in 1912 (about six years after the purported miracle), the chapel was dedicated and an annual procession inaugurated in which the image was carried from the chapel to the imposing Church of the Ascension in Donaldsonville.[1]

The annual procession became an occasion to celebrate the Italian heritage of the region. Contemporary devotees recall Musco's visits to the homes of Italian families to raise money for the festival that followed the procession on the chapel grounds, and the local parish clergy supported the annual devotion by supplying a priest who could hear confessions and deliver a sermon in Italian. By the 1940s the procession had gained enough prominence to attract the attention of the local novelist Frances Keyes, who, in collaboration with the famed folklife photographer Elemore Morgan, included the procession in an anecdotal travelogue entitled *All This Is Louisiana*.[2] The photographs of the 1947 procession that Morgan contributed depict a proud Tony Musco leading the group along River Road, with his son Lucien—now a middle-aged adult—helping to carry the image of Amico. Within twenty years, however, the devotion was in decline, affected by Tony Musco's death in 1960 and the changing ethos of devotionalism in the wake of the Second Vatican Council. In the late 1970s a new parish priest refused to permit the image access to the church grounds, arguing that Amico was not a legitimate saint. Although the procession continued, Amico was forced to "watch" from a private lawn across the street from the church while devotees attended Mass. After approximately fifteen years of this indignity, a new pastor allowed the image to be returned to the church, but only a few faithful remained to continue the annual procession. Even this was ended in 2001 when the remaining devotees determined that they were too few and too elderly to continue the tradition.[3]

The life and death of Donaldsonville's devotion to St. Amico might be read as yet another example of the failure of a European devotion to find continued success in North America, in this case due, in part, to Amico's obscurity as a holy figure and his inability to symbolize a larger Italian nationalist identity in the manner of St. Joseph or Madonna del Carmine. However, there are anomalies in the devotion to Amico that make such a judgment preliminary and hasty. The Donaldsonville devotion was not imported but indigenous; it celebrated no "old world" miracles but rather the apparition of the saint among the faithful of south Louisiana. In addition, clearly, at least for a time, the image of the obscure saint as a "dark man" appealed to the Italian immigrant community of the region even if this appeal could not be sustained longer than two generations. In other words, the devotion to St. Amico may tell us little about the transmission of a European devotion to American shores, but it may provide insight on how Amico functioned as an image through which a community could in fact imagine itself.

In 1971 Peter Brown both challenged and changed the prevailing scholarly opinion regarding the cult of the saints in late antiquity. Arguing that the persistence of provincial pagan practices was insufficient to explain the rise of the "holy man" in Christianity, Brown suggested that the emergence of the holy man instead be regarded "as one of the many surprising devices by which men in a vigorous and sophisticated society . . . set about the delicate business of living."[4] The veneration of martyrs and confessors was not a leftover fragment of classical polytheism that was baptized into Christianity, Brown asserted, but rather an innovative adaptation to the transformations of late antiquity. As an ascribed attribute, sanctity was not so much a characteristic of the holy man as it was a reflection of the society that assigned it; thus, Brown proposed that the task of a scholar was not to pursue the authenticity of the image of the saint but "to analyze this image as a product of the society around the holy man."[5]

Although Brown was principally concerned with the desert ascetics of the fifth and sixth centuries, his insights are instructive for the larger examination of saints and their cults, particularly before the conferral of canonicity became an institutionalized process controlled by ecclesiastical bureaucrats. The determination of individual sanctity in the premodern era was a social process wherein the figure of the saint came to be imagined in a multitude of ways depending on the needs of various constituencies. For ecclesiastical authorities, saints were exemplars of heroic virtues, but the promotion of a cult or devotion usually owed as much to politics as to religious virtuosity. Local political authorities likewise stood to gain tangible benefits when a shrine became a place of miracles and a destination for pilgrims. Communities looked to their divine patrons for protection but also enjoyed the prestige brought by particularly efficacious relics or association with significant figures, and individuals sought out the saints for healing or assistance in a multiplicity of ways. In each case, the figure of the saint might be imagined in ways both subtle and surprising, both complementary and contradictory. From miracle stories to hagiographies, from paintings to prayers, the image of the saint was subject to a process of continuous definition and reinterpretation that reflected the conditions imposed by the larger social context. Thus, the saint was at once both a product and a commodity of the cultic community.

This process can be traced in the history of the cult of St. Amico. By all measures, Amico is a rather obscure figure, but this obscurity has paradoxically been the single feature most responsible for the endurance of his cult. With no unique miracles or thaumaturgic specialties, the figure of Amico has presented a blank slate on which diverse images have been inscribed by various constituencies seeking to create a "usable" image of the saint to meet their own requirements. Since little evidence remains of the historical figure behind these images, the ways in which these communities have imagined Amico have come to define the cult of the saint. Whether heralded as the supernatural protector of a small Italian village or as a monastic reformer, the figure of Amico has been subject to a constant process of construction and redefinition according to the needs and historical situations of the communities of the devout.

The various cultic images of Amico are grounded in a historical figure who lived from about the mid–tenth century to the mid–eleventh century. According to the two *vitae* published in the *Acta Sanctorum*,[6] he was born of a noble family in the town of Camerino in the Italian Marches and probably lived a large part of his adult life in the rugged Abruzzi region of central Italy. In typical hagiographic fashion, the anonymous authors of the *vitae* cared little about the mundane details of his life—preferring to focus on his miracles—but certain clues do suggest ways in which the saint might be placed within some of the currents of central Italian religious life during what was a rather tumultuous period.

Central Italy during the tenth and eleventh centuries was contested ground, a border region between German, Lombard, Byzantine, and papal territories. Not until the end of the eleventh century, with the end of Byzantine influence and the rise of Norman military power, did some degree of political stability come to the region, and this was quickly followed by the ecclesiastical reforms associated with Pope Gregory VII in the twelfth century. While the Norman and Gregorian periods have commanded the attention of many historians, some recent scholars have argued that the Gregorian reform was merely the culmination of a much larger movement for reform that began within the monastic tradition almost a century before Gregory—himself a former monk—assumed the papacy in 1073. According to Phyllis G. Jestice, this reform movement had its foundation in the appearance of certain "wayward monks" who, by their unorthodox practices, began the lengthy process of redefining monastic life in the late tenth and early eleventh centuries.[7] The principal expressions of this redefinition were a growing emphasis on individual endeavors and the concomitant rejection of the cenobitic life for either a greater engagement with the secular world outside the monastery or, alternatively, a life lived in heroic solitude as a hermit or a recluse.

This new eremitism may have in fact been influenced by the influx into the region of Orthodox monks who came seeking refuge from Arab-Muslim rule in Sicily. Attracted by the rugged mountains and dense forests of Byzantine-controlled regions in Calabria and Apulia, Greek-speaking ascetics began arriving in the region in the late ninth century to live either as recluses or in small communities of hermits. C. H. Lawrence has argued that "[t]he founding fathers of the Italian eremitical movement" were to be found in Byzantine figures such as St. Nilus, a Greek-speaking monk from Calabria who made a celebrated visit to Montecassino in the late tenth century.[8] Indeed, despite continuous jurisdictional disputes between Rome and Constantinople in southern Italy, many Greek saints made pilgrimages to Rome in the years prior to the schism, and there are enough obvious parallels between these Byzantine ascetics and the new breed of holy hermits who began to inhabit the Apennine wilderness in the tenth century to suggest that the latter were motivated by more than their own pious rejection of wealthy monasteries and worldly monks.

The historical Amico appears to have been one of these hermits, and as is the case with the others, the factors that drove him to seek solitude in central Italy's rugged terrain have long since been buried under the pious hagiographical convention that he abandoned the cenobitic life out of disgust at his brother monks who "turned aside from the right path most destructively . . . [and] were obstinately occupied much more in worldly practices."[9] Although the two hagiographies that are preserved in the *Acta Sanctorum* largely present a traditional image of Amico as an itinerant preacher and thaumaturge, the opening chapters capture the spirit of a wandering hermit who lived in "deserted, desolate lands."[10] At one point, according to the author of the second *vita,* Amico "ascended to the summit of a mountain, and sought out a cave, prepared for him by divine providence . . . [and] having prayed and made the sign of the cross around himself, he entered the cave where he stayed for the space of three years, without the comfort of any men, and he was supported only by divine friendship."[11] His reputation as a holy man, however, soon led to the formation of a small body of disciples who finally prevailed upon him to move to a more easily accessible grotto. Even so, he continued to practice an extreme asceticism for the next twenty years, during which "he enjoyed no other nourishment except mushrooms or fruits of the woods; and likewise, throughout forty years, he made his body weak with so much abstinence that he was satisfied with neither bread nor sleep."[12]

The factors that influenced and informed Amico's eremitic life remain unknown. Clearly, however, his initial years as a wandering ascetic fit the pattern of the "wayward monks" who roamed the region in the late tenth and eleventh centuries, although unlike contemporaries such as Nilus or St. Romuald (founder of the Camaldolese order), Amico never came to be celebrated as a hermit saint. Indeed, his eremitism and solitude made him a marginal and unusable figure for his hagiographers, who—writing years later under the influence of the great monastic center at Montecassino—found it necessary to "domesticate" him as an exemplar of cenobitism. Fortunately for these writers, Amico apparently abandoned the eremitic life prior to his death and spent his final years in a newly founded monastery in San Pietro Avellana, a small village located on the banks of the Sangro River in remote Alto Molise. His pious death there in or about the year 1045 gave the new monastery its first—and only—saint.

Amico's death at San Pietro Avellana also began the transformation of the holy hermit into a local patron. Fully half of the miracles reported by the author of the

Vita prima, the longer and more substantial of the surviving hagiographies, are "shrine stories" designed to demonstrate the authenticity of Amico's own sanctity through his posthumous miracles at his tomb in San Pietro Avellana, especially his aptitude for healing hernias (a peculiar specialty that he shared with some other medieval saints). According to the *vitae,* as Amico lay dying, he had instructed his closest disciple to tie a rope around his legs and drag his body to an unmarked hole for burial—an appropriately pious death for one renowned for his asceticism. However, the hermit who had sought solitude during most of his life apparently desired acknowledgment after death, and his unmarked tomb became a place of potent supernatural power. According to a story recounted in the longer *vita,* a visiting bishop had his foot suddenly paralyzed when he stepped unknowingly on Amico's grave; and only after it was determined that this was indeed the burial place of the holy man was the bishop healed. The experience proved enough to convince the ecclesiastic of Amico's sanctity and power, and he vowed to return annually and bring "an ass weighted down with sacred oil" to the site. According to the hagiographer, though, the bishop proved unfaithful and broke his vow; thus he was "never without the torment of his entire body" for the remainder of his life.[13]

Amico's vengeance on the impious bishop—both in his initial paralysis and in his later torments—grates against modern sensibilities but fulfills the expectations that medieval Christians would have had for their patron saints. An old hermit living on crumbs in a small cell might inspire some individuals to similar feats of piety, but a powerful saint who could wreak vengeance on those who neglected to pay him proper respect garnered respect not only for himself but for his shrine as well. Imagined as patron, Amico was not only placed in a new relationship of mutual obligations with the villagers, but he also helped to define the new community, enhance its reputation, give status to its inhabitants, and defend them against various external assaults.

Indeed, Amico's association with the village came early after its founding. The death in 981 of Pandulf "Ironhead" I, the ruler of the powerful Lombard state of Capua-Benevento in central Italy, produced a frenzied land grab by noble families in the region, and the once centralized state was fractured into thirty-four separate counties.[14] Among the beneficiaries of the dissolution of Pandulf's state was the Count of Marsia, Oderisio Borello I ("Borello the Great"), who gained control of the county of Molise in the southern Abruzzi and established a short-lived dynastic state.[15] Borello sought to secure his authority in this wild and sparsely populated region by establishing new villages and endowing new monastic foundations. In 1026 he established the monastery of San Pietro Avellana in an area "previously uninhabited" between Montemiglio and the Sangro River.[16] The opportune arrival and death of Amico there during the earliest years of the monastery were critically important events for both the new monastery and the nascent village that was beginning to form nearby. Although the monastery and, eventually, the local parish were dedicated to St. Peter, the chief apostle was, in a classification scheme proposed by William A. Christian, only the "titular" patron of San Pietro Avellana, while Amico became the more significant "active" patron.[17] Amico's role had thus changed significantly, from that of a charismatic ascetic and exemplar of piety to the supernatural advocate and representative of the village—both to the local authorities and, more importantly, to God. As Michael Carroll has noted, however, the relationship between a locality and its supernatural patron was not just a reciprocal one of protection in exchange for devotion but rather entailed the actual creation of the community as an identifiable "geographical unit" that "defined . . . a particular physical space."[18] Amico's shrine, his relics, and the demonstrations of his power through the miracles became the nucleus of communal identity, and an annual procession of the image of Amico through the streets of the village delineated both the municipal boundaries and the identity of its occupants as those under the saint's protection.

Whether or not the Borellos recognized their good fortune in so quickly obtaining a patron for their new village, they apparently did little to promote a cult of devotion there. Rather, Oderisius and his successors repeatedly plundered the monastery and its associated settlement until 1069, when Borello II, the oldest son of Oderisius, ceded the monastery and its surrounding lands to Abbot Desiderius of Montecassino in an act that was probably designed to keep the area from falling into Norman hands. Montecassino's acquisition of San Pietro Avellana solidified the cult of Amico by adding him to the Benedictine pantheon of martyrs and confessors. Despite its remoteness, the monastery at San Pietro Avellana quickly became "a particularly important dependency" of the great Benedictine abbey during its most expansive feudal period, and numerous churches in the region were placed under the care of the local abbot.[19] As feudal lords, the abbots of Montecassino also fortified the village and ended the depredations of the Borellos and other local counts. When the Normans established political control over the southern peninsula in the latter eleventh century, San Pietro Avellana's status as a fief of the great archabbey protected it from plunder because of the Norman alliance with Montecassino. With such significant support, the cult of Amico flourished for the next three centuries, although it remained localized in the Alto Molise region.

The mid–eleventh century was the golden age of Montecassino, under the able administration of Abbot Desiderius (later to become Pope Victor III). The fall of the city of Bari to the Normans in 1071 eliminated the final stronghold of Byzantine rule in southern Italy, and both Montecassino and the nearby monastery of San Vincenzo al Volturna sought to consolidate networks of feudal dependencies, driven as much by political concerns as by religious revival. Due to its location in the heart of territories contested by Norman, Lombard, German, and papal forces, Montecassino was showered with privileges and prerogatives by popes and the emperors of both the East and the West, as well as the emerging Norman rulers. As abbot, Desiderius managed to steer a course of reconciliation and realpolitik in the midst of these competing interests, preserving both the abbey's traditional immunity as an independent political dominion and its exemption from local ecclesiastical authorities.[20] As the instigator of the eventual accord between the papacy and the Normans, Desiderius was named the papal vicar for all of the monasteries of southern Italy, including those in the former Byzantine territories of Apulia and Calabria that bordered Molise. The principal symbol of his administration at Montecassino came with the building of a new basilica there. Its dedication in 1071 drew "one of the most illustrious gatherings of the eleventh century" of political and ecclesiastical figures, including the various counts of the Borello family, who were then at the height of their power.[21]

Desiderius's acquisition of formerly independent monasteries such as the one at San Pietro Avellana must be understood in light of both the extension of feudal prerogatives and the monastic revival of the eleventh century of which Montecassino was an important center. One method by which both ends could be achieved was through the promotion of local cults. As H. E. J. Cowdrey observed, the local villages were "establishing their identity by elaborating their patrons' cultuses, by adding to their relics, and by amplifying local funds of legends, liturgies, and festival," and "Montecassino's hagiographical literature shows how the skills of its monks were not only directed towards the cultus of St. Benedict and the saints of Montecassino, but were also available to the monks, bishops, and people of other monasteries, churches, and localities, in order to build up their own devotion and civic pride."[22] Throughout southern Italy, Montecassino's hagiographers "baptized" the earlier hermits into the Benedictine tradition and appropriated their independent monastic foundations into the expanding Cassinese reform.

This was undoubtedly the process through which Amico came to be associated with Montecassino. According to the testimony of the twelfth-century chronicler of Montecassino, Peter the Deacon, it was a Cassinese monk named Bernard who first "described the miracles of the holy confessor Amico, a monk of Montecassino."[23] The Bollandist Carlos De Smedt, who edited the Latin *vitae* of Amico in the *Acta Sanctorum,* judged the work of Bernard to be the shorter *Vita secunda* based on Peter's comment that he had recorded only the miracles (rather than the life) of Amico, but in fact both *vitae* are primarily collections of miracle stories. Neither places Amico at Montecassino nor identifies him in any way with the great abbey; rather, both focus solely on his association with San Pietro Avellana.

Nonetheless, the *vitae,* by their inclusion in the developing canon of Cassinese saints, claimed the former hermit for Montecassino's own cenobitic revival.

This posthumous and anachronistic relationship between Amico and Montecassino brought certain advantages to the devotion. First of all, it gave Amico the benefits of support and promotion that came with his association with a religious order, and the great collections of Benedictine martyrologies (such as that compiled by Jean Mabillon in the seventeenth century) never fail to include a version of his *vita.* More importantly, as a Benedictine saint, Amico was raised to the altar at Montecassino and included in its liturgies. These actions truly transfigured the devotion from local cult to "catholic" status.

In 1441 the last Cassinese monk to serve as abbot in San Pietro Avellana began his term in office; shortly thereafter the monastery was abandoned in the aftermath of a devastating earthquake.[24] The village of San Pietro Avellana remained a feudal and ecclesiastical dependency of Montecassino until 1785. This long association between the village and the abbey meant that Amico's roles as village patron and Cassinese exemplar merged, and subsequent lives of the saint had to account for the inherent contradictions. Eventually, Amico, like his great contemporary Dominic of Sora,[25] came to be viewed not as a solitary holy man but as a missionary of the Cassinese revival, the "principal patron and benefactor of San Pietro Avellana . . . who left behind the walls of Montecassino, by divine inspiration, [and] came into this region to sanctify it with [his] preaching and penitence."[26]

Despite the closure of the monastery in San Pietro Avellana in the fifteenth century, the monks of Montecassino did not abandon their adopted saint. On September 22, 1623, Don Bernadino of Saavedra, the reigning abbot, presided over a great festival during which Amico's remains were solemnly translated from their original burial site to a new stone sarcophagus that was located beneath the altar of a small chapel attached to the parish church.[27] The occasion that brought such a rekindled interest in the cult of Amico after the neglect of almost two centuries remains unclear, but it may be connected to the rise of an alternative cult that identified Amico not as a Benedictine monk but as a Cistercian abbot who lived and died at the Abbey of Santa Maria Rambona in the province of Macerata, well to the north of San Pietro Avellana and outside the realm of Montecassino's influence.

In many ways the identification of the eremitical Amico with the Cistercians presents a more appropriate fit than was the case with the cenobitic revival at Montecassino. Although the Cistercians remained within the larger Benedictine tradition, their stringent interpretation of the Rule of St. Benedict made them attractive to those individuals who sought a rigorous ascetic ideal within the context of community. Unlike other orders founded in the High Middle Ages that were little more than communities of hermits (such as the Calmodolese), the Cistercians offered a popular balance between eremitism and cenobitism that caused them to emerge as among the most powerful rivals of the more conservative Benedictines of Montecassino.[28]

The monastery at Rambona actually predated the founding of the Cistercian order by many centuries. Initially founded in the late ninth century by Ageltruda, the Lombard wife of Guy III, Marquis of Spoleto and Camerino, who became the first non-Carolingian to hold, briefly at least (891–94), the title of emperor,[29] the abbey grew to possess numerous churches, dependencies, and other assets. At some point between the twelfth and fifteenth centuries, Rambona became a leading center for the Cistercian reform movement in central Italy, but its sack in the middle of the fifteenth century by Milanese soldiers, who pillaged the monastery's wealth and set fire to the edifice, was a blow from which it was unable to recover.

Beneath the ruined abbey church, a small crypt claims to hold the relics of a monk named Amico who ruled as the abbot of the monastery there in the late tenth century. Whether this Amico is understood to be the same as San Pietro Avellana's saint or as a different individual by the same name, the two figures led parallel lives. Both were born in the region of the Marches; both initially lived as hermits and then later in a monastic cell attached to a church; both developed a postmortem specialty in healing hernias; and both died on November 2 (or in some accounts November 3). Even if these two Amicos were historically distinct figures, clearly their cults had merged by the seventeenth century. Thus, the translation of Amico's relics and the construction of his new tomb in San Pietro Avellana may have been Abbot Bernadino's response to this expanding devotion and the potential eclipse of the Benedictine Amico by his Cistercian doppelgänger.

While there is no *vita* of Amico of Rambona to match those of Montecassino's saint, he is named in a critically important historical document, Peter Damian's famous epistle traditionally entitled the *Liber Gratissimus.* Unfortunately, the brief mention by Damian provides few tangible details: only that this Amico had died within the living memory of Damian's correspondents and that he had been recognized as a saintly figure despite his ordination by a simoniac bishop.[30] Since Damian was the abbot of the Camaldolese monastery of San Pietro at Fonte Avellana in the northern Apennines (not the Benedictine monastery in Molise), his epigrammatic note has only added to the confusion between the two Amicos.[31] Further, while Damian's comment indicates that Amico of Rambona had died by the middle of the eleventh century, the iconographic depictions of this Amico always place him in a white Cistercian habit—an anachronism that associates him with the reform movement a full century before the Abbey of Rambona could have even adopted it.

Despite the lack of documentary evidence concerning the Amico of Rambona, the iconographic evidence suggests a much more significant and geographically more dispersed cult than was ever the case with the Amico of San Pietro Avellana. Images, paintings, and frescoes of the Cistercian abbot appear throughout the Marches, Umbria, and as far south as L'Aquila in central Abruzzo, while the cult of the Benedictine Amico remained confined to the more immediate area near its Molisano shrine.[32] Apart from the different habits, however, there are no other iconographic distinctions between the two Amicos. Both can be depicted as either old or young, bearded or clean shaven. The key iconographic symbols of both are an ax and a wolf (often leashed) that reflect the same miracle credited to both saints. According to later oral tradition (it is absent from both *vitae*), Amico had once gone into the woods for firewood, taking along a mule outfitted with saddlebags to haul the wood back to his cell. While the saint was chopping wood, a wolf killed the mule, and when Amico returned, he scolded the wolf, who felt such shame that he agreed to carry the firewood-laden saddlebags back to the village. The miracle of the taming of the wolf may be read as a symbolic tale of Christian virtue taming the rugged wilderness of the central Apennines, but it may have also inspired (or been inspired by—the chronology is unclear) the analogous and more famous story of St. Francis's taming of the wolf of Gubbio. Both Gubbio and Assisi were in the same general region as Amico's birthplace, and not far from the abbey at Rambona, but the similarities of the stories may demonstrate only the fluidity of the oral tradition of this miracle tale in this region. The primary significance of this story is that it gives to the cult of Amico its principal iconographic symbols and allows us to identify the late sixteenth and early seventeenth centuries—when the majority of these depictions of the saint were completed—as a period during which the cult flourished in central Italy.

In 1887 Sabatino Frazzini, then the parish priest at the church in San Pietro Avellana, published a short and pious account of Amico and his association with the village—the first vernacular account of the village's patron saint.[33] Frazzini's booklet reflected a renewal of interest in the cult as Amico began to assume a new role as a symbol of communal memory even as the village and surrounding region were undergoing the stresses and strains of emigration and depopulation. Unlike the heavily industrialized north, southern Italy was still a land of subsistence farming, and the land reforms introduced by the new government in Rome after the unification of the peninsula in 1870 had succeeded only in displacing peasants who had few other options than to leave for new lives. These emigrants viewed themselves not as citizens of a nation-state but as *paesani* of their local villages or region, and it was this identification that helped the emigrants respond to the social dislocations they faced—whether through physical return, continued communication, the establishment of diasporic "colonies," or, in many cases, simply a continued devotion to the local saints and Madonnas of the *paese*. Indeed, as William A. Douglass has noted in his study of emigration from Agnone (located about thirty-six kilometers from San Pietro Avellana), not only did such strategies provide a means whereby the immigrants could create familiar worlds of meaning in their new situations, but also their former residences "consciously attempted to retain the loyalties and orchestrate the activities of the immigrants" for the benefit of the village.[34] Immigrants who succeeded financially became a source of economic support for the village as well as for its churches and local cults.

Frazzini's booklet thus provided emigrants from San Pietro Avellana with a tangible and portable identity with the *paese* through the stories of its patron. One measure of their response was the dedication in 1906 of a new St. Amico chapel in the woods just outside of town, built with donations from emigrants from San Pietro Avellana. The new chapel not only illustrated the continued devotion of expatriate *sampietrese* to their village guardian but also allowed for their symbolic incorporation into the annual procession that now made its way from the seventeenth century shrine to the new edifice.

It would be simplistic to assign the origin of the devotion in Donaldsonville to this reinvigoration of the cult as a response to the pressures of emigration, although certainly such factors cannot be easily dismissed. However, in the same way in which the image of Amico had been constructed by various constituencies throughout the course of the history of the devotion, the devotees in south Louisiana creatively utilized the figure of Amico to symbolize their own identity. Their annual procession was not an attempt to replicate the traditions of San Pietro Avellana (indeed, there is no evidence to suggest that a substantial number of the Donaldsonville devotees were from San Pietro Avellana) but was rather a means of creating a new corporate identity that could be publicly affirmed and negotiated. Like the monks of Montecassino or the Cistercians of Rambona, the devotees in Donaldsonville ascribed to the image of St. Amico an identity that reflected their own.

The key to interpreting the Louisiana devotion in this way lies in the belief of the devotees that Amico had appeared among them as a "dark man." The immigrants who arrived in south Louisiana during the late nineteenth and early twentieth centuries found themselves in the midst of an increasing climate of racial tension in the Jim Crow South. This was especially true for those who made their way into the state's "sugar bowl" region, where the departure of African Americans after Reconstruction had created an acute crisis of labor. The owners of the sugar plantations in the area saw immigrant labor as providing an answer to the labor problem, and during the 1890s they had begun an aggressive campaign to recruit southern Italian emigrants. Although initially regarded as "white labor" in distinction to the black labor of former slaves, the dark-skinned Italians quickly

Fig. 1. (left) The image of St. Amico at the chapel in Donaldsonville, Louisiana, following the annual procession. The saint is represented here as a Benedictine monk and wears a stole to which various ex-votos have been attached. Photograph by Rodger Payne (April 1996).

Fig. 2. Fresco of St. Amico depicted as a Cistercian monk. Note the iconographic symbols of the ax and the wolf on a leash. Church of Santa Maria della Grazie, Cucollo, Italy. Photograph by Rodger Payne (October 2000).

found themselves a racially suspect community in a climate of increasingly antagonistic racial categories.[35] By assuming the work formerly performed by slaves and freedmen, by living in and among the remaining African American laborers, and by their own ignorance of the severity of southern segregation laws and customs, the Italians encountered the same discrimination that southern blacks endured, including the horrors of lynching. In three famous cases between 1891 and 1899, Italians faced such vigilante justice at the hands of those who perceived that they had, in the words of John Higham, violated "the white man's code."[36]

In such a climate as this, Amico's obscurity served the Italian immigrant community of south Louisiana well. By appearing as a "dark man" in a region where "black" and "white" had become the only markers of racial identity, Amico's own racial ambiguity—as a dark saint represented by a light-skinned image—reflected that of his immigrant devotees. The procession provided a public expression of this identity as well as the opportunity for a limited amount of racial integration since, as the photos of Elemore Morgan vividly depict,[37] the devotees were accompanied from the chapel into Donaldsonville and back again by an African American brass band. As the Italians eventually came to be accepted as "white," however, the significance of the image of a racially indeterminate Amico to symbolize the community began to fade. With no corporate memory of the *paese* to preserve, devotees have abandoned Amico for other saints and devotions.

While the devotion to St. Amico in south Louisiana represents the most unusual adaptation of the image of St. Amico to meet the needs of corporate self-identity, it is certainly not unique in this regard. Whether as hermit or patron, abbot or monk, the only constant theme in the devotion to Amico has been the ability of the saint to be imagined in ways that meet the needs of the devout community.

Notes

1. Jennie Musco Salemi, *A True Story of Saint Amico* (privately printed account of the apparition in Donaldsonville distributed at the chapel, n.d.).

2. Frances Parkinson Keyes, *All This Is Louisiana* (New York: Harper and Brothers, 1950), 204–7.

3. The pastor who allowed the return of the image to the church also encouraged the devotees to shift the festival from the ecclesiastically irregular Sunday after Easter to a time closer to Amico's feast day (November 2) in order to gain the full support of the parish, but they declined, citing their lingering bitterness over the years of the image's exile.

4. Peter Brown, "The Rise and Function of the Holy Man in Late Antiquity," *Journal of Roman Studies* 71 (1971): 82.

5. Ibid., 81.

6. *Acta Sanctorum* (hereafter *AASS*), Nov. II, part 1 (Brussels, 1894), 92–102. The *vitae* are preceded by Carolo De Smedt's "Commentarius praevius," 89–92. My translation of these texts was prepared by Kit Smoot.

7. Phyllis G. Jestice, *Wayward Monks and the Religious Revolution of the Eleventh Century* (Leiden: Brill, 1997).

8. C. H. Lawrence, *Medieval Monasticism: Forms of Religious Life in Western Europe in the Middle Ages,* 2nd ed. (London: Longman, 1989), 152.

9. *AASS,* 93.

10. Ibid., 100.

11. Ibid.

12. Ibid., 101.

13. Ibid., 98.

14. Barbara Kreutz, *Before the Normans: Southern Italy in the Ninth and Tenth Centuries* (Philadelphia: University of Pennsylvania Press, 1991), 103–6; William A. Douglass, *Emigration in a South Italian Town: An Anthropological History* (New Brunswick, N.J.: Rutgers University Press, 1984), 32–33.

15. Cesare Rivera, "Origini dei Borelli conti di Sangro," *Archivo storico per le province napoletane* 44 (1919): 48–91.

16. Herbert Bloch, *Monte Cassino in the Middle Ages,* 3 vols. (Cambridge, Mass.: Harvard University Press, 1986), 1:362–63; Rivera, "Origini dei Borelli," 62–65.

17. William A. Christian, *Person and God in a Spanish Valley* (New York: Seminar Press, 1972), 68.

18. Michael P. Carroll, *Madonnas That Maim: Popular Catholicism in Italy since the Fifteenth Century* (Baltimore and London: Johns Hopkins University Press, 1992), 38.

19. Bloch, *Monte Cassino,* 1:362.

20. H. E. J. Cowdrey, *The Age of Abbot Desiderius: Montecassino, the Papacy, and the Normans in the Eleventh and Twelfth Centuries* (Oxford, U.K.: Clarendon Press, 1983), xxxii–xxxiii.

21. Ibid., 4, 62, 122; Rivera, "Origini dei Borelli," 81.

22. Cowdrey, *Age of Abbot Desiderius,* 39.

23. Petrus Diaconus, *De viris illustribus Casinensis coenobii,* in *Patrologia Latina,* ed. J.-P. Migne (Paris, 1895), vol. 173, col. 1043.

24. Bloch, *Monte Cassino,* 1:368.

25. Like Amico, Dominic was a peripatetic holy man of the eleventh century whom tradition credits as the founder of numerous monasteries in south-central Italy. Likewise, his hagiographer, Alberic of Montecassino, incorporated him into the Cassinese cenobitic tradition, asserting, in fact, that Dominic was the actual founder of the monastery at San Pietro Avellana two decades prior to Borello's endowment.

26. Michele Messore, *Sant'Amico in San Pietro Avellana* (Rome: Editrice Missioni O. M. I., 1961), 96.

27. Giambattista Masciotta, *Il Molise dalle origini ai nostri giorni,* vol. 3, *Il circondario d'Isernia* (Campobasso: Editrice Lampo, 1983), 356; Pasquale Settefrati, *S. Amico di San Pietro Avellana: Il Santo amico Dio e degli uomini* (Teramo: Edigrafital, 2001), 186–87.

28. Peter King, *Western Monasticism: A History of the Monastic Movement in the Latin Church* (Kalamazoo, Mich.: Cistercian Publications, 1999), 168–70.

29. Chris Wickham, *Early Medieval Italy: Central Power and Local Society, 400–1000* (Totowa, N.J.: Barnes and Noble Books, 1981), 170; Kreutz, *Before the Normans,* 66.

30. The *Liber gratissimus* is a lengthy letter composed by Damian in 1052 regarding the validity of ordination by simoniac bishops (a practice that Damian defended). The citation is to the English translation in Peter Damian, *Letters of Peter Damian,* vol. 2, trans. Owen J. Blum (Washington, D.C.: Catholic University of America Press, 1990), 187.

31. E.g., Butler's *Lives of the Saints* follows De Smedt's argument in his introduction to the *vitae* in the *Acta Sanctorum* that the two are distinctly different individuals, but then it confusedly locates the Benedictine Amico at Damian's monastery in Fonte Avellana.

32. George Kaftal, *Iconography of the Saints in Italian Paintings from Its Beginnings to the Early XVIth Century,* 3 vols. (Florence: Sansoni, 1952), 2:48; Settefrati, *S. Amico di San Pietro Avellana,* 157–85.

33. Sabatino Frazzini, *Vita di Santo Amico: Eremita e monaco cassinese* (Isernia, 1887).

34. Douglass, *Emigration in a South Italian Town,* 114.

35. Jean Ann Scarpaci discusses these racial tensions in her article "Immigrants in the New South: Italians in Louisiana's Sugar Parishes, 1880–1910," *Labor History* 16 (1975): 165–83. See also Rodger Payne, "*Patronus Obscurus:* Devotion to St. Amico and the Italian 'Other' in South Louisiana," in *Journey into Otherness,* ed. Ada Savin, 39–56 (Amsterdam: VU University Press, 2005).

36. John Higham, *Strangers in the Land: Patterns of American Nativism, 1860–1925,* 2nd ed. (New Brunswick, N.J.: Rutgers University Press, 1988), 169.

37. Keyes, *All This Is Louisiana,* 205–6.

Seeking the Holy Child of Tierra Adentro

The Historical Origins of the Santo Niño de Atocha, 1704–1848

Juan Javier Pescador

Right on the imaginary line that divides North American deserts from central Mexico's tropical lands lies the Sanctuary of Plateros in the state of Zacatecas, Mexico. A mining town in colonial times, Plateros owed its existence to silver ores and its location on multiple borders and roads. Since the sixteenth century Plateros has been part of a chain of silver towns that stretched along the Camino Real between Zacatecas, Durango, Chihuahua, and Santa Fe. The silver is long gone, but Plateros remains a meeting place for people of Mexican descent. Pilgrims from northern and central Mexico, Mexican immigrants living in the United States, and U.S.-born Mexicans pack its dusty streets with their cars, vans, and pickups, especially in December and in the summer, to pay their respects to the Santo Niño de Atocha.

Originally a mere attachment to the Holy Virgin of Atocha, a colonial religious icon, the Santo Niño became a special saint for the people of the borderlands in the nineteenth century. Devotion to the Santo Niño quickly spread: first along the Camino Real de Tierra Adentro from Zacatecas all the way up to northern New Mexico, then in the 1880s with the Atchison Topeka and Santa Fe Railroad and Ferrocarril Central Mexicano railroad lines between Mexico City, El Paso, and Santa Fe. Poor people in general, but especially miners, prisoners, pregnant women, travelers, migrants, pilgrims, soldiers, muleteers, the sick and disabled, railroad workers, captives, prostitutes, and even thieves found a religious entity they could relate to in the Santo Niño. The lower class in the great Chihuahuan desert and its outer limits developed a local veneration for the Niñito, the Morenito, the Tejanito, or the Santo Niño de Atochita, as he is variously referred to. Without the official sponsorship of the Catholic Church and sometimes in spite of its blatant opposition, people in the area established a chain of shrines to venerate the Niñito from Plateros to Chimayó in northern New Mexico, especially in Chihuahua, Durango, Jiménez, El Paso, and Española.

In the early twenty-first century, devotion to the Santo Niño has moved well beyond the Camino Real de Tierra Adentro. As Mexican immigration to the United States reaches its highest point in history and the Mexican American population spreads beyond the United States Southwest, the Santo Niñito's humble hat and sandals can be recognized in New York City, Iowa City, Los Angeles, and Chicago. Each year since the beginning of the 1990s, the Sanctuary of Plateros has received—by mail, by hand, or via intermediaries—an average of four thousand letters addressed to the Santo Niño de Atocha. Three-quarters of this correspondence originates in the United States. Although the majority of these letters come from the U.S. Southwest where the Mexican presence has deep historical roots, an increasing number of missives arrive from other areas, especially the Midwest and the East Coast, mirroring new trends in the destinations of Mexican immigrants and Mexican Americans.[1] In July 1998 the image of the Santo Niño de Atocha was taken to the church of Nuestra Señora Reina de Los Angeles, or La Placita, in Los Angeles, California, and was revered by more than one hundred thousand pilgrims.[2]

This essay examines the social conditions that led to the development of this cult and stresses the fluid character of popular devotions associated with religious icons in late colonial and early national Mexico (1750–1850). It illustrates how religious veneration reflects social, political, and demographic conditions.[3]

As a background to the veneration of the Holy Child of Atocha, it should be noted that devotion to his mother, Our Lady of Atocha, was promoted by the Dominicans in Castille in the sixteenth century and probably brought by them to Zacatecas, where they founded a monastery in 1604.[4] The first reference to her veneration in Mexico, identified by the Zacatecan historian Bernardo del Hoyo, dates from 1664. The inventory of Lorenzo Ruíz Tostado, a miner in Zacatecas, from 1664 lists a private chapel in Tostado's mining estate, where there was "a statue of Our Lady of Atocha with a silver crown."[5]

The Holy Child is first mentioned forty years later, in a letter from September 29, 1704, written by Bizente de Medina, a resident of Fresnillo, to the bishop of Guadalajara requesting a permit to build a chapel on the outskirts of the mining town in honor of the Santo Cristo de los Plateros (also known as the Señor de los Plateros), a local crucifix with a miraculous reputation. Medina was the *mayordomo* (director of the board) of a confraternity recently created to venerate this image of Christ. Attached to Medina's petition was an inventory of the images under the brotherhood's custody. After the Christ of Plateros, an image of Our Lady of Atocha was listed: "One statue of more than one staff's height of Our Lady of Atocha with silver crown and sceptre that weighed one mark and one and a quarter ounce with her child Jesus, two mantles, one made with blue wool and the other yellow. [And] a little royal sceptre."[6]

The confraternity also commissioned masses in honor of Our Lady of Atocha, and Diego de Sotomayor, the parish priest in Fresnillo, testified that he had sung Mass in honor of the Virgin of Atocha every year in recent times. On October 9, 1704, the bishop of Guadalajara authorized the foundation of the brotherhood and the erection of the chapel.[7]

The confraternity of the Señor de los Plateros was only one of many such organizations among the region's provincial elites vigorously promoting the miraculous reputations of their own religious images. These lay confraternities functioned as social vehicles to re-create networks between families and immigrants from the same villages and provinces in the Old Country. They embodied the local desire among Spanish elites to emulate Iberian translocal devotions with an identifiable colonial core, such as that already adopted in Zacatecas. Moreover, these devotions expressed their aspiration to appear as social benefactors and civic leaders with patriarchal ties to their workers.

Funds to build the chapel dedicated to the Lord of Plateros were provided by one of the wealthiest men in the region: Don Fernando de La Campa y Coz, *Conde* (Count) of San Mateo Valparaiso. In 1732 Manuel Gutierrez de Avila, a senior scribe in Zacatecas, recorded that he had "noticed that in the past years in the Mining district of Fresnillo [the Count of San Mateo] had under his charge the building of the Santo Christo de Plateros' church, whose shrine is placed a league and half away [from Fresnillo], . . . which was decorated and furnished with everything possible at his own expense."[8]

Devotion to Our Lady of Atocha did not flourish during the eighteenth century. In March 1789 Fresnillo's parish priest, Don José María Díaz, initiated the building of an entirely new shrine to the Señor de Plateros; Díaz gathered economic support from different neighbors in Fresnillo by 1792 and had completed a new chapel next to the old one, as Díaz proudly reported to the bishop of Guadalajara.[9] However, Díaz's report, which lists masses and novenas, indicates that masses in honor of Our Lady of Atocha had ceased at some point in the eighteenth century.

In 1822 nine different confraternities existed in Fresnillo, but none of them venerated Our Lady of Atocha.[10] The most important local religious associations, after El Señor de Plateros, were dedicated to St. Joseph, Jesus of Nazareth, Our Lady of Sorrows, and the Souls in Purgatory. Three more modest confraternities were in charge of venerating St. Anne, St. Nicholas, and the Virgin of Tránsito. Fresnillo's parish priests supervised all local confraternities but were especially involved with the shrine of Plateros, which was under their direct authority.

The devotion to Our Lady of Atocha in Zacatecas most likely failed to grow due to the existence of previous Marian devotions with similar colonial contents. In the city of Zacatecas, the veneration to La Virgen del Patrocinio certainly eclipsed any other Marian advocation, while in Fresnillo the devotion to the Virgin of La Purificación, sponsored by the local clergy as the local patroness, certainly limited the chances of developing other Marian venerations. By the time a new church was constructed in 1789, official masses to Our Lady of Atocha had ceased.

An even more important change took place by late colonial times in Fresnillo: the Santo Niño de Atocha attained not only an autonomous status but also a unique reputation. In fact, the Santo Niño replaced the Señor de Plateros as the most important religious icon inside the shrine. Miracles were now performed not by the crucifix but by the Holy Child. The association of the Holy Child with the parish priests of La Purificación in Fresnillo must have played a role in this devotional change. Fresnillo's priests used the image of the Santo Niño as an itinerant figure who visited the parish church at Christmas and on February's *fiesta de la Candelaria* or *fiesta de la Purificación,* the Virgin's Purification, also known as Candlemas. Moreover, as the shrine inventories indicate, Fresnillo's priests were in charge of dressing the Santo Niño's image with several different outfits in order to emphasize different seasonal festivities in the liturgical calendar. The fact that he was removed from and returned to the Virgin of La Purificación in the parish church at various times every year would contribute to the Santo Niño's reputation in the area for wandering.

By the late eighteenth century the parish priests of Fresnillo had begun to exert more influence over the chapel's affairs and incorporated the brotherhood's activities into a set of local rituals between the church of La Purificación in Fresnillo and the chapel in Plateros. The parish priests transformed this rural chapel into a processional station that hosted and sent out religious images with strong local reputations as miraculous. Plateros thus became a sacred space in the ritual orbit of the church of La Purificación and served as a processional center on Easter and other religious festivities. The leadership of Fresnillo's priests was also seen in the construction of the new church in 1789.

As Plateros was absorbed into Fresnillo's ritual geography, local documents ceased to identify it as an independent religious space. In 1797 Fresnillo's mayor (*alcalde mayor*) Juan Antonio Evía drew a detailed map of the jurisdiction including "towns, villages, congregations and haciendas" but failed to mention Plateros.[11] One cause may be the fact that Plateros's mining potential was long extinguished by the end of the eighteenth century, and the area's small population consisted of a scattered community that worked on a ranch of the same name. Of the 231 ranches in the jurisdiction of Fresnillo, the Ranch of Plateros was among the smallest.[12] Even the ranch did not manage to survive as an independent unit and was absorbed by the hacienda of Nuestra Señora de los Dolores del Paso del Jaral, one of the many haciendas owned by the heirs of the Conde de San Matheo.[13]

A Traveler in Sandals, 1810–48

On February 15, 1816, Don Manuel Díaz de los Ríos, elected *mayordomo* of the Señor de los Plateros's confraternity, proceeded with the scribe José María García to make an inventory of goods, properties, images, and garments under his custody in the Sanctuary of Plateros. The image of the Niño de Atocha is described here for the first time as separated and different from that of the Madonna: "Her Child with purple dress, sandals, sceptre, and a little globe made of silver, and various *milagros* (ex-votos) and silver coins."[14]

Dressed as a little prince, with an orb and a scepter in his hands to denote his authority over the world, the Holy Child appears as a focus of devotion in his own right. In spite of the evidence of the *milagros* attached to his purple dress, devotion to the Holy Child had not developed enough to provide a specific niche for him in the church, nor even to justify a suitable setting to welcome his visitors. The inventory notes that the Holy Child stood above an old table and two used mirrors, one of which was broken. Subsequent additions to the inventory do not register a change in this setting. However, the *milagros* attached to his apparel witness to devotion to him. The most important factor in this miraculous reputation was, beyond doubt, the two thanksgiving paintings (*retablos*) standing at the Holy Child's feet, one sponsored by Don Juan Antonio de Evía and the other by Doña Bárbara Dovalina. The *retablos* are listed as regular in size, but their written content is, unfortunately, not transcribed in the inventory. Evía and Dovalina, both prominent Spanish-criollo *vecinos* (citizens of white Spanish descent) in Fresnillo, were likely the first devotees to express thanks to the Santo Niño with a *retablo.*

The chapel of Plateros was experiencing a rapid transformation in the internal hierarchy of its religious images. Despite the miraculous reputation attached to the Señor de Plateros, local people in Fresnillo were developing an increasingly important veneration for the Holy Child of Atocha. Such veneration was strikingly absent in all the chapel documentation since the building's construction in 1704. As late as the 1790s local records in Plateros failed to mention the Holy Child as a miraculous image or even as a religious icon separate from the Lady of Atocha; the Señor de Plateros remained the most prominent figure at the main altar in the chapel. However, the Holy Child, sustained by the Madonna of Atocha, soon began to take credit for divine interventions on behalf of the local faithful. The *retablo* tradition, manifested first by two local Spanish-criollo neighbors, appears to have been documented for the first time in 1816 but never in association with Our Lady of Atocha's image.

Various factors may explain the new development of this devotion in Fresnillo. The Mexican Independence Wars (1810–21) had a disastrous impact on the entire region; the military conflict that had started in the Bajío region soon spread to Los Altos de Jalisco and Zacatecas. The local criollo and mestizo population provided enthusiastic support to the *insurgentes,* while the significant peninsular population fully sided with the *realistas.* As internal class and ethnic divisions surfaced with the conflict, the region became completely involved in the struggle, and its prominent urban areas, Zacatecas city, Fresnillo, and Sombrerete, became obligatory targets for troops on both sides.

The postindependence period brought significant changes in the political landscape for Fresnillo and the entire region. Shifting away from its traditional union with Guadalajara and the kingdom of Nueva Galicia, Zacatecas became an independent federal state in 1823. Dominated by liberal nationalists, Zacatecas promulgated its first constitution in 1825, curbing the church's influence and granting extensive powers to municipalities.[15] Zacatecas's political autonomy from Guadalajara did not materialize in the formation of a new and separate diocese, however, and the archbishop of Guadalajara continued to control local ecclesiastical affairs.

As the new independent liberal regime developed in Zacatecas, the municipal and state government agencies increased their influence on local life everywhere. In 1826 the state government created the first normal school in the hemisphere, in a serious effort to challenge the primacy of the Catholic Church in the formation of teachers and local education.[16] The state government also declared as holidays the fourth of July and the fourth of October, to commemorate respectively the birth of Zacatecas as a federal state and Zacatecas's first constitution.[17]

In addition, liberals in Zacatecas challenged the economic primacy of the church through different means. In 1828 the state government established La Dirección del Diezmo (the Bureau of Tithes) with the purpose of regulating, supervising, and overseeing the final distribution of contributions to the local church. Some religious properties were secularized, and they were placed under direct state supervision and their properties confiscated.[18]

The liberal regime's socioeconomic reforms profoundly affected local life in Fresnillo. In 1824, as a result of the new territorial delimitation, the state government created the new municipalities of Tlaltenango and Jerez at the expense of Fresnillo's territories.

More importantly, in 1830 the state legislature expropriated the mines of Proaño in Fresnillo with the purpose of resuming silver production under state government control. Considered a crucial component of the region's economic development by the state government, Proaño's success became a priority for local politicians in Zacatecas. Prisoners from the state penitentiary system were drafted to work in Fresnillo, and the state government invited other states to contribute with their own inmates.[19] Governor Francisco García Salinas formally established a prison to house this captive labor force. In fact, the terms for workers, prisoners, and miners sometimes became interchangeable in local documentation.

As Proaño's expansion drew more investments, infrastructure, and workers, Fresnillo's population increased dramatically in the 1830s. In 1831 Fresnillo counted two thousand residents, but according to the 1832 census, the local population had already surpassed seventeen thousand.[20]

The silver bonanza in Fresnillo gave birth to an instantaneous economic and demographic boom. In the 1830s Proaño produced five hundred thousand silver pesos annually and had investments for more than two million, employing more than thirty-five hundred workers. Employing the newly developed steam-based technology and aggressively recruiting British companies and managers to design and supervise the production, Proaño became an economic miracle in the region. In 1834 the population in Fresnillo surpassed thirty-six thousand inhabitants.[21] In 1834 municipal authorities requested funds and guidance from the state government to create a modern police department, given the new demographic conditions prevalent in Fresnillo.[22] As local life was profoundly transformed and altered by state agencies, British companies, and a new labor force composed of outside prisoners and migrant workers, Proaño's enormous dividends provided the state of Zacatecas with a considerable source of income, which enabled it to achieve a new political status within the Mexican Federation.

Meanwhile, external military threats to the lives of Fresnillo residents had expanded since the Independence Wars (1810–21), and the increasing involvement of the state of Zacatecas in national affairs had resulted in heavy enrollment of young men in the civic militias. Based on the income generated in Proaño, the liberal government in Zacatecas openly challenged the centralist regime in Mexico City. In 1832 a rebellion led by Zacatecas against Mexico's centralist president Anastasio Bustamante resulted in an open confrontation in the Bajío region. Local militias from Zacatecas and San Luis Potosí, fighting on behalf of their own states and Tamaulipas, Jalisco, and Durango, were defeated by the national army.

Three years later, in 1835, Zacatecas rose up against the national government of Antonio López de Santa Anna. In May 1835 Santa Anna's troops routed the local militias in Guadalupe, south of Zacatecas City.[23] The state capital was looted, and Zacatecas's liberal regime was replaced by a conservative government while losing its southernmost district, which became the state of Aguascalientes.

In Fresnillo the rapid economic and political changes soon impacted local religious predilections. Devotion to the Santo Niño de Atocha expanded considerably in the midst of this political turmoil, civil unrest, and open confrontation between local church and government. In 1838 Teodoro Zapata, *mayordomo* of Plateros's chapel since 1828, recorded a new inventory. Again following the hierarchy of religious images and space, Zapata described the entirely new altar dedicated to the Señor de Plateros: "One niche where the miraculous image of the *Señor de los Plateros* is placed, with three glass cases . . . at his feet, another little regular niche, that serves as *sagrario* where the *Niño de Nuestra Señora de Atocha* has been placed, with its glass case, lock and key."[24] According to the inventory, not only had the image of the Santo Niño been relocated from the side altar where it stood in 1816 and placed in the main altar, but the Santo Niño had also been completely detached from the image of Our Lady of Atocha, situated in 1838 on a secondary altar below the itinerant image of the Señor de los Plateros that the confraternity used to collect alms. Significantly, Zapata's report also listed thirty-two *retablos* dedicated to the Santo Niño de Atocha and the Señor de los Plateros, five of which had been framed.[25]

The 1838 statue of the Santo Niño was decorated with the same silver-embroidered outfit that emphasized his role as child-prince of the world: orb and scepter in his hands, plus a miniature rosary and a belt.[26] The sanctuary also listed a pair of sandals and twenty-nine distinct *tuniquitos* (little capes) for the Santo Niño de Atocha to wear on different occasions.[27]

According to the 1838 inventory, the images of Our Lady of Atocha and the Santo Niño were not actually present at the chapel of Plateros at the time but instead were located as "guests" in the parish church of La Purificación in the town of Fresnillo. Zapata, the confraternity's *mayordomo,* consequently included the description of those two itinerant images as follows:

> In the parish of this city [Fresnillo] is found the following pertaining to the Most Holy Lady of Atocha who is currently located in this city:
> One white tunic from Cambray as the underdress.
> One white satin tunic with gold finishings.
> Three steel chains as adornments.
> One silver gilded crown.
> One craped white cloth to cover her head.
> Some silver gilded *mantillas.*
> One bouquet of flowers in her right hand.
>
> The Santo Niño has the following:
> One fine white linen tunic as the underdress.
> One yellow satin tunic with white finishings.
> Sandals, sceptres and a golden rod in his hand.
> One little bouquet of flowers in his hand.[28]

This inventory clearly illustrates how the position of the Santo Niño de Atocha in Plateros had changed in the independent era. From being a secondary icon with a rather modest reputation for miracles in the 1810s, after having none in the previous century, the Santo Niño de Atocha had developed a remarkable tradition as a divine intercessor, as witnessed by the increasing number of *retablos* and *milagros*. Inside the Sanctuary of Plateros, the Santo Niño was no longer placed on a side altar; instead, his image stood at the center of the main altar, below the Señor de los Plateros and completely separated from the statue of Our Lady of Atocha.

As the 1838 inventory indicates, the Plateros confraternity and especially the parish priests in Fresnillo had created an entirely new function for the Santo Niño and Nuestra Señora de Atocha; these images became *itinerant* religious icons who traveled back and forth between Plateros and Fresnillo to fulfill different religious functions.

This ritual traffic of religious images between La Purificación parish in Fresnillo and Plateros chapel in the countryside had started with the Easter ceremonies centered on the image of the Señor de los Plateros and expanded later to include other religious icons and festivities. From the parish priests' perspective, such circulation of itinerant images emphasized the connections and subordination between urban Fresnillo and rural Plateros, between a private chapel and a parish church, between a lay confraternity and a religious authority. Moreover, the circulation of images between Plateros and La Purificación underscored the importance of a local sacred geography where open-air rituals were used to reinvigorate the church's spiritual authority over the local life. As the increasing influence of liberal and anticlerical governments in Zacatecas posed a significant threat to the Catholic Church's authority over local life, Fresnillo priests and confraternities responded by accentuating the character of religious images as sacred guardians of local geography and enhanced their attributes as itinerant sacred images. The expansion of the sacred image of the Santo Niño's abilities beyond the boundaries of the local chapel and parish church represented a response to local uncertainties and anxieties resulting from the unprecedented mining boom, the arrival of immigrant laborers from outside the region in large numbers, and the presence of non-Catholic foreigners as new leaders in the local economy.

In the 1830s Fresnillo entered an accelerated process of economic and social transformations triggered by the mining industry boom. External and secular influences on the town became an increasing source of concern to local religious authorities and the faithful. The mining companies, owned by the liberal and anticlerical state government in Zacatecas and supervised by British Protestants, were at the core of these broad economic and social transformations. Even after the defeat and fall of Francisco García Salinas's liberal regime in 1835 and the reinstatement of a conservative government in Zacatecas, the sociodemographic and political processes unleashed by the mining boom remained unchallenged. In demographic terms, the immigration flux from distant areas did not stop, and the demand for mine workers remained steady. Moreover, since the traditional mining towns in northern and central Mexico did not regain momentum, the rate of recruitment of outside workers and prisoners to work in the mines was maintained.

In the social arena, the increasing influence of nonlocal agencies did not diminish with the fall of the liberal faction in Zacatecas. The federal government replaced the state of Zacatecas as "rightful owner" of the mines, which were from then on administered not from the state capital but from Mexico City. The presence and influence of Protestant foreigners, especially British workers, were not reduced either as they were welcomed by Santa Anna's bureaucracy in Mexico City to keep running the mines. In 1835 the Compañía Zacatecano Mexicana became the new formal owner of Proaño mines and resumed production at the eighteen different sites.[29]

The Spanish colonial presence in Fresnillo had dwindled since the 1820s as a result of the liberal policies implemented by the state in the early national period. The Zacatecas government expelled its Spanish citizens in 1827, just days before the federal law expelled them nationwide.[30] In December 1828 rioters in Fresnillo looted and burned many stores to the ground, in a local rendition of the Parián riots in Mexico City two months earlier.[31] As the anti-Spanish Iberian sentiments ran high in the local sphere, the social visibility of prominent Spaniards became a concern for them and their families, for they could be subjected to legal deportation and/or ethnic animosity in the streets. Consequently, many Spanish residents opted for exile, as did José de Retegui, the last peninsular owner in Proaño, or decided to keep a low profile and retired from public functions, politics, and local celebrations. Many Spaniards who were traditionally the leaders of religious festivities as directors and organizers in the confraternities opted for more limited participation in processions, Easter celebrations, and other functions. At the center of such activities was the devotion to the Señor de los Plateros, an icon traditionally associated with Spanish miners and the Spanish colonial empire in the local world. Accordingly, the local clergy in Fresnillo faced a serious crisis in the 1830s as the Spanish colonial primacy faded away and the participation of Spanish citizens as custodians of the faith was significantly curbed.

In a local religious life maimed by the collapse of Iberian leadership, the political crisis of the Catholic Church, and the growing influence of liberal and centralist regimes in local affairs, the veneration of traditional religious icons gave way to more adaptable symbols. In the 1830s dozens of *retablos* began to accumulate in Plateros to thank the Santo Niño de Atocha as the reputation of this representation of the Holy Child spread through different networks. The parish priests in Fresnillo, as guardians and chaplains of the sanctuary, displayed the *retablos* as a sign of Fresnillo's recently developed privileged status as the region's economic heart. The seasonal transporting of the image between Plateros and Fresnillo at Christmas and Candlemas, organized by both the parish priests of Fresnillo and the confraternity, also contributed substantially to the local reputation of the Santo Niño as an ambulatory figure.

While the devotions to the Señor de Plateros and Our Lady of Atocha fell in disarray as the social leadership of Spaniards in the area drastically diminished, the reputation of the Santo Niño de Atocha developed to new levels, especially among the mine workers, the prisoners, and their families, most of whom were recently relocated in Fresnillo. Mining workers, as either recruited laborers outside Fresnillo or former incarcerated men compelled to work, constituted the core of this newly developed devotion.

In 1844 José Cipriano Taboada, parish priest of Fresnillo, reported to the bishop of Guadalajara that the Holy Child was the most venerated icon in the church: "Our Lady of Atocha is venerated in the Sanctuary of Plateros, but more as a devotion to the Santo Niño, whom all venerate . . . [and to whom they] make pilgrimages and give small contributions that are collected by the shrine custodian inside the church. The custodian keeps daily record of it in a notebook and gives the funds to the *mayordomo,* who puts them together with the *Señor de Plateros*'s funds, although the records specify what belongs to the Virgin and the Holy Child."[32] Taboada added in his report a petition to allocate the Santo Niño's funds to the building of a separate side altar for the religious image: "it is desirable that the contributions to the Santo Niño, although it is very little that gets collected, be destined for a side altar, even one made of stone, because the actual place of the Virgin is on an old wooden stand reclined against the wall, without design, decency or neatness."[33]

In 1848 the Imprenta de Oñate (printing press of Oñate) in Guanajuato published the *Nueva Novena dedicada al milagrosísimo niño de Atocha. . . .*[34] The *Nueva Novena* was a composition by Calixto Aguirre, a Guanajuato resident who vowed in 1841 to thank the Santo Niño de Atocha for his help with a novena in his honor. In the middle of a serious infection in his "lower parts," Aguirre prayed to the Santo Niño and promised to praise him in exchange for his recovery: "I vowed to him [the Santo Niño] to compose this novena out of the rudeness of my discernment, describing one of his miracles every day, to increase devotion to him, from those thanksgiving paintings that hang in his sanctuary . . . and for that purpose I visited that deserted place."[35]

After his recovery Calixto Aguirre fulfilled his promise and made a trip to Fresnillo from Guanajuato, initiating his thanksgiving acts with a pilgrimage.

Once in Fresnillo, and with the help of Francisco Munguía, the confraternity's director, and Luis Vadillo, the shrine's guardian priest in Plateros, Aguirre transcribed nine miracles from the *retablos* hanging in the sanctuary and used them as inspirational themes for each day's prayer. Fray José María de Jesús Belaunzarán, former bishop of Monterrey, gave ecclesiastical approval to Aguirre's novena.[36] The *Nueva Novena* came along with nine *viñetas,* or engravings, illustrating the miracles granted by the Santo Niño and, more importantly, his first popular representation as a holy traveler.

The 1848 *Nueva Novena* represents a landmark in the history of devotion to the Santo Niño for several reasons. First, it provided a visual representation of the Santo Niño as an autonomous icon completely detached from Our Lady of Atocha. Second, the Santo Niño appeared no longer as a baby Jesus but as an older boy with unique apparel that emphasized his traveling abilities instead of his colonial attributes of royal authority. The dress ascribed to the Santo Niño de Atocha in the *Nueva Novena* is no longer a medieval prince's; rather, his clothing indicates his attributes as a traveler. Instead of wearing a small crown, he wears a wide-brimmed hat. The orb in his left hand was replaced by a little food basket, and the scepter in his right hand was replaced by a walking stick with a gourd hanging from it. The gourd, an unequivocal symbol of pilgrimage and traveling, also represented resurrection and redemption in religious art. In Christian art, St. James the Greater, Jonah, and sometimes the archangel Raphael are depicted bearing gourds.[37] The new image of the Santo Niño as a young traveler was created to conform to the miraculous reputation of the Holy Child as a wanderer and to better mirror the stories contained in the thanksgiving *retablos* in the shrine.

The *Nueva Novena* had a tremendous impact both to the north and to the south of Zacatecas, for soon after 1848 an enormous number of copies were printed in different places in Mexico, New Mexico, and Central America. In Guatemala alone three editions were printed before 1885: in 1853, 1863, and 1884.[38] Catholic printing houses in Mexico City, Guadalajara, Guanajuato, and Puebla reprinted several copies of the *Nueva Novena.*[39] In most cases the reprints had no year or place.

Several factors explain the *Nueva Novena*'s popularity. It was written in colloquial Spanish, and more important, it mirrored—for the most part—Mexican pronunciation and conjugational forms, giving the relationship between the faithful and the Holy Child a local accent that traditional novenas lacked since they followed Iberian conjugational forms and pronunciation. Traditional devotions in Mexico sponsored by the Catholic Church still contained deferential forms in Iberian Spanish.

Far from being an isolated incident, Aguirre's novena was a response to the increasing reputation of rival images in western and northern Mexico, in particular to the publication of an extremely popular novena dedicated to the Virgin of San Juan de Los Lagos in 1845.[40] In the absence of effective leadership from the pulpit, novenas became indispensable vehicles for shaping the local devotions of Mexican families in times marked by the breakdown of Spanish leadership in the Catholic Church, increasing hostility between the national governments and the ecclesiastical authorities, and the transference of territories to the United States after the Mexican-American War (1846–48).

The abundance of affordable novenas, pilgrimages, inexpensive religious stamps, and affordable tin paintings constituted the material base from which a popular devotion expanded from Zacatecas to the north, along the Camino Real de Tierra Adentro, and reached northern New Mexico. To the south, a similar process took place to reach Guanajuato, Mexico City, and Guatemala. It was in the borderlands, however, where the devotion to the Santo Niño developed a unique profile and reached levels of popularity unparalleled in other places.

The miracles narrated in the *Nueva Novena* played a crucial role in spreading and developing the holy reputation of the Santo Niño to its highest level. The first miracle in the *Nueva Novena* refers to the story of Maximiana Esparza,[41] a woman from La Encarnación who was jailed in 1829 and exiled to Catorce, where she was arrested again. After being exiled to Saltillo, Esparza was imprisoned one more time because of her immoral behavior (*malas costumbres*). From Saltillo's prison, she was sentenced to exile in Durango, where she spent a full year in prison.

According to Aguirre's novena, during her imprisonment in Durango, Esparza sincerely prayed to the Santo Niño de Atocha for her liberation. Later she received a visit from Manuel de Atocha, a "handsome youth" who brought her food "on behalf of his mother, María de Atocha." He claimed to be her attorney and promised her a prompt release. In the next hearing she was released and placed under the young advocate's custody. He instructed her to leave the city and walk with him to his house in Fresnillo. Esparza followed her liberator and walked all night but lost his track near a lagoon. At dawn she approached Fresnillo and asked the residents for directions. After telling the parish priest of La Purificación her story, Esparza and the minister went to the Sanctuary of Plateros, where she immediately recognized the face of the Santo Niño de Atocha as her liberator. Overwhelmed, Esparza fell to the ground and gave thanks with tears for the divine help. She placed a *retablo* in the sanctuary as testimony of this miracle.[42]

Esparza's story illustrates the "modern" qualities of the Santo Niño as an intermediary who can successfully interact with the newly adopted legal system in independent Mexico. Despite being tried, convicted, incarcerated, and exiled because of her *malas costumbres* three times, Esparza was not once represented by an attorney or, as the story phrases it, had anybody "who spoke on her behalf."

Esparza's crimes are not revealed in the novena, but her repeated dubious behavior placed her in a continuous conflict with the law. She is also a poor woman, an immigrant, an individual separated from her family by legal actions taken in a mechanical and impersonal way. Uprooted like many other people in the region, Esparza loses her connection to any parish church, confraternity, or religious institution. The Santo Niño's intervention begins with a restoration of Esparza's human condition, for he brings her a basket of bread on behalf of his mother. Esparza is reconnected to a family, the Santo Niño's, and recognized as a person with basic human needs. The next step in the story is the Santo Niño's prophecy that a judge will sympathize with Esparza's ordeal and set her free. The Santo Niño's intervention consists of influencing the authority's judgment in a way that acknowledges Esparza's sufferings and humanity. After the judge sets her free, the Santo Niño leads Esparza out of Durango to a place where she can start a different life.

Once in Fresnillo, Maximiana Esparza is not only fully redeemed but also reshaped as a witness and recipient of a divine intervention. Rescued by the Santo Niño from a vicious circle of bad behavior and punishment by an indifferent legal system that punishes by incarceration and exile, Esparza arrives in Fresnillo as a different person. The direction of Esparza's travels is circular since, among all of her various destinations, Fresnillo is the closest place to La Encarnación. In Fresnillo, Esparza completes a circle in both geographic and spiritual terms. At the end of her Encarnación-Catorce-Saltillo-Durango-Fresnillo itinerary she becomes a new person, or better said, she becomes a person. Her two-year journey of punishment and exile becomes a spiritual pilgrimage and her sufferings a meaningful ordeal. However, unlike in the standard colonial narratives of miraculous redemptions, Esparza does not become a nun or join a religious confraternity; she is not placed under the supervision of ecclesiastical authorities or made a servant in a prominent family. In fact, as soon as she recognizes the Santo Niño's favor with a *retablo* she completely disappears from the narrative. Moreover, by invoking the Santo Niño's help in the solitude of her cell, Esparza appears as the only initiator in such intervention. Although the parish priest of Fresnillo plays a role in the story, his intervention does not go beyond the role of qualified witness to the miracle. He certifies Esparza's account and leads her to Plateros but, according to the story, has no part in the relationship between Esparza and the Santo Niño de Atocha.

The second miracle in the novena takes place in Fresnillo on May 4, 1834. While working late at night Don José María Delgado, a shopkeeper, is the victim of an attempted robbery by a group of men in the store. Armed with swords and inebriated, the assaulters insult him and severely hurt him with a stab that perforates his body from side to side. Wounded and hopeless, Delgado invokes the

Santo Niño and, two days after the attack, begins a slow but firm recuperation. Interestingly, the novena mentions neither Delgado's nor anyone else's ethnic background, although Delgado occupies a position traditionally dominated by Spanish immigrants.

The third and fourth miracles take place in 1836 in the mines of Barreno in Fresnillo. Mariano García, a mine worker, is saved from death as the result of a serious fall when he becomes trapped in the machinery. Jorge García, a mine worker, and his assistant are hit by a rock and trapped when the wagon car turns upside down inside the pit. After requesting the Santo Niño's divine intercession, both men are rescued by other workers.[43] These men, trapped by the mechanical and impersonal new technology, resorted to the Santo Niño as their last resource against the perils of labor conditions in the mines that had significantly changed with the arrival of British miners to Fresnillo.

In the novena's fifth miracle a woman named María Eleuteria García is repeatedly stabbed by "a despicable man" while sitting on her front porch talking to a friend. García's friend, María Catalina Rivera, seeing her severely wounded in the neck and face, invokes the Santo Niño. When García recovers, the two friends visit the sanctuary and leave a thanksgiving *retablo.* In the sixth miracle, dated 1838, Albino Ibarra is healed from an incurable burning in his lower body. These two miracles, based on the restoration of health and bodily integrity, emphasized the reputation of the Santo Niño as a doctor or "divine physician."[44]

The seventh miracle follows the structure and themes presented in Esparza's ordeal and dates from 1839. José María Díaz goes "through the misfortune of killing someone by stabbing him in a fight." Arrested by Fresnillo's local authorities, Díaz is convicted and sentenced to ten years in prison. When he hears his punishment, Díaz invokes the Santo Niño and prays to him for freedom, justice, and mercy. After a year Díaz leaves jail as a free man.

The eighth miracle takes place in 1840 in the nearby town of Jerez. Here, Doña Juliana Codina is cured from a strong pain in her side provoked by fatigue. In the ninth, and last, miracle narrated in the *Nueva Novena,* Calixto Aguirre places himself as the beneficiary of the Santo Niño's intercession.

Aguirre's novena played a crucial role in consolidating the supernatural reputation of the Santo Niño de Atocha as a protector against misfortune, violence, disease, and tragedy. This reputation became manifest in three different areas. First, he was a saint for the body's restoration, a *divino médico* (divine doctor) who could restore health to those affected by diseases and severe injuries. He cured Albino Ibarra of his "internal" infirmity, cured Doña Juliana Codina, and healed Aguirre's severe inflammation in his lower parts.

A second area of intervention is the workplace, as in the cases of the miners injured in Proaño and the shopkeeper attacked before closing the store. The Santo

Niño appears here as a patron against external threats that workers faced in the area on a regular basis: accidents, injuries, robberies, assaults.

A third area consists of prison and legal ordeals, in which ordinary people face punishment and incarceration with little or no resources. As the stories of Maximiana Esparza and José María Díaz illustrate, the Santo Niño protects repeat offenders against an indifferent penitentiary system that displaces people and punishes with excessive severity. The Santo Niño appears in this area as an intermediary between authorities and criminals in order to restrain the abuses of the former against the latter.

Both Díaz, who stabs his opponent in a street fight, and Esparza, who repeatedly falls into *malas costumbres,* find in the Santo Niño's intervention the fairness and compassion they should have gotten from the judicial authorities in the first place. They do not walk out free as a result of their prayers to the Santo Niño; instead, they obtain a less harsh punishment and, more importantly, a chance for rehabilitation. Instead of more time in prison and exile, Esparza undertakes a spiritual journey to Fresnillo, where she is rehabilitated by rediscovering the Santo Niño's image, while Díaz spends only a year in jail, a sentence barely comparable with the length of imprisonment he originally faced.

The identification of the Santo Niño with liberal professions (physician, attorney) certainly reflects the concerns of the faithful with the increasing influence of modernizing agents on the lower classes' everyday lives. A common feature in these stories highlighted by Aguirre's novena is the border between domestic spaces and external threats, between street and house, body and disease, work and injury, and incarceration and reintegration into society—all processes notably exempt from a proactive ecclesiastic supervision.

Aguirre's novena, however, is not exempt from clerical influences, and the narratives in the miracles naturally appear to be retouched by an ecclesiastical authority. The invocations of the Santo Niño in the case of accidents and life-threatening situations are depicted as motivated in part by the need to survive at least long enough to receive the last rites (although this could be important to laypeople as well as clergy). However, the narratives do not portray religious authorities in pivotal roles, and in no case do they appear as the initiators or facilitators in the miraculous intervention. Priests and other members of the institutional church remain, according to the stories, outsiders in the relationship between the faithful and the Santo Niño de Atocha. This autonomy is seen not only in terms of the invocation, which is always produced independently by the requesters and never suggested, triggered, supervised, or advised by a priest, but also regarding the act of thanksgiving or ritual reciprocation; these never involve the participation of official clergy. In Aguirre's novena no votive masses are said to thank the saint and no sacraments are administered as a result or consequence of the miracles. The essential connection is between the faithful and the saint, and priests do not participate directly in it.

Mirroring the new socioeconomic conditions of Fresnillo in the early national period, the reputation of the Santo Niño presents a deliberate contrast with colonial religious icons. His miracles, for instance, are completely dissociated from the type of miracle attributed to the crucifixes patronized by the upper classes—for example, recovery of property, the validation of racial hierarchies, and the subordination of the faithful to the church authorities. Instead, the recipients of the Santo Niño's help are individuals who have been deprived of ideal original conditions (health, freedom, safe environment) in the interaction with threatening and modernizing social spaces (the mining technology implemented by British companies, the national and liberal legal system, the diseases and conditions associated with sexual behavior, the street violence). Unlike the miracles associated with the crucifixes in the region in colonial times, requested by the local employers on behalf of their workers and servants, in the Santo Niño's stories the requesting parties are always the individuals directly affected and, consequently, the ones who give thanks for the intercession.

In 1857 Severiano Medina, a *vecino* of Chimayó in northern New Mexico, began a practice that would be repeated all over the borderlands in following times. After a pilgrimage to Plateros, Medina built a private shrine to venerate the Santo Niño locally. This shrine is particularly important because it had no room for an image of Our Lady of Atocha inside its walls and represented an image of the Santo Niño modeled on the 1848 novena by Calixto Aguirre. The image in Chimayó soon became a devotional icon on its own merit and replaced the worshiping of a black Christ (Our Lord of Esquipulas) as the region's most important veneration.[45]

In the reinvented image of a vulnerable child in sandals and pilgrim's attire, Mexican families, from Zacatecas to New Mexico, took a colonial icon originally meant to inculcate Spanish colonial values, and transformed it into a meaningful symbol to facilitate their way out of the post-Spanish colonial era. The story of the Santo Niño de Atocha and its followers is also the story of the struggle by Mexican families in the Camino de Tierra Adentro to create new ways in which they could relate to the sacred in accordance with the challenges of new times and without accepting the subordinate status inherited from the colonial era.

Notes

1. Juan Pereira Nieves, Presbítero Licenciado, *Cartas al Santo Niño de Atocha: Expresiones de religiosidad popular* (Fresnillo: Santuario de Plateros, Librería del Niño, Parra y Cía, 2000), 3ff.

2. See Emma Trujillo, "La esperanza de la humanidad está en la niñez: El Santo Niño de Atocha atrae a 100,000 peregrinos a la parroquia de Los Angeles," *La Cruz de California,* September 1998, Artículos sect. 3.

3. For studies on late colonial and early national religious practices in Mexico, see Brian F. Connaughton, *Ideología y sociedad en Guadalajara (1788–1853)* (Mexico City: Conaculta, 1992); Juan Javier Pescador, *De bautizados a fieles difuntos: Familia y mentalidades en una parroquia urbana; Santa Catarina de México, 1568–1820* (Mexico City: El Colegio de México, 1992); and William B. Taylor, *Magistrates of the Sacred: Priests and Parishioners in Eighteenth-Century Mexico* (Stanford, Calif.: Stanford University Press, 1996). Scholarship on Mexican communities in the late colonial and early national periods includes Deborah E. Kanter, "Hijos del Pueblo: Family, Community and Gender in Rural Mexico, the Toluca Region, 1730–1830" (Ph.D. diss., University of Virginia, 1993); Rodolfo Pastor, *Campesinos y reformas. la mixteca, 1700–1856* (Mexico City: El Colegio de México, 1987); and Deena J. González, *Refusing the Favor: The Spanish Mexican Women of Santa Fe, 1820–1880* (New York: Oxford University Press, 2000).

4. D. Joseph Ribera Bernárdez, Conde de Santiago de La Laguna, *Descripción breve de la muy noble y leal Ciudad de Zacatecas [1732],* in *Testimonios de Zacatecas,* selected by Gabriel Salinas de la Torre, intro. by Juan B. Iníguiz (Mexico City: Imprenta Universitaria, 1946), 51–107, quotation from 77.

5. "Ejecucion hecha en los bienes de lorenzo tostado, difunto, en 10,926 rs. Inventario 1664 de la hacienda de minas de beneficio por azogues que quedo por fin y muerte de Lorenzo Ruiz Tostado . . ." (Archivo Histórico del Estado de Zacatecas [hereafter AHEZ], Real Hacienda Judicial box 1, file 1, 1645–52, fol. 51).

6. "Yten una Ymagen de bulto de mas de bara de Nuestra Señora de Atocha con corona y zetro de plata que peso un marco una onza y una quarta con su niño Jezus, dos mantos uno de lana azul y el otro de mandacin amarillo" (Archivo de la Arquidiócesis de Guadalajara [hereafter AAG], Fresnillo, box 1, folder 2, 1704–1817, under the year 1704).

7. AAG, Fresnillo, box 1, folder 2, 1704–1817, 1704.

8. AHEZ, Cargos y Oficios, Certificaciones de Raza, box 1, 1732, document identified by Bernardo del Hoyo.

9. The following is from AAG, Fresnillo, box 1, folder 2, 1804–17, 1792:

> Yllustrisimo I Reverendisimo Señor Maestro Don fray Antonio Alcalde mi Señor.
> Yllustrisimo y Reverendisimo Señor
> Besa los pies de Vuestra Señoria Ylustrisima su mas obediente subdito, obligado servidor y agradecido capellan.
> José María Díaz. Rúbrica

10. AAG, Fresnillo, box 2, folder 2, 1822.

11. AHEZ, Planos, "Plano de 1797 elaborado por Juan Antonio Evia, Alcalde Mayor de Fresnillo. . . . "

12. AHEZ, Relacion de los Terrenos, Pueblos y Haziendas que se comprehenden en esta Jurisdiccion 1792–93.

13. AHEZ, Romo/Folletos, *Informe que rinde el licenciado José María Hernández a los vecinos del pueblo de Plateros* (Zacatecas: Imprenta de Villagrana, 1882).

14. "Su niño con tunico morado, cacles; potencia y mundito de plata dorados y varios milagros y medios de plata" (AAG, Fresnillo, box 1, "Ynventario . . . ," 1816, fol. 12).

15. Flores Olague et al., *Breve historia de Zacatecas* (Mexico City: El Colegio de México–Fondo de Cultura Económica, 1996), 102–3.

16. Roberto Ramos Dávila, ed., *Zacatecas: Síntesis histórica* (Zacatecas: Centro de Investigaciones Históricas, Gobierno del Estado de Zacatecas 1995), 125.

17. Ibid., 131.

18. Ibid., 133.

19. Guadalupe Dávalos Macías, *Fuentes para el estudio del Mineral de Fresnillo, 1566–1872* (Zacatecas: Patronato del Museo de Minería, 2000), 87ff.

20. Ibid., 88.

21. Ibid., 90.

22. Ibid., 89.

23. Olague et al., *Breve historia de Zacatecas,* 110ff.

24. AAG, Fresnillo, box 1, "Ymbentario de las Alajas . . .," 1838, fol. 1.

25. "Cinco retablos presentables con bidrieras del Señor de Plateros y del Santo Niño, mas veinte y siete de las mismas Ymagenes, sin vidrieras" (AAG, Fresnillo, box 1, "Ymbentario de las Alajas . . ." [1838]).

26. Ibid.:

> Un par cacles, potencias y un mundito de plata del niño de Nuestra Señora de Atocha.
> Un par de sarcillos de concha chiquita de la misma ymagen.
> Un rosario chiquito con cruz de oro.
> Un cordoncito de alambre de plata con pendiente de lo mismo.

27. "Veintinueve tuniquitos de distintos generos del niño de Nuestra Señora de Atocha" (ibid.).

28. The following is from AAG, Fresnillo, box 1, "Ymbentario de las Alajas . . ." (1838):

> En la Parroquia de esta ciudad se halla lo siguiente que tiene la Santisima Virgen de Atocha por estar actualmente en esta ciudad
>
> Un tunico blanco de Cambray en lo interior
> Uno dicho razo blanco con galon de oro en las orillas y en lo exterior.
> Tres cadenitas de azero en el adorno
> Una corona de plata sobredorada
> Un paño blanco con crespon que le cubre la cabeza
> Unas mantillas de plata sobredoradas
> Un ramo de flores en la mano derecha.
>
> En el Santo Niño con los siguientes
> Un tunico de lienzo fino blanco en lo interior

Uno dicho de razo amarillo con encaje blanco
Unas sandalias, unas potencias y un mando en la mano sobredorado.
Un pañito atravesado de lienzo fino
Un ramito de flores en la mano.

29. See *Compañía de Minas Zacatecano-Mexicana: Escritura de asociación . . .* (Mexico City: Imp. Ignacio Cumplido, 1835); *Compañía de Minas Zacatecano-Mexicana: Informe que da a la Junta menor permanente, del estado de la negociación del Fresnillo en el primer semestre del año de 1838* (Mexico City: Imp. Ignacio Cumplido, 1838); *Compañía de Minas Zacatecano-Mexicana: Informe que da a la Junta menor permanente, del estado de la negociación del Fresnillo en el segundo semestre del año de 1839* (Mexico City: Imp. Ignacio Cumplido, 1840); *Compañía de Minas Zacatecano-Mexicana: Informe que da a la Junta menor permanente, del estado de la negociación del Fresnillo en el primer semestre del año de 1841* (Mexico City: Imprenta de Vicente García Torres, 1841); *Compañía de Minas Zacatecano-Mexicana: Informe que da a la Junta menor permanente, del estado de la negociación del Fresnillo en el año de 1842* (Mexico City: Imprenta de Vicente García Torres, 1843).

30. Dávila, *Zacatecas,* 134.

31. Ibid., 135.

32. The following is from AAG, Fresnillo, box 2, folder 2, 1844–52:

Yll[ustrisi]mo S[eñor] Provisor.

1. En el decreto con que su Yll[ustrisi]ma aprobo las cuentas del S[eñ]or de Plateros se previene que el cura del Fresnillo informe a esa superioridad sobre la funcion anual que se le hace a dicha Imagen, y sobre la de N[uestra] S[eñora] de Atocha. Y para cumplir con esta prevencion, digo: que siempre fue costumbre traer de su santuario la imagen: Martes de Pascua se le hacia su funcion con novenario, misa muy solemne, fuegos artificiales, sermon, iluminacion y procesion, todo por beneficio de las aguas. Para sufragar los gastos se colectaba limosna en la ciudad, hacienda y ranchos, y lo que faltaba para el completo se tomaba de los fondos lo cual todo consta en los libros.

2. El año de [18]42 el finado Prefecto Don Jose Maria Linares prohivio la qüestacion acostumbrada y tubo ese año que hacerse la funcion toda de los fondos, moderandose lo posible los gastos, y como yo pusiere en conocimiento del Ill[ustrisi]mo S[eñor] Ob[is]po, asi tambien la de que el Ayuntamiento no quizo asistir como lo tenia de costumbre, y habiendo agregado de que los fondos los dejo exahustos el mayordomo Zapata, el Yll[ustrisi]mo S[eñ]or [Obispo] libro orden para que en lo sucesibo ya no bajasen al S[eñor] de su nicho, sin orden ni licencia superior, y en tal virtud el año pasado solo se canto su misa solemne en su santuario costeandose los gastos de los fondos.

33. Ibid.

34. *Nueva Novena dedicada al milagrosísimo Niño de Nuest[r]a Señora de Atocha, que se venera en el Santuario de Plateros, a extramuros de la ciudad del Fresnillo: Con un milagro en cada día, de los mismos que en retablos se halla en su Santuario: Con una jaculatoria y*

oracion diaria y diversa, y una oracion á su Santísima Madre . . . / dispuesta por un devoto del Santísimo Niño (Guanajuato: Oñate, 1848).

35. "Prólogo. / . . . Le protesté componerle esta novena de la rudeza de mi ingenio, para aumentar su devoción, poniéndole un milagro en cada día, de los que constan y están en su Santuario, para cuya adquisición ocurrí á aquel desierto . . ." (ibid.).

36. *Nueva Novena* (1848). Fray José María de Belaunzarán y Ureña, O.F.M., was bishop of Monterrey from 1831 to 1834, when he abandoned his seat. See Carlos E. Castañeda, *Our Catholic Heritage in Texas: 1519–1936,* 7 vols. (Austin, Tex.: Von Boeckmann-Jones Company, 1950), 6:344, 355.

37. See James Hall, *Dictionary of Subjects & Symbols in Art,* rev. ed. (New York: Harper & Row, 1979), 141.

38. See *Novena dedicada al milagroso Niño de Nuestra Señora de Atocha que se venera en el Santuario de Plateros, a extramuros de la ciudad del Fresnillo* (Guatemala City: Imprenta de la Aurora, 1884); *Novena del Santo Niño de Atocha, por un devoto: Reimpresa en Guatemala* (Guatemala City: Imprenta de la Aurora, 1853); *Novena del Santo Niño de Atocha por un devoto* (Guatemala City: Reimpresa por L. Luna, 1863); *Nueva Novena dedicada al milagrosísimo niño de n[uestr]a s[ecor]a de Atocha: Que se venera en el santuario de Plateros y extramuros de la ciudad del Fresnillo* (Las Vegas, N.M.: Imprenta de la Revista Católica, 1886).

39. See, for instance, *Nueva Novena dedicada al Milagrosísimo Niño de Nuestra Señora de Atocha que se venera en el Santuario de Plateros a Extramuros de la ciudad del Fresnillo* . . . (Mexico City: Edición de M. Murguía, 1867).

40. See *Novena dedicada a la Purísima e inmaculada Virgen María, nuestra señora, y en honra de su portentosa imagen intitulada de "María Santísima de San Juan de Los Lagos" que se venera en la villa de este nombre, perteneciente al Arzobispado de Guadalajara: Escrita por un sacerdote misionero, de la filiacion del suprimido Colegio Apostólico de Propaganda Fide, de María Santísima de Zapopan* (Guadalajara: Imprenta de Narciso Parga, 1875), foreword, 4.

41. *Nueva Novena* (1848), 9.

42. "Y al ver la citada Maximiana el bello relicario del S[an]to Niño, postrada en tierra y anegada en lagrimas, le tributa infinitas gracias en recompensa de tan admirable prodigio, le patentiza su fé y su amor con el presente milagro, demostrando a los devotos del Santo Niño de Atocha la mas singular maravilla que con ella hizo, haciendolo ver con su retablo que le puso en el santuario de Plateros, para certificarlo a todo devoto o afligido que implore del Santo Niño su proteccion" (ibid., 10).

43. "En el año de 1836, á primero de Marzo, aconteció á Mariano García . . ." (*Nueva Novena* [1848], 16–18).

44. This and following quotes are all from the *Nueva Novena* of 1848, cited in the previous note.

45. See Stephen F. de Borhegyi, "The Miraculous Shrines of Our Lord of Esquípulas in Guatemala and Chimayó, New Mexico," *El Palacio* 60, no. 3 (March 1953): 83–111; Stephen F. de Borhegyi, "The Cult of Our Lord of Esquípulas in Middle America and New Mexico," *El Palacio* 61, no. 12 (December 1954): 387–401; Elizabeth Willis DeHuff,

Say the Bells of Old Missions: Legends of Old New Mexico Churches (London: B. Herder Book Co. 1948); Alexander M. Frankfurter, "A Gathering of Children: Holy Infants and the Cult of El Santo Niño de Atocha," *El Palacio* 94, no. 1 (Summer/Fall 1988): 30–40; Ramón A. Gutiérrez, "El Santuario de Chimayo: A Syncretic Shrine in New Mexico," in *Feasts and Celebrations in North American Ethnic Communities,* ed. Ramón A. Gutiérrez and Geneviève Fabre, 71–86 (Albuquerque: University of New Mexico Press, 1995); Sam Howard and Enrique R. Lamadrid, *Pilgrimage to Chimayó: Contemporary Portrait of a Living Tradition* (Santa Fe: Museum of New Mexico, 1999); Elizabeth Jey, *Chimayo Valley Traditions* (Santa Fe: Ancient City Press, 1987); Tey Marianna Nunn, "Santo Niño de Atocha: Development, Dispersal, and Devotion of a New World Image" (M.A. thesis, University of New Mexico at Albuquerque, 1993); William Wroth, "New Mexican Santos and the Preservation of Religious Traditions," *El Palacio* 94, no. 1 (Summer/Fall 1988): 4–18.

Prayers in Plaster and Plastic

Catholic Kitsch as Ritual Habit

Robert Westerfelhaus

The streets that lead to the Basilica of Our Lady of Guadalupe in Mexico City are lined with shops that overflow with religious paraphernalia. On the vast plaza that fronts the basilica, venders tend small, stationary carts or walk about hawking their wares. The items these shops and vendors offer for sale, in common with devotional aids found throughout the Roman Catholic world, range from cheap, garishly colored plaster and plastic statues to expensive rosaries made of precious metals and stones. For Catholics, such objects derive religious significance from what they represent, and not from their aesthetic worth or the value ascribed to the materials used in fashioning them. Thus, it is not uncommon to see masterfully carved marble sculptures placed side by side with gaudy, mass-produced plaster or plastic statues in Catholic homes and places of worship.

Art of the latter kind, often referred to as kitsch, is a pervasive part of a popular Catholic piety that shapes the religious life of Catholicism's estimated one billion adherents. The term "kitsch" is derived from the German noun *Kitsch,* which literally means "trash." The term is used denotatively to refer to art—ranging from architecture to comic books—that significantly deviates from the aesthetic standards of "high art," however these standards are defined within a given culture. Connotatively, the term "kitsch" is often used in reference to art that is deemed "inferior" because it conspicuously flouts the conventions of high art and yet possesses a naive charm capable of eliciting pleasure, even from those trained in aesthetic appreciation. In this essay I propose that the devotional practices associated with Catholic kitsch are expressions of what I term *ritual habit,* defined as a kind of communication in which form takes precedence over content. In making my argument, I focus on how this habit is expressed in relation to one of Catholicism's most famous images, that of Our Lady of Guadalupe.

Theory and Method

My understanding of the role Catholic kitsch plays in popular Catholic piety draws on anthropological, devotional, historical, and theological literature. In order to examine how this role is enacted in the religious lives of contemporary adherents of the Guadalupan cult, interviews were conducted with pilgrims in the vicinity of the Basilica of Our Lady of Guadalupe immediately prior to, during, and after the annual feast day honoring her[1] (December 12). A team consisting of six native Spanish speakers working under the direction of the author conducted these interviews. Two of the interviewers have training and experience in conducting social scientific interviews.[2] The other four are professionals who engage in ethnographic research and conduct interviews as means of assessing viewing habits for the Mexican television network Televisa.[3] The interviews were recorded, translated,[4] and transcribed. The research team conducted forty-one interviews with seventy-five pilgrims: forty-five men and thirty women. Twelve interviews were conducted with groups of pilgrims, five with couples, and twenty-four with individuals. The interviews, which averaged in length from twenty to thirty minutes, were conducted outside the basilica, on the plaza that fronts it, and atop Tepeyac (the hill on which Juan Diego claimed to have experienced the Meso-American manifestation of the Virgin Mary now known as Our Lady of Guadalupe). Pilgrims were never interrupted while entering a church or at prayer. Attempts were made to conduct interviews with men and women, young and old, individuals, couples, and groups. Given the crowded, chaotic circumstances under which the research team worked (over four million people visited the basilica grounds during the festival time we worked there), interviewees were chosen as opportunities occurred. In order to preserve their privacy, they are referred to by gender and age and not by name. These interviews were conducted as part of a broader study into Marian apparitional cults in general and the cult of Our Lady of Guadalupe in particular.[5]

This study is informed by two communication theories: semiotics and Carey's theory of ritual communication.[6] Semiotics is a field of communication studies that investigates how meaning is created and shared.[7] The smallest unit of meaning is the sign, defined as anything capable of containing and conveying meaning, such as a word, an image, or a ritual practice.[8] According to semiotic theory, signs are neither used nor understood in isolation from one another. Rather, the uses and meanings ascribed to signs are determined by codes. As defined by Fiske, "A code is a rule-governed system of signs, whose rules and conventions are shared amongst members of a culture, and which is used to generate and circulate meanings in and for that culture."[9] Relevant to this study are two ways that codes ascribe meaning to signs: iconicity and indexicality. A sign is meaningful as an icon through resemblance to the thing it represents.[10] A classic example of an icon is a portrait, which is rendered meaningful through its resemblance to the person it portrays. A sign is meaningful as an index through some existential connection it has with that which it represents. Medical diagnoses, meteorological forecasts, and the findings of forensic science are all semiotic undertakings that rely on the interpretation of indexical signs. Bowen argues, "The semiotic approach [is] particularly useful in pointing out two ways that religious objects convey meaning. The first way is through the *history of physical contact* [that is, an indexical connection] between an object and a spiritual or sacred being. . . . A second way objects take on a powerful religious meaning is through their *resemblance* [that is, iconicity] to a sacred or powerful being."[11]

The sign that is at the center of this study is the image of Our Lady of Guadalupe. This image, which is reputed to have been given to a sixteenth-century Aztec farmer through miraculous means, is the devotional focus of the Virgin's cult. This cult is the largest and most popular of the Catholic Church's many Marian cults.[12] For adherents of the Virgin's cult, a system of signification that I refer to as the code of Catholic kitsch governs how they use and understand reproductions of Our Lady of Guadalupe's image. Iconic resemblance and indexical connections are central to this code. For believers, these qualities imbue reproductions of the image with powers akin to what anthropologists refer to as imitative and contagious magic.[13] Like iconicity, imitative magic is based on the similarity that one thing has to another. Contagious magic, on the other hand, is indexical in that it depends on existential connections, which are often established through direct physical contact. The supernatural power ascribed to reproductions of the image of Our Lady of Guadalupe is based on the similarity of such reproductions to the original image. Images are believed by cult adherents to obtain additional power when they are brought to, or purchased at or near, the basilica shrine in Mexico City where the original image is displayed. Through physical contact with the sacred shrine, as well as through their resemblance to it, reproductions of the image are thus indexically connected to the original.

Another key feature of the code of Catholic kitsch is that it defines the sacred—and those things believed to be imbued with that quality—in opposition to the profane. A binary opposition of this kind is an "elementary structure of signification."[14] As Barley explains, "The mechanism of opposition suggests we know what something means, in part, by knowing what it does not mean."[15] The term "up," for example, derives meaning from its opposition to the term "down." The logic of Catholic kitsch, like that of the broader religious tradition of which it is a part, defines those things deemed sacred as separate and distinct from the commonplace and everyday: sacred things are thus seen as being in the world but not of the world.

In addition to semiotic theory, this study also borrows from, and extends, Carey's theory of ritual communication. According to Carey, this form of communication "is linked to terms such as sharing, participation, association, and the possession of a common faith."[16] As explained by Carey, "A ritual view of communication is not directed toward the extension of messages in space but the maintenance of society in time; not the act of imparting information but the representation of shared belief."[17] This view of communication drastically differs from the traditional transmission view of communication, which continues to inform most humanistic and social scientific inquiry into human communication. According to Carey, "The transmission view of communication is the commonest in our culture. . . . It is defined by terms such as imparting, sending, transmitting, or giving information to others."[18] Unlike communication intended to inform or control, ritual communication is defined by Carey as being similar to "attending a mass: a situation in which nothing new is learned but in which a particular view of the world is portrayed and confirmed."[19] As we shall see, kitsch renderings of the Virgin impart little information about her or about the religious tradition to which she belongs. Rather than being a weakness, however, it is my contention that this lack of communicative transmission allows kitsch to bind cult adherents to one another precisely because they need not share a common view, and it enables them to fashion a devotion to the image that simultaneously affirms and challenges the beliefs and practices of orthodox Catholicism.

Art and Objects in Catholic Piety

The Roman Catholic Church is a discerning patron of the arts. As such, the church commissioned the great Gothic cathedrals, the Renaissance frescoes of Michelangelo and Raphael, and such modern masterpieces as Tokyo's St. Mary's Cathedral. As a religion, Roman Catholicism values the use of art to promote spiritual purposes. The *Catechism of the Catholic Church* sums up the church's teaching regarding the role of religious art in this way: "*Sacred art* is true and beautiful when its form corresponds to its particular vocation: evoking and glorifying, in faith and adoration, the transcendent mystery of God. . . . Genuine sacred art draws man [*sic*] to adoration, to prayer, and to the love of God, Creator and Savior, the Holy One and Sanctifier."[20] Within the Catholic tradition, art is used not only to inspire worship but also as a means of effecting communication between living Catholics inhabiting the mundane material world and deceased Catholics who dwell in heaven, the latter of whom the church refers to as saints. Such communication is deemed possible because, as Morgan explains, the church holds that there is "a uniform, homogeneous continuity between this life and the next such that the merits of the saints compiled here during their exemplary lives transferred, as it were, to a celestial account by which they could be accessed through a material economy of intercessions and indulgences. From the late medieval world to the twentieth century, such heavenly assistance has been communicated through a variety of sacred acts and objects including the rosary, holy water, scapulars, medals, the Blessed Sacrament, pilgrimage, and icons."[21]

For Catholics, such objects—known as "sacramentals"—serve as material vehicles that mediate between the worldly sphere of human existence and the spiritual realm. The use of sacramentals is prevalent in the *popular piety* of Roman Catholics, that is, the religious beliefs and practices that develop and flourish outside the church's core traditions. Some of these, such as the rosary and the stations of the cross, have won the approval of the institutional church. Others have not. Regarding popular piety, the church's *Catechism* states: "These expressions of piety extend the liturgical life of the Church, but do not replace it."[22] The official policy of the church holds that it is the responsibility of local bishops to "purify" the popular Catholicism expressed within their dioceses. In practice, however, bishops tend to tolerate some deviation from the strictest adherence to Catholic orthodoxy/orthopraxy. This tolerance has allowed the use of sacramentals to flourish in ways that are sometimes at odds with the beliefs and practices promoted by the institutional church.

According to the teaching of the institutional church, as explained by Wilhelm, "statues, pictures, etc. are not prayed to as having power of themselves; rather they remind us of God's presence."[23] He goes on to warn his fellow Catholics: "We should use sacramentals reverently, but also avoiding superstition. What we derive from them depends on God's will, the Church's prayer, and our own faith and devotion. We must be careful not to look on them as magical, producing effects automatically. If we use them with a living faith, they are wonderful ways to make us aware of God's presence in our lives, in everyone and everything around us."[24] This orthodox Catholic understanding of sacramentals was echoed by one of the pilgrims interviewed for this study, a female in her midthirties who, when asked why she had expended the time, energy, and money required to travel from her home to the Basilica of Our Lady of Guadalupe, explained, "It's because of the image. We revere the image. We know She's not there, but we know She's listening to us. And on the other hand, we're not adoring [the image], because if we were doing that, we would be adoring the picture, the frame, and not Our Lady of Guadalupe. So, adoring the frame wouldn't mean anything." The description offered by most of the pilgrims of their beliefs and practices regarding the Virgin's image, however, reflects a popular piety that deviates from the official teachings of the institutional church. The image and reproductions of it are believed by adherents of the Virgin's cult to possess in themselves supernatural power capable of, for example, healing and protecting.

A work's aesthetic value (however and by whomever defined) can differ significantly from its spiritual value. As O'Flaherty observes, one can find placed "in the niches of great Gothic cathedrals plaster-of-paris images garishly painted . . . and these tawdry, funky icons are still infused with great power."[25] According to Morgan, such aesthetic juxtapositions are commonplace within religious settings:

"The sublime and the prosaic go hand in hand—they always have. This is the pastiche of everyday life."[26] Both the mass-produced plaster image and the laboriously crafted stone cathedral give expression to and engender religious experience by giving material form to the immaterial. Regarding the role of kitsch within Roman Catholicism, Morgan observes, "The inexpensive mass-produced broadside, pilgrimage medal, dashboard saint . . . form a vital part of the material culture of Christianity without which many generations of believers could not have practiced their beliefs in the characteristic ways they have."[27] Because most expressions of Catholic kitsch are typically small and relatively inexpensive, kitsch renderings of religious subject matter are the most accessible forms of art for the vast majority of Catholics.

The Sacred as Separate

In the *Power of Myth*, Joseph Campbell discusses the famous vision of Black Elk in which the Native American prophet said he saw himself atop Harney Peak in South Dakota, the central mountain and thus regarded as the sacred center, of his people's religious tradition. Black Elk says that during that vision he came to the realization that "the central mountain is everywhere."[28] As Campbell explains, Black Elk saw that access to the sacred is not confined to a special place but is possible everywhere. As will be seen, this view regarding access to the sacred was shared by several pilgrims to Our Lady of Guadalupe. However, in general, orthodox Catholicism strictly separates the sacred from the profane. This separation reflects the twin influences of Judaism and the traditions of the ancient Roman religion.

The concept that sacred spaces are clearly demarcated from the profane is expressed early and often in the Hebrew Bible (which is referred to by some Christians as the Old Testament). In Genesis, for example, God is said to have set aside the seventh day of the week as special, blessing and sanctifying it as a day of rest. Indeed, the Hebrew scripture in general and the Pentateuch in particular[29] set other things aside and define them as sacred within the Jewish tradition: the temple is set aside as a hallowed place, the Levites as a priestly tribe, certain feasts as holy times of the year. Moreover, the Hebrew scripture defined the Hebrews as a special people set apart from all others because they were called to and consecrated by God. The Catholic tradition, which regards the Hebrew Bible as part of its sacred scripture, has incorporated the view expressed in it of the sacred as something separate and distinct.

The *terms* "sacred" and "profane" originated in distinctions that ancient Romans drew regarding space. According to Colpe, "To the Roman, *sacrum* meant what belonged to the gods or was in their power."[30] The Romans contrasted the sacred space of their temple precinct with the mundane space that lay immediately in front of it, which they referred to as the *profanum.* As Colpe explains, "Originally, *profanare* meant 'to bring out' the offering 'before the temple precinct (the *fanum*),' in which a sacrifice was performed. *Sacer* and *profanus* were therefore linked to specific and quite distinct locations; one of these, a spot referred to as *sacer,* was either walled off or otherwise set apart, that is to say, *sanctum* —within the other, surrounding space available for profane use."[31] Though the terms "sacred" and "profane" originated as designating spatial distinctions, over time their usage has broadened to include objects, people, time, and other things. In the religious life of the Western world, which still reflects the influence of the ancient Hebrews and Romans, this distinction has been so pervasive that Durkheim argued that it is central to the development of all religious traditions.[32] Many contemporary religious studies scholars, however, dispute whether this distinction is as universal as Durkheim believed it to be.[33]

Sacred Space and Objects in Modern Marian Devotion

Though the distinction between the sacred and the profane may not be universal as Durkheim claimed, this binary opposition has certainly influenced the development of Catholic approaches to the material and spiritual dimensions of the human experience. As in other religious traditions, such distinctions frequently focus on indexical connections and/or iconic resemblance.

In the case of a purported Marian apparition, a place is made sacred through its indexical connection with a quasi-historical event: a purported vision in which a person claims to have had spiritual rather than physical contact there with some localized manifestation of the Blessed Virgin Mary.[34] Whether this spiritual event "actually" occurred is irrelevant. When someone claims to have experienced such a vision and the claim is believed by enough people and/or endorsed by the church, the place where the Blessed Virgin is said to have manifested herself is defined as a sacred site. Important examples of such sites include Aparecida, Brazil; Fatima, Portugal; Lourdes, France; Medjugorje, Bosnia and Herzegovina; and Kibeho, Rwanda. Each of these places has a shrine dedicated to the local version of the Virgin who is said to have appeared there in apparitional form. Because of their historical/indexical connection with a Marian apparition, these shrines are considered sacred by adherents of the Virgin's various cults. Objects purchased at or near them, or brought to them, are rendered sacred through their contact with and connection to the shrines.

The most popular of the Marian apparitional shrines attract millions of pilgrims annually. Indeed, during the last century there was a significant shift in Catholic pilgrimage practices. In the past, sites purported to possess the relics of a saint, or which possessed historical importance, were the primary foci of Catholic pilgrimages; today, however, more than 80 percent of Catholic pilgrimages are made to Marian shrines associated with apparitions of the Virgin.[35] Currently no Marian shrine attracts more pilgrims than does that of Our Lady of Guadalupe, located in Mexico City. Between ten and twenty million people are estimated to visit the shrine each year. Only the Vatican attracts more Catholic pilgrims.[36] The Basilica of Our Lady of Guadalupe is located just below Tepeyac, the small hill atop which Juan Diego claimed he encountered the Meso-American manifestation of the Virgin Mary now known as Our Lady of Guadalupe. As a result of Juan Diego's claim, and of its later endorsement by the Catholic Church, the hill is regarded as sacred and serves as the center of the Guadalupan cult's sacred geography.

The Image of Our Lady of Guadalupe as an Object of Cultic Devotion

As important as Tepeyac is as a sacred site, the primary focus of the cult's devotional attention is the image of Our Lady of Guadalupe. According to a legend first recorded in the *Nican Mopohua*,[37] which was written in the Aztec language of Nahuatl sometime between 1548 and 1560, a recent Aztec convert to Roman Catholicism, Juan Diego, experienced a series of visions at Tepeyac in which he saw and spoke with a woman who claimed to be the Mother of God.[38] This woman instructed Juan Diego to report to the local bishop and tell him to build a church atop the hill[39] in her honor. When he visited the bishop, the skeptical prelate dismissed the farmer, who left discouraged.

In another vision the woman instructed Juan Diego to gather flowers in his cloak and present them to the skeptical bishop. The flowers, which were blooming out of season, would serve as miraculous proof that Juan Diego's visions were genuine. Dutifully, Juan Diego gathered the flowers as the Virgin instructed him, and then he once again sought an audience with the bishop. When Juan Diego opened his cloak in the presence of the prelate, the flowers fell to the ground, revealing an image imprinted on his cloak depicting the woman he claimed to have seen in his visions, which adherents of the Virgin's cult believe was miraculously placed there.

In the image the Virgin is depicted as a brown-skinned woman. Hands clasped, head tilted to her right, eyes slightly averted, she stands on a crescent-shaped sliver of moon upheld by a childlike angel. She is clothed in a cloak studded with stars and is framed by the golden rays of a hidden sun. This image is pervasive throughout Mexico and in places outside Meso-America where large numbers of Mexican immigrants live. Indeed, as reported by Anthony DePalma: "The Virgin of Guadalupe is so adored by Mexicans that a reproduction of the image she is said to have left on Juan Diego's cloak over 465 years ago appears in nearly every home and workplace, including the windshields of city buses and the bumpers of long-haul trucks."[40] Ignacio Corona confirms the image's popularity:

"She is everywhere. On T-shirts, tattooed on biceps and chests, etched into the back windows or lacquer enameled on the back trunks of low riders, on murals, on tiles and medals. Even on cowboy boots. An El Paso boot maker designed a pair that sells for $1,500, although the workers had to be convinced of the propriety."[41] According to Richard Vara, the image of Our Lady of Guadalupe even adorns some Mexican American Protestant places of worship.[42] These ubiquitous images of the Virgin are clearly part of people's daily lives, and yet these same images are regarded as being apart from the mundane world as well. Even when rendered as tattoos, pasted on bumpers, or depicted in mosaics made from discarded plastic soft-drink bottles,[43] kitsch reproductions of the image are regarded as sacred because they resemble and represent the Virgin depicted in the original.

Iconic and Indexical Power

Images of Our Lady of Guadalupe are believed to possess imitative power because of their iconic resemblance to the Virgin. When purchased near, or brought to, the Virgin's shrine, these images are believed to obtain contagious power through this indexical connection to the shrine. The power such items are believed to possess is illustrated in the following explanation offered by a woman in her early forties regarding why she had purchased several religious items from vendors operating near the basilica: "I usually buy scapulars for my sons so they can wear them around their necks and they can carry Our Lady of Guadalupe around with them all the time, so that She can protect them. For instance, I have a son who is a truck driver, so I usually give him a scapular so he can wear it, and I know that Our Lady of Guadalupe is gong to protect him on the road, from any danger, from any accident. I know She is going to protect him all the time." Indeed, most of the pilgrims interviewed for this study, in accordance with the beliefs of popular Catholicism, stated that they believe that reproductions of the image of Our Lady of Guadalupe possess great power. Although some pilgrims, such as the woman cited above, reported that they bought images of the Virgin from the shops or vendors that sell religious items in and around the area of the basilica, others said that they brought images they already possessed to the basilica with the intention of having them specially made sacred through the blessing of a priest. One woman in her early twenties explained, "I made a promise that I would bring this image here [to the basilica], so I am doing that today. And also I am going to ask the priest to bless the image for me." The Catholic Church teaches that any priest could have blessed the image anywhere in the world. However, as understood by the woman cited above, the priestly blessing takes on greater significance when it is given at the shrine because the item then derives some of its power from the indexical connection established through its own presence at, and the priest's association with, the shrine.

Reproductions of the image render the sacred portable and thus accessible to more people. Images that have been brought to the basilica in which the original image is displayed extend the sphere of that place's sacred space when taken back home. The following story, told by a man in his late thirties, illustrates this: "What happens is that I was working with some firemen in another village, and they had [an image of the] Virgin, so they said, 'Oh, we would like to get this Virgin blessed.' And so, they say, 'We have another one if you want it.' So, I decided to bring both of them and I asked my friends if they wanted to come here with me. So we are going to get both Virgins blessed here by the priest. And then we'll take them back. And we'll keep one and return the other one." One pilgrim, a man in his midtwenties, described his response to otherwise mundane places made sacred: "If I go to any other place and I see an image of or a shrine to Our Lady of Guadalupe, I honor that; because anywhere She is the same, so we can pray to Her anyplace."

Reproductions of the image help to establish connections not only between the basilica shrine of Our Lady of Guadalupe and other places but also between the Virgin and her followers. One female pilgrim in her midthirties explained the special sense of connection fostered by such images: "Some people carry Her in medals and little pictures. I have a little picture. But we know that She can be anywhere, and that we don't need any of those things to know that She is with us. She can be anywhere. But people carry things at work or have little shrines or have a little medal in their pockets or their wallets or their purses, so that they can feel closer to Her. But we know that She can be anywhere. That's the very special thing about Her." As another pilgrim, a woman in her midtwenties, put it, "They [images of Our Lady of Guadalupe] mean that She will always be with us. For instance, any day that I feel alone I can just grab one of these pictures or images and feel closer to Her."[44]

Reproductions of the image also enable pilgrims to establish and maintain spiritual connections between the Virgin and those unable to visit her shrine. As one pilgrim, a woman in her midtwenties, explained: "We bought some scapulars and some pictures of Our Lady of Guadalupe; and we are taking them back to our town, and we'll give some as gifts and some of them we'll keep. And one thing I wanted to add about the scapulars is that some of them will even go to New York. We will send them to our relatives in the U.S." Indeed, in interviews conducted for this study, the exportation of Guadalupan religious items to Mexican émigrés in the United States was a common theme. When asked what he planned to do with the religious items he had purchased, a man in his midtwenties responded: "Actually, they're for me, because I have a house back in town and I didn't have any picture of Our Lady of Guadalupe. So I need some pictures and images. And I will also buy some key rings for some friends and for my relatives, especially for my brother who is in the United States. He believes strongly in Our Lady of Guadalupe, so I'm going to buy a key ring and a T-shirt with the image of Our Lady of Guadalupe for him because by me being here, it's like he has been here too. So I'm going to send him a few things." In this way, this pilgrim feels that he is able to share his pilgrimage experience with his brother. Such connections between people who are geographically separated are fostered by the indexical logic of Catholic kitsch.

Kitsch as Ritual Habit

One wonders what influence such images might exercise in perpetuating core Catholic beliefs and the practices associated with these beliefs. Some scholars, such as O'Flaherty, contend that "the myths[45] that endure best, on any cultural level, are those that are free of kitsch."[46] Other scholars, such as Morgan, argue that myths do not survive in spite of their being expressed in kitsch art but rather because of this expression. With respect to Catholic kitsch in particular, and religious kitsch in general, I suggest that there is truth in both arguments. If by mythic survival one means the continuation of the specific *content* of myths, kitsch has not proven itself to be the best vehicle of effecting such continuation. If, however, mythic survival is defined as the perpetuation of a myth's elemental *forms,* then I contend that kitsch is wonderfully suited to the task of perpetuating such forms. Kitsch of the kind that constitutes Catholic sacramentals, such as the images of Our Lady of Guadalupe, captures in visual form frozen moments or key characters from the church's mythic traditions, often in exaggerated caricatures of the original images. These forms are readily recognizable to believers. However, kitsch art provides neither a narrative context nor an exegetical framework for the mythic forms to which they give material expression. In this respect, Catholic kitsch's seeming inability to transmit important information about itself and the religious tradition of which it is a part suggests that it has much in common with other forms of communication defined as ritual by Carey.

Kitsch as Perpetuation of Mythic Form

Through widespread dissemination of kitsch reproductions, the image of Our Lady of Guadalupe is easily recognized throughout Central America and much of the Roman Catholic world beyond. The story of the image's origin, however, is not so well known or widespread among those who adore her. Indeed, when asked to recount the story of Juan Diego and his apparitional encounters with Our Lady of Guadalupe, only a couple of the pilgrims interviewed were able to provide informed answers.[47] The following interview exchange, with a man in his late thirties, is typical of the sketchy responses provided by most pilgrims:

Q: Do you believe in the story that says Our Lady of Guadalupe appeared to Juan Diego?
A: Yes, we are all believers.
Q: What can you tell us about the story?
A: What else can I tell you? Basically, what we were taught about the story. That's what we know.
Q: And what were you taught about the story?
A: To believe, to respect Her, to believe the story. That's what we have been taught.

When pressed further, this pilgrim was unable to provide any details regarding that story. Most of the pilgrims we interviewed openly admitted to knowing little about Juan Diego's story; the following admissions of ignorance are typical:

— "I believe in the story of Juan Diego but I don't know much about it. I really don't know" (a man in his early thirties).
— "I don't know much about it either. We see that everyone goes up there [Tepeyac hill], and we know that that's the original site, so that's why we decided to go up there. But we don't know much about the story" (woman in her early thirties).
— "Well honestly, there's not much I can tell you" (woman in her early forties).
— "The truth is I can't tell you [the story]. To be honest, as I said before, I didn't have much education so I can't tell you much about it. But I do believe in the story" (a man in his midtwenties).

As these statements suggest, a lack of knowledge about the story behind the Guadalupan image does not necessarily correspond with a lack of faith in the spiritual value of the image or the Virgin it depicts. In fact, many of those who admitted to knowing little or nothing about the story professed strong belief in the story's central figure, Our Lady of Guadalupe.

Familiarity with and participation in a myth's elemental forms in the absence of (much) knowledge about the myth's content (that is, narrative, meaning, exegetical apparatuses) exemplifies a socioreligious practice I term *ritual habit.* Contemporary examples of ritual habit are easy to find. In the United States these include the hanging of stockings on Christmas Eve, the hiding of eggs at Easter, and the throwing of rice at couples who have just been married. Most of those who engage in such behaviors know little, if anything, about the historical background or the meanings ascribed to these activities originally or by those religiocultural traditions that later appropriated them. Still, there is the expectation, if not outright insistence, that the formal expression of these rituals be carried out.

There is a great deal of variation, however, in the way ritual habits are realized. There are neither uniform practices associated with nor standard material expressions of such ritual habits as Christmas stockings, Easter eggs, and the throwing of rice (and now quite often birdseed) after weddings. In much the same way, reproductions of the image of Our Lady of Guadalupe are often only loosely related to the original image.[48] License is taken with the posture and positioning of the Virgin, with the color of her clothing, and with the image's astronomical and floral symbolism. Like depictions of the American version of Santa Claus, as long as the Virgin is even vaguely recognizable as Our Lady of Guadalupe, she may be rendered in any way an artist desires. (This fluid approach to religious art, it should be noted, differs drastically from the strict codification found in other Christian artistic traditions. The rules governing the creation of Byzantine icons, for example, promote a high degree of standardization.) This variation in visually rendering the Virgin's image is accompanied by variations in beliefs and practices associated with devotion to her. In this way, Catholic kitsch differs from most communication defined as ritual. While dissemination of kitsch art serves to perpetuate the image that is the focus of cultic devotion, and is thus instrumental in maintaining the most important feature of the cult, kitsch does not promote a shared view of the world but rather allows for multiple views—some complementary, some conflicting—to exist side by side.

Kitsch Adaptability and Multivocality

Much contemporary Catholic kitsch celebrates some version of the Virgin Mary. Seen in semiotic terms, the Blessed Virgin Mary is a sign open to multiple artistic reinventions and religious (re)interpretations. As Bowen notes:

> Catholic images, and especially the image of the Virgin Mary, have served to mediate translations of religion across vast social and cultural divides, first within Europe, and then across the seas with the expansion of the Church. But the very capacity of the image to carry multiple meanings—which I have called the "multivocality" of the image—has allowed subordinate groups to contest the dominant meanings. Spanish villagers insist on their own Mary's capacity to protect and nurture; Mexicans, of the Virgin of Guadalupe's role as a national symbol; Brazilians, of Yemanja/Mary's powers over the seas; Christians throughout the world, on Mary's willingness to appear to them and deliver messages of hope and struggle. Each set of claims to Mary is asserted over and against official counterclaims that underscore the unity of Mary and Christ and the authoritative voice of Rome.
>
> In the center of this tension between center and many peripheries lies the image. The multiplicity of the image, its capacity to be replicated and to carry many meanings, gives it this powerful role, and shapes the color and experience of the Catholic religious tradition.[49]

In practice, the Virgin's multivocality[50] has resulted in the adoration of many Marys. What Carroll says of the multiple Italian Madonnas is true throughout the Catholic world: "While these different madonnas may indeed be associated vaguely with the official Mary, each madonna nevertheless has a separate identity, and each is the object of distinct cultic devotion."[51]

When rendered with the fluid artistic freedom of kitsch, and in the relative absence of mythic content, these many Marys invite additional reinventions and interpretations. The image of Our Lady of Guadalupe, for example, is seen by some scholars as a Christian icon in the traditional religious sense of the word[52] and by others as a kind of Aztec codex.[53] The pilgrims interviewed as part of the broader study of which this examination is a part also expressed radically divergent views regarding the image. Some saw it as a religious icon symbolic of the triumph of Christianity over the indigenous Aztec religious system, while others saw the same image as a codex celebrating the Meso-American peoples and their cultures.[54] Given this multiplicity of possible interpretations, Guerrero argues that the image of Our Lady of Guadalupe is a wonderful example of what Catholic theologians call *inculturation,* which is the Catholic theological position that, since potential reception of the Gospel message is implanted in all cultures, the Christian message can and should be given culturally specific expression among different peoples.[55] For this reason, the material expression and cultural practices of the Catholicism one finds in Ireland, for example, differ a great deal from the material expression and cultural practices of Filipino Catholics. Accordingly, from a Catholic perspective it should not be surprising that Europeans and Meso-Americans might view the same image of the Virgin in radically different ways using quite different interpretive apparatuses.

It is easier to import an image than the theology supporting it from one culture to another. Today, devotion to the image of Our Lady of Guadalupe has spread to places as culturally and geographically removed from one another as Ethiopia, France, Italy, Japan, Kenya, Poland, Spain, Sweden, and the United States. With this spread, the image central to this cult is being reinvented through inexpensive kitsch reproductions that deviate, sometimes radically, from the original and which reflect the cultures of these very different places.[56] These reproductions render the Virgin economically and culturally accessible to her new adherents. They also invite new interpretations that might have little if anything to do with either the story of Juan Diego or the Marian/Meso-American mythology in which the image has played such an important role. In this respect, of course, these new kitsch reproductions, like other forms of ritual habit, perpetuate the image's mythic form in the absence of substantive mythic content, and in doing so, such images invite multiple interpretations, some at odds with the Catholic religious tradition of which they ostensibly are part. In addition, like

American Christmas customs that have been transplanted to places where both Christianity and the U.S. secular culture associated with the holiday are alien, the forms of the ritual habit are continued in the absence of the cultural beliefs and practices that have supported it.

Implications

In this essay I have identified iconicity and indexicality as the main features of the semiotic code informing Catholic kitsch, explained how this code defines some things as separate in that they are deemed sacred, described how the code creates connections, and pointed out how Catholic kitsch promotes a ritual habit that is adaptable and multivocalic. These latter two qualities of Catholic kitsch have several important implications. First, these features of Catholic kitsch provide those outside the institutional church's center of power with a means of challenging that power and reshaping Catholicism in ways that respond to and reflect their own culture and historical circumstances. The Virgin depicted in that image dresses and looks like an Aztec maiden of the early sixteenth century and not like the European version of the Blessed Virgin Mary that the Spanish conquistadors had brought with them and sought to impose on the Aztecs. In responding to the Meso-American features of the Virgin depicted in the image imprinted on Juan Diego's cloak, the Aztecs embraced this New World re-envisioning of the Virgin with a rapidity and enthusiasm that stunned the Spanish missionaries and local church officials. In the decade following Juan Diego's initial report regarding the apparitions he said he had experienced, over ten million Meso-Americans are reported to have embraced a version of the Catholic faith associated in the popular mind with the image of the woman who had purportedly appeared to Juan Diego.[57] This remains the largest unforced conversion in the history of Christianity.

This mass conversion illustrates the power of an image to attract adherents. This is a power that the Catholic Church has had a long history of exploiting, not only in art produced under the patronage of the church, but also through deliberate appropriations of the images of other religious traditions. The traditional Madonna-and-child imagery, for example, was imported wholesale from the once-popular Mediterranean cult of Isis. Indeed, such appropriation was so open at one point during the late Roman era that statues of Isis and her son Horus were placed in Christian churches, with their original inscriptions scratched off and new ones carved into their stone identifying the pair as Mary and Jesus. The practice of appropriation proved to be such an effective means of proselytizing that Pope Gregory the Great, as Bede records in his *Ecclesiastical History of the English People,* advised a missionary to claim and Christianize whenever possible pagan places, practices, and objects of worship.[58] This policy reflects, and in all likelihood prompted the development of, the church's theology of inculturation, and, of course, it reflects as well the ability of places, practices, and objects to carry multiple meanings.

As Westerfelhaus and Singhal point out, the same multivocality that served the church as it expanded its sphere of influence also enables the church's adherents to challenge—sometimes unknowingly—the teachings and practices promoted by the institutional church.[59] The image of Our Lady of Guadalupe, for example, includes astronomical and floral imagery, religious symbols, and an aesthetic sensibility that are distinctively Aztec.[60] Today the image and its numerous reproductions continue to provide adherents of the Virgin's cult with means of challenging traditional Catholicism. The image is the devotional focus of an ostensibly Marian cult that incorporates key features of the precontact Aztec religious tradition. In doing so the cult of Our Lady of Guadalupe incorporates much that is at odds with the present-day teachings of the institutional church.[61] In this respect, it has much in common with views promoted by many of the other cults that populate Catholic popular piety and which celebrate, for example, other Marian entities, various saints, the Sacred Heart, and the Infant of Prague. Each of these cults contains beliefs and associated practices contrary to orthodox/orthoprax Catholicism, and each makes use of kitsch images of the cult's object of devotion as means of expressing and engendering religious devotion. These cults celebrate such images and accord them a central role. It is these images, and not any specific beliefs or practices, that are central to the religious devotion of the cults' adherents. In fact, adherents of such cults often develop personal beliefs and practices regarding the images that not only deviate from those of the church but also are a departure from those beliefs and practices typically associated with the images' cults. In addition, in many cases those who hold heterodox beliefs and engage in heteropraxic practices contrary to those promoted by the church or by an officially sanctioned Catholic cult are unaware of the oppositional nature of their beliefs and behaviors. Ironically, naive profession of such beliefs and participation in such practices by nominal adherents of the church allow Catholicism to expand its sphere of influence while at the same time unintentionally weakening that very influence by diluting Catholic doctrines.

This kind of adherence is tied to another implication of the fluidity and adaptability of kitsch images: the ability of such images to foster connections between Catholics that transcend time, place, cultures, and even differences of belief. Though the formal expression of such images as that of Our Lady of Guadalupe is fluid, there is still some consistency in the way they are rendered or else they would no longer be recognizable with respect to what they are intended to represent. Such consistency enables these images to transcend time and place and allows them to respond to diverse cultural preferences and fashion's changing tastes, while also making it possible for people from different times and different cultures to recognize and respond to variations of the same image. This enables adherents of an image's cult to share in a ritual habit that binds them across time and place, and yet which does not demand that they share similar beliefs about, or engage in similar practices with respect to, an image.

In this way, Catholic kitsch provides adherents of the church's various cults with what I call the "continuity of comfort," a deep and satisfying sense of "communitas" enjoyed by people who have little more in common than the ritual they share.[62] Understood thus, kitsch religious art can be viewed as a form of ritual communication that, in common with other kinds of ritual communication, serves to bind believers together rather than to convey information. In contrast to the conventional conception of ritual communication, however, kitsch renderings of religious images do not reaffirm a shared view of the world. Indeed, the lack of informed responses by those pilgrims interviewed as part of this study indicates that such a shared view does not exist, given the absence of even a basic knowledge of Our Lady of Guadalupe, her history, and the Marian theology that informs the orthodox Catholic view of the Virgin. Instead, as I have argued regarding Catholic kitsch as ritual habit, it is the mythic form of the image itself that is reaffirmed, the image that is shared, the image that is the focus. In the words of one of the pilgrims cited earlier, "It's because of the image. We revere the image." As long as this remains true, kitsch renderings of cult images will continue to play an important role within the Catholic religious tradition, serving both to affirm and to challenge that tradition.

Notes

1. Although I follow contemporary publishing conventions in my own text, when transcribing the interviews of the adherents of Our Lady of Guadalupe, I respectfully follow their convention of capitalizing the first letters of the pronouns "Her" and "She" when these refer to Mary.

2. Rafael Obregon (Ph.D., Pennsylvania State University) and Yolanda Uresti (M.A., Ohio University).

3. Carmen Rosiles Arrendondo, Jannet Velencia Flores, Veronica Mondragon, and Marissa Hernandez Perez. Their time was made available for this study through the generosity of Heriberto Lopez of Televisa.

4. The interviews were translated into English by Rafael Obregon, who was one of the interviewers. Having only one translator helped to ensure consistency in the quality of the translations.

5. Robert Westerfelhaus, "She Speaks to Us, for Us, and of Us: Our Lady of Guadalupe as a Semiotic Site of Struggle and Identity," in *Communicating Ethnic and Cultural Identity*, ed. Mary Fong and Rueyling Chuang, 105–20 (Oxford, U.K.: Rowman and Littlefield, 2004); Robert Westerfelhaus and Arvind Singhal, "Difficulties in Co-opting a

Complex Sign: Our Lady of Guadalupe as a Site of Semiotic Struggle and Entanglement," *Communication Quarterly* 49 (2002): 95–114; Robert Westerfelhaus, Arvind Singhal, and Rafael Obregon, "Meso-American Devotion to Our Lady of Guadalupe as Celebration of Self: An Examination of an Inverted Icon/Addressee Relationship," *Kentucky Journal of Communication* 20 (2001): 41–70; Robert Westerfelhaus, "An Examination of th Cult of Our Lady of Guadalupe from Two Communication-Based Perspectives: Diffusion of Innovations and Socio-semiotics" (Ph.D. diss., Ohio University, 1999).

6. James W. Carey, "A Cultural Approach to Communication," *Communication* 2, no. 1 (1975): 1–22.

7. This field has its roots in the work of the American pragmatist philosopher Charles Sanders Peirce and the Swiss structural linguist Ferdinand de Saussure. Peirce's works on semiotics were originally published in various magazines and journals toward the end of the nineteenth century; Saussure first published his *General Linguistics* during the first decade of the twentieth century.

8. Umberto Eco, *A Theory of Semiotics* (Bloomington: Indiana University Press, 1976); M. Gottdiener, *Postmodern Semiotics: Material Culture and the Forms of Postmodern Life* (Cambridge, MA: Basil Blackwell Inc., 1995).

9. John Fiske, *Television Culture* (New York: Methuen, 1987), 4.

10. Charles Sanders Peirce, *Peirce on Signs: Writings on Semiotic* [*sic*] *by Charles Sanders Peirce* (Chapel Hill: University of North Carolina Press, 1991).

11. John R. Bowen, *Religions in Practice: An Approach to the Anthropology of Religion* (Boston: Allyn and Bacon, 1998), 143.

12. That is, cults devoted to some version of the Blessed Virgin Mary. My use of the term "cult" in this sense conforms to the conventional usage of the word in anthropological and theological literature to denote a complex of beliefs and ritual practices that has a particular focus. Within Catholicism, such foci include, for example, devotions to Mary and to local and universal saints. This usage differs from the popular use of the term "cult," which has a negative connotation.

13. Alice B. Child and Irvin L. Child, *Religion and Magic in the Life of Traditional Peoples* (Englewood Cliffs, N.J.: Prentice Hall, 1993); James George Frazer, *The Golden Bough* (New York: Simon & Schuster, 1996)—a classic study that was published first in two volumes in 1890 and later as a twelve-volume work in 1911–15; Brian Morris, *Anthropological Studies of Religion: An Introductory Text* (New York: Cambridge University Press, 1987).

14. Algirdas Julien Greimas, *Semantique Structurale* (Paris: Larousse, 1966). See also Terence Hawkes, *Structuralism & Semiotics (New Accents)* (London: Methuen, 2004).

15. Stephen R. Barley, "Semiotics and the Study of Occupational and Organizational Cultures," *Administrative Science Quarterly* 28 (1983): 397.

16. Carey, "Cultural Approach," 6.

17. Ibid.

18. Ibid., 3.

19. Ibid., 8.

20. *Catechism of the Catholic Church: Revised in Accordance with the Official Latin Text Promulgated by Pope John Paul II* (Huntington, Ind.: Our Sunday Visitor, 2000), §2502.

A catechism is a summary of church teachings. The catechism cited here is the first formal catechism of the Roman Catholic church since the catechism produced by the Council of Trent in the sixteenth century.

21. David Morgan, *Visual Piety: A History and Theory of Popular Religious Images* (Berkeley: University of California Press, 1998), 66.

22. *Catechism,* §1675.

23. Anthony Wilhelm, *Christ among Us,* 2nd ed. (New York: Paulist Press, 1975), 180.

24. Ibid., 181.

25. Wendy Doniger O'Flaherty, *Other People's Myths: The Cave of Echoes* (Chicago: University of Chicago Press, 1988), 39. Note: After the publication of the book cited here, this scholar dropped O'Flaherty from her name and once again published under Wendy Doniger, by which name she is better known.

26. Morgan, *Visual Piety,* 24.

27. Ibid.

28. Joseph Campbell with Bill Moyers, *The Power of Myth* (New York: Doubleday, 1988), 89.

29. The five books that comprise the Pentateuch are Genesis, Exodus, Leviticus, Numbers, and Deuteronomy.

30. Carsten Colpe, "The Sacred and the Profane," in *The Encyclopedia of Religion,* ed. Mircea Eliade (New York: Macmillan, 1987), 12:511.

31. Ibid.

32. Emile Durkheim, *The Elementary Forms of the Religious Life* (1915; repr., London: Allen & Unwin, 1964).

33. Regarding which dispute, see Morris, *Anthropological Studies of Religion.*

34. Sandra L. Zimdars-Swartz, *Encountering Mary: From La Salette to Medjugorje* (Princeton, N.J.: Princeton University Press, 1991).

35. As reported by Westerfelhaus, Singhal, and Obregon, "Meso-American Devotion."

36. As reported in "Marian Shrines: Signs of the Pilgrimage Church," *Marian Library Newsletter* 32 (1996): 1–2.

37. Authorship of the *Nican Mopohua* is traditionally ascribed to Antonio Valeriano, a well-educated Aztec nobleman, who recorded the facts as he knew them less than a generation after the visions were said to have occurred (see Charles Wahlig, "First Author of Historic Account on Guadalupe: Don Antonio Valeriano," in *A Handbook on Guadalupe,* ed. [Brother] Francis Mary, 51–54 [New Bedford, Mass.: Franciscan Friars of the Immaculate, 1997]). Some scholars question Valeriano's authorship; see, for example, Stafford Poole, *Lady of Guadalupe: The Origins and Sources of a Mexican National Symbol, 1531–1797* (Tucson: University of Arizona Press, 1995).

38. Janet Barber, trans., "*Nican Mopohua,*" paper presented at Our Lady of Guadalupe symposium, Pontifical College Josephenum, Columbus, Ohio, December 12, 1996; Wahlig, "First Author."

39. Tepeyac had been the site of a shrine, destroyed by the Spanish, that was dedicated to the Aztec goddess Tonantzin. The cult of Our Lady of Guadalupe has absorbed several

elements from the cult of this goddess, such as some of the dances performed in front of the basilica in celebration of the feast of Our Lady of Guadalupe (see Westerfelhaus and Singhal, "Difficulties").

40. Anthony DePalma, "Let Heavens Fall, Mexicans Will Revere Virgin," *New York Times,* June 21, 1996, A4.

41. Ignacio Corona, "Guadalupismo: Popular Religiosity and Cultural Identity," paper presented at Our Lady of Guadalupe symposium, Pontifical College Josephenum, Columbus, Ohio, December 12, 1996, 18.

42. Richard Vara, "The Lady of Guadalupe: From Mexican Shrine to Houston Auto Shop, Tributes to Mary Abound," *Houston Chronicle,* December 9, 2000, E1, E3.

43. A mosaic image of Our Lady of Guadalupe made of soft-drink bottles can be found in Houston's Sixth Ward.

44. This tactility, which complements the visual appeal of the Virgin's image, is an important feature of Meso-American Catholicism and is one reason why sacramentals play such a prominent role in the Catholic popular piety of Mexican and Mexican American Catholics.

45. Here the term "myth" is used to denote a complex of religious beliefs.

46. Doniger O'Flaherty, *Other People's Myths,* 51.

47. These were well-educated women from the United States who had read a great deal about the image of Our Lady of Guadalupe and its history prior to visiting Her shrine.

48. Felipe Ehrenberg, "Framing an Icon: Guadalupe and the Artist's Vision," in *Goddess of the Americas / La Diosa de las Américas: Writings on the Virgin of Guadalupe,* ed. Ana Castillo, 170–83 (New York: Riverhead Books, 1996).

49. Bowen, *Religions,* 169.

50. Or polysemy, to use semiotic terminology, which in common with the anthropological term "multivocality" is defined as the ability of a sign to mean different things to different people, and thus to convey multiple meanings.

51. Michael P. Carroll, *Madonnas That Maim: Popular Catholicism in Italy since the Fifteenth Century* (Baltimore: Johns Hopkins University Press, 1992), 59.

52. Columban Hawkins, "The Iconography of Guadalupe," in *Handbook on Guadalupe,* 63–67; see also Ehrenberg, "Framing an Icon."

53. Janet Barber, "The Sacred Image Is a Divine Codex," in *Handbook on Guadalupe,* 68–73; Janet Barber, "The Codex That Breathes Life," in *Handbook on Guadalupe,* 75–80. Aztec codices, which make use of colorful, richly detailed, and highly stylized pictographic glyphs to convey symbolic meanings, are invaluable sources of information about Meso-American culture, cuisine, history, medicine, and religion. Many of the codices still extant were collected in book form during the post-Columbian contact period. Some include glosses in Spanish and Nahuatl, the latter language rendered using the Roman alphabet. There are two ways in which an image of Our Lady of Guadalupe can be read as a codex. First, like a codex, the image includes traditional Aztec glyphs such as the quincunx situated on the Virgin's cloak. As Barber explains in "Sacred Image," this floral glyph represents "the four compass points of the world, with heaven and the

underworld vertically encountering earth in the center, in the 'navel' of the world, or, to use the metaphor, in the navel of the moon as they call the Valley of Mexico" (72). The placement of this flower with respect to the Virgin's womb signifies to the Aztecs and their heirs that the baby she is carrying has strong cultural and geographic ties to their world. The image can also be read as a codex in that its floral and astronomical symbolism taps into the same religio-cultural logic that both informs and is given expression by conventional Aztec codices.

54. The image of Our Lady of Guadalupe depicts a woman standing atop a crescent moon. A conventional Catholic reading sees such an image as representing the Blessed Virgin Mary's triumph over an indigenous mother goddess, who is symbolically represented by the moon. From a precontact Meso-American perspective, this same image can be read as representing the emergence of an indigenous version of the Virgin Mary, with the crescent moon symbolizing the Valley of Mexico (see Westerfelhaus, "Examination of the Cult of Our Lady of Guadalupe" and "She Speaks"; Westerfelhaus and Singhal, "Difficulties").

55. José Luis Guerrero, "The 'Nican Mopohua': A Magnificent Example of Inculturation," paper presented at Our Lady of Guadalupe symposium, Pontifical College Josephenum, Columbus, Ohio, December 12, 1996.

56. For example, in an Asian mall on the west side of Houston, Tex., I saw several Chinese versions of the Guadalupan Virgin.

57. (Father) Maximilian, "Our Lady of Guadalupe—Model of Prayer and Holiness," in *Handbook on Guadalupe,* (see note 37), 80.

58. (Venerable) Bede, *Ecclesiastical History of the English People* (New York: Penguin, 1990), 92. Pope Gregory's letter was written in 601 C.E. Bede's history was written in 731 C.E.

59. Westerfelhaus and Singhal, "Difficulties," 107–9.

60. See Thomas J. Ascheman, "Guadalupe: Good News for All People," in *Handbook on Guadalupe* 116–20; Barber, "Codex" and "Sacred Image"; Frank Gonzalez-Crussi, "The Anatomy of a Virgin," in *Goddess of the Americas / La Diosa de las Américas,* 1–14; Guerrero, "Nican Mopohua."

61. For example, devotees of Our Lady of Guadalupe see Her as a miracle worker. The church, however, teaches that only God can work miracles and that miracles attributed to the Virgin, as well as other saints, are the products of their intercession on behalf of those who pray to them.

62. Robert Westerfelhaus, "The Comfort of Continuity: The Tridentine Mass as Symbolic Equipment for Living," *Virginia Journal of Communication* 11 (1998): 105–21.

Massachusetts Miracles

Controlling Cures in Catholic Boston, 1929–1930

Patrick J. Hayes

Cultic aspects of Catholic devotions to the miraculous have for centuries pitted the wills of church officials against those of believers. Although some Catholic prelates have been receptive to the emergence of these cults in their own sees, particularly in connection to an established local saint, there are instances when a bishop has sought to quash rumors of miracles.[1] The appeal of miracles is not at issue because their stories help bind Catholics together through a common imagination.[2] No bishop would assert his authority against miraculous phenomena in principle, and yet particular stories that arise within his see remain subject to episcopal oversight. When bishops do act, it is not uncommon for there to be resistance to their authority. A prime illustration of such a struggle arose from a string of miracle stories current in Boston around the time of the great stock market crash of 1929. The miracles were attributed to Father Patrick Power, a man who had been deceased for sixty years.

Power's early life is not well attested. Records found in the archives of the Archdiocese of Boston indicate that he was born in Bantry, county Cork, Ireland, on October 20, 1844. He came to the United States at an early age. There is some question over his citizenship; there is no record of a passport or visa application filed with the U.S. District Court in Boston. In any event, Power was the youngest of six children and was orphaned at age four and sent to America to live with relatives. Two of his cousins were priests in the United States, and they resided in Charlestown, Massachusetts. One of them, Father John J. Power, eventually became a vicar general in the Diocese of Springfield in western Massachusetts when it separated from the Archdiocese of Boston in 1870.

The young Power was eventually sent to pursue studies at Laval University beginning at age seventeen. He then enrolled in St. Joseph's Seminary in Troy, New York. Power was ordained at Holy Cross Cathedral in Boston before being sent to study canon law at the University of Louvain, but he stayed there less than a year. His last assignment was as a curate in Holy Redeemer Church in East

Boston, where Father James Fitton, his mentor, was stationed. Fitton had already had a long career as a missionary throughout the New England states and was the first to organize Catholics in western Massachusetts.

In one of his early assignments, Power served at Holy Name of Jesus Church in Chicopee, Massachusetts, a parish initially visited by Fitton in the 1830s. A plaque on the edifice signals its importance.

Although Power was able to minister in a relatively new church, the adjacent rectory preceded it. He was there, off and on, for about seven months in 1869. Its poor construction has made it uninhabitable today, though generations of priests have made it their home. As a junior curate, he was probably given a room in the house that was susceptible to drafts. It is likely that the rough New England weather affected Power adversely, and by the time he moved on to his next assignment in East Boston, his health had deteriorated to a point beyond recovery. He died of tuberculosis on the Feast of the Immaculate Conception, December 8, 1869, at the home of his brother in Brookline. He was twenty-five years old.

When he was laid to rest in the priest's section of the Holy Cross Cemetery in Malden, Massachusetts, there was only one other priest buried in the lot. Power's corpse was placed within a small mound in the open air. There was no more to be said about the man until sixty years later, during the week of the stock market crash in 1929.

The so-called Black Thursday of October 24, 1929, was the beginning of a week of panic among traders.[3] The volatility of the market caused some financial institutions to collapse, but it also provided a chance for schemers to capitalize on a general feeling of uncertainty and insecurity. This was no less true in the religious realm than in the financial world. It was at precisely this tragic moment in American financial history that a rumor began to circulate about a miracle cure at Power's grave.

No officially authenticated miracle had to this point ever been attributed to any church, shrine, or person in postcolonial New England. Several hundred "documented" healings had taken place in connection with Boston's mission church, the Basilica of Our Lady of Perpetual Help, located in the Roxbury section of the city. Beginning in August 1871 with the healing of a protruding bone in Louisa Julia Kohles's leg, the church quickly became a site for pilgrims. The Redemptorist Fathers, in whose care the church remains to this day, promoted these cures. Years later the healing of four-year-old Grace Hanley's "shattered spine" caused a sensation due to the prominence of her father—a Civil War colonel—but the cure was never given official approbation.[4] Dubbed "Lourdes in the Land of the Puritans," the church has supplied numerous testimonies to the power of the image of Our Lady of Perpetual Help, especially among Boston's poor, but the icon seemed powerless in the face of the most recent national crisis.

The miracle stories attributed to Power began to multiply within a relatively short period. There now seemed to be an opportunity for Catholics in Boston to raise a symbol of hope amidst the tears of the preceding days, as well as to advance the cause of the nation's first potential saint.[5] By November 2, 1929, scores of rosaries, pins, rings, and other jewelry littered the grave site as tokens of thanksgiving. By noon on that day, an estimated fifteen hundred people were keeping vigil.[6]

As it was later reported in the *Nation,* the pastor of a parish near the cemetery made an announcement from the pulpit at Sunday Mass that cures related to the grave site had been reported to him. Any additional cures were to be made known to him promptly. In Mass that morning were two individuals associated with rival Boston newspapers, and these two quickly set the media's machinery in motion, spreading the story throughout the region. It is difficult to pin down the "first reported cure." One reporter, approximately fifty years after the fact, wrote that Mrs. Mary O'Hearn of Everett, Massachusetts, was the first reported cure, and the *Boston Sunday Post* reported that her "cure" occurred on October 29. She had gone to pray by the grave three times, and on the day after the third visit, her hearing was restored.[7]

O'Hearn's case was complemented in the many stories of children who were positively affected by visits to Power's grave. Sometime after November 4 the mother of six-year-old James Panora of Revere, Massachusetts, took him to the cemetery. James had been a deaf-mute since his early childhood. After praying there, "they stood up and when his mother spoke his name he answered, 'What?' She then asked him to say 'Father Power' and he repeated the words. Mrs. Panora became hysterical with joy and several hundred people dropped to their knees in thanksgiving."[8] The following day Vincent O'Neill, age nine, who was blind in one eye, went to the cemetery with his grandmother. After praying before the grave, the two entered a small chapel at the entrance to the cemetery. Then, while staring at the statues in the chapel, the child blurted out, "Grandma, I can see tall white people!" Other children, after visiting the grave site, took off their leg braces and walked away happy. One anonymous pilgrim to the grave simply left a pair of eyeglasses there with a note that read, "Cured, thank you Father Power."[9]

Interestingly, one did not have to be present at the grave to receive favors. A six-year-old South Boston native named William Gaul, who was hospitalized with respiratory problems, had a tube inserted down his throat to help him breathe. His parents, fearing for their child's life, went to the cemetery and, after nearly a two-hour wait, managed to touch a handkerchief to some rainwater that had collected in the chalice etched into Power's tombstone. When they later applied the cloth to the young man, he began to breathe on his own.

Healing narratives no longer remained confined to simple crosstown stories but began to include accounts from the West Coast as well. One story about Power came in a news report from Santa Barbara, California, where a nun in a monastery of Poor Clares described how an eye ailment was cured after a picture of the young priest was applied. She touched the photo to her face and asked for healing if it were God's holy will. By the time she sang Matins that night, the ailment had subsided without any pain and she was able to read from the Divine Office without glasses. Writing to the Boston chancery, she claimed, "It is now over a week since I invoked Father Power's aid and my eye has been, and still is, perfectly normal. I am writing this, at my Superior's suggestion, in thanksgiving for the favor I received."[10]

Power's intercession went beyond physical cures. For example, a letter from Baltimore describes how a petition for a financial windfall was favorably granted.[11] A hymn, "O Father Power of Holy Cross," was written in his honor and was a small financial boon to its composer. Its refrain extols Power as a great intercessor:

Saintly priest, oh, hear our prayer
Friend of God, His works declare
O Father Power, so meek and just
In thy mercy, pray for us.[12]

Power's appeal cut across both economic and religious divisions. Among the believers, simple people rubbed shoulders with Boston's most famous citizens. Jack Sharkey, who was then the reigning heavyweight-boxing champion, stood in line to pray for his daughter, Dorothy, who had been born blind in one eye. Boston's mayor-elect James Michael Curley came and knelt in a steady drizzle to pray for the health of his wife. Though the Catholic community claimed Power for themselves, at least one Jewish man, Sam Sidman of Dorchester, was photographed standing unaided for the first time in years; he abandoned his wheelchair in the cemetery.[13] By now the miracle stories were legion and demanded an official response.

Cardinal William O'Connell, a burly Irishman and former rector of the North American College in Rome, made a few brief appearances at the cemetery, which were covered by the local press. Aloof and authoritarian, O'Connell typified *Romanità* among American prelates.[14] He was described as "Monsignor Pomposity" and as an impressive figure, "as an elephant is impressive."[15] In the cardinal's view, the church found its greatest expression as part of a papal apparatus, a vast network of local churches—and there was no doubt among his priests and their parishioners that he was in charge of Boston. As he made his way through the crowds, he blessed those he saw gathered in the field of mud surrounding the grave. His silence probably signaled as much disdain for the spectacle as it did prudential judgment. He departed without answering any questions, except to say, "All we know is what we see with our eyes, and you can see as much as I can."[16]

However, when he arrived at the chancery, he made it clear to his staff that no official comment was to be made about the miracle stories and that care was to be taken over the security of the cemetery property. The cardinal's repeated visits to the cemetery reinforced his instruction on silence; he gave no further remarks to the press. Moreover, he instructed his brother Edward, who was the cemetery's superintendent, to make sure that the crowds did not behave in an undignified manner. Edward dutifully complied.

The crowds continued to grow at the site. On November 11, 1929, the headline for the Monday morning *Boston Globe* read: "Crush of 100,000 at Priest's Grave Knocks Stone Down—Cemetery Thronged throughout the Day." Boston's Catholics came out in droves, forcing the transit authority to authorize additional trolley service between the city and Malden. It was estimated by Malden police that one-seventh of all registered vehicles in the Commonwealth of Massachusetts passed through the city on November 10. The people pushed one another to jockey for a position nearest the tomb and ended up tipping over a large six-foot cross. The Catholic press as far away as Switzerland had received word that "600 policemen could not keep them in check and that the militia had to be called out."[17]

Local clergy were put on alert, including the vicar for the cemetery, Father Patrick Walsh. The archdiocesan vicar general, Father Richard Haberlin, wrote a memorandum on November 12, 1929, that read: "The Cardinal saw Rev. P. H. Walsh on November 12th and instructed him to have two young men take care of the people gathering about the Chapel and to see to it that these young men keep order and collect whatever offerings are made by the faithful. These offerings are to belong to the Cemetery Corporation. The Vicar General saw Father Walsh on the same day and communicated those same instructions to him."[18]

Haberlin also penciled some additional marginal notes about the crowds in the cemetery. The people were to be orderly and respectful, and an advertisement to this effect was to accompany a request that the faithful abstain from coming to the cemetery in large numbers. Boardinghouses near the cemetery were not to be patronized since they were interested only in making money from those pious pilgrims who had traveled great distances and who were often in desperate financial circumstances already. Those hawking goods were also to be avoided, and state and municipal authorities were put on notice that such individuals were annoying those genuinely interested in visiting their deceased loved ones.[19]

Other schemes were in the wind. In New York City, and without the cardinal's approval, a group of Irish Americans formed the Reverend Patrick J. Power Pilgrims League, whose goal was "to spread the knowledge of the reported cures effected at Father Power's grave and to gather the correct data of all such reported cures and after having this material certified to cause its presentation to the ecclesiastical authorities with a view to have Father Power beatified."[20] Haberlin wrote more than one letter forbidding group pilgrimages to Power's grave. A woman from Jermyn, Pennsylvania, had been contemplating such a pilgrimage tour and asked the cardinal his views. Haberlin wrote back: "I take this occasion to inform you that such action on your part is prohibited. In the event that such a Pilgrimage does come, admission to the Cemetery will be refused."[21]

Despite these actions, the week before Thanksgiving did not yield further calm. An advance press release of a story about to be filed for the *Nation* made its way into the chancery building.[22] The release put the public on notice that the journal was running a story describing the author's "horror at the suffering and at the apparent violation of the human intellect in some of the actions comprising the demonstration of faith." In the story filed November 23, but appearing December 4, Gardner Jackson attacked popular belief in the cures and suggested that it illustrated how vulgar and base the pilgrims were. Jackson wrote,

> The spectacle is repellent beyond words and at the same time stirs feelings of intense pity. The commercialism involved is shocking: the slab over the grave covered with money dropped by the kneelers; the two waste-baskets filled with money and emptied two or three times a day; . . . the hot-dog stands and food tents on the adjacent streets; the hawking of celluloid buttons, just like campaign buttons, bearing the likeness of Father Power; the making way every now and then for the movie men to get good shots and spread the word around the country; the screams of hysterical women, the tears, the faintings, the fine dust into which the turf has been pulverized around the grave. It is a scene that violates the most elementary principles of mental and physical health.[23]

Some journalists took the occasion of the miracle stories to explain the religious excitement as a revival of will that was being tested by the nation's economic crisis. Yet even some in the Catholic press echoed how the scene reeked of commercialism and linked the degradation to recent stock market woes. One editor wrote in the Catholic journal *Commonweal,* "In Wall Street we are told the remedy needed is restoration of the true and inherent value of the stock. It may be that such a restoration of values is needed in our souls."[24]

The cardinal had had enough, and on November 22 he suspended night visits to the cemetery. On Thanksgiving Day he ordered the cemetery closed until further notice to what was estimated to be around fifty thousand daily visitors. Only funeral processions and relatives of those visiting loved ones would be allowed to enter, and only then to their family plots—not to Power's grave. A battery of Irish cops was dispatched to guard the entrances and, at the chancery's suggestion, ushered the peddlers and food venders from in front of the gates. On December 7, 1929, the *Pilot* ran a front-page banner headline proclaiming Cardinal O'Connell's seventieth birthday, which would occur on the following day, December 8. This coincided with the sixtieth anniversary of Power's death, but there was no mention of Power in all the editions subsequent to December 7. Boston's Catholic newspaper was under the editorial control of its publisher, Cardinal O'Connell. The paper's silence on Power's case is conspicuous, and it appears that O'Connell did not want to be upstaged on his birthday by a sixty-year-old corpse. In addition, he probably hoped to avoid the appearance of sanctioning the growing cult.

The faithful raised a huge outcry. A woman from Poughkeepsie, New York, who was nearly en route with her invalid child learned of the cemetery closing and complained to His Eminence, "it seems to me that the Catholic Church should welcome another glorious chapter of its history at the hands of the intercession of one of its priests after 60 years of his death. It may be the will of God to manifest his power to check those Christians and others who have gone far in their ignostic [*sic*] state of mind and who are 'scientists' in their faith." She concluded her letter in anguish: "If you could only see or even conceive my suffering poor child and how much agony I go through every minute I see her for ten months past, you could not with a heart of flint but grant my wish and permit my visit."[25]

Additionally, several groups sent petitions to Cardinal O'Connell demanding that the cemetery be reopened. One of the longer ones contained in the archdiocesan files was from a group who were "all good Catholics and working women." Some sixty-three signatories, "many of us being afflicted with infirmities both slight and serious," and all of whom worked at the same factory, could not hope to visit before its closing time without losing their daily wages. They asked the cardinal to have the cemetery remain open until at least 8:00 P.M. so that they could "journey to this holy spot."[26] Most of these women were from Jamaica Plain or Roxbury, two heavily Irish American neighborhoods within the city limits. At the time, these were areas dominated by hoi polloi, and mayor-elect Curley, who came from "JP," never forgot the base of his support. Given the hour's trolley ride to Malden from these neighborhoods, the social, political, and spiritual bonds of these women would have been reinforced on a daily basis. With the cardinal's directive, their newly found comradeship ceased.

However onerous to the faithful his orders may have been, the cardinal might have been simply observing the conventions of canon law in force at the time. The question for any ordinary in O'Connell's situation was twofold. First, how could episcopal vigilance be upheld with respect to public worship, including devotional life, within his see? In this regard, he was to see to it that no canonical irregularity was promoted, nor any superstitious practice carried out. Second, how could the veneration of a sacred site or person by a cult conform to the longstanding practices of the church?[27]

What was needed was an attitude of discretion and patience in order to properly authenticate a "heroically virtuous life."[28] Only then could the miracles be assessed—two for beatification, two more for canonization.[29] Much of the 1917 Code of Canon Law's section on causes leading to beatification is colored by the "founder of the modern science of juridical history," Pope Benedict XIV (1675–1758).[30] This pontiff's eighteen-year papacy must be seen in light of his previous twenty years as a curial official, which included the position of promoter of the faith, the highest office within the Congregation of Rites. This congregation was responsible for identifying saints, and Benedict's massive treatise *De servorum Dei beatificatione et beatorum canonizatione,* written while he was a curial cardinal, continues to guide the work of the present-day Congregation for the Causes of Saints. Benedict's insistence on cautious judgments on the part of the local ordinary are supplemented by his advice in classifying types of miraculous cures—some of which also required a reasonable time for evaluation.[31] For a miraculous cure to be authentic, the following criteria needed to be satisfied:

> First, That the disease be considerable, dangerous, inveterate, and such as commonly resists the strength of known medicines. . . . 2dly, That the disease be not come to its crisis, in which it is natural to look for a remission of its symptoms and cure. 3dly, That the ordinary helps of natural remedies have not been used, or at least there be just reason to presume from the time elapsed since taking them, and from other circumstances, that they could have no influence on the cure. 4thly, That the cure be sudden and instantaneous. . . . 5thly, That the cure be perfect and entire. 6thly, That there happened no crisis, nor any sensible alteration which might have naturally wrought the cure. 7thly, That the health recovered be constant and not followed by a speedy relapse.[32]

These concerns were at the heart of any future investigation of the veracity of the miracle stories, but there was another pressing matter on the cardinal's mind. In mid-December 1929 O'Connell personally instructed the chancellor to order three priests to oversee the exhumation of Power's body.[33] It would be moved to lower ground within the priests' lot, but not simply as a matter of convenience for visitors. Already the cardinal must have had it in mind that if the stories were going to prove true, an inspection of the priest's remains would be necessary to detect any signs of corruption. "Incorruptibles" such as Mother Cabrini in New York City were widely understood as possessing special sanctity. There was also a need to confirm the actual presence of Power's remains, rather than those of another person, in the tomb.

On review, indeed, Power's flesh had long since decayed. As the spokesman for the group, Father Patrick H. Walsh later attested that the bones were all intact and that nothing out of the ordinary was visible.[34] All the bones were translated into a new concrete vault to prevent grave-robbing for the relic trade. Incredibly, none of Power's relatives were notified of the disinterment. When they read about it through the news reports, they complained bitterly,[35] but none of their complaints received replies. After Power's reinterment, the new grave was then fenced in.

As the news coverage of Power's shrine increased over the winter months, a long string of requests came in asking Cardinal O'Connell for special permission to visit the locked cemetery. There are scores of letters in the files of the archdiocesan archives, and some of these come from a considerable distance. O'Connell received letters from as far away as Costa Rica, the Philippines, and Spain. Requests from American cities—Kansas City, New York, Chicago—peppered the chancery for "a bit of earth" from Power's grave. Some had the hope of bringing potential converts, such as a New York woman who asked to bring "a girl there who has been cripple [*sic*] for the past few years." The treatment of specialists had yielded no positive result, she continued. "This girl however is not a Catholic, but I am sure she would be willing to accept the Faith were such a cure possible." In contrast, another sought a healing cure for her stomach: "I ask help in the name of God so I can work to help my children," the writer said, but she "wouldn't want the letter published as a lot of Protestant people would make light of it. If you please send me the sand and water, send it C.O.D. and I will gladly pay the charge."[36]

The chancellor of the Archdiocese of Boston, Monsignor Francis A. Burke, was assigned the unenviable task of having to reply to these letters, which must have consumed hours of his time. At first they were a curiosity and were treated as individual requests, but as the numbers of cemetery visitors grew, so did the amount of correspondence. To give an idea of the numbers of those who traveled to the cemetery, estimates range from a low of 400,000 to nearly 1.5 million over the course of the month of November 1929. There are hundreds of requests for earth in the chancery files.

Each of the letters displays a simple piety, and almost all exhibit a mixture of desperation and friendly optimism. About a month after the stories broke, a letter arrived from Jacksonville, Florida. F.H., a disabled American veteran who served in World War I, wrote that he had contacted "the Superintendent of the Cemetery" and that "he sent me some soil from the grave with no instructions." He wondered if the cardinal could write back telling him "what to do with it, as it must be sacred."[37] Some of the letters were sent on behalf of others, as if the miracles could take effect only under the condition of charitable anonymity. A letter from R.J. to the cardinal instructs him not to reveal the fact that she is writing on behalf of a family friend whose child suffered from some palsy.[38] For the miracle to work, its narrative had to be concealed; only then could it be considered "pure charity."

O'Connell never replied to any of these missives. As for his staff, there is only one instance among the several hundred requests when Burke sent anything from Power's graveside. These were in the form of "religious articles" sent originally by Joseph Beaubien of Detroit to be returned after they had touched Power's grave. Beaubien had written directly to Burke four times complaining that he wished his items returned. The ever-dutiful Burke probably made his way to Malden one night, touched the articles to the tomb, and shipped them off the next day.[39]

People were still writing to O'Connell well into July 1930 for a bit of earth or water that had collected in the chalice sculpted into Power's tombstone. Of course, not everyone was convinced of the miracle cures. Apart from the liberal press, the medical establishment also weighed in. Dr. Charles Mayo of the Mayo Clinic, for instance, denounced such stories as superstition and as an affront to science and the medical profession.[40] Psychologists explained that the "cures" were the result of self-convincing by persons in high emotional states.[41]

Father Ovid L. Chaput, the assistant chancellor of the Archdiocese of Boston, was assigned the task of investigating the veracity of the stories that had appeared in the local papers. On December 13, 1929, he sent several handwritten letters asking pastors, doctors, and others to investigate the claims of those "cured."[42] Over the course of the next several months, reports flowed in from pastors and physicians, along with testimonials from the cemetery's superintendent and others from around the country.

One of the responses to Chaput's inquiry came from Fr. John Gorham at St. Charles Parish in Woburn. His letter is brief but typical:

December 16, 1929

Rev. O. L. Chaput,
Assistant Chancellor,
Lake Street
Brighton, Massachusetts.

Dear Father Chaput:

I received your letter of December 13, concerning the Gonsalves child of this parish who was brought to the grave of Father Power in Malden. There seems to be nothing worthy of an official inquiry in the case. I have seen the child and his parents.

The child is Ayres Joseph Gonsalves, born May 31, 1925, of Joseph Gonsalves and Mrs. Stella Gonsalves, residing now at 10 Lake Avenue, Woburn, Mass. The boy is ailing since birth with some brain trouble which causes paralysis of his left side and lower limbs. The mother brought him to the Cemetery on Monday, November 11, 1929, and prayed for him at the grave of Father Power and also in the Cemetery Chapel. She rubbed him with earth taken from the grave, and on the following days, Tuesday and Wednesday, the father brought the child and prayed for him in the same manner at the grave and in the Chapel. After these visits to the priest's grave they noticed no change in the condition of the child up to the present time. The child is being treated in the Children's Hospital in Boston. He is getting some benefit from the hospital treatment and there is hope of a natural cure of his ailment.

I shall be pleased to give any other information you may desire about this case.

Very sincerely yours in the Lord,
John R. Gorham, Parish Priest.[43]

Other priests' reports gave similar judgments, including one that indicated explicitly that his case was "outside the sphere of the miraculous."[44] While diocesan clergy usually formed a negative opinion on their parishioners' claims, this was not the case among members of religious orders. Fathers E. J. Bertrand and Regis Sirois of the Society of Mary reviewed the case of Cecile Croteau. Here is their report:

> Testimony of Mother: Child had not been able to see with the right eye ever since six months after birth. The eye was covered with a grayish membrane and caused much pain. The two eyes converged towards each other in an extremely abnormal way. The child had always been weak and sickly. The cause of the trouble had never been found by doctors and the case was said to be helpless. On a second visit to Father Power's grave the child left there her glasses and saw with both eyes.
> Condition of the child when visited: Child is in perfect health. She sees with both eyes. The eye in fact would be normal at least in appearance if it were not still converging towards the other—a defect which is said to have improved and still improving greatly.[45]

After the spring of 1930 these documents became more sporadic, but they were still arriving as late as 1934. With all the data before him, Chaput drafted an undated memorandum to the cardinal on the thirty-five cases he had investigated. He broke these into five classes: "1) a miraculous cure testified by physicians; 2) what appears to be a miraculous cure but unsupported by testimony of physicians; 3) cases in which there is no doubt of very great improvement; 4) cases in which there is considerable improvement; 5) cases in which there is some or little improvement."[46]

Chaput found only one instance of the first class, and according to a witness, the miracle occurred after the subject swallowed some of the earth from Power's grave.[47] The miracle belonged to "Miss Laura Moody, a girl about 17 years old, who was afflicted with what is known as a poker back which was encased in a cast. The physician who attended her at the City Hospital and the physician who treated her at her home testify that in their belief there is an absolute cure which cannot be other than a miracle. Miss Moody now goes about with no appearance of any previous ailment."[48] The attestation of Dr. Harold W. Dana, M.D., a self-described "non-Catholic who believes that God still performs miracles on this earth," convinced Chaput that there was something to Moody's recovery that could not be explained by ordinary medical means.[49] Dana's opinion was supplemented and affirmed by a more detailed testimonial from Dr. Edward J. Leonard, M.D., of Boston City Hospital.[50]

During the investigation, the chancellor received word from the business manager of the *Brooklyn Tablet* newspaper that "there is circulating in Brooklyn, at the present time, a medallion bearing the photograph of Rev. Patrick Power, containing particles of earth alleged to be from the original grave of Father Power, . . . which you will note sells for $2.75."[51] Long before, by late February and early March of 1930, the chancery was able to trace the medallion to Thomas F. McNamara of Brooklyn, New York. McNamara sought to capitalize on Power's fame by issuing certificates and medals for sale, of which a portion of the proceeds would be given over as a donation to the Archdiocese of Boston. Although this was clearly a moneymaking scheme and was promptly decried by Monsignor Burke, McNamara went on undeterred, simply indicating in his advertisements that the church had no connection to his firm's offer. In perhaps his greatest bit of hucksterism, McNamara attempted to convince buyers to purchase medallions by throwing into the deal free dirt alleged to be from Power's grave.

The same procedure was followed in addressing the hopes of another New York businessman, P. J. O'Sullivan, who, after test-marketing his medallion, indicated that "people seem to feel the time is right for a Catholic Irish American Saint."[52] On the orders of the cardinal, Burke shot back that no medallion was to be struck and that because no official sanction would be forthcoming, any attempt to do so would be considered "offensive to public Catholic sentiment."[53]

State troopers were still protecting the nation's largest Catholic cemetery after January 1930, and when the gates were reopened to the public in April, crowds of between five and six thousand continued to gather each weekend until the first week of May. From then on the numbers dwindled. By the late spring of 1930 it had become clear that the Power miracles could not be authenticated to the satisfaction of the cardinal, even though I have found no official document closing the case. In fact, letters came into the hands of chancery officials for years afterward and were merely filed among the Power records without any indication that the stories they relate were ever investigated.[54] Moreover, there is no documentary indication that anyone at the chancery actively assembled information on the life of Power or any miracles that may have occurred in the years prior to 1929.[55] No dossier was made, for instance, that gathered evidence of demonstrable virtue or sanctity, other than the number of baptisms and weddings celebrated by Power.

If the enthusiasm for instructing a cause for sainthood was waning in the halls of the chancery, this tendency mirrored the public's interest as well. By the middle of 1930 only a few of Boston's Catholics were still coming to the cemetery. Such individuals continued to visit the grave and undoubtedly influenced their children's understanding of Power's cult, so that even today locals recall the fervor of their parents' piety. As they struggled through the Depression, these devotees clung to a symbol of hope in a young priest cut down in his prime and now doling out favors for the living like so much political patronage. This may reflect a decrease in the American Catholic preoccupation with Old World devotions, reflecting instead an increase in their attempts at assimilation, even while preserving religious unity. It is during these same months and years that Christian America turned introspective and brought the cultivation of the moral self into greater focus.[56] Nonetheless, even today Power's grave remains a site of popular piety, a curiosity to outsiders but a place where some of the locals explain that Power is still "one of us." The field of mud once surrounding his grave has been replaced with new sod. On the fence surrounding the tomb, faded rosaries wave in the breeze alongside those of a more recent vintage, one bead linked to the next, connecting the past to the present.

Notes

1. For the European context, see, e.g., Michael P. Carroll, *Veiled Threats: The Logic of Popular Catholicism in Italy* (Baltimore: Johns Hopkins University Press, 1996); Craig Harline, *Miracles at the Jesus Oak: Histories of the Supernatural in Reformation Europe* (New York: Doubleday, 2003); Robert Kreiser, *Miracles, Convulsions, and Ecclesiastical Politics in Early Eighteenth Century Paris* (Princeton, N.J.: Princeton University Press, 1978); Thomas Kselman, *Miracles and Prophecies in Nineteenth Century France* (New Brunswick, N.J.: Rutgers University Press, 1983); Mary Lee Nolan and Sidney Nolan, *Christian Pilgrimage in Modern Western Europe* (Chapel Hill: University of North Carolina Press, 1989).

2. On miracles' appeal to Catholics' religious imagination, see Robert Bruce Mullin, *Miracle and the Religious Imagination* (New Haven, Conn.: Yale University Press, 1996), esp. chap. 5. In this fascinating book Mullin considers why people choose to embrace the miraculous or not and how their decisions impact their views of nature or history. The decisions often acted as litmus tests either for a person's rationality or a person's orthodoxy. Within those religious bodies that accepted miracles as articles of faith, their precise nature and the corresponding responses to them were mixed. For instance, in the eighteenth and nineteenth centuries some Protestants took it as a mark of their own identity to acknowledge biblical miracles and to deny any extracanonical phenomena as bogus inventions of

"papists." Catholic miracles, they insisted, concentrated not on the power of God but on the sorcery of priests. By contrast, from the early modern period onward, Catholics saw it as a mark of their own identity not only to acknowledge the biblical miracles, but also to demonstrate to Protestants that their errors prevented them from enjoying postbiblical signs of God's intervention in the world—not to mention how false their churches were. To deny miracles was to deny the saints who performed them. Miracle stories, moreover, were viewed as persuasive in missionary activity among unbelievers. Miracles had the power to convert, and any authentic conversion was a conversion to Catholicism.

3. See John Kenneth Galbraith, *The Great Crash, 1929* (Boston: Houghton Mifflin, 1988); Maury Klein, *Rainbow's End: The Crash of 1929* (New York: Oxford University Press, 2001); David E. Kyvig, *Daily Life in the United States, 1920–1939: Decades of Promise and Pain* (Westport, Conn.: Greenwood Press, 2002); Cabell Phillips, *The New York Times Chronicle of American Life: From the Crash to the Blitz, 1929–1939* (New York: Fordham University Press, 2000), 17–35.

4. See Charles W. Currier, "History of the Church of Our Lady of Perpetual Succor in Boston," *Records of the American Catholic Historical Society of Philadelphia* 2 (1886–88): 206–24.

5. About a year prior to this, Cardinal George Mundelein of Chicago ordered a formal investigation to be begun on the merits of the life of Mother Frances Xavier Cabrini, who would be canonized in 1949. The first American-born saint was Mother Elizabeth Ann Bayley Seton, and while her investigation began in 1882 by order of Cardinal James Gibbons of Baltimore, she was not canonized until 1959.

6. See Victor DeRubeis, "The 'Miracle Priest' of 1929, Part 1: Hundreds of Thousands Sought 'Cure' at Grave," *Malden Evening News,* December 10, 1979, 11.

7. Ibid., 1. See also Thomas E. Kissling, *Father Power: A Biography* (Baltimore: Belvedere Press, 1931), 31–32. The *Boston Sunday Post* issued a "Father Patrick J. Power Memorial Booklet" that lists O'Hearn as the first cure. It can be found in the Archives of the Archdiocese of Boston (hereafter AAB), Power, Rev. Patrick J., M-1587 files. I thank Robert Johnson-Lally and his staff for their helpful assistance in collecting images and documents related to Power.

8. Bill Lombardi, "Out of the Past: The Grave in the Holy Cross Cemetery in Malden, Massachusetts," *Branch 34's Clan* (October 1994): 7.

9. Ibid.

10. "Sister Tells Experience with Father Power's Picture," clipping in AAB, Power, Rev. Patrick J., M-1587 files.

11. L.P.W. to O'Connell, December 14, 1929, in AAB, Power, Rev. Patrick J., M-1587 files.

12. AAB, Power, Rev. Patrick J., M-1587 files, folder 6.

13. See the collage of photographs culled from the *New York Journal* of January 11, 1930, entitled "Latest Facts about the Miracles Reported at the Malden Shrine," clipping in AAB, Power, Rev. Patrick J., M-1587 files, folder 1.

14. See James M. O'Toole, *Militant and Triumphant: William Henry O'Connell and the Catholic Church in Boston, 1859-1944* (Notre Dame, Ind.: University of Notre Dame Press, 1992), 16–18.

15. See Charles R. Morris, *American Catholic: The Saints and Sinners Who Built America's Most Powerful Church* (New York: Vintage, 1997), 120.

16. "Scores Faint in Record Pilgrimage of 200,000 to Shrine of Malden Priest," undated news clipping in AAB, Power, Rev. Patrick J., M-1587 files.

17. Fr. Schweizer to the Right Reverend Chancellor, November 18, 1929, in AAB, Power, Rev. Patrick J., M-1587 files. About seventy-five uniformed members of Malden's American Legion Post 69 stood watch. See "Scores Faint in Record Pilgrimage of 200,000 to Shrine of Malden Priest," clipping in ibid.

18. Haberlin memorandum, November 12, 1929, in AAB, Power, Rev. Patrick J., M-1587 files.

19. Undated notes, AAB, Power, Rev. Patrick J., M-1587 files.

20. "Dear Friend" letter of JTM on behalf of the Reverend Patrick J. Power Pilgrims League (printed on National Irish American Press Bureau stationery), November 14, 1929, in AAB, Power, Rev. Patrick J., M-1587 files.

21. Haberlin to Mrs. F. E., November 21, 1929. See also similar letters to Mrs. T.R.G. of Wilkesbarre, PA, and to Mrs. J.C. of Scranton, PA, both dated November 21, 1929, in AAB, Power, Rev. Patrick J., M-1587 files.

22. "Immediate Release: 'Miracles' at Malden," in AAB, Power, Rev. Patrick J., M-1587 files.

23. Gardner Jackson, "'Miracles' at Malden," *Nation* 129 (December 4, 1929): 662.

24. "Reviews," in clippings in AAB, Power, Rev. Patrick J., M-1587 files.

25. F.S.B. to O'Connell, December 2, 1929, in AAB, Power, Rev. Patrick J., M-1587 files.

26. Petitioners to O'Connell, November 22, 1929, in AAB, Power, Rev. Patrick J., M-1587 files.

27. *Codex Iuris Canonici* (Rome: Typis Polyglottis, 1917), cc. 1261.1 and 1261.2; the commentary of T. Lincoln Bourscaren and Adam C. Ellis in *Canon Law: A Text and Commentary* (Milwaukee: Bruce, 1957), 689–90. The church's Sacred Congregation of the Holy Office had been relatively silent on repressing certain pious practices until the 1930s.

28. See Robert Sarno, "Diocesan Inquiries Required by the Legislator in the New Legislation for the Causes of Saints" (J.C.D. diss., Pontificia Università Gregoriana, 1987), 77, reprinted in William H. Woestman, ed., *Canonization: Theology, History, Process* (Ottawa: Faculty of Canon Law, Saint Paul University, 2002), 44.

29. See Kenneth L. Woodward, *Making Saints: How the Catholic Church Determines Who Becomes a Saint, Who Doesn't, and Why* (New York: Simon and Schuster, 1996), 85.

30. John A. Hardon, "The Concept of Miracle from St. Augustine to Modern Apologetics," *Theological Studies* 15 (1954): 220–57, here at 234 citing the *Enciclopedia cattolica,* 2:1283. On Pope Benedict XIV, see Philippe Levillain, ed., *The Papacy: An Encyclopedia,* 3 vols. (New York: Routledge, 2002), 1:168–72; and Fabijan Veraja, *Le cause di canonizzazione Dei santi: Commento alla legislazione e guida pratica* (Vatican City: Libreria Éditrice Vaticana, 1992), passim.

31. Benedict also indicated a "sixty-year rule," which separated recent from ancient causes. Ancient causes would be initiated more than sixty years after the death of the

servant of God. Recent causes were initiated within sixty years of death. See Sarno, "Canonical Procedure for Canonization," in Woestman, *Canonization,* 95.

32. Cited in Mullin, *Miracle,* 110. See also George Hay, *The Scripture Doctrine of Miracles Displayed,* 2 vols. (New York, 1851), 2:216.

33. Burke to Walsh, December 2, 1929, in AAB, Power, Rev. Patrick J., M-1587 files.

34. Testament of Revs. Patrick H. Walsh, Daniel W. Lenehan, and George A. Gately and Mr. Edward J. O'Connell to Burke, January 6, 1930 (and notarized on January 8, 1930), in AAB, Power, Rev. Patrick J., M-1587 files.

35. Two letters from James S. Power of Brooklyn, N.Y., survive in the archives. The first indicates that James S. Power, a nephew of the priest, was the administrator of his father's estate whose legacy survived the death of the priest in 1869. See James S. Power, "Dear Sir," December 19, 1929, in AAB, Power, Rev. Patrick J., M-1587 files. Several weeks later Power again attempted to get satisfaction by asking who had given permission to have the priest's remains unearthed. Power also wondered "what became of the money and jewels left to Father Power as they belong to the Power family." See James S. Power, "Dear Sir," January 13, 1929, in AAB, Power, Rev. Patrick J., M-1587 files.

36. G.F.L. to O'Connell, November 23, 1929, and G.M.C. to O'Connell, November 25, 1929, in AAB, Power, Rev. Patrick J., M-1587 files.

37. F.H. to O'Connell, November 30, 1929, in AAB, Power, Rev. Patrick J., M-1587 files.

38. R.J. to O'Connell, December 19, 1929, in AAB, Power, Rev. Patrick J., M-1587 files.

39. Burke to Beaubien, December 13, 1930, in AAB, Power, Rev. Patrick J., M-1587 files.

40. "Dr. Mayo Scores Cures at Shrine," unsigned news clipping, in AAB, Power, Rev. Patrick J., M-1587 files.

41. F. Lauriston Bullard, "Malden—In Retrospect and Prospect," *Atlantic Monthly* 145 (April 1930): 537–45.

42. Chaput letters, December 13, 1929, in AAB, Power, Rev. Patrick J., M-1587 files.

43. Gorham to Chaput, December 16, 1929, in AAB, Power, Rev. Patrick J., M-1587 files.

44. Delaney to Chaput, December 27, 1929, in AAB, Power, Rev. Patrick J., M-1587 files.

45. Sirois and Bertrand to Chaput, February 27, 1930, in AAB, Power, Rev. Patrick J., M-1587 files.

46. Memorandum from Chaput to "Your Eminence," in AAB, Power, Rev. Patrick J., M-1587 files.

47. Testimonial letter of Alexander MacKinnon, February 1, 1930, in AAB, Power, Rev. Patrick J., M-1587 files.

48. Memorandum from Chaput to "Your Eminence," in AAB, Power, Rev. Patrick J., M-1587 files.

49. Dana to O'Connell, November 30, 1929, in AAB, Power, Rev. Patrick J., M-1587 files.

50. Leonard to Father Richard Haberlin, January 11, 1930, in AAB, Power, Rev. Patrick J., M-1587 files.

51. C. M. Becker to Burke, November 30, 1932, in AAB, Power, Rev. Patrick J., M-1587 files.

52. O'Sullivan to O'Connell, March 17, 1930, in AAB, Power, Rev. Patrick J., M-1587 files. An earlier letter from O'Sullivan on behalf of his partners states that "when the matter first appeared in the papers we felt sure every thing was alright and being both Catholics we thought perhaps the earlier we started the better, rather than wait for the Jews, who have strangled the religious goods market to get into it" (O'Sullivan to O'Connell, March 5, 1930, in AAB, Power, Rev. Patrick J., M-1587 files).

53. Burke to McNamara, March 25, 1930, in AAB, Power, Rev. Patrick J., M-1587 files.

54. See, e.g., B.A.M. to O'Connell, June 26, 1938, in AAB, Power, Rev. Patrick J., M-1587 files.

55. Father Patrick Walsh, cemetery chaplain, and the cemetery superintendent, Edward J. O'Connell, may have intimated to a reporter that there were prior miracle stories; see Bullard, "Malden," 538–39. Bullard recounts the story of "a priest" (Walsh?) who, "in conversation with the writer," gave details on the first reported cure "accomplished at the grave about a third of a century ago. A spike had been driven into a man's leg, a friend wrenching it away tore the flesh, gangrene set in, and the wound appeared incurable. A sister anointed the limb with water from the chalice above the grave. There were several applications. Slowly, not instantaneously, the leg healed. Said the priest: 'He told me it was like magic. That was his word—magic.'"

56. This is seen perhaps most eminently in Walter Lippmann's *A Preface to Morals* (New York: Macmillan, 1929), in which he laments the passing of the "ancestral order" into a more debauched age. It can also be seen in the early work of a young academic at the Catholic University of America, Fulton Sheen, who would go on to challenge the nation on his widely viewed *Catholic Hour* television show in the 1950s (see Fulton Sheen, *Religion without God* [New York: Longmans, Green, 1928]; idem., "Religion and Values," *New Scholasticism* 2 [July 1929]: 39–43). For analysis of Sheen's impact, see Mark S. Massa, *Catholics and American Culture: Fulton Sheen, Dorothy Day, and the Notre Dame Football Team* (New York: Crossroad Publishing, 1999).

Our Lady of Prompt Succor

The Search for an American Marian Cult in New Orleans

MICHAEL PASQUIER

IN 1809 SISTER ST. MICHEL GENSOUL VOWED, "O most holy Virgin Mary, if you obtain for me a prompt and favorable answer, I promise to have you honored at New Orleans under the title of Our Lady of Prompt Succor."[1] The Ursuline nun from Montpellier, France, sought Mary's *prompt secours,* or quick help, as she sent a letter to Pope Pius VII requesting a transfer to the fledgling Ursuline convent of New Orleans.[2] The likelihood of a response from Rome was low because of Napoleon's military occupation of Italy and his having placed the pope under house arrest.[3] Two months later, however, Sister St. Michel received a positive reply. True to her word, she commissioned an artisan to sculpt a wooden statue of Our Lady of Prompt Succor holding the infant Jesus, and this was painted in gold. The Ursuline nun and the new statue of Mary then immigrated to a city awash in political, social, and religious instability. The Louisiana Purchase of 1803 opened New Orleans to an unprecedented level of American immigration, thus diversifying an already heterogeneous population reflecting French, Spanish, African, and Caribbean influences.[4] Moreover, a power struggle between liberal and conservative priests weakened the authority of the Diocese of New Orleans. Father Antonio de Sedella, the controversial Capuchin pastor of St. Louis Cathedral, supported the "French ethos" of Creole Catholicism and the notions of religious tolerance and racial equality.[5] The Anglo-Catholic hierarchy of Baltimore moved to replace radical liberals with more conservative clerics.[6] The Ursuline order, a fixture in the Crescent City since 1727, represented a source of religious constancy in the otherwise volatile urban world of the lower Mississippi Valley.[7]

In the midst of such social commotion, the Ursulines refrained from introducing the cult of Our Lady of Prompt Succor to the public until the 1815 Battle of New Orleans. Catholic citizens identified the miraculous intercession of Mary as a factor in the American victory over the British army. Afterward, between 1815 and 1928, Our Lady of Prompt Succor received ecclesiastical support comparable to the most famous cults of Our Lady of Guadalupe, Our Lady of Lourdes, and Our Lady of Fatima. Pope Pius IX authorized a canonical feast day in 1851. Pope Leo XIII granted a solemn coronation of the statue in 1894, the first of its kind in the United States.[8] In 1928 Rome designated Our Lady of Prompt Succor as the "Patroness of Louisiana," and the Archdiocese of New Orleans constructed a national votive shrine in the statue's honor. The Catholic hierarchy, in short, institutionalized a marginal cult of the Virgin Mary as a symbol of unification among the diverse, often antagonistic, Catholic population of New Orleans. Yet, despite the obvious favor granted to the cult during the late nineteenth and early twentieth centuries, popular devotion to Our Lady of Prompt Succor never reached the heights of similarly recognized cults of the Virgin Mary.

This historical examination traces the transatlantic origins of Our Lady of Prompt Succor, the Catholic hierarchy's interest in recasting the cult as indigenous to America, and the laity's haphazard response to ecclesiastical mandates. It illustrates the limitations of "new" popular devotionalism in the United States and the resilience of ethnic ties to non-American cults. During the 1890s—a decade wrought with controversy over America's place in the Catholic Church—Rome and the Archdiocese of New Orleans used their institutional resources to elevate the cult of Our Lady of Prompt Succor to a position of authority among the pantheon of Catholic saints. Moreover, they tried to use the figure of Mary to ease the cultural tension between ethnic communities as well as the conservative-progressive rift in the American Catholic Church. Such ecclesiastical motivations and investments, however, ran contrary to the development of Marian devotionalism on both the American and world stages. In the United States, the Catholic hierarchy customarily supported ethnic-specific cults of the Virgin Mary but stopped short of initiating nationwide devotional movements.[9] In the cases of transnational cults—those that reached an international audience of devotees—an enthusiastic laity initiated and legitimized the supernaturalism of sacred statues and sites, while the church responded to lay demand with the imposition of liturgical and theological parameters.[10] Rome and the Archdiocese of New Orleans tried to do something different with Our Lady of Prompt Succor. They wanted a relatively mundane, unpopular cult to transcend ethnic boundaries and thus incorporate a broader range of Catholics in America. However, without the initial ferment of a popular movement, and without a supernatural tradition to activate the imaginations of potential devotees, Our Lady of Prompt Succor never became what the Catholic hierarchy had intended—an American Mary with multiethnic appeal.

The Ursuline Cult of Our Lady of Prompt Succor

In January 1815 General Andrew Jackson and his "American" army defended New Orleans against General Edward Pakenham and his British expeditionary force.[11] The ragtag defenders of the Crescent City, outnumbered five to one by the Royal Army, included French and Spanish Creoles, Native Americans, free and enslaved African Americans, Caribbean pirates, and volunteers from Kentucky and Tennessee. Portions of the city's noncombatant population—primarily women, children, and the elderly—fled in prayer to the Ursuline Chapel on the eve of battle. Neither the Ursulines nor the laity, however, intended to invest Our Lady of Prompt Succor with miraculous significance. The cult was a private Ursuline affair generating only limited lay involvement prior to the Battle of New Orleans.[12] Catholic citizens went to the chapel because they considered the Ursulines a source of charity and spiritual stability in a city known for its irreligiosity and ecclesiastical problems. The Ursulines held the distinction of being the first female religious order to serve New Orleans. They managed a hospital, an orphanage, and a boarding school. Moreover, at the time of the battle, the Ursuline Chapel was the temporary seat of the diocese due to an empty episcopal seat and a pastoral dispute at St. Louis Cathedral. Father Antonio de Sedella, popularly known as Père Antoine, had rejected the appointment of Father William Dubourg as vicar apostolic of the cathedral.[13] Dubourg, as a consequence, relied on the support of the Ursulines to exhibit some level of institutional authority. On the eve of battle, as Dubourg led a prayer vigil in the chapel, the Ursulines transferred the statue of Our Lady of Prompt Succor from their private choir to the main altar. The mother superior asked Our Lady of Prompt Succor "in the name of the community" to provide victory for the "American Army."[14] In exchange, she promised that the Ursulines and the new devotees would sing an annual mass of thanksgiving in the statue's honor.

The following morning, January 8, 1815, a messenger interrupted Mass to announce the American victory. Those in attendance attributed military success to the miraculous intercession of Our Lady of Prompt Succor. Jackson, however, disregarded the role of Mary and chose instead to recognize the "signal interposition of heaven" during the battle.[15] The citizens celebrated the victory with a rally in the French Quarter's Place d'Armes and a mass of thanksgiving in St. Louis Cathedral.[16] The outdoor crowd included twelve thousand citizens and soldiers. A six-columned arch stood opposite the cathedral. Young ladies representing each state of the union formed an alley for Jackson and threw flower petals at his feet. One of the girls crowned the general with laurels while another sang "Yankee Doodle." A prominent female citizen then thanked Jackson on behalf of the State of Louisiana. After the speech, Jackson reached the door of the cathedral where Dubourg thanked both God and the general for victory.[17] The Ursulines remained cloistered during the celebration.[18]

Despite the attribution of a miracle to Our Lady of Prompt Succor, the cult did not produce a significant level of popular devotion after the Battle of New

Orleans. Of the approximately eighteen thousand citizens of New Orleans in 1815, only a few hundred encountered the first introduction of the Ursuline devotion on the eve of battle. The postcombat festivities, moreover, did not include a public presentation of the statue or a common recognition of a miracle. The Catholic population of French and Spanish Creoles chose instead to identify Jackson as the savior of New Orleans. For the next eighty years the cult of Our Lady of Prompt Succor remained at the margins of the disparate religious atmosphere in New Orleans. The Ursulines kept their vow to offer annual masses of thanksgiving in honor of Mary's intercession. They did not, however, articulate a miraculous narrative conducive to popular dissemination. Without a clear framework for devotion and without a strong corps of lay devotees, the Ursulines' Creole constituency largely disregarded the significance of Our Lady of Prompt Succor and continued in their dismissive attitude toward observance of religious norms. Written accounts of antebellum travelers typically described "New Orleans [as] a dreadful place in the eyes of a New England man. They keep Sunday like we in Boston keep the fourth of July."[19] They expressed dismay at the Creoles' "excessive devotion to pleasure" and participation in dueling and extramarital affairs.[20] Even after the death of Père Antoine in 1829 and the establishment of a conservative hierarchy, the Creole laity preserved their Latin laissez-faire bearing.

The social and political upheaval of antebellum New Orleans undercut the diocese's claim to religious authority and eclipsed the role of Our Lady of Prompt Succor in the everyday lives of Catholics. From 1830 to 1860 New Orleans became the nation's second-largest port city, the second-largest immigrant destination, the largest slave market, and the fifth-largest city in total population.[21] The shift from a Franco-Hispanic culture to a thriving multicultural settlement complicated diocesan efforts to control the anticlerical, antiauthoritarian antics of Catholic Creoles. During one of Dubourg's first sermons at St. Louis Cathedral, Benjamin Latrobe recounted how the Creole parishioners "sneezed, coughed, spat, and, as decency required, rubbed out their spittle on the floor with their feet."[22] By the 1850s Charles Gayarré, a Catholic Creole member of the Know-Nothing Party, contended that Creoles in Louisiana were "free from those gross superstitions which you attribute to the church of Rome. . . . We acknowledge no other power in the head of our church than one which is purely spiritual . . . Louisianans are enlightened Catholics, who would not permit the most distant ecclesiastical interference with politics."[23] The diocese tried to gain some semblance of ecclesiastical order by relying on the "Americanized brand" of Irish Catholicism, with its respect for authority and plain-styled rituals.[24] The Catholic hierarchy mustered more considerable lay support, however, by justifying the Creole and Irish interest in the preservation of slavery. Church officials published a letter from Auguste Martin, the bishop of Natchitoches, Louisiana, in which he regarded the institution of slavery as "the manifest will of God" and castigated abolitionists for "upset[ting] the will of Providence."[25] To the satisfaction of the white Catholic population, the Archdiocese of New Orleans extended its proslavery position to support the secession of Louisiana and the formation of the Confederate States of America. "Our country . . . has become involved in a bloody war," Archbishop Jean Marie Odin announced to the New Orleans public; "justice is on our side . . . let us fervently beseech the Lord that he may be pleased to shield them with his powerful arm, to protect our rights, and to preserve our liberties untouched."[26]

The Ursuline convent survived the tumult of unprecedented population growth and a civil war, but not without losing much of its core constituency to religious indifference, along with its position as the only female religious order in the archdiocese. Female religious education remained the central duty of the Ursulines.[27] The majority of the students came from wealthy Creole families, while a smaller segment of impoverished whites received scholarships.[28] The students comprised the heart of the cult of Our Lady of Prompt Succor. The cult, however, remained private inasmuch as the Ursulines made little effort to develop lay devotion beyond the student body. The parents of the children, especially the fathers, were among the Catholic citizens known for religious indifference. The waves of Catholic immigrants rarely encountered Our Lady of Prompt Succor because of their collaboration with ethnic-specific religious orders. Furthermore, as racial animosity reached its zenith during the Civil War, the black Catholic community all but separated itself from the institutional authority of the archdiocese.[29]

Archbishop Antoine Blanc sanctioned at least nine new female religious groups to meet the needs of the Catholic immigrants, particularly the Irish, Germans, and African Creoles. Blanc's dedication to the maintenance of new orders, however, did not diminish his respect for the Ursuline convent.[30] As a result, he collaborated with Pope Pius IX to authorize a liturgical feast day for Our Lady of Prompt Succor on every eighth day of January.[31] "This latter favor," Archbishop Joseph Rummel wrote almost one hundred years later, "is remarkable because it implies . . . an interruption of the Octave of the Feast of the Epiphany of Our Lord, which is one of the most solemn Octaves in the liturgical year."[32] The Ursulines, nevertheless, refused to interpret the papal partiality as a mandate for public promulgation of the cult. They still did not use the publicity to articulate an archdiocesan-wide narrative of Our Lady of Prompt Succor. In 1878, when the Ursulines produced the first written description of Sister St. Michel's original vow to Mary and the miracle of the Battle of New Orleans, the records remained inaccessible to public dissemination.[33]

The Institutional Cult of Our Lady of Prompt Succor

The tempered exposure of the Ursuline cult of Our Lady of Prompt Succor changed in 1894 when Mother St. Ignace Gardette, "the Mother Superior of the Sisters of the Order of St. Ursula of [the New Orleans] monastery, asked the pope to issue a decree that the Blessed Virgin's statue be crowned."[34] Pope Leo XIII did not grant approval until Archbishop Francis Janssens of New Orleans supported the Ursuline recommendation during an audience in Rome on June 17, 1894. At the meeting, Janssens gave the pope a picture of the statue and a list of miracles attributed to her.[35] Four days later a special delegation of the Sacred Congregation for the Propagation of the Faith granted official approval.[36] Two papal decrees arrived at New Orleans soon thereafter. In the first letter Leo XIII introduced indulgences for the Confraternity of Our Lady of Prompt Succor.[37] The second letter announced the coronation of the miraculous statue. Rome named Janssens implementer of the decree, "mandat[ing] that there be a solemn coronation of the Our Lady of Prompt Succor statue and that it be exposed for public veneration in the aforesaid [Ursuline] chapel."[38]

The papal coronation of a Marian statue was not a common occurrence. Before 1894 Rome had never given such special consideration to a cult developed in the United States. However, in recognition of Leo XIII's strong attachment to the cult of the Virgin Mary, the Ursulines asked the pope to authorize the coronation of Our Lady of Prompt Succor. Archbishop Janssens defended the nuns' request because of the order's position of institutional stability and charity among a highly diverse Catholic population. Janssens's biographer, Annemarie Kasteel, explained that the Dutch archbishop and Mother St. Ignace were good friends and, as such, supported each other's positions in the archdiocese.[39] The Ursulines required the oversight of Janssens to prevent the encroachment of other religious orders on their missionary territory and ethnic constituency.[40] Janssens needed the backing of the Ursulines on account of the severe opposition to his episcopacy by many subordinate priests. The secular clergy at the time contained a large number of Frenchmen. Also, all of the preceding bishops during the nineteenth century were French. As a result, when Rome appointed a Dutchman to the post, French priests commented that "they might as well have chosen a Chinaman" and petitioned the pope to reassign a French prelate.[41] To counter the clerical antagonism, Janssens earned the trust of the various ethnic groups and religious orders, including the traditionally French Ursulines.[42] Janssens's approval of the Ursuline request for a papal coronation was a product of their collaboration in archdiocesan affairs and their awareness of current trends in Rome. In effect, the Dutch archbishop appropriated a French symbol, Our

Lady of Prompt Succor, and transformed it into a unifying symbol of New Orleans.

Janssens, confronted by an array of ethnic interests, was following the "progressive" Catholic movement to "Americanize" the large immigrant population. The words "progressive" and "Americanize," in Roman Catholic circles, meant different things to different people. Simply put, progressive Catholics at the end of the nineteenth century thought that the correct way to improve the lives of Catholic immigrants was to Americanize them, or reduce their ties to the Old World by encouraging them to conform to American culture. The conservative Catholic hierarchy opposed the liberal progressive movement out of concern for the loss of Catholic faith during the process of Americanization.[43] Before his appointment to New Orleans, Janssens worked closely with James Cardinal Gibbons, the archbishop of Baltimore and a progressive leader, thus placing him squarely in the progressive school.[44] Janssens's biographer argues that he was the first archbishop to begin the process of Americanization in New Orleans.[45] The historian Thomas McAvoy notes two hindrances to the Americanization process: "Loyalties to old world traditions and customs"; and "the American dominant culture" of Protestantism.[46] Janssens, however, faced a different situation. While New Orleans did contain a large immigrant population with strong transatlantic ties, the prevalence of Catholicism in the city limited the infiltration of Protestantism into the ranks of the faithful. The archdiocese, therefore, was less concerned with losing Catholics to Protestantism than with alleviating tension between disparate ethnic groups, as well as tension between the American hierarchy and Rome.

Leo XIII maintained a keen interest in the immigration of European Catholics to the United States. He issued the 1888 encyclical *Quam aerumnosa* to discuss "how sad and fraught with trouble is the state of . . . the scattered sons of Italy."[47] New Orleans, as a major port of entry in the American South, deserved special consideration. The influence of Catholicism in New Orleans gave the pope some assurance that the loss of faith would not be as significant as in other urban areas. Leo XIII and Janssens, consequently, concerned themselves less over the use of progressive or conservative measures and more on the prospect for Catholic unification. This simplification of concerns, however, did not eliminate the fact that the Archdiocese of New Orleans suffered from severe ethnic tension. The dominant French clergy held an uneasy relationship with priests who served particular immigrant groups.[48] Religious orders and charitable organizations claimed different constituencies, causing one scholar of the Society of the Sacred Heart to note how "each congregation carefully guarded its niche."[49] Ethnic enclaves and national parishes formed cultural borders between the lay French and Creoles, Irish, Italians, Germans, and African Americans. The geographic borders, however, were more fluid by the 1890s, as seen in the positioning of the Irish parish of St. Alphonsus and the German parish of St. Mary's Assumption across the street from each other. Such fluid interaction often turned tension into violence, demonstrated by the March 14, 1891, lynching of eleven Italians suspected in the murder of the Irish police superintendent.[50] Also during the bishopric of Janssens, controversy surrounded the formation of the African American parish of St. Katherine.[51] All of this disunion fell under the context of a "Creole brand of Latin Catholicism" in which "hostility to ecclesiastical authority" was the rule.[52]

The severity of ethnic tension, and its implications for the future order of the archdiocese, made it difficult for Janssens to implement Leo XIII's directive "that religion, and religion only, can create the social bond; that it alone maintains the peace of a nation on a solid foundation."[53] The cultural atmosphere of New Orleans was not always kind to religious authority. Janssens stood amidst a whirlwind of antagonistic forces, including an anticlerical Creole aristocracy, a collection of growing and needy immigrant groups, the largest black Catholic community in the United States, and non-Catholic religious and secular interests.[54] Like most cities in the South, New Orleans also suffered from inadequate police and fire departments, sanitation problems, xenophobia, class conflict, and racism.[55] The renewal of society, as far as Leo XIII was concerned, required the renewal of religion. In one of his first encyclicals, Leo XIII deplored the evils of society—antiauthoritarianism, worldliness, self-interest, modernism—and identified the Catholic Church as a source of social reform.[56] In recognition of these social ills, the pope conceived a system of ecclesiastical authority different from earlier notions of papal supremacy. He walked the line between, on the one hand, the religious and temporal authority of the church and, on the other hand, the rights and liberties of the individual. The encyclicals *Libertas* (1888) and *Rerum novarum* (1891) demonstrated this balance. The Magisterium still regulated the parameters for "true virtue," but now with a keener eye toward the dignity of humans. Endowed with intelligence and reason, man "is 'in the hand of his counsel' and has power over his actions."[57] It was the responsibility of the Catholic hierarchy to defend human rights, especially "the rights and duties of Capital and Labor," against the injustice of state and special interests.[58] In the case of American society, Rome was in the process of formulating an official position on the role of the Catholic Church in the United States during the early 1890s. The 1895 encyclical *Longinque oceani* praised the advancement of the American republic but warned against the American error of "dissevered and divorced" church and state.[59]

The cult of the Virgin Mary, according to Leo XIII, represented a potential instrument of mediation between the profane world and the sacred church, as well as a source of spiritual fortification and Catholic identity. New Orleans would be a proving ground for this theory. Leo XIII gave special consideration to the cult of the Virgin Mary during his pontificate.[60] He issued eight encyclicals on the devotion to the Rosary. In them, he described his program to increase Marian devotionalism. "To all the Patriarchs, Primates, Archbishops and Bishops of the Catholic World in the Grace and Communion of the Apostolic See," Leo XIII declared, "the more you have at heart the honour of Mary, and the welfare of human society, the more diligently [you must] apply yourselves to nourish the piety of the people towards the great Virgin, and to increase their confidence in her. We believe it to be part of the designs of Providence that, in these times of trial for the church, the ancient devotion to the August Virgin should live and flourish amid the greatest part of the Christian world."[61] According to Leo XIII, therefore, "nothing is more natural, nothing more desirable than to seek a refuge in the protection and in the loyalty of [Mary]," the "glorious intermediary" between God and humanity.[62] He also recognized Mary—neither modern nor American, and wholly Catholic—as an intermediary between conservative and liberal Catholic leaders. The cult of the Virgin Mary did not offend either party, and thus signified a basis of compromise for bishops trying to uphold the immigrant Catholic Church in an American context. By instituting new forms of Marian devotion in a world of cultural differences, the church saw the potential for an improvement in both ecclesiastical authority and multiethnic group identity. The cult of the Virgin Mary, moreover, was a symbol for both institutional cohesiveness and individual agency, both of which were prerequisites for Leo XIII's notion of an ordered society.

Janssens considered Our Lady of Prompt Succor a potentially unifying devotion for New Orleans. In general, the cult of the Virgin Mary figured prominently in the minds of Catholics regardless of ethnicity. It was common for individuals to form strong devotions to particular statues or images of Mary, which often translated into strong group identities.[63] The cults of Our Lady of Lourdes in France and Our Lady of Guadalupe in Mexico exemplified this hope for solidarity in the nineteenth century. Their appeal surpassed national borders, and they became popular to Catholics in Louisiana and the world over.[64] In fact, Janssens attended the coronation ceremony of Our Lady of Guadalupe in Mexico just weeks before crowning Our Lady of Prompt Succor.[65] With these successful Marian devotions in mind, Janssens prayed to Our Lady of Prompt Succor for the same results: "I am going to offer up to her the heart of everyone here, everyone in the state of Louisiana, that she may preserve us all from sin and protect us also in our temporal interests and be a mother to us, each and everyone, every day of our lives, and finally at the moment when we lie upon our deathbeds."[66] Janssens considered Our Lady of Prompt Succor to be the "Patroness of Louisiana" because of her singular status as a cult native to Louisiana, inasmuch as the Ursulines did not reveal the statue to the public until the Battle of New Orleans. Furthermore, the cult that developed under the auspices of the Ursuline order during the nineteenth century bore few if any divisive attributes, nothing to challenge or offend Catholics regardless of cultural background. In short, Our Lady of Prompt Succor was a safe, uncontroversial Mary.

With the papal decree in hand, Janssens led the crowd of devotees in the coronation of the statue of Our Lady of Prompt Succor on November 10, 1895. The day's events called for an open-air ceremony to accommodate the expected ten thousand people on the Ursuline grounds, but poor weather conditions forced a move into the chapel and a reduction in attendance. Five bishops joined Janssens.[67] Other archdiocesan clergymen, representatives from charitable and educational institutions, "the leading Catholic gentlemen of the city," and "a delegation of ladies from the congress of advanced women" also obtained access to the chapel.[68] The Ursulines joined in the opening procession and remained cloistered for the rest of the ceremony. Organizers moved the statue down from above the main altar to a small pedestal on the ground. Janssens blessed the two crowns fashioned out of donated jewelry, one for Mary and the other for the infant Jesus.[69] He then started the pontifical High Mass. Bishops Janssens, Theophile Meerschaert of the Oklahoma Territory, and T. Heslin of Natchez gave homilies. Heslin opened with remarks in English for the congregants in the chapel, while Meerschaert offered words in French to the outdoor crowd in the cold rain. Janssens temporarily transferred the statue out to the courtyard and gave a short speech in English, led the Hail Mary three times, and sang the Te Deum. After Mass, the prominent indoor participants moved to a banquet held at the convent.[70]

The only written coverage of the coronation ceremony appeared in the *Daily Picayune,* the leading newspaper of New Orleans. Although it was a secular publication, Janssens said of the *Daily Picayune,* "I have always been an object of the kindest consideration at the hands of the newspaper men. I have always found them ready to do what was asked of them and often willing to do much more."[71] Prior to the coronation, the Ursulines' private documents contained the only written version of the devotional story, but they were inaccessible to the public. After the coronation, the readers of the *Picayune* were for the first time able to clarify and compare their understanding of the oral tradition to the archdiocesan-supported narrative. The *Picayune,* in effect, became the de facto instrument of the church to promote the cult of Our Lady of Prompt Succor. It verified the miracles attributed to the "Patroness of Louisiana" and the integral role of the Ursulines throughout the nineteenth century. Moreover, it allowed archdiocesan officials to attach new, more modern interpretations to the role of Our Lady of Prompt Succor. "The church is accused by the thoughtless as slow and behind the times," Bishop Heslin preached. "We live in a time of rapid transit and communication.

. . . Not only do we wish to be heard, but to be speedily heard. Men grow impatient with delays, even from above, and because they are not listened to at once they are prone to give up asking. The devotion to Our Lady of Prompt Succor will remedy this evil and remove the excuse for not persevering in prayer."[72] The archdiocese wanted to appeal to "modern," impatient Catholics outside the customary Ursuline constituency of French Creoles since Our Lady of Prompt Succor "shed her blessings every day upon every family in the state of Louisiana."[73]

The coronation article, in addition to telling the official story of the cult, described the different participatory roles of the clergy and the Ursulines during the coronation ceremony. Janssens and the other bishops stood at the top of the religious hierarchy. Jesuit and secular priests filled the remaining space around and directly in front of the altar. The Ursulines remained cloistered. The homiletic texts of the three bishops contained brief references to the Ursuline involvement in the devotion. Janssens especially thanked "our good Ursuline Sisters, who for the last 170 years have done so much good in this and adjoining states."[74] Yet, despite the recognition of the Ursulines, the coronation marked a clear shift in devotional control from the nuns to the Archdiocese of New Orleans. The Ursulines remained a private thread of devotional constancy, while the archdiocese took a proactive, highly public role in the development of a popular devotion. In short, Our Lady of Prompt Succor was no longer an Ursuline devotion. Instead, as Heslin stated, "it is an authorized devotion. The holy father has approved it, and expressly sanctioned this solemn and unique ceremony . . . Our Lady of Prompt Succor, hasten to help us."[75] The participation of several thousand devotees at the coronation ceremony demonstrated a foundation for devotional growth. The promotion of the confraternity of Our Lady of Prompt Succor to an archconfraternity in 1897 exhibited a further increase, first, in the number of parish priests supporting lay devotion and, second, in the organizational outreach of the archdiocese to potential devotees.[76]

The application of new miracles to Our Lady of Prompt Succor was a vital component to the archdiocese's conception of a devotional narrative. While the Ursulines had not attributed any major miracle to Our Lady of Prompt Succor since the 1815 Battle of New Orleans, archdiocesan officials added two miracles to the popular story before the turn of the nineteenth century. The first addition involved Bishop Theophile Meerschaert of the Oklahoma Territory. One month after participating in the coronation, doctors diagnosed Meerschaert with Bright's disease and predicted that he would live only one more week.[77] He immediately left for New Orleans, whereupon the Ursulines started a novena to Our Lady of Prompt Succor for a quick recovery. On the fifth day of the novena, Meerschaert passed his largest stone and doctors found a 70 percent reduction in the albumin. Doctors and priests agreed: "there was no doubt that [his] cure was absolutely miraculous."[78] Janssens, according to the narrative, received the second post-coronation miracle. On June 9, 1897, Janssens set sail for France to raise funds for the archdiocese and died of a heart attack during the first night of the voyage. The chancellor of the archdiocese implored the captain to return the body of Janssens to New Orleans, but he refused; the archbishop would have to be buried at sea. That night passengers prayed to Our Lady of Prompt Succor for a way to go back ashore and bury Janssens. The next morning a ship sailing for New Orleans passed the outgoing vessel. The crews reportedly transferred the body of Janssens under the arch of a rainbow, and he was buried in the city. The archdiocese touted "the miracle of the sea" as evidence of Our Lady of Prompt Succor's capacity for intercession.[79]

The development of a popular narrative continued under the auspices of the Society of Jesus, and devotional promoters identified Our Lady of Prompt Succor as a distinctly American cult. In 1907 Father J. A. Hogan, a Jesuit, wrote the first devotional guide, entitled *The Pilgrimage of Our Lady of Prompt Succor.*[80] The small book became the definitive work on the history and motifs of the cult. Hogan characterized the Battle of New Orleans as the most exemplary and formative event for the twentieth-century devotee. In addition to the miraculous intercession of Mary, Hogan emphasized the roles of Andrew Jackson and his "American" army during the battle. "Heaven . . . made of [Jackson] its vessel of election to carry out its merciful designs . . . [and] though not a Catholic, he had a strong Christian faith in God."[81] Jackson admitted the "signal interposition of heaven, in giving success to our arms against the enemy," but he did not acknowledge the intervention of Mary.[82] Hogan disregarded Jackson's omission of Mary, instead recognizing two saviors of New Orleans—Our Lady of Prompt Succor and Andrew Jackson.[83] The Jesuits sponsored a second publication, *The Ursulines in New Orleans and Our Lady of Prompt Succor, 1727–1925.*[84] Like Hogan, its author focused on the Battle of New Orleans miracle. In this work Jackson earned the title "Saviour of New Orleans" and received an ovation "unprecedented in this vast republic."[85] The two publications appealed to the patriotic sensibilities of Catholics by attaching an American identity to the cult of Our Lady of Prompt Succor. As an "American" Mary, and not an Ursuline or Creole Mary, the Jesuits saw an opportunity "to counteract the impious spirit . . . [of] bad Catholics" and reach a wider audience of devotees.[86]

With a widely accessible narrative in place, the German Archbishop James Hubert Blenk sponsored a drive to construct a national votive shrine of Our Lady of Prompt Succor. The journal entitled the *Messenger of Our Lady of Prompt Succor* became the archdiocese's primary instrument of devotional outreach and fund-raising.[87] As the journal was an organ of the archconfraternity and the Ursuline Alumnae Association, "the object of Our Lady of Prompt Succor's Messenger

[was] to propagate devotion to the august patroness of Louisiana, and to promote the erection of her Votive Shrine."[88] The archdiocese directed the endeavor, and the Ursulines assumed the responsibility of collecting material, writing, and formatting the journal. For the first time the archdiocese permitted the laity to articulate their personal devotion to Our Lady of Prompt Succor in a public format. The prayers and petitions of the laity ranged from unspecified requests for "special favors" to more detailed needs related to health, work, weather, and family. A typical passage in the "Favors Received" section read, "The favor that we have been praying for since April has been granted, and you will remember I promised to give one dollar per month for the period of one year. Thank you very kindly for the prayers."[89] Another caption sent from Baton Rouge, Louisiana, simply stated, "Enclosed find one dollar for the Votive Shrine of Our Lady in thanksgiving for a favor received."[90] The editors never named the supplicants, adding to the difficulty in determining ethnicity and gender. However, they did record where the devotees lived. New Orleans, not surprisingly, was the most common place of habitation. Most of the remaining letters originated in south Louisiana, especially in Baton Rouge, Houma, Lafayette, and Alexandria, all of which represented major concentrations of Catholic population. Outside Louisiana, areas of devotion followed the locations of other Ursuline convents around the United States, Canada, and France.[91]

Finally, after seven years of fund-raising, Archbishop John William Shaw blessed and dedicated the new Votive Shrine to Our Lady of Prompt Succor on January 8, 1924.[92] Then on January 6, 1928, the national shrine opened to the public with a solemn mass of consecration. The nave of the Romanesque chapel measured eighty feet long and forty feet wide, with a hundred-foot steeple. The statue of Our Lady of Prompt Succor stood on a pedestal above the main altar. Artists modeled the stained glass windows after those of the cathedral of Notre-Dame de Chartres. Outside the chapel resided a replica of the statue with the inscription "To Mary, the Victorious."[93] Bishop Gunn of Natchez, Mississippi, called the votive shrine a "super-church," built as a "loving tribute of Louisiana's gratitude to Our Lady of Prompt Succor."[94] The *Times Picayune,* however, reported only on a mass of thanksgiving in remembrance of the Battle of New Orleans, not once mentioning the new shrine.[95]

Conclusion

With the opening of the national votive shrine, the Archdiocese of New Orleans reduced its role in the promotion of the cult of Our Lady of Prompt Succor and thus transferred the primary responsibility of devotional articulation to the Ursulines and the laity. The Ursuline nuns and the lay alumnae of the Ursuline Academy continued to publish the *Messenger* until the 1950s. The content of the journal, however, shifted emphasis away from Our Lady of Prompt Succor and toward more recognizable and universal Catholic devotions to the Immaculate Conception, the Blessed Sacrament, and the lives of saints and popes. After the 1950s the public narrative, instead of emphasizing the applicability of Mary to the present, tended to focus more on the past glory of Our Lady of Prompt Succor at the Battle of New Orleans and the papal coronation.[96] By failing to demonstrate the miraculous vitality of Our Lady of Prompt Succor—by not effectively publicizing private miracles—the cult could not distinguish itself from other, more powerful, more active, manifestations of Mary.

Today the majority of devotees to Our Lady of Prompt Succor are students and alumnae of the Ursuline Academy. Some followers still observe the weekly novenas and masses held at the national votive shrine, but attendance "usually does not exceed twenty-five old ladies."[97] The January feast day, commemorating Our Lady of Prompt Succor's intercession at the Battle of New Orleans, remains the only event capable of drawing a crowd. It is, however, worth noting that the archdiocese promotes Our Lady of Prompt Succor for protection against hurricanes.[98] During hurricane season, from June to November, the archdiocese permits its church parishes to pray to Our Lady of Prompt Succor for protection against the destruction of hurricanes. The exact origin of this tradition is unknown. However, it definitely was not a feature of the cult during the nineteenth century.[99] Archival evidence suggests that the archdiocese highlighted the association of Our Lady of Prompt Succor with miraculous weather phenomena during the Mississippi River flood of 1927. Archbishop Shaw offered a thanksgiving mass to the Patroness of Louisiana, who "again . . . turned the tide and saved the City" from levee breaks and flooding.[100] He did not mention the intentional dynamiting and subsequent flooding of Plaquemines and other parishes in order to save New Orleans, an event renowned as one of the most despicable political acts in Louisiana history.[101] In 2002 the archdiocese thanked Our Lady of Prompt Succor for protection against Hurricane Lili, a category-four storm that inexplicably reduced its strength to category two just before hitting the coast of Louisiana.[102] Our Lady of Prompt Succor was again invoked against Hurricane Katrina in 2005. Rodger Payne reports:

> While it is still much too early to assess the impact that this disaster will have on the devotion to Our Lady of Prompt Succor, a preliminary investigation of newspaper accounts and Internet Web sites (including weblogs) suggests that devotees actively petitioned their patroness for protection prior to Katrina's arrival and then tried to come to terms with the destruction that followed in the wake of the hurricane. While some questioned whether Our Lady of Prompt Succor was "out to lunch" (as one blogger phrased it) on

> that horrible day, others noted that as it made landfall, Katrina turned slightly to the east and thus spared New Orleans the direct hit that would have truly destroyed the city. These devotees argue that their prayers were efficacious, that New Orleans suffered only minor damage from this powerful storm, and that the most substantial damage was caused by the failure of the human-engineered levee system and not the hurricane itself. Although the Ursuline Convent and Academy were damaged by flood waters, the national shrine itself was relatively unharmed, and the annual Thanksgiving Mass was celebrated there on January 8, 2006, by Archbishop Alfred C. Hughes.[103]

During the nineteenth and early twentieth centuries, the Archdiocese of New Orleans and the Vatican imagined Our Lady of Prompt Succor as a source of social stability and Catholic solidarity among the diverse ethnic population of New Orleans. The Catholic hierarchy created an American Marian cult by appropriating a specialized devotion of the Ursulines and adapting it to the multiethnic context of American Catholicism. Yet, in spite of the church's unprecedented investment in an American Mary, Our Lady of Prompt Succor has remained a marginal Marian manifestation within the highly competitive arena of popular Catholic devotionalism. The cooperative efforts of American and Roman bishops to authorize a feast day, a coronation, and a national votive shrine in the name of Our Lady of Prompt Succor—all firsts in the history of Catholicism in the United States—failed to evoke a popular multiethnic movement. Catholic leaders, in effect, wanted more of Our Lady of Prompt Succor than the laity was willing to permit. They wanted the Patroness of Louisiana to reach the popular heights of Our Lady of Guadalupe and Our Lady of Lourdes, but they failed to create the fundamental prerequisites of a transnational cult of the Virgin Mary—a critical mass of enthusiastic lay devotees and a widespread acceptance of the supernatural power of a local Marian devotion. Unlike the cults of the Marys of Lourdes and Guadalupe, and later Fatima and Medjugorje, the cult of Our Lady of Prompt Succor did not begin as a lay movement; it was the creation, first, of a female religious order and, then, of a male clergy. Moreover, the narrative of Our Lady of Prompt Succor did not advocate any miraculous apparition or profound message; it provided little to stimulate the imaginations of the laity. Thus, the institutionalization of Our Lady of Prompt Succor did not translate into the popularization of an American Mary, although it managed to produce a core of devotees in Louisiana. The Catholic hierarchy and laity have never formed a lasting agreement on the legitimacy of an American-made transnational cult of the Virgin Mary.

Notes

1. "Coronation Ceremonies," *New Orleans Daily Picayune,* November 11, 1895. I would like to thank Sister Joan Marie Aycock, archivist at the Ursuline convent of New Orleans, for her kindness and generosity. I would also like to express my gratitude to Dr. Rodger Payne, associate professor of religion at Louisiana State University, who guided me as an undergraduate and continues to enrich my education as a graduate student.

2. Obituary of Francois Agatha Gensoul (Sister St. Michel), May 1822, in "Obituaries," 54, Ursuline Archives of New Orleans (hereafter cited as UANO). "Obituaries" is a collection of Ursuline biographies from 1728 to 1835.

3. Margaret M. O'Dwyer, *The Papacy in the Age of Napoleon and the Restoration: Pius VII, 1800–1823* (Lanham, Md.: University Press of America, 1985), 103.

4. For a discussion of American migration to New Orleans, see Lewis William Newton, *The Americanization of French Louisiana: A Study of the Process of Americanization between the French and the Anglo-American Populations of Louisiana, 1803–1860* (New York: Arno Press, 1980).

5. Jerah Johnson, "Colonial New Orleans: A Fragment of the Eighteenth-Century French Ethos," in *Creole New Orleans: Race and Americanization,* ed. Arnold R. Hirsch and Joseph Logsdon, 12–57 (Baton Rouge: Louisiana State University Press, 1992), quote from 12; Joseph G. Tregle, "Creoles and Americans," in *Creole New Orleans,* 131–85.

6. Caryn Cossé Bell, *Revolution, Romanticism, and the Afro-Creole Protest Tradition in Louisiana, 1718–1868* (Baton Rouge: Louisiana State University Press, 1997), 69–74.

7. For a scholarly treatment of the Ursulines of New Orleans, see Sister Jane Francis Heaney, *A Century of Pioneering: A History of the Ursulines in New Orleans, 1727–1827* (Chelsea, Mich.: Ursuline Sisters of New Orleans, 1993).

8. Pope Leo XIII authorized the crowning of only three Marian statues in North America. Our Lady of Guadalupe received a coronation on October 12, 1895, in Mexico; Our Lady of Prompt Succor on November 10, 1895, in New Orleans; and Our Lady of Mount Carmel on July 10, 1904, in Harlem, New York.

9. For analyses of ethnic-specific cults of the Virgin Mary in America, see Robert Orsi, *The Madonna of 115th Street: Faith and Community in Italian Harlem, 1880–1950* (New Haven, Conn.: Yale University Press, 1985), 60; Thomas Tweed, *Our Lady of the Exile: Diasporic Religion at a Cuban Catholic Shrine in Miami* (New York: Oxford University Press, 1997). Orsi mistakenly referred to Our Lady of Prompt Succor as "Our Lady of Perpetual Help."

10. For analyses of international cults of the Virgin Mary, see Ruth Harris, *Lourdes: Body and Spirit in the Secular Age* (New York: Viking, 1997); D. A. Brading, *Mexican Phoenix: Our Lady of Guadalupe: Image and Tradition across Five Centuries* (New York: Cambridge University Press, 2001); Stafford Poole, *Our Lady of Guadalupe: The Origins and Sources of a Mexican National Symbol, 1531–1797* (Tucson: University of Arizona Press, 1995).

11. Robert V. Remini, *The Battle of New Orleans* (New York: Viking, 1999); Leonard V. Huber, *New Orleans as It Was in 1814–1815* (New Orleans: Battle of New Orleans 150th Anniversary Commission of Louisiana, 1965).

12. The contemporary narrative of Our Lady of Prompt Succor states that Mary saved the Ursuline convent from a citywide fire in 1812. However, the archivist of the Ursuline Archives admitted confusion over the exact date of the conflagration, joking that "if you can get all of the fires in New Orleans straight, then let me know." See Fire Miracle Footnote, "Private Archives," 1878, 1:127, UANO; Sister Joan Marie Aycock, interview by author, May 22, 2000, UANO. The statue involved in the fire miracle was not the original statue of Our Lady of Prompt Succor. Rather, it was a *petite statue de la Ste. Vierge* brought by a French nun to New Orleans in 1785. See Sister Eugenia O'Laughlin, "Sweetheart," pamphlet, OMI Missions, c. 1960, UANO.

13. Charles Edward O'Neill, "'A Quarter Marked by Sundry Peculiarities': New Orleans, Lay Trustees, and Pere Antoine," *Catholic Historical Review* 76 (1990): 235–77. New Orleans did not have a bishop after the retrocession of Louisiana from Spain to France in 1802. Antonio de Sedella, commonly known as Père Antoine, was the Spanish pastor of St. Louis Cathedral, where he received considerable support from the liberal, anticlerical Creole community. When Archbishop John Carroll appointed William Dubourg to the post of vicar apostolic, Père Antoine denied him access to the cathedral.

14. "Victoire emportee sur les Anglais par l'intercession de Notre Dame de Prompt Secours," 1878, "Private Archives," 1:123, UANO. "Private Archives" is a three-volume collection of documents related to the history of the Ursuline convent in New Orleans. The Ursulines wrote the first volume in 1878 and then recopied its contents into two more volumes during the 1910s and 1920s.

15. Andrew Jackson to William Dubourg, New Orleans, January 19, 1815, UANO.

16. The Place d'Armes was the central square of the French Quarter and is now known as Jackson's Square. It is also the site of St. Louis Cathedral. It is unknown why Dubourg, and not Père Antoine, celebrated the thanksgiving mass at the cathedral.

17. Leonard Huber, *Jackson Square: Through the Years* (New Orleans: Laborde Printing Co., 1982).

18. There is some confusion over whether or not Jackson visited the Ursulines after the Battle of New Orleans. Volume 1 of "Private Archives" describes the Battle of New Orleans miracle, but it does not describe a visit by Jackson to the convent. See "Victoire emportée sur les Anglais." The 1820 obituary of the mother superior, Sr. St. Marie Olivier de Vezin, does not discuss the battle. The 1822 obituary of Sr. St. Michel contains a footnote on the battle miracle, but it is unclear whether or not the footnote was added later. The first mention of Jackson's visit to the convent appeared in "Coronation Ceremonies," *New Orleans Daily Picayune*, November 11, 1895.

19. Liliane Crété, *Daily Life in Louisiana, 1815–1830*, trans. Patrick Gregory (Baton Rouge: Louisiana State University Press, 1978), 71. The use of the word "creole" is problematic for many reasons. For the purposes of this article, the title "Creole" refers to Spanish and French natives of Louisiana who identified themselves as white. Creoles who identified themselves as black, or who were identified by others as black, did not develop

strong ties to the Ursuline convent and as a result did not develop any marked association with the cult of Our Lady of Prompt Succor. For further consideration of the definition of "creole," see Virginia Dominguez, *White by Definition: Social Classification in Creole Louisiana* (New Brunswick, N.J.: Rutgers University Press, 1986).

20. Crété, *Daily Life in Louisiana,* 71–72; Jean Boze, "de Gentilly Bulletin No. 3," March 15–27, 1837, Ste Geme Family Papers, Historic New Orleans Collection (hereafter cited as HNOC); Jean Boze to Le Baron Henri de Ste-Geme, Gentilly, La., December 1, 1834, Ste Geme Family Papers, HNOC.

21. For depictions of the social growth and upheaval of antebellum New Orleans, see Newton, *Americanization of French Louisiana;* Edward Magdol and Jon Wakelyn, eds., *The Southern Common People: Studies in Nineteenth-Century Social History* (Westport, Conn.: Greenwood Press, 1980); Thomas Ingersoll, *Mammon and Manon in Early New Orleans: The First Slave Society in the Deep South, 1718–1819* (Knoxville: University of Tennessee Press, 1999); Walter Johnson, *Soul by Soul: Life inside the Antebellum Slave Market* (Cambridge, Mass.: Harvard University Press, 1999).

22. Benjamin Latrobe, *Impressions Respecting New Orleans: Diary and Sketches, 1818–1820,* ed. Samuel Wilson, Jr. (New York: Columbia University Press, 1951), quoted in Crété, *Daily Life in Louisiana,* 146.

23. *New Orleans Daily True Delta,* September 18, 1855, quoted in Leon Cyprian Soulé, *The Know Nothing Party in New Orleans: A Reappraisal* (Baton Rouge: Louisiana Historical Association, 1961), 66.

24. For more on the relationship between the Irish immigrants and the Archdiocese of New Orleans, see Michael Doorley, "Irish Catholics and French Creoles: Ethnic Struggles within the Catholic Church in New Orleans, 1835–1920," *Catholic Historical Review* 87, no. 1 (2001): 38–42; Earl F. Niehaus, *The Irish in New Orleans, 1800–1860* (Baton Rouge: Louisiana State University Press, 1965); David T. Gleeson, *The Irish in the South, 1815–1877* (Chapel Hill: University of North Carolina Press, 2001).

25. For a transcript of Auguste Martin's pastoral letter, see *American Catholics and Slavery: 1789–1866: An Anthology of Primary Documents,* ed. Kenneth Zanca (Lanham, Md.: University Press of America, 1994), 219–20. See also Maria Genoino Caraviglios, "A Roman Critique of the Pro-Slavery Views of Bishop Martin of Natchitoches, Louisiana," *Records of the American Catholic Historical Society of Philadelphia* 83 (June 1972): 67–81; Elisabeth Joan Doyle, "Bishop Auguste Marie Martin of Natchitoches and the Civil War," in *Cross, Crozier, and Crucible: A Volume Celebrating the Bicentennial of a Catholic Diocese in Louisiana,* ed. Glenn R. Conrad, 135–44 (Chelsea, Mich.: Archdiocese of New Orleans in cooperation with the Center for Louisiana Studies, 1993).

26. Jean Marie Odin, Pastoral Letter for the Lent of 1862, New Orleans, February 16, 1862, Archdiocesan Archives of New Orleans (hereafter cited as AANO).

27. Heaney, *Century of Pioneering,* 284–300.

28. During the colonial and early antebellum periods, the Ursulines welcomed some free black students into their school, while at the same time owning some slaves. By 1860, with the increase in racial hostility, the Ursulines limited admission to white students.

29. For a study of the black Catholic community in the Archdiocese of New Orleans during the Civil War, see Stephen Ochs, *A Black Patriot and a White Priest: André Cailloux and Claude Paschal Maistre in Civil War New Orleans* (Baton Rouge: Louisiana State University Press, 2000).

30. Earl F. Niehaus, "Catholic Ethnics in Nineteenth Century Louisiana," in Conrad, *Cross, Crozier, and Crucible*, 48–69.

31. J. A. Hogan, *The Pilgrimage of Our Lady of Prompt Succor* (New Orleans: J. G. Hauser, 1907). The original papal decree is not held at the Ursuline Archives of New Orleans. Hogan's transcription is the only source available.

32. Joseph Francis Rummel, "The Holy See and Our Shrine," in *The Messenger of Our Lady of Prompt Succor*, c. 1945, UANO.

33. "Origine de la devotion a Notre Dame de Prompt Secours," 1878, "Private Archives," 1:61, UANO; "Victoire emportee sur les Anglais." The contemporary archivist of the Ursuline Archives noted that the "Private Archives" are just that—private—thus diminishing the possibility that the 1878 document increased popular devotion (Sister Joan Marie Aycock, interview by author, New Orleans, December 12, 2000).

34. Leo XIII, "Solemn Coronation of the Miraculous Statue of Our Lady of Prompt Succor," decree, June 21, 1894, UANO.

35. "Janssens' Visit to Rome," letter, n.d., UANO. It is unclear which miracles Janssens chose to list.

36. "Coronation of Our Lady of Prompt Succor," file, UANO.

37. A copy of the confraternity papal decree is not available. The archdiocese promoted the confraternity to an archconfraternity in 1897. A confraternity, or sodality, is "a voluntary association of clergy or laity established under church authority; an association of the faithful" (Peter M. J. Stravinskas, ed., *Catholic Encyclopedia* [Huntington, Ind.: Our Sunday Visitor, 1991], 248).

38. Leo XIII, "Solemn Coronation."

39. Annemarie Kasteel, *Francis Janssens, 1843–1897: A Dutch-American Prelate* (Lafayette: Center for Louisiana Studies, 1992), 226.

40. The Ursuline constituency included primarily wealthy French and Creole families. Forty-two of sixty-eight Ursuline Academy students in 1895 had French surnames. The 1888 annual tuition was $188 per year plus expenses. See "Ursuline Academy, on the River Front in the Lower Limits of New Orleans," commencement booklet (New Orleans: T. Fitzwilliams & Co., 1895). Other religious orders in New Orleans by 1894 included Daughters of Charity of St. Vincent de Paul (1830), Sisters of the Holy Family (1842), School Sisters of Notre Dame, Little Sisters of the Poor (1868), Marianites of the Holy Cross (1849), Sisters of Mercy (1869), Dominican Sisters (1859), Sisters of Mount Carmel (1883), and Discalced Carmelites (1877). The Sisters of the Blessed Sacrament arrived in 1915.

41. Annemarie Kasteel, "Archbishop Francis Janssens and the Americanization of the Church in Louisiana," in Conrad, *Cross, Crozier, and Crucible*, 156–69.

42. Patricia Lynch, "Mother Katherine Drexel's Rural Schools: Education and Evangelization through Lay Leadership," in Conrad, *Cross, Crozier, and Crucible*, 262–74. Most notably, Janssens founded a seminary for native Louisianans and permitted Mother

Katherine Drexel to minister to the African American community and Mother Francis Cabrini to minister to the Italians.

43. For an examination of the Americanist controversy, see Margaret Mary Reher, "Pope Leo XIII and 'Americanism,'" *Theological Studies* 34 (1973): 679–89; David P. Killen, "Americanism Revisited: John Spalding and *Testem Benevolentiae,*" *Harvard Theological Review* 66 (1973): 413–54.

44. John Tracy Ellis, *The Life of James Cardinal Gibbons: Archbishop of Baltimore, 1834–1921* (Milwaukee: Bruce Publishing Co., 1952). Gibbons was born in New Orleans. Archbishop Antoine Blanc warned the young Gibbons of ecclesiastical problems between priests of different ethnic backgrounds in New Orleans and thus compelled him to pursue the priesthood elsewhere.

45. Kasteel, "Archbishop Francis Janssens," 156–69.

46. Thomas T. McAvoy, *The Americanist Heresy in Roman Catholicism 1895–1900* (Notre Dame, Ind.: University of Notre Dame Press, 1963), 16.

47. Leo XIII, *Quam aerumnosa,* Rome, December 10, 1888. This and other encyclicals can be found at http://www.vatican.va/offices/papal_docs_list.html (accessed October 6, 2006).

48. Niehaus, "Catholic Ethnics," 48–69.

49. Sally K. Reeves, "The Society of the Sacred Heart in New Orleans," in Conrad, *Cross, Crozier, and Crucible,* 219.

50. Niehaus, "Catholic Ethnics," 48–69.

51. Lynch, "Mother Katherine Drexel's Rural Schools," 262–74; Dolores Egger Labbe, *Jim Crow Comes to Church* (Lafayette: University of Southwestern Louisiana, 1971).

52. Doorley, "Irish Catholics and French Creoles," 38–39.

53. Leo XIII, *Au Milieu des Solicitudes,* Rome, February 16, 1892.

54. For a general history of the Archdiocese of New Orleans, see Roger Baudier, *The Catholic Church in Louisiana* (New Orleans: A. W. Hyatt Stationary Mfg. Co., 1939). For a survey of black Catholics in New Orleans, see Cyprian Davis, *The History of Black Catholics in the United States* (New York: Crossroad Publishing Co., 1991).

55. Bennett H. Wall, ed., *Louisiana: A History* (Wheeling, Ill.: Harlan Davidson, 1997), 223–38; Roger Shugg, *Origins of Class Struggle in Louisiana: A Social History of White Farmers and Laborers during Slavery and After, 1840–1875* (Baton Rouge: Louisiana State University Press, 1939).

56. Leo XIII, *Inscrutabili Dei consilio,* Rome, April 21, 1878.

57. Leo XIII, *Libertas,* Rome, June 20, 1888.

58. Leo XIII, *Rerum novarum,* Rome, May 15, 1891.

59. Leo XIII, *Longinqua oceani,* Rome, January 6, 1895. For more on the modernist controversy in the United States, see R. Scott Appleby, *Church and Age Unite: The Modernist Impulse in American Catholicism* (Notre Dame, Ind.: University of Notre Dame Press, 1992).

60. For an ecclesiastical biography of Leo XIII, see Bernard O'Reilly, *The Life of Pope Leo XIII: From an Authentic Memoir Furnished by His Order* (London: John C. Winston Co., 1903). Though Leo XIII was a strong proponent of Marian devotionalism, the biography does not cover the topic in any comprehensive fashion.

61. Leo XIII, *Supremi apostolatus officio,* Rome, September 1, 1883.

62. Leo XIII, *Octobri mense,* Rome, September 22, 1891.

63. Ann Taves, *The Household of Faith: Roman Catholic Devotionalism in Mid-Nineteenth-Century America* (Notre Dame, Ind.: University of Notre Dame Press, 1986).

64. The first Louisiana church parish named for Our Lady of Lourdes was established in 1887, and the first in New Orleans was in 1905.

65. Francis Janssens to the Archdiocese of New Orleans, Mexico D.F., October 13, 1895, UANO. Bishop Theophile Meerschaert joined Janssens at the coronation in Mexico.

66. "Coronation Ceremonies," *New Orleans Daily Picayune,* November 11, 1895.

67. The five other bishops were Forest of San Antonio, Verdaguer of Laredo, Dunne of Dallas, Meerschaert of Oklahoma, and Heslin of Natchez.

68. "Coronation Ceremonies," *New Orleans Daily Picayune,* November 11, 1895. Segments of the article read like a New Orleans society column, with over a hundred names of prominent clergy and citizens.

69. Receipt, Feeley Jewelry, Providence, RI, 1895, UANO. The *Daily Picayune* estimated the price of the crowns at fifteen hundred dollars for the gold and jewelry donations, and between six thousand and eight thousand dollars for the craftsmanship.

70. "Coronation Ceremonies," *New Orleans Daily Picayune,* November 11, 1895.

71. Ibid.

72. Ibid.

73. Ibid.

74. Ibid. The article quotes each of the three bishop's speeches.

75. Ibid.

76. "Constitution of the Archconfraternity of Our Lady of Prompt Succor," UANO. An archconfraternity is an organization of confraternities. The Ursuline Chapel was the headquarters of the archconfraternity. Confraternities were then established at other church parishes, which in turn reported to the archconfraternity.

77. Bright's disease is a kidney ailment called nephritis and characterized by albuminuria and heightened blood pressure.

78. "Sermon of Bishop Meerschaert on the centenary of Our Lady of Prompt Succor's arrival," transcript, January 8, 1911, UANO. After the incident, Meerschaert placed a statue of Our Lady of Prompt Succor in the personal chapel of the bishop of Oklahoma.

79. Gloria Day, "The Miracle of the Sea," UANO. There is a painting of the sea exchange at the museum of the Ursuline convent in New Orleans.

80. See note 31 above.

81. Hogan, *Pilgrimage,* 133.

82. Ibid., 135.

83. Jackson received no credit for victory by the Ursulines in "Victoire emportée sur les Anglais."

84. Henry Semple, *The Ursulines in New Orleans and Our Lady of Prompt Succor, 1727–1925* (New York: P. J. Kennedy & Sons, 1925). Father Semple, president of Loyola University in New Orleans, received credit for authorship, but in fact he only edited the book. An Ursuline nun, Mary Teresa Wolfe, actually wrote the work.

85. Ibid.

86. Hogan, *Pilgrimage,* 18.

87. The *Messenger of Our Lady of Prompt Succor* was published in New Orleans by L. Graham Co., Ltd., from 1917 to 1950.

88. *Messenger of Our Lady of Prompt Succor* 1, no. 1 (1917): 1.

89. *Messenger of Our Lady of Prompt Succor* 6, no. 4 (February 1923): 24.

90. *Messenger of Our Lady of Prompt Succor* 7, no. 2 (August 1923): 21.

91. The hard copies of the letters do not exist due to the annual practice of burning them on the January feast day.

92. The votive shrine resides at 2705 State Street, New Orleans, Louisiana, on the grounds of the Ursuline Academy.

93. "National Shrine of Our Lady of Prompt Succor," file, UANO.

94. Semple, *Ursulines in New Orleans,* 136.

95. "Ursuline Convent has Celebration," *New Orleans Times Picayune,* January 7, 1928.

96. For the most popular contemporary devotional literature, see Gerald Muller, *Our Lady Comes to New Orleans* (Notre Dame, Ind.: Dujarie Press, 1957); Harnett Kane, *The Ursulines: Nuns of Adventure* (New York: Farrar, Straus, & Cudahy, 1959).

97. Joan Marie Aycock, interview by author, May 22, 2000.

98. "Prelates Attend Mass for Coronation Jubilee," *Catholic Action of the South* (New Orleans), November 22, 1945; Francis B. Schulte to Archdiocese of New Orleans, "Feast of Our Lady of Prompt Succor," January 8, 1995, AANO; Francis B. Schulte, "We Still Pray to Our Lady of Prompt Succor," *Clarion Herald* (New Orleans), November 16, 1995; "Celebration of Our Lady," *New Orleans Times Picayune,* November 20, 1995; Bruce Nolan, "Mass Raises Questions of Ethics," *New Orleans Times Picayune,* January 10, 1998.

99. In the Ursulines' "Private Archives" no. 4, the sisters related the incident of "a terrible hurricane that blew away the roof of our church" in 1812 (57). The narrative, however, makes no reference to Our Lady of Prompt Succor.

100. "Grateful Orleanians Gather at Shrine for Thanksgiving Service," *Morning Star* (New Orleans), July 9, 1927, UANO.

101. John M. Barry, *The Great Mississippi River Flood of 1927 and How It Changed America* (New York: Simon & Schuster, 1997).

102. Julie Mickles, "Our Lady of Prompt Succor Protects LA [*sic*] from Danger," *Catholic Commentator* (Baton Rouge), October 16, 2002, 7–8.

103. Rodger Payne, e-mail communication, January 2006.

Wars of Religion in the Circum-Caribbean

English Iconoclasm in Spanish America, 1570–1702

Nicholas M. Beasley

Attacks on religious imagery, both polemical and physical, became increasingly common in early modern Europe. Social historians of the Reformation have pointed to iconoclasm as a popular expression of the impulse toward reform, as a physical reaction to the theologizing of Calvin and Luther, and as an example of agency among the lower classes. Iconoclasm also attracts attention in the circles of cultural history, where it can be seen as a public display of identity formation, an act that draws a distinct line between self and other, or as an elite attempt to manipulate popular piety. Yet scholars of iconoclasm among the English have done little to consider the export of iconoclasm to distant shores. This essay seeks to explore the redirection of English iconoclastic activity into the Spanish Empire in the Americas. England's long war with Spain was partly economic, partly geopolitical, and partly cultural and religious. The privateering, piratical, and naval voyages of the late sixteenth through early eighteenth centuries combined these elements. Held up alongside one another, they demonstrate an emerging vocabulary of image destruction that extended across the decades. Destructive actions spoke to some Englishmen's aspirations both for religious reform at home and for dominance abroad. By symbolically degrading Catholic images and ritual objects, English mariners rejected Spanish and Catholic hegemony in the Americas and fashioned a distinct and vigorous English Protestant identity in the early modern Atlantic world.[1]

To understand English behavior in Spanish America, which resists categorization along lines of secular or religious motivation, it is necessary to take a broad look at what sorts of acts constituted iconoclasm. It is quite clear that the voyages of Francis Drake, John Oxenham, and William Jackson, and Oliver Cromwell's "Western Design" to conquer Santo Domingo involved deliberate destruction of particular pieces of Spanish religious imagery. These journeys also included the theft, rather than destruction, of valuable religious objects such as vestments and chalices. While clearly examples of plunder, these thefts also indicate a degree of theological critique and symbolic degradation, especially when the English made everyday clothing of chasubles or drank ordinary wine from sacred vessels. Thomas Cavendish, James Moore, and others made a policy of leaving Spanish ports and their churches "burnt and spoiled," without recording more specific acts of destruction.[2] While this general arson may be less clearly iconoclastic, its effects on Catholic worship were the same. The English tendency to beat and humiliate friars was another means of accomplishing the symbolic degradation of all things Spanish and Catholic. Indeed, English mariners did not view their pursuit of profit and plunder as particularly distinct from their religious goals. They viewed the Americas as the key to Catholic Europe's wealth and power. Breaking images and plundering warehouses were parallel efforts in defense of Protestantism.

These acts were inspired by a long Reformation that led the English to become some of the most virulent iconomachs in the early modern world.[3] Yet, apart from the criticism of Lollards, late medieval English religion had been as heavily invested in saintly imagery as any other region in western Christendom. The saints were claimed as "friends and helpers" by men and women of various social ranks.[4] Saints were to be imitated in their holiness, petitioned for their intercessions, and celebrated for the miracles they wrought.[5] Moreover, the Communion of Saints was no mere abstract clause in the creed. It was a reality much incarnated by the presence of their images, which "filled the churches, gazing down in polychrome glory from altar-piece and bracket, from windows and niches."[6] Whether statues or panels, these images attracted the devotion of the people, who endowed their lights and provided for their repair and augmentation.

Popular devotion to the saints and their images was but one branch of a wider stream of devotion to physical manifestations of important spiritual realities in the medieval church. Saints' images were often connected to relics, the physical remnants of a saint's body or life. Relics were foci of devotion and pilgrimage, but the church that lacked an important relic could hope that a well-executed or miraculous image might make it a destination for regional pilgrimages. Though the veneration of the saints and their relics was highly important, the central act of worship in the later Middle Ages was the Eucharist. Its physical elements of bread and wine attracted the attention and devotion of the people weekly, sometimes daily, allowing their participation in the mystery of Christ's death on the cross. The realism of medieval eucharistic theology thus undergirded a theology of divine immanence, in which the numinous was mediated to sinners through a material element.[7] Simply put, the veneration of images, relics, and the elements of the Eucharist were part of the same strand of medieval piety, one that encouraged believers to approach the numinous through visual elements and their own bodies.

The Protestant Reformation marked an abrupt break with that long tradition. Luther's followers were generally less anxious about imagery than were those of Calvin and Zwingli. Once the "idols of the heart and mind" were destroyed, Luther expected that a limited number of physical images might be used appropriately. Though his colleague Kaarlstadt (Andreas Bodenstein) disagreed, the use of limited imagery, especially the crucifix, remained unexceptional in Lutheran churches. The image tradition received greater condemnation in Geneva and among its spiritual descendents. The sharp distinction that Calvin drew between nature and grace and his insistence on the absolute primacy of the Word quickly turned image veneration into idolatry. Thus, "iconoclasm was an inevitable outcome of Reformed ideology." Geneva "became the exporting center of the Reformed faith in Western Europe," and its second product was the iconoclasm that spread across France, the Low Countries, and to England.[8]

Considering the generally conservative stance that Henry VIII took toward religious reform in England, it is surprising that the attack on religious imagery began as early as it did. Popular iconoclasm increased in the 1520s and 1530s and found some degree of official approval in the royal injunctions of 1536, in which Thomas Cromwell ordered the clergy of the realm to ensure that no one should "set forth or extol any images, relics or miracles for any superstition or lucre."[9] The critique intensified with the publication of new injunctions in 1538, when "feigned images" were connected to "that most detestable offence of idolatry." All lights before images were forbidden, and parishioners were to be taught that images existed only for the benefit of those unable to read the Bible. The reign of Edward VI saw further erosion of the use of images when any image that had been an object of veneration or pilgrimage was ordered destroyed.[10] The campaign against images was more general than a mere attack on "abuses," however. As confirmed by Elizabeth after the Marian interlude, the Edwardian reformation was for the English an almost complete break with the image tradition in western Christianity. Though Elizabeth and the early Stuarts would temper some of the Edwardian enthusiasm, the majority of English people remained iconophobic.

The shift from widespread use of images in worship was paralleled by a shift away from the most theologically realistic understandings of the nature of Christ's presence in the Eucharist in the circles of official theology. Though Thomas Cranmer and other church leaders were initially restrained by Henry's conservatism on the sacrament, evangelical ascendancy during the next reign allowed for rapid changes in official eucharistic theology.[11] By the summer of 1548 Cranmer was prepared to move the church in a much more reformed direction, as he did in 1550's *Defence of the True and Catholic Doctrine of the Sacrament of the Body and Blood of Our Saviour Christ.*[12] His thinking carried the day in the Church of England for many generations and was enshrined in the Articles of Religion, which affirmed that "the body of Christ is given, taken and eaten in the supper only after an heavenly and spiritual manner; and the mean whereby the body of Christ is received and eaten in the supper is faith."[13]

These two theological shifts, away from the use of images in worship and away from a realistic understanding of the Eucharist, paved the way for the tradition of English iconoclasm. As a pervasive sense of divine immanence retreated in the face of Protestant doctrine, successive generations of Protestant Englishmen were educated with a loathing for anything that smacked of idolatry, the rubric under which images and transubstantiation were understood. This sense was inculcated through schooling, catechizing, and preaching and through publishing for those with access to books. Indeed, one of the homilies approved for public reading was entitled *On the Perils of Idolatry.*[14] In Margaret Aston's words, "in the sixteenth century, idolatry became deeply engraved on the English conscience."[15] The soldiers, sailors, and adventurers discussed below would incorporate this English iconoclastic tradition into their voyages to the Americas.

For more than forty years, however, Englishmen of all sorts deferred to Elizabeth I and her strong opinions in matters of liturgy. Elizabeth's insistence on achieving a golden mediocrity in religion displeased her most zealous subjects, whether their zealotry ran in directions Catholic or Protestant, and may have intensified the critique of images inherent in acts of destruction. Elizabeth combined her mother's evangelicalism with her father's conservatism on many ecclesiastical issues, leaving her with a religious policy not readily labeled. She would probably have preferred a celibate clergy who presided over a very traditional-looking Eucharist, with the chasuble and unleavened wafers used on a stone altar with either cross or crucifix.[16] Though forced to concede much to her evangelical bishops, the queen kept a crucifix and candles on the altar in her chapel and shouted down the dean of St. Paul's Cathedral in 1565 when he broached the topic in an Ash Wednesday sermon.[17] When iconoclasts destroyed the crucifix in 1562 and 1567, it was quickly replaced.[18] The queen's personal tastes in liturgical apparatus were clearly more catholic than those of her bishops and many of her people.

Of wider import was Elizabeth's insistence on a variety of other liturgical details bound to antagonize her most Protestant subjects. She succeeded in requiring the use of the linen surplice for officiating at prayers and the Eucharist, a vestment far too popish for most Puritans.[19] Her 1559 Act of Uniformity made few changes to the Book of Common Prayer, and those were more appealing to Catholics than to hotter Protestants. Especially striking was the resurrection of the words for administering the Eucharist from the first prayer book, which could easily support a realistic eucharistic theology.[20] She used Archbishop Whitgift to crush Puritan criticism of her religious settlement so effectively that issues such as the use of the cross in baptism and kneeling for communion would not surface again until after her death.[21] Her reign also saw the articulation of the *via media* theology of Richard Hooker, which became the intellectual underpinning of the high-church liturgical movement of William Laud during the reign of Charles I.[22]

Thus, Elizabeth's religious settlement was moderate above all else and makes it clear that the high point of official evangelical fervor in Tudor England was reached before her time, during her half-brother's reign. The fight over the legacy and extension of reformation that would consume the regime of Charles I was prefigured in her days, though she and her bishops managed it far more effectively. The anxiety of Englishmen who regarded their church as "but half reformed" will be palpable in the accounts examined below, in which iconoclasm became an act in the defense of international Protestantism. Men such as Walter Raleigh, Francis Drake, and John Oxenham harbored an antipathy for Spain and its Catholicism that was probably only heightened by the knowledge that their own national church was viewed with considerable suspicion by the more thoroughly reformed churches on the Continent. Smashing images, sacking churches, and humiliating and attacking Catholic clergy in the Spanish dominions were powerful ways of asserting the vigorous Protestantism of the English nation. Sailing "beyond the line" was an opportunity to put their more radical religious mores to good use.

Nonetheless, it is not prudent to offer any single explanation for English acts of iconoclasm. Students of art history sometimes draw a distinction between iconoclasm and vandalism, the former having more symbolic value than the latter.[23] Others would differentiate between simple "aggressive" iconoclasm and "ideological" or "symbolic" iconoclasm, the first being basic mean-spiritedness and the latter a violent but considered critique of a rejected culture, group, or system of belief.[24] Whatever its inspiration, iconoclasm is clearly connected to "magical-symbolic acts of degradation" and to the "rituals of humiliation" common in early modern societies.[25] In the examination below, it will be difficult to isolate particular motivations for iconoclasm. These acts spoke a symbolic language loudly, voicing rejection of Catholicism, Spanish culture, and Spanish policy in the Americas by subjecting Spanish Catholic ritual objects to violent rites of symbolic degradation.[26] While speculation about motivation and meaning may be fruitful at times, it cannot always fill the gaps left by acts so relentlessly inarticulate.

War with Spain created the opportunity for both privateering and iconoclasm. Excommunicated by the pope in 1570, Elizabeth had been reluctant initially to bear the Protestant standard in Europe, avoiding the imbroglio of the war in the Netherlands for as long as possible.[27] Her tortured decision to execute the deposed Queen of Scots in February 1587 made war with Spain inevitable, as did

Leicester's indiscretions in the Netherlands.[28] The war created enormous opportunities for men with a spirit of adventure and some capital to prey on the extended supply lines of the Spanish Empire.[29] Formally excluded from New World trade by Spanish policy and the papal division of the Americas, English merchants were cut off from the profits generated by the tropical luxuries that the Indies provided. When Philip II seized English ships in Iberian harbors, Elizabeth became willing to offer letters of reprisal, documents that marked the subtle difference between piracy and privateering.

Even before the beginning of official hostilities, some Englishmen, including the most famous, Francis Drake, had taken to preying on Spanish shipping. There are hints to the direction that Drake's practical theology would take in his upbringing in Devon. His father, Edmund Drake, was both a cloth worker and a priest. He married in 1539, some ten years before the act permitting the marriage of priests became law. Francis Drake was probably born in 1540 and was living in the household of his cousins, the Hawkins family of Plymouth, by 1548.[30] Drake's first experiences at sea were on the Hawkinses' voyages to Africa, the Canary and Cape Verde Islands, and the Caribbean. He must have taken note of the way his elder cousin John Hawkins required the crew to gather twice daily to recite psalms and for prayers. Each Sunday, Hawkins would read to the crew from Erasmus's *Paraphrases,* adding his own words as a sort of homily.[31] During Drake's own 1577 circumnavigation voyage, he usurped the role of the ship's chaplain, leading prayers, reading from the Bible, and preaching on occasion.[32] While there is little evidence to suggest that Drake was a devout man, he seems to have learned the usefulness of religion early in his career.

After some years of quasi-apprenticeship in the Hawkins operation, Drake was ready to take his own command. In this new role, Drake and his men were instrumental in establishing many of the patterns that would inform English behavior in the New World for generations. Raiding off Panama in 1571, Drake prompted a local official called Garcia de Paz to write to Philip II from Nombre de Dios (Panama) to report that Drake's men had seized a frigate and "maltreated and stripped a friar who was on board, insulting and affronting him, from which it was understood that these corsairs are Lutheran, enemies of our holy Catholic faith."[33] In attacking a friar, Drake thus engaged in one of the broadly iconoclastic acts typical of Englishmen in the Spanish Caribbean. Members of the mendicant orders attracted a disproportionate share of Englishmen's hatred for Catholicism in the Caribbean. The records rarely indicate any justification for these attacks such as physical resistance from the friars.[34] Instead, it seems probable that friars were attractive targets for the sort of ritual degradation inherent in more classic expressions of iconoclasm. On this first voyage, when images were not readily available for destruction, Drake was content to make an image of the friar, a pattern to be seen in several of the accounts that follow.[35] Acting in equal parts as Protestant and pirate, Drake made a tremendous success of this journey, emptying ships, riverboats, and warehouses. Spanish claims totaled some 250,000 pesos, and total profits are estimated to have been at least £100,000.[36]

In 1572–73 Drake made contact with the maroons of the Panamanian forest, slaves who had liberated themselves from Spanish control.[37] Again, Drake established a pattern that would be repeated in subsequent history. Taking the position that the enemy of my enemy is my friend, the maroons assisted Drake in his exploits on the isthmus. One crew member subsequently reported that the maroons had "no kinde of Priests, only they held the Crosse in great reputation; but at our Captaine's perswasion they were contented to leave their Crosses, and to learne the Lord's prayer, and to be instructed in some measure concerning God's true worship."[38] As he sought plunder across the isthmus, Drake was accompanied by a party of maroons that outnumbered his own force. Seeking to ambush a mule train bound for Nombre de Dios, Drake's forces killed a Dominican friar.[39] This voyage proved to be both a financial success and important in setting patterns for subsequent voyages, establishing a connection between the English and the maroons and between plunder and Protestantism in the actions of men such as Drake.[40]

As Drake learned much of his technique from the Hawkins family, John Oxenham learned much from Drake in his role as cook on the voyage of 1571. Though Drake was no model of civility, Oxenham took Drake's methods to new levels in his own voyage that commenced in April 1576. Oxenham lacked the patina of legitimacy as a privateer with which Drake managed to cover himself. When captured, Oxenham affirmed to the Spanish authorities from Lima that "the sovereign of England knew nothing of his coming."[41] The cautious and religiously moderate queen would certainly not have endorsed Oxenham's behavior. His violent interaction with Catholic Spaniards and with Catholic religious culture can thus be interpreted as a departure from the queen's studiously moderate religious policy. Where Drake was somewhat restrained by his connections to Elizabeth, Oxenham's lack of royal letters allowed him to act out fantasies of Protestant aggression in the New World, forging an English identity more vigorously Protestant than Elizabeth allowed at home.

Oxenham told his captors that he came to Panama to find the maroons "rich in gold and silver" and to offer them "cloths, hatchets, *machetes*" in exchange for their precious metals.[42] Find them he did, and they struck a bargain requiring Oxenham to kill any Spanish prisoners he might take and to allow the maroons to seize any slaves they encountered.[43] From the maroon stronghold near the middle of the isthmus, the mixed force made its way down a river valley toward the Pacific. Oxenham's men then constructed a launch, which enabled them to sail into the Pacific and to the Pearl Islands, just off the coast of Panama.[44] Besides providing the gold and silver that Oxenham found among the inhabitants of the islands, the location proved to be a useful base for intercepting a ship from Quito well laden with precious metals.[45]

In addition to their booty, the Pearl Islands offered opportunity to engage in some vividly recorded attacks on Catholicism. Island resident Diego de Sotomayor alleged that "wherever they went [they] broke to pieces all the images they found, both of Our Lord Jesus Christ and of His glorious Mother, the Holy Virgin Mary." They were guilty of "destroying consecrated altars, chalices, profaning articles used in celebration of mass, and with great boldness and audacity uttering many blasphemies and heresies of the evil sect of Martin Luther . . . seconded by nine *cimarrones* they had with them to whom they taught his dogma."[46] This coalition of English Protestants and anti-Spanish maroons proved to be most destructive to the Pearl Islands and a continuing source of anxiety for Spanish authorities.

Arriving on the island of Chapera before sunrise on the first morning during Lent, Oxenham and his band invaded the home of the deponent Sotomayor. They began by examining the books Sotomayor had in his home, sorting through them with an aggressively Protestant bias. They told him that his pontificals "were lies, adding that the pope was a . . ." (omission in the original). Picking up the "bulls of the holy crusade," the corsairs insisted to Sotomayor that the pope promulgated them only for the income they produced, "whereat they threw the bulls upon the floor and trampled on them and tore them." One Englishman who spoke Spanish took up a "child's lesson book" and mocked the Catholic version of the Decalogue found in it.[47] Eventually the corsairs found a copy of the New Testament in Spanish, and they urged that Sotomayor "read that book, because it was a good book . . . in as much as the others were fabrications and all lies."[48] Even in this strange setting, Oxenham's men dramatically displayed the biblicism typical of English Protestants.

From books the corsairs proceeded to images, an action more likely to demonstrate Protestant identity and cement the maroon alliance than sorting through a stack of books. Breaking into the man's clothing chest, they found a crucifix. Oxenham "looked deponent in the face wrathfully and holding up the crucifix in his hands demanded: What hast thou this?" He threw the crucifix at Sotomayor, but it struck a stand, "which broke the crucifix to pieces." Oxenham turned his attention to "a veronica framed" and "demanded to know why he had so many gods." He then slashed the image, tore it from its backing, "broke off a piece and threw it upon the floor and trampled upon it."[49] Having degraded Sotomayor and all of the images in his house, the corsairs left for the home of his father-in-law, Juan Manzaneda. At Manzaneda's, they "smashed the consecrated altar he had there . . . that they might walk over it, as they did." Receiving their attention next was the church, where the English cook "took the alb used in the ceremony of the mass and put it on and danced about in it, ridiculing everything." He later cut the bottom off of the alb and wore the top portion for a shirt. The maroons witnessed all of this and "gave great evidence of their pleasure." One remarked "I, English; pure Lutheran."[50]

The English probably interpreted this maroon identification with them as a preference for Protestantism and English culture over Spanish Catholic culture. It is far more likely, however, that the African speaker was adding a weapon to his anti-Spanish, antihegemonic arsenal on his own terms. The ritual degradation practiced by the English and the maroons was highly important in identity formation for both parties. Disparaging Catholic belief and practice identified Oxenham and his men as good Englishmen. By participating in those actions, the maroons also claimed a distinction from the Spanish for themselves. Building on Drake's initial contact with the Panamanian maroons, Oxenham continued to develop a tradition of cooperation between English marauders and persons subjugated among the Spanish. Their shared goal of undermining Spanish hegemony was symbolized and cemented in these acts of ritual degradation.

Oxenham also re-created Drake's attacks on Spanish clergy in dramatic fashion. During the eight-day sojourn that followed the corsairs' arrival, two priests arrived from the mainland, unaware that the island was in English and maroon hands. Juan Constantino was a secular cleric and commissary of the Inquisition. Since he was untonsured, the English seem not to have recognized him as a priest, for "they let him alone and did nothing to him."[51] The tonsured Franciscan Miguel de los Angeles, however, gave the English another Catholic ritual object to abuse, the person of a priest. The friar remembered that "the English captain took the wafers which they were bringing for the celebration of Mass, and forced one into deponent's mouth, saying: Behold your God! Is this your God?"[52] Oxenham kicked an image of the Virgin into the sea and destroyed books and rosaries. Some of the English argued with Constantino in the days ahead, "the Spaniard valiantly defending Catholicism, the English as hotly abusing the pope and every distinctly Catholic dogma."[53] This strange colloquium continued for several days as early modern Africans, Englishmen, and Spaniards fought out their theological-cultural differences on an island in the Pacific.

The corsairs further developed the disdain for friars that had become a mark of English Protestantism. At the home of Sotomayor, the corsairs had urged "deponent and his wife not to believe the saints or the friars, because it was all witchcraft, and they sinners like the rest of us."[54] When harassing the friar, the English knelt before him and babbled in Latin, mocking his office of announcing absolution.[55] Things became more serious when "the captain of the English . . . struck him a heavy blow upon the head with his sheathed sword, crying: '——, to deceive Christians'" (omission in original).[56] They later threatened to crucify and burn him before they departed.[57] In a moment rich with symbolism and perhaps a little humor, they "put a chamber-pot upon his head and struck him many fisticuffs." Having crowned their prey with a container for excrement, the English spared the friar the fulfillment of their worst threats but made his ritual degradation complete through this almost creative manipulation of symbolic objects and persons.

Just as the English and maroons used these sorts of actions to draw a line between themselves and the Catholic other, the Spanish in the Indies could use English and maroon iconoclasm to attract metropolitan assistance and resources. Residents had a healthy fear of corsairs, but the constant threat of the maroons was far more pressing and had not been addressed by the crown. Maroon alliances with Drake and Oxenham and their iconoclastic activities gave settlers a useful issue. The Pacific port of Panama petitioned Philip II with a litany of Oxenham's misdeeds against the church and begged him "to forbid that here in this new land the sect of Luther be implanted. The *cimarrones* are already as Lutheran as the English, and so by their acts and words declare and manifest themselves to be. They are easily taught any doctrine, evil or good, which is presented to them."[58] The danger of the alliance of maroons and English became a refrain in official documents that lamented that "the English and the negroes should have combined against us, for the blacks are numerous."[59] The Spanish in America recognized the danger of any cultural and religious identification between the English and subjugated Africans and played all necessary rhetorical cards to gain royal support.[60]

The Spanish response to Oxenham's raid was swift and effective. His tactical mistakes destroyed the alliance with the maroons, and most of his party were killed in the forest or captured by a force dispatched from Lima. The Audiencia of Panama reported that "these corsairs and *cimarrones* who were taken alive are being subjected to investigation under torture."[61] The maroon villages were destroyed, and those who remained at large were forced into hiding deep in the wilderness. The commander of the forces from Peru reported, "well punished are these blacks, and sorry they ever let the English pass!"[62] The English survivors, including Oxenham, were transported to Lima. They were condemned as pirates and hanged by the Inquisition.[63]

As Oxenham awaited execution in Lima, Drake was sailing and raiding up the coast of Chile, having entered the Pacific through the Straits of Magellan late in 1578. One of Drake's victims later reported that during this voyage "offences and sacrileges had been committed such as the said English would naturally do, being, as they were, Lutheran heretics."[64] Even before the close of the sixteenth century, iconoclasm and Protestant proselytizing became stereotypical manifestations of

English identity in the Americas.[65] Spanish records of the circumnavigational voyage are replete with references to Drake's opposition to the pope, to religious imagery, and to the orders of clergy, as well as his use of John Foxe's *Acts and Monuments* (1563) and Protestant worship on his ship. Though Drake's profit motive cannot be doubted, his efforts to combine profit with a Protestant crusade should not be neglected.

Drake's men first destroyed Catholic images and ritual objects on the eastern side of the Atlantic, in the Cape Verde Islands. The fleet's chaplain, Francis Fletcher, recorded his realization that "the inhabitants were . . . superstitious accordeing to the popes antechristian traditions." From the ship, he saw that "upon every cape, & small head land they sett up a cross; one most wherof is ingraven an evill faced Picture of christ." Fletcher and "others did breake down" one of the crosses.[66] After arriving in the Pacific, Drake's forces intercepted several Spanish vessels. Seizing a bark belonging to Rodrigo Tello off the coast of Nicaragua, Drake's men found a crucifix, which "they broke to pieces, trod under foot and cast into the sea."[67] These episodes were preludes to the more dramatic events at Guatulco on the Pacific coast of New Spain.

Drake apparently allowed some of his men to go ashore ahead of him, and the church received their prompt attention. The vicar returned the next day to find "the church profaned and plundered, and the images broken and slashed, and the altar picture and a crucifix and the altar stone broken to pieces." Besides these broken items, the English showed their fiscal realism by stealing "all the sacred vestments, and the bell, and the chalices and monstrance, lamp and water and wine vessels, and other silver things of great value; also canopies and altar cloths, and the canopy of the sacrament."[68] "One of the said Lutherans" was later seen by a Spanish prisoner "wear[ing] a chasuble from the said church."[69] Seemingly valueless unconsecrated eucharistic wafers "were strewn on the floor and trampled upon."[70] Later, in the home of Francisco Gomez Rengifo, the boatswain smashed other images and told Rengifo to be sorry not for the images but because "you are not Christians but idolaters, who adores stocks and stones."[71] The action in Guatulco would prove typical of English behavior in Spanish America. The English expressed their theological convictions by smashing images and altars but carried off eucharistic vessels and vestments made of valuable materials.

After Oxenham's execution and his own triumphal circumnavigation, Drake again sailed for the West Indies by way of Spain and various Atlantic islands in 1585–86. Drake parlayed the fame and wealth of his feat into considerable investment in the West Indian voyage, including at least ten thousand pounds from the queen.[72] This voyage had the same complex set of goals seen in other Drake ventures, including plunder and weakening Spain and Catholicism. Drake would emphasize the latter when corresponding with official England, as he did in a

1587 message to Francis Walsingham. His men were ready "to stand for our gracious Queen and country against Antichrist and his members." But iconoclasm was patriotic, for Drake expected to find the Spanish enemy to be "for the most part enemies to the truth and upholders of Baal or Dagon's image, which hath already fallen before the ark of our God with his hands and arms and head stricken off."[73] At least rhetorically, Drake seemed to place iconoclasm at the center of his mission in the Caribbean.

Again Drake began near the Iberian Peninsula. His fleet of over thirty vessels arrived near Bayona in northwestern Spain in late September. Some seven hundred men were landed on a small island. The writer of the log kept on the *Primrose* noted "3 or fowre Images in that chapple which wee brake & burned." An English resident of the island added some color to that account, noting that one of the images they destroyed was Our Lady of the Borge. The English "were so bold as to take the clothes from her, and when they had done so, they took both her and all the rest of her company of the church that she was wont to have."[74] Seizing a ship in the harbor, they found "a Chest filled with Coapes . . . and suche other Churche trashe belonginge to the hyghe church."[75] Though the chronicler called the contents of the trunk "trashe," his general found in it "one cross . . . as much as a man might carry, being very fine silver of excellent workmanship." This cross was certainly not consigned to the flames.[76] English iconoclasm could be cost conscious.

As the fleet worked its way across the Atlantic and into the Caribbean, the keeper of the *Primrose* log lamented lost opportunities for booty and for iconoclasm. It appears that residents of the towns now accustomed to the visits of Protestant corsairs had learned how to protect their personal and corporate assets. At São Tiago in the Cape Verde Islands, he noted that the "town has 3 churches in it but their best images were carried away with them."[77] At Santo Domingo, the writer expressed disappointment that residents "had carried out their treasure and a great image of silver out of their church, which was of great value."[78] With advance warning, Spanish subjects took care to remove the material the English needed to accomplish either theft or symbolic destruction.

Yet opportunities for plunder and symbolic destruction were eventually found. At Santo Domingo the English "burned all of their images of wood, [and] brake and destroyed all their fairest work within their churches."[79] The dean and the chapter of Santo Domingo reported that "they treated this city as an enemy of their religion." The English burned "all its churches and monasteries and nunneries, its hospitals and hermitages, excepting the Cathedral." Even there they destroyed "its altars, retables, crucifixes, images, choir, screens, organs, bells, and all other objects." Once purged, the English used the great church for their headquarters, "where they dealt in and negotiated their evil affairs. It was their warehouse and dispensary, and served them for even viler purposes."[80] The Audiencia of Santo Domingo named some of those viler purposes. In the process of "heaping ignominy and vituperation upon our religion," the English "opened the sepulchers of the dead and into them threw filth and offal of cattle they slaughtered in the churches, which they converted to slaughter pens."[81] The English thus converted graves into chamber pots, degrading sacred space much as Oxenham had degraded sacred objects and persons.

Other cities suffered as well. The cathedral at Cartagena was mostly destroyed by artillery fire well after the English took the city, though Spanish and English sources do not agree on whether the English did this on purpose.[82] On his way up the Florida coast, Drake paused to sack St. Augustine, where he "burned the church with its images and crosses and cut down the fruit trees."[83] Perhaps the only exception to the Drake policy of destruction of religious imagery and buildings was at Punta de la Canoa in Cuba, where Drake allowed the churches and cathedral to be ransomed for 110,000 ducats.[84] Spanish officials could do little more than write to Spain in frustration, as Rodrigo Fernández de Ribera did from Santo Domingo, lamenting that "we have seen our enemies trample and burn its images and churches and blaspheme against the Christian religion, while we, miserable creatures, stood by, unable to offer defence!"[85]

Drake also used another form of pillage rich in symbolic potential, the seizure of bells from churches. Valuable for their metal alone, bells were also the voices of churches, and their use had become controversial among some Protestants. By stealing them, Drake both silenced his Catholic opponents and gained valuable goods, neatly pairing the goals of his voyage in a single act. Beginning on the eastern side of the Atlantic, Drake's forces seized bells wherever they stopped. At São Tiago in the Cape Verde Islands, the *Primrose* chronicler remembered that "we took all the bells out of the steeple" of the great hospital.[86] In Santo Domingo the bells were cut down from the steeple and "fell upon the dome and demolished part of the sacristy."[87] In Cartagena the English "brought away all their bells, and all other metals we could find."[88] This pattern would be repeated in 1592 by Christopher Newport, who "took three bells out of their church, and destroyed their images" at Puerto de Caballos.[89] Even the Earl of Cumberland, who sought to minimize damage to churches during his raids, seized "certeyn Belles to some good value" on his 1598 voyage to Puerto Rico.[90] Silent churches were left behind, unable to summon the faithful to worship.

We have already seen how Drake and Oxenham, in earlier voyages, used iconoclasm to build alliances with the maroons of Panama. On this voyage as well, Drake's forces drew support from slaves or Indians at most every stop. Even before leaving England, Drake hired a black guide who had been a slave in Bayona and "promised this negro that if we could take the Spaniard that the negro before was slave unto, then the Spaniard should be slave unto the negro."[91] At Santo Domingo the Audiencia complained that "many negroes belonging to private persons . . . went with them of their own free will."[92] An officer of Cartagena wrote to the Audiencia at Turbaco in Panama that "some soldiers, especially the Moors, deserted to the Englishmen, as did the black slaves, whom they find very useful."[93] The Indians of La Florida used Drake's attack on St. Augustine as an opportunity to steal everything that was in the houses and burn all that was left.[94] Subjugated peoples clearly recognized that whatever Drake's motivations, the disorder he created and symbolized most dramatically through iconoclasm was an enormous opportunity for liberation or revenge.[95]

Drake's last voyage to the Caribbean in 1595–96 was an unmitigated disaster. Both Drake and John Hawkins died of fevers on the voyage, little plunder was taken, and no iconoclasm was celebrated in the surviving accounts.[96] The accession of James I in 1603 meant that the Scots' peace with Spain became reality in England as well. For the next forty years some Englishmen would pine for the days of Drake and his colleagues, when they imagined that England had been stout in defense of the Reformed faith and against the overweening Spaniards. Various persons, often Puritans opposed to Stuart policy, pursued personal anti-Hispanism through efforts to settle Providence and Association islands in the Caribbean.[97] However, it was not until Parliament and Charles I fell out in the 1640s that royal policy (or lack thereof) would permit a sustained return to the tradition of English iconoclasm in the Spanish Americas.

The years of the early Stuarts were also marked by conflict over church furnishing and decoration, much of it associated with the rise of Archbishop William Laud. Laud insisted on the full use of the rites and ceremonies of the Book of Common Prayer and had little patience for tender Puritan consciences.[98] Ceremonies, the physical component of liturgy, were at the center of Laud's understanding of the church's discipline. They were, he wrote, like "the hedges that fence the substance of religion from all the indignities which profaneness and sacrilege too commonly put upon it." Laud did not consider the aural experience of the Word sufficient for demonstrating loyalty and orthodoxy, saying that he felt "bound to worship with body as well as soul"[99] and labeling the altar "the greatest residence of God upon earth."[100] Along with this sacramentalism came a renewed emphasis on church decoration, especially ornate altar rails, communion tables in their pre-Reformation position, and some new stained glass. For Puritans, these changes signaled a retreat from reformation. It was not surprising that iconoclasm, both at home and abroad, became a feature of parliamentary policy after the outbreak of the civil war.[101]

Concurrent with the beginning of the war was the Caribbean voyage of Captain William Jackson in 1642. Jackson's forces lost the element of surprise early on, finding in many places that the Spanish "had carried away their wealthe, and left us nothing but the bare walls to gaze upon."[102] His ports of call included beleaguered Puerto Cabello in modern-day Venezuela, where the inhabitants had abandoned the town and taken their possessions, leaving the houses "unprovided of all furniture fit for entertainment." "In revenge of which discourtesy, wee took away their Saintsbell from the chapel, and spoyled their crucifixes without the least scruple of Sacralege."[103] At Talon, near Cartagena, they fired the three hundred houses but strangely "exempted 3 fair churches." Still, the keeper of the journal derided the residents, "leaving them to coudle their Crosses in dust and ashes."[104] Near Campeche in the Yucatán, the keeper of the journal recorded bursting into a friary at night. They caught "two of these Epicures in the night time, whilst they were drinking and reveling, with their whores." Their punishment was the theft of all the church's silver vessels.[105] Even after an interlude of almost half a century, the patterns of English iconoclasm in the New World had not changed much. English identity was still being acted out in opposition to Spanish Catholicism and through the destruction of its material cultural elements.

Jackson's vessels also visited Santiago de la Vega in Jamaica, where the keeper of the journal saw great opportunities for economic development. He wished that it "were in the possession of such as would employ the same towards the advancement of God's Glory and the propagation of the Gospell: for now the greatest revenue of these American Regions are conferred towards the maintenance of the Papall Kingdome and confirmation of all Anti-Christian monarchs."[106] This nicely summarizes the evolution in thinking about the New World that shaped Cromwell's Western Design. Rather than seeing Spanish America as merely a field for plunder and a theater for iconoclasm, Cromwell and others wanted to augment English power and coffers by seizing major Spanish possessions. The riches that would flow from a tropical plantation possession would fund continued war against Europe's Catholic powers.

Cromwell sought to make that Puritan fantasy reality with the campaign against Santo Domingo led by Admiral William Penn and General Robert Venables.[107] The recriminations that followed the failure to capture Santo Domingo produced a defense from Venables, in which the old patterns of iconoclasm are still readily discernible. After landing in Santo Domingo, Venables' forces found a plantation chapel "furnished with good store of popish trumperie, which we wasted."[108] The next plantation chapel featured "a large statue of the Virgin Mary, well accoutered"; the men "pelted her to death with oranges."[109] Henry Whistler, sailing master of Penn's own vessel, reported a similar incident at a friary. Finding that "the Ballpated friars" had abandoned "all thayer Imedges," the soldiers set to work. The "richlie clad" image of the Virgin was brought out on the head of a soldier. "The souldgers did fall a flinging of orringes att her, and did sodainelly deforme her."[110] Though the use of citrus in the degradation of images may be a parliamentary innovation, it is clear that iconoclasm had become a cultural habit for the English in the Caribbean. No longer constrained by equivocating monarchs, Englishmen of the parliamentary era reveled in their freedom to destroy Spanish religious objects.

Finding various footholds on the North American mainland in the seventeenth century, the English carried their iconoclastic tradition north. While Puritan New Englanders might be expected to have best preserved the iconoclastic drive, supposedly religiously lax Carolinians actually found the greatest opportunity to sponsor iconoclastic raids. As invading Carolinians made their way toward St. Augustine in 1702, they overran Spanish missions to the Indians. Each time, Spanish friars and military men took pains to remove statuary and church valuables ahead of the English arrival.[111] Seeking help from Havana, Florida's governor cited his responsibility to "protect the holy images, ornaments, jewels of the church, the clergy, [and] friars."[112] He thus demonstrated an accurate knowledge of English behavior in the Americas, perhaps even down to their willingness to attack clergy when objects were not available. James Moore used the Franciscan church for his headquarters and burned at least ten churches during the expedition, thus destroying most of the physical plant of Florida Catholicism and permanently impairing the province's ability to attract clergy.[113] Spanish efforts to prevent destruction of religious imagery suggest that this brief incident in the War of Spanish Succession was as much an act of religious aggression as a moment in the struggle for empire.

To suggest that a vocabulary of iconoclasm emerged in the age of Elizabethan privateering and carried through Carolinians' raids on Florida is not to suggest that the meaning of these actions was fixed. Even on a single voyage or in a single period, the meaning of violence against Catholic imagery could shift as different actors took center stage in different ports. One smashed crucifix may signal Protestant revulsion from Catholic imagery. A broken crucifix might also reveal English rejection of Spanish claims to govern the Americas. Plain meanness is another possibility, for destroying images could certainly express the temporary interpersonal domination that the privateer enjoyed over his captives. The best explanation will likely allow that all three meanings, and many more, can be found in these actions.

Like most aggressive acts, these behaviors reveal much about the origins of the aggressors. Between the accession of Elizabeth I and the execution of Charles I, the most radical English Protestants were effectively muzzled at home. Elizabeth and the early Stuarts pursued a moderate religious policy, retaining catholic orders of ministry, a liturgical tradition, and limited forms of traditional imagery. The liturgical and mildly iconophilic anti-Calvinist movement sustained by Richard

Hooker, Lancelot Andrewes, and William Laud generated great anxiety for the most Protestant of Englishmen. War with Spain and distance from the careful queen allowed men such as Drake to articulate their aspirations for the further reform of the Church of England by destroying the Catholic imagery of the Spanish. Once iconoclasm again found official sanction under the parliamentary regime, English Puritans were quick to export it via the Western Design. The struggle for the soul of English Protestantism is thus a vital subtext of iconoclasm in the Americas.

All explanations of image destruction must recognize an English effort to symbolically degrade their Spanish Catholic enemies. It is also clear that the forms of iconoclasm were remarkably constant across the decades under consideration, even as the particular emphases of meaning shifted. Smashing images, stealing eucharistic vessels, and abusing friars were basic ways of acting out Englishness in the Spanish Americas. Spanish acts of veneration and English acts of iconoclasm attached new and revised symbolic import to the Madonnas, crucifixes, and altars of the Spanish world. When English raiders visited, their violence toward these objects was an attempt to invalidate one sort of symbolic power and impose another. Like the acts of veneration that honored Christ and the saints through their images, English iconoclasm became a ritual behavior in its own right, readily repeatable and available as a cultural tool.

When the iconoclasts departed for the next port, damaged images were not left devoid of symbolism. On Capera Island, Diego de Sotomayor collected the fragments of the crucifix that John Oxenham had smashed, giving them to the precentor of the church in Panama. He carried his broken veronica to his deposition, "with the marks of these wounds and blows upon it; which veronica he exhibited."[114] Oxenham's marks added meaning as Sotomayor dramatically exhibited his image's wounds, though certainly not the meaning Oxenham intended. Whether repaired, buried, or left broken to testify to Protestant depravity, images continued to accrue layers of symbolic power. Never static, the meaning of images and the actions used to manipulate them were powerful cultural markers in the early modern world. As Catholic Spain and Protestant England struggled for dominance, attacks on images emerged as a lingua franca in the Americas, readily recognized by all as a symbol of English identity. There is thus not a little irony in the fact that Englishmen turned, as they had since the Middle Ages, to images of the saints when they sought to make profound statements about their identities.

Notes

1. Alain Besançon, *The Forbidden Image: An Intellectual History of Iconoclasm* (Chicago: University of Chicago Press, 2000); David Morgan, *Visual Piety: A History and Theory of Popular Religious Images* (Berkeley: University of California Press, 1998); Carlos

Eire, *War against the Idols: The Reformation of Worship from Erasmus to Calvin* (London: Cambridge University Press, 1986); Sergiusz Michalski, *The Reformation and the Visual Arts: The Protestant Image Question in Western and Eastern Europe* (London: Routledge, 1993).

2. Letter of Thomas Cavendish, 1588, in Philip Edwards, ed., *Last Voyages: Cavendish, Hudson, Ralegh, The Original Narratives* (Oxford, U.K.: Clarendon Press, 1988), 50.

3. This useful term designates persons hostile to images but who may not have made the transition to destroying images. On iconoclasm in England, see Eamon Duffy, *The Stripping of the Altars: Traditional Religion in England, 1400–1580* (New Haven, Conn.: Yale University Press, 1992); John Phillips, *The Reformation of Images: Destruction of Art in England, 1535–1660* (Berkeley: University of California Press, 1973); Margaret Aston, *England's Iconoclasts,* vol. 1, *Laws against Images* (Oxford, U.K.: Clarendon Press, 1988); Michael O'Connell, *The Idolatrous Eye: Iconoclasm and Theater in Early-Modern England* (New York: Oxford University Press, 2000).

4. Duffy, *Stripping of the Altars,* 160.

5. Ibid., 169–70.

6. Ibid., 155.

7. "Realistic" in the theological sense, i.e. the real, objective presence of Christ in the bread and wine of the Eucharist.

8. Eire, *War against the Idols,* 279. See also Phyllis Mack Crew, *Calvinist Preaching and Iconoclasm in the Netherlands, 1544–1569* (New York: Cambridge University Press, 1978); Carl C. Christiansen, *Art and the Reformation in Germany* (Athens: Ohio University Press, 1979).

9. Gerald Bray, ed., *Documents of the English Reformation* (Minneapolis: Fortress Press, 1994), 176.

10. Injunctions of 1547 in ibid., 249.

11. Diarmaid MacCulloch, *Thomas Cranmer: A Life* (New Haven, Conn.: Yale University Press, 1996), 357.

12. Diarmaid MacCulloch, *The Boy King: Edward VI and the Protestant Reformation* (New York: Palgrave, 1999), 92.

13. Article 28/29 in Bray, *Documents,* 302.

14. Bray, *Documents,* 305.

15. Aston, *England's Iconoclasts,* 1: 343.

16. Patrick Collinson, *The Religion of Protestants: The Church in English Society, 1559–1625* (Oxford, U.K.: Clarendon Press, 1983), 31.

17. Ibid., 34.

18. Aston, *England's Iconoclasts,* 1: 313.

19. Collinson, *Religion of Protestants,* 32.

20. John Guy, *Tudor England* (Oxford: Oxford University Press, 1988), 261.

21. Ibid., 306–7.

22. Peter Lake, "Calvinism and the English Church, 1570–1635," in *Reformation to Revolution: Politics and Religion in Early Modern England,* ed. Margo Todd (New York: Routledge, 1995), 186.

23. See Dario Gamboni, *The Destruction of Art: Iconoclasm and Vandalism since the French Revolution* (New Haven, Conn.: Yale University Press, 1997).

24. Aston, *England's Iconoclasts,* 1: 44.

25. Michalski, *Reformation and the Visual Arts,* 90.

26. A very useful contribution to the literature on iconoclasm is Joel Budd, "Rethinking Iconoclasm in Early Modern England: The Case of the Cheapside Cross," *Journal of Early Modern History* 4, nos. 3–4 (2000): 379–404. Budd argues that "religious images evoked a complex variety of associations, not all of them necessarily religious in a direct sense." Thus iconoclasm is less a "generalized attack on traditional religion" and more "one ritual among many that shaped the meaning of images" (402).

27. Guy, *Tudor England,* 281–89.

28. Ibid., 338.

29. The literature on the seafaring English is vast, much of it focused on the development of naval policy and the British Empire. See the works of Kenneth R. Andrews, including *The Spanish Caribbean: Trade and Plunder 1530–1630* (New Haven, Conn.: Yale University Press, 1978); "English Voyages to the Caribbean, 1596–1604: An Annotated List," *William and Mary Quarterly* 31, no. 2 (April 1974): 243–54; *Elizabethan Privateering: English Privateering during the Spanish War, 1585–1603* (Cambridge: Cambridge University Press, 1964); *English Privateering Voyages to the West Indies, 1588–1595,* Works Issued by the Hakluyt Society, 2nd ser., 111 (Cambridge: Cambridge University Press, 1959); *Trade, Plunder, and Settlement: Maritime Enterprise and the Genesis of the British Empire, 1480–1630* (Cambridge: Cambridge University Press, 1984). See also Kris E. Lane, *Pillaging the Empire: Piracy in the Americas, 1500–1750* (Armonk, N.Y.: M. E. Sharpe, 1998); Peter R. Galvin, *Patterns of Pillage: A Geography of Caribbean-Based Piracy in Spanish America, 1536–1718* (New York: Peter Lang, 1999).

30. Harry Kelsey, *Francis Drake: The Queen's Pirate* (New Haven, Conn.: Yale University Press, 1998), 7–9. See also K. R. Andrews, *Drake's Voyages: A Re-assessment of Their Place in Elizabethan Maritime Expansion* (New York: Scribner, 1968).

31. Kelsey, *Francis Drake,* 33.

32. Ibid., 170.

33. Irene A. Wright, ed., *Documents Concerning English Voyages to the Spanish Main, 1569–1580,* Works Issued by the Hakluyt Society, 2nd ser., 71 (London: Printed for the Hakluyt Society, 1932), 20, 23.

34. I mean to say that there was no proximate cause consisting of resistance or aggression on the part of the friars attacked. There is ample evidence of clergy supporting Spanish attempts to resist the English. A Spanish soldier wrote to Fray Bartolomé de la Barrera y Castroverde in 1596, recognizing that "the bullets you made and blessed with your hands must have been well-made, for we have had great success in punishing those accursed men" (K. R. Andrews, ed., *The Last Voyage of Drake and Hawkins,* Works Issued by the Hakluyt Society, 2nd ser., 142 [Cambridge: Cambridge University Press, 1972], 226).

35. Of course, the reverse was true as well, as the bodies of captured privateers and pirates were used for very public purposes. Captain Diego Lopez of Trujillo reported his success against Andrew Barker to the crown in 1577. During the Spanish attack, which

came "with a Hail Mary," Barker was killed. Lopez brought the severed head of Barker and the hands of twelve of his men to the municipal authorities and petitioned the king to add them to his coat of arms. See Wright, *Documents,* 197.

36. Kelsey, *Francis Drake,* 50.

37. All of the voyages treated here include landings and attempts to extract goods and ransom from coastal towns. Most privateering was restricted to attempts to seize cargo and ships at sea. That sort of privateering naturally offered fewer opportunities for iconoclasm.

38. Sir Francis Drake, *Sir Francis Drake Revived* (London, 1592), printed in Wright, *Documents,* 298. This account ends on a paradoxical note. The return to Plymouth harbor occurred at service time on Sunday, August 9, 1573. News of Drake's return passed quickly through the church, leaving the worshipers so filled with "desire and delight to see him, that very few or none remained with the Preacher, all hastening to see God's love and blessing towards our Gracious Queene and Country, by the fruite of our Captaine's labour and successe." Thus the great Protestant corsair disrupted good Protestant worship. See Wright, *Documents,* 326.

39. Wright, *Documents,* 45n1.

40. See Georges Baudot, "Corsaires Iconoclastes en 1572–1574," *Cahiers du Monde Hispanique et Luso-Brésilien* 45 (1985): 79–85. Baudot argues that French Protestant corsairs operating off the Yucatán Peninsula similarly established patterns that would carry into the seventeenth-century golden age of buccaneering. Baudot sees their vandalism as iconoclastic in the broader sense, as seeking "to live without fetters, beyond the constraints of European societies." This argument probably holds for many of the lesser figures involved in Caribbean privateering, including John Oxenham. Drake and the Parliamentarians discussed below operated at a different and more official level.

41. Deposition of Oxenham, October 20, 1577, in Wright, *Documents,* 174.

42. Ibid., 170.

43. Ibid., 172.

44. Ibid.

45. Ibid., 173.

46. Deposition of Sotomayor, April 17, 1577, in Wright, *Documents,* 117.

47. Ibid., 118.

48. Ibid., 119.

49. Ibid. A veronica was an image of the face of Christ.

50. Deposition of Sotomayor, April 17, 1577, in Wright, *Documents,* 120.

51. Ibid., 120–21.

52. Deposition of los Angeles in Wright, *Documents,* 122.

53. Summary of deposition of Constantino in Wright, *Documents,* 122.

54. Deposition of Sotomayor, April 17, 1577, in Wright, *Documents,* 119.

55. Ibid., 121.

56. Deposition of los Angeles in Wright, *Documents,* 122.

57. Deposition of Sotomayor, April 17, 1577, in Wright, *Documents,* 121. Around this time, the privateer Andrew Barker was operating in Caribbean waters off Panama. If accurately reported, his attack on two friars was particularly brutal. "They castrated two

Franciscan friars," both of whom died of their injuries. See Wright, *Documents,* 187. Barker did not live to provide an account of his actions.

58. City of Panama to the crown, April 15, 1577, in Wright, *Documents,* 113.

59. Municipal Council of Panama to the crown, February 24, 1573, in Wright, *Documents,* 50.

60. The Spanish response is treated in Roland D. Hussey, "Spanish Reaction to Foreign Aggression in the Caribbean to About 1680," *Hispanic American Historical Review* 9, no. 3 (August 1929): 286–302; and in Paul E. Hoffman, *The Spanish Crown and the Defense of the Caribbean, 1535–1585* (Baton Rouge: Louisiana State University Press, 1980).

61. Audiencia of Panama to the crown, May 1, 1577, in Wright, *Documents,* 139.

62. Diego de Frias Trejo to the crown, February 18, 1578, in Wright, *Documents,* 202.

63. Richard Hawkins, *The Observations of Sir Richard Hawkins, Knight, in His Voyage to the South Seas, Anno Domini 1593* (London, 1622), in Wright, *Documents,* 341.

64. Deposition of Gaspar de Vargas, May 14, 1580, in Zelia Nuttall, ed., *New Light on Drake: A Collection of Documents Relating to His Voyage of Circumnavigation,* Works Issued by the Hakluyt Society, 2nd ser., 34 (London: for the Hakluyt Society, 1914), 341.

65. Deposition of Vargas, May 14, 1580, in Nuttall, *New Light on Drake,* 341.

66. N. M. Penzer, ed., *The World Encompassed and Contemporary Analogous Documents Concerning Sir Francis Drake's Circumnavigation of the World* (New York: Cooper Square Publishers, 1969), 97. The quote is from Francis Fletcher's notes, Sloane MS No. 61, in the British Museum. The use of *u* and *v* has been modernized here.

67. Deposition of Giusepe de Parraces, May 1579, in Nuttall, *New Light on Drake,* 188.

68. Deposition of Simon de Miranda, May 15, 1580, in Nuttall, *New Light on Drake,* 349.

69. Deposition of Bernardino Lopez, May 15, 1580, in Nuttall, *New Light on Drake,* 346.

70. Deposition of Lopez, May 15, 1580, in Nuttall, *New Light on Drake,* 344.

71. Deposition of Francisco Gomez Rengifo, February 18, 1580, in Nuttall, *New Light on Drake,* 353.

72. Kelsey, *Francis Drake,* 240. Much more on privateering as an investment can be found in the works of Kenneth R. Andrews (cited in notes 29 and 30 above) and in W. R. Scott, *The Constitution and Finance of English, Scottish, and Irish Joint Stock Companies to 1720* (New York: Peter Smith, 1951).

73. Two dispatches to Francis Walsingham in Julian S. Corbett, ed., *Papers Relating to the Navy during the Spanish War, 1585–1587,* Publications of the Naval Record Society, vol. 11 (London: Naval Record Society, 1898), 103, 133.

74. *Primrose* account in Mary Frear Keeler, ed., *Sir Francis Drake's West Indian Voyage, 1585–86,* Works Issued by the Hakluyt Society, 2nd series, 148 (London: Hakluyt Society, 1981), 181n4. This edition includes the *Primrose* account along with documents from other ships.

75. *Tiger* account by Christopher Carleill and Edward Powell in Keeler, *Drake's West Indian Voyage,* 84.

76. Dispatch of Christopher Carleill to Walsingham, October 4–11, 1585, in Corbett, *Papers Relating to the Navy,* 46.

77. *Primrose* account in Corbett, *Papers Relating to the Navy,* 8. Another account of the attack on São Tiago includes this interesting distinction between the plain cross of St. George and more elaborate forms of Christian imagery. The commanders "sent the great ensigne, which had nothing in it but the plaine English crosse, to be placed towards the Sea, that our Fleete might see Saint Georges cross flourish in the enemies fortresse" (Richard Hakluyt, ed., *The Principal Navigations, Voyages, Traffiques & Discoveries of the English Nation,* 12 vols. [1598–1600; repr., Glasgow: J. MacLehose and Sons, 1903–5], 10:104; this is the account of Walter Bigges, prepared for printing by Thomas Cates).

78. *Primrose* account in Corbett, *Papers Relating to the Navy,* 15.

79. Ibid., 18.

80. Dean and chapter of Santo Domingo to the crown, February 19, 1586, in Irene A. Wright, ed., *Further English Voyages to Spanish America 1583–94,* Works Issued by the Hakluyt Society, 2nd series, 99 (Glasgow: Robert MacLehose and Co., 1951), 28.

81. Audiencia of Santo Domingo to the crown, February 24, 1586, in Wright, *Further English Voyages,* 34–35. While the English sources gladly own up to the destruction of images, these attacks on the dead are unrecorded in English sources. Could this be a more personalized form of iconoclasm, one akin to the attacks on mendicants? We should also note the possibility that Drake's men murdered at least one friar in Santo Domingo, which, though not reported in Spanish sources, is indicated by English sources.

82. Corbett, *Papers Relating to the Navy,* 20. The *Primrose* account calls it an accident, caused by an artillery piece's recoil. The Spanish thought it intentional. See the report of Pedro Fernández de Busto to the crown, May 25, 1586, in Wright, *Further English Voyages,* 143.

83. Dean and chapter of Santo Domingo to the crown, February 19, 1586, in Wright, *Further English Voyages,* 28.

84. Diego Daça to the Municipal Authorities of Havana, April 8, 1586, in Wright, *Further English Voyages,* 61.

85. Rodrigo Fernández de Ribera to the crown, June 30, 1586, in Wright, *Further English Voyages,* 178.

86. Corbett, *Papers Relating to the Navy,* 9.

87. Wright, *Further English Voyages,* 28.

88. Corbett, *Papers Relating to the Navy,* 21.

89. Andrews, *English Privateering Voyages,* 192. This account was written by John Twitt, a corporal on the voyage. It can be verified in Wright, *Further English Voyages,* by consulting the report of Diego Martin de Angelo to the crown, June 15, 1592. For Newport, see K. R. Andrews, "Christopher Newport of Limehouse, Mariner," *William and Mary Quarterly* 11, no. 1 (January 1954): 28–41.

90. G. C. Williamson, *George, Third Earl of Cumberland (1558–1605): His Life and His Voyages* (Cambridge: Cambridge University Press, 1920), 184, account of Captain William Meysey. On this voyage one soldier was condemned to death (though later pardoned) for defacing a church (ibid., 192). Bell theft or, more usually, destruction was also

a feature of North American Indian attacks on Spanish missions. Archaeologists working on the site of Santa Catalina de Guale in present-day St. Catherine's Island (S.C.) have found bell fragments that "show punch and axe marks, indicating that the bells were deliberately destroyed" (David Hurst Thomas, "The Archaeology of Mission Santa Catalina de Guale: Our First 15 Years," in *The Spanish Missions of La Florida,* ed. Bonnie G. McEwan, 1–34 [Gainesville: University Press of Florida, 1993], quotation from 18). Thomas suggests that Indian attacks on bells manifested their rejection of Spanish domination of their time and labor, as symbolized by the bells' ordering of the day. While English interest in bells was more pecuniary, the symbolic import of both Indian and English attacks cannot be ignored. For information on Cumberland, see Richard T. Spence, *The Privateering Earl* (Stroud, U.K.: A. Sutton, 1995).

91. *Primrose* account in Corbett, *Papers Relating to the Navy,* 10.

92. Audiencia of Santo Domingo to the crown, February 24, 1586, in Wright, *Further English Voyages,* 35.

93. Pedro Fernández de Busto to the Audiencia at Turbaco, Panama, March 12, 1586, in Wright, *Further English Voyages,* 54.

94. Deposition of Alonso Sancho Saez and Miguel de Valdés, August 12, 1586, in Wright, *Further English Voyages,* 200.

95. On this point, see David B. Quinn, "Turks, Moors, Blacks, and Others in Drake's West Indian Voyage," *Terrae Incognitae* 14 (1982): 97–104.

96. See Kelsey, *Francis Drake,* chap. 13.

97. For this period, see David Delison Hebb, *Piracy and the English Government, 1616–1642* (Aldershot, U.K.: Scolar Press, 1994). Also useful is W. Frank Craven, "The Earl of Warwick, A Speculator in Piracy," *Hispanic American Historical Review* 10, no. 4 (November 1930): 457–79. For the evolution of Providence Island from Puritan colony to pirates' nest, see Karen O. Kupperman, *Providence Island 1630–1641* (Cambridge: Cambridge University Press, 1993); and A. P. Newton, *The Colonising Activities of the English Puritans: The Last Phase of the Elizabethan Struggle with Spain* (New Haven, Conn.: Yale University Press, 1914).

98. Kevin Sharpe, *The Personal Rule of Charles I* (New Haven, Conn.: Yale University Press, 1992), 288.

99. Ibid., 329.

100. Julian Davies, *The Caroline Captivity of the Church: Charles I and the Remoulding of Anglicanism* (Oxford, U.K.: Clarendon Press, 1992), 53, quoting *The Works of the Most Reverend Father in God, William Laud, D.D.* (Oxford, U.K.: J. H. Parker, 1847–60), 6:51–57. More fully, he said, "The altar is the greatest place of God's residence upon earth. I say the greatest, yea greater than the pulpit, for there 'tis *Hoc est corpus meum,* 'This is my Body,' but in the pulpit 'tis at most *Hoc est verbum meum,* 'This is my Word.'"

101. See Michael O'Connell, *The Idolatrous Eye: Iconoclasm and Theater in Early Modern England* (New York: Oxford University Press, 2000); Julie Spraggon, *Puritan Iconoclasm during the English Civil War* (Rochester, N.Y.: Boydell Press, 2003).

102. "A Briefe Journall or a Succinct and True Relation of the Most Remarkable Passage Observed in That Voyage Undertaken by Cap. William Jackson to the Western Indies

or Continent of America," in *Camden Miscellany,* vol. 13, 3rd ser. (vol. 34) (London, 1924), 33. This is a printing of British Library Sloan MSS 793/894. The keeper of the journal is not identified but seems to have been an eyewitness.

103. Ibid., 7.

104. Ibid., 29.

105. Ibid., 33.

106. Ibid., 15–16.

107. See S. A. G. Taylor, *The Western Design: An Account of Cromwell's Expedition to the Caribbean* (Kingston: Institute of Jamaica and the Jamaica Historical Society, 1965); Lucie Street, *An Uncommon Sailor: A Portrait of Admiral Sir William Penn* (New York: St. Martin's Press, 1988).

108. C. H. Firth, ed., *The Narrative of General Venables, with an Appendix of Papers Relating to the Expedition to the West Indies and Conquest of Jamaica, 1654–1655,* Royal Historical Society Publications, 60 (1900; repr., New York: Johnson Reprint Corp., 1965), 129.

109. Ibid., 130.

110. Ibid., 152. *The Journal of Henry Whistler* is also printed in this volume; it is British Library Sloane MS 3926.

111. Charles W. Arnade, *The Siege of St. Augustine in 1702* (Gainesville: University of Florida Press, 1959), 14.

112. Ibid., 20, 24.

113. Ibid., 47, 57; Robert L. Kapitzke, *Religion, Power, and Politics in Colonial St. Augustine* (Gainesville: University Press of Florida, 2001), 162. Kapitzke also records the efforts of a priest during the 1728 British attack on St. Augustine; this priest exposed himself to great danger by taking the reserved sacrament out of the church and into the Castillo, "where he could protect it to prevent the indecencies that the heretics might execute." (159).

114. Deposition of Sotomayor, April 17, 1577, in Wright, *Documents,* 119.

The Influence of Pilgrimage on Artistic Traditions in Medieval Ireland

Tessa Garton

The early Irish concept of pilgrimage was one of restless wandering, often without a well-planned itinerary. Kathleen Hughes has characterized the typical early Irish saint as "constantly moving from place to place" and "sometimes even entrusting himself to the seas without oars or rudder."[1] Pilgrims appear to have imitated the ideal practiced by the saints they sought to visit. Irish pilgrimage sites are generally in remote and isolated locations, such as mountaintops or islands, and frequently involve difficult access and arduous journeys. The focus of pilgrimage was characteristically related to an Irish saint and was often associated with a feature such as a holy well or a sacred stone.[2] Corporeal relics of the saints or shrines containing them are rare, though there are a few surviving examples, such as the free-standing carved stone tomb-shrine at Clones in county Monaghan and a simple triangular-shaped slab-shrine at Temple Cronan in county Clare (see fig. 2). Here pilgrims could reach through a hole in the side to touch the bones of the saint.[3] Most of the surviving Irish shrines and reliquaries contain associative relics, such as bells, books, or crosiers, that were believed to have belonged to the saints.[4] Such objects were important symbols of sainthood in Ireland and also appear to have been associated with pilgrimage. Writing at the end of the twelfth century, Gerald of Wales noted that "the people and clergy of both Wales and Ireland have a great reverence for bells that can be carried about, and staffs belonging to the saints, and made of gold and silver, or bronze, and curved at their upper ends. So much so that they fear to swear or perjure themselves in making oaths on these, much more than they do in swearing on the gospels."[5]

Harbison has suggested that images of figures carrying such items, as on the stone pillars at Carndonagh in county Donegal and at Killadeas in county Fermanagh, may represent saints or possibly pilgrims.[6] The figure on the Carndonagh pillar carries a bell and a book or satchel and has a drop-headed staff or crosier beneath his feet, while the stone at Killadeas shows a figure holding a bell

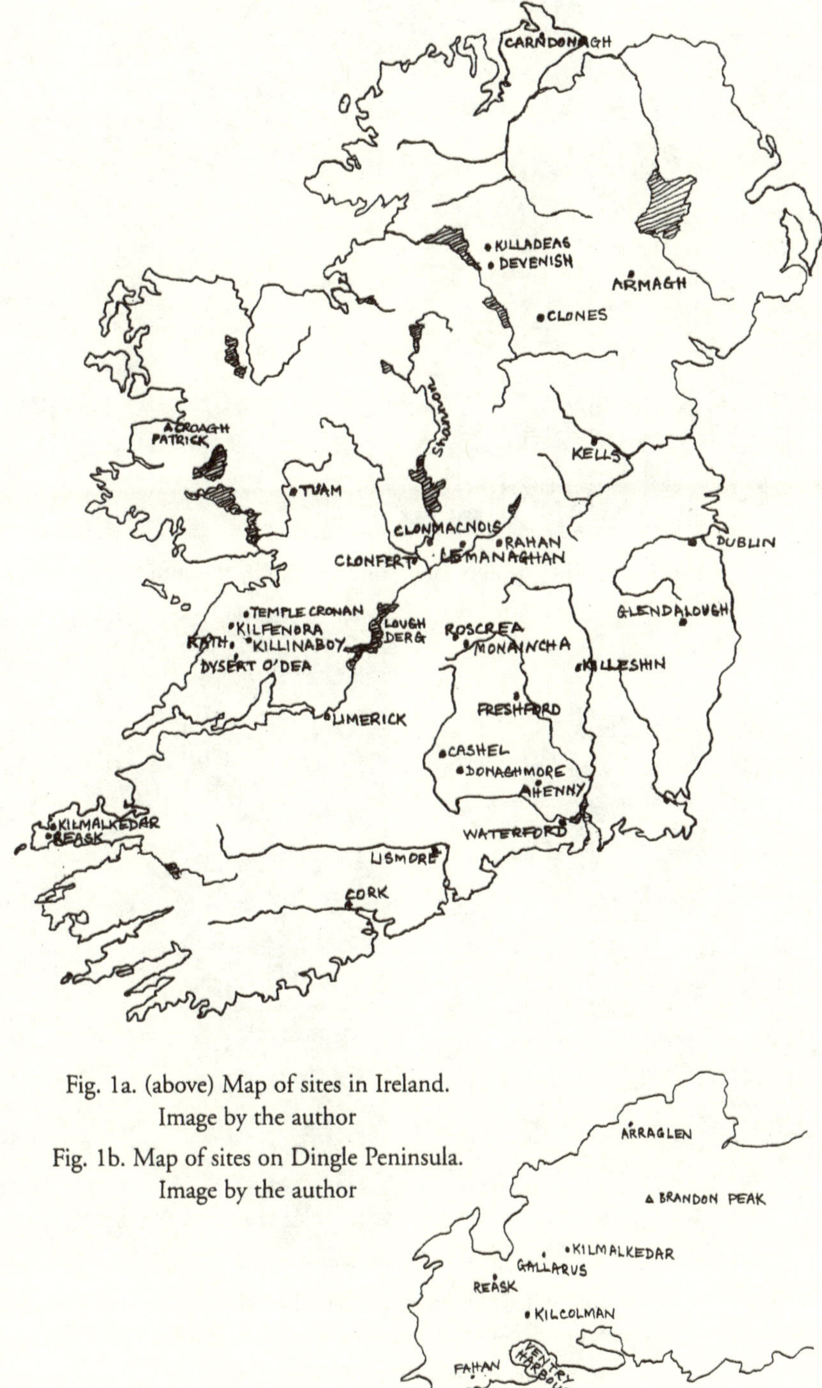

Fig. 1a. (above) Map of sites in Ireland.
Image by the author

Fig. 1b. Map of sites on Dingle Peninsula.
Image by the author

Fig. 2. Temple Cronan (Clare), tomb. Image by the author

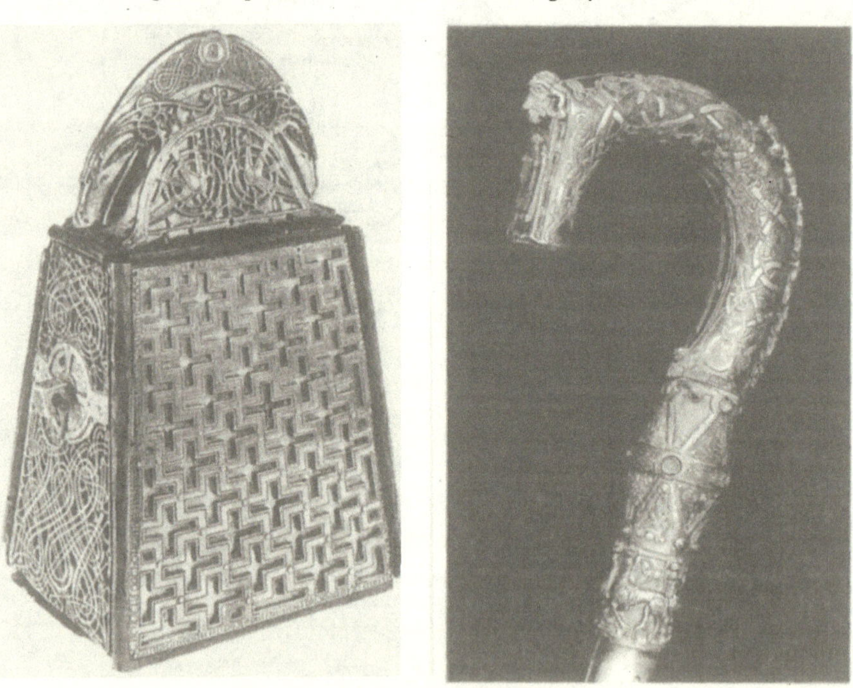

Fig. 3. (left) Shrine of St. Patrick's Bell.
Courtesy of the National Museum of Ireland, Dublin

Fig. 4. Crosier of the abbots of Clonmacnoise.
Courtesy of the National Museum of Ireland, Dublin

and a crosier. The pillars at Carndonagh have been dated between the seventh and ninth centuries and appear to be connected with a pilgrimage associated with St. Colum Cille.

The bells, books, and crosiers associated with Irish saints were enshrined in elaborate reliquaries, typically reflecting the form of the objects within. A remarkable number of metalwork reliquaries remain from the eleventh and twelfth centuries, indicating an increased interest in relics as well as a flowering of high-quality craftsmanship during this period.[7] Such reliquaries—for example, the Shrine of St. Patrick's Bell (see fig. 3)[8] or the crosier of the abbots of Clonmacnoise (see fig. 4)[9]— are distinctive to the traditions of Irish saints. They are decorated predominantly with zoomorphic interlace and geometric ornament.

While these richly decorated reliquaries often have inscriptions recording the names of patrons or artists, the architectural monuments associated with Irish pilgrimage are relatively simple and are not as well documented. This essay examines a selection of early medieval pilgrimage sites and monuments and suggests a relationship between the decoration of metalwork reliquaries and the sculptural decoration of Romanesque churches and high crosses connected with pilgrimage sites.

Pilgrimage to Holy Mountains in the West of Ireland

One of the better-documented early Irish pilgrimages, still practiced in modern times, is to the summit of Croagh Patrick in county Mayo, where St. Patrick is reputed to have fasted for forty days and forty nights.[10] Attacked by birds, St. Patrick defended himself with a bell, which has been identified with one known as Clog Dubh, or Black Bell.[11] The bell probably dates from the seventh century to the ninth century and was first recorded in 1098 as a relic venerated at Croagh Patrick.[12] Another bell traditionally considered to have been used by St. Patrick and buried in his tomb is enshrined in a reliquary made in the late eleventh or early twelfth century (see fig. 3 above).

Croagh Patrick is a remote and inhospitable site involving a dangerous journey; in 1113 thirty pilgrims were killed by lightning while fasting on the mountain.[13] Documents record an oratory on the summit from as early as 824,[14] and excavations in the 1990s uncovered the remains of a rampart, circular huts, and an oratory that can be radiocarbon-dated between 568 and 770.[15] The oratory was a dry-stone structure similar to Gallarus oratory on the Dingle Peninsula in county Kerry.

Gallarus oratory is situated close to another remote mountain pilgrimage site on the summit of Mount Brandon (see fig. 1b above). The mountain is the most significant peak at the western end of the Dingle Peninsula and was probably the center of an earlier pagan cult that may have become connected with St. Brendan the Navigator due to the similarity in name.[16] The early medieval pilgrimage to

Mount Brandon is not as well documented as that to Croagh Patrick, but the route preserves a series of early medieval monuments exemplifying many of the characteristic features of Irish pilgrimage sites.

The "Saint's Road" that leads to Mount Brandon appears to start near the coast at the southwestern part of the Dingle Peninsula, possibly at Kilcolman. At this site an earthwork encloses some beehive huts, a possible church site, and a boulder carved with two equal-armed crosses and an ogham inscription requesting a prayer for Colman the pilgrim.[17] The road passes through Kilmalkedar, where there is a twelfth-century church with a carved doorway (see figs. 5a and 5b), and continues to the summit of Mount Brandon, where the remains of an oratory were discovered in 1868. Elaborately carved stones, now lost, were found at this site.[18] They were recorded as being similar to those on the twelfth-century doorway at Kilmalkedar (fig. 5b), suggesting a more elaborate Romanesque oratory than the earlier dry-stone structure on Croagh Patrick. The embellishment of the churches at Mount Brandon and Kilmalkedar in the twelfth century indicates the importance of the pilgrimage during this period. In addition to the carved doorway, the Romanesque church at Kilmalkedar is enriched with a decorated chancel arch and with a blind colonnade along the interior of the nave walls.

While Kilmalkedar functioned as a station on the Saint's Road south of Mount Brandon, it was itself the focus of a pilgrimage dedicated to a more obscure local saint, Malkedar.[19] Harbison has suggested that the local cult of St. Malkedar probably predated the association of St. Brendan with the Dingle Peninsula and Mount Brandon. This co-option of a local pilgrimage shrine into the cult of a more significant national saint is also evident in the development of the cult of St. Patrick at Lough Derg.[20]

The site at Kilmalkedar includes features typically found at medieval pilgrimage sites in Ireland. Inside the church is a fragment of a cross-decorated stone with an inscription in early Irish,[21] and to the west of the church are an ogham stone, a simple stone cross, and a sundial that is decorated on the reverse with an equal-armed cross. There are small, undecorated crosses in the burial ground around the church, two holy wells close by, a two-story building of uncertain use,[22] and the remains of a dry-stone oratory in a nearby field. This cluster of holy sites and monuments suggests a shrine of early origin (probably pre-Christian) that remained in use throughout the Middle Ages and gained particular importance in the twelfth century, no doubt in connection with the pilgrimage to Mount Brandon.

There may have been more than one route to Mount Brandon, and the exact path of the Saint's Road is uncertain, but it evidently included a variety of monuments along the way, such as cross-inscribed slabs and ogham stones, as well as beehive huts and dry-stone oratories. Numerous sites with beehive huts, such as

Fig. 5a. Kilmalkedar Church (Kerry), view from west. Image by the author

Fig. 5b. Kilmalkedar Church, detail of west doorway. Image by the author

those at Fahan and nearby Caherconor, are situated along the coast close to Ventry harbor and the start of the pilgrimage route. There are many more remains of beehive huts in this area than in any other part of Ireland, and Harbison has proposed that these may have served as accommodations for pilgrims who traveled by sea to Ventry harbor and had to wait for good weather to continue their pilgrimages.[23] Although the dry-stone beehive huts cannot generally be dated with any certainty, some have provided evidence of an early medieval date.[24] The Early Christian site at Reask, west of Kilmalkedar, has a stone-walled enclosure, or *cashel*, containing the remains of some beehive huts; an oratory; some cross-decorated stones, one of which is carved with an equal-armed cross in a circle and the word *domine (dne)* (see fig. 6).[25]

Some cross-decorated stones appear to have been used as markers along the pilgrimage route. The crosses are often inscribed in a circle, and some of the stones have ogham or Latin inscriptions.[26] The cross-decorated stones at Kilfountain and Faha mark routes to and from the summit of Mount Brandon. A tall stone at Arraglen, north of Mount Brandon, is located at a height of about two thousand feet on a saddle close to the summit. It is carved on two faces with equal-armed crosses and with an ogham inscription, "Ronan the priest son of Comgan." As Harbison has argued, a stone at this altitude, close to the summit of Mount Brandon, is unlikely to have served as a burial monument or a boundary marker, and its erection by a priest suggests a connection with Christian pilgrimage.[27]

Fig. 6. (left) Reask (Kerry), cross-decorated stone. Image by the author

Fig. 7. (right) Ahenny (Tipperary), north cross. Image by the author

Fig. 8. (far right) Kells (Meath), cross of Sts. Patrick and Colum Cille. Image by the author

High Crosses of the Ninth to Tenth Centuries

The simple cross-decorated stones marking sites connected with pilgrimage may have provided a precedent for the more elaborately carved high crosses of the ninth to tenth centuries at sites connected with Irish saints. As Dorothy Verkerk has demonstrated, medieval accounts of the lives of Irish saints provide evidence of the use of crosses to mark important sites connected with the saints' births, miracles, or places of prayer.[28] Crosses were frequently named for saints; five crosses named respectively for Coemgall, Colum Cille, Brigit, Sechnall, and Eogan were erected at Armagh, and one of the crosses at Kells has an inscription naming Sts. Patrick and Colum Cille (see fig. 8 below).[29]

The earliest stone crosses in Ireland, such as those at Ahenny, which probably date from the eighth or ninth century (see fig. 7), were typically decorated with nonfigurative ornament based on designs of Insular origin, such as spirals, interlace, fret patterns, and animal ornament. This decoration appears to be a translation into stone carving of patterns used in metalwork, so that the high crosses can be seen as monumental versions of small-scale crosses in precious metals. The rounded angle moldings and ornamental bosses on the Ahenny crosses closely resemble the coverings and rivet-heads of metal-plated processional crosses.[30]

In the ninth and tenth centuries this abstract decoration was enriched by the appearance of figurative and narrative imagery, as on the Cross of Sts. Patrick and Colum Cille at Kells (see fig. 8) or the Cross of the Scriptures at Clonmacnoise. This development of monumental figure sculpture is particularly remarkable in the context of Insular art, with its emphasis on abstract and decorative forms rather than figural representation. There is no comparable monumental stone sculpture in Europe from this period. Verkerk has proposed that the introduction of figurative imagery on Irish stone crosses was a response to the experiences of Irish pilgrims in Rome, where Early Christian sarcophagi played a prominent role in the display of the relics of the apostles and martyrs. She suggests that the images on the Irish high crosses may have imitated Early Christian sarcophagi out of a "desire to create a Rome in Ireland," and that the images may represent the local Irish saints as typological manifestations of apostolic and biblical heroes.[31] This theory is supported by the literary evidence for a shift in the nature of Irish pilgrimage around the ninth century. The early concept of the pilgrim wandering with no specific destination appears to have been replaced by the concept of pilgrimage to specific shrines, with an emphasis on those of the apostles in Rome. However, the popularity of overseas pilgrimage to Rome also appears to have generated a countercurrent in favor of pilgrimage within Ireland to the shrines of early Irish saints. Verkerk has argued that the desire to validate local Irish pilgrimages may have influenced the creation of the figurative crosses by encouraging the creation of surrogates for Roman monuments in Ireland.

Irish Pilgrimage to Santiago de Compostela

If monuments related to pilgrimage in ninth- to tenth-century Ireland were inspired by the decoration of the shrines of Early Christian Rome, one might expect that the twelfth-century Irish monuments connected with pilgrimage would reflect those of the road to Santiago de Compostela, which rivaled Rome in popularity and importance as a destination for European pilgrimage in the eleventh to twelfth centuries.[32] Twelfth-century pilgrims from Britain and Ireland to Santiago generally traveled by sea to the west coast of France. There must have been considerable numbers making the trip since in 1210 a hostel was built in Dublin for pilgrims waiting for boat passage to Santiago.[33] The pilgrims would have landed at one of the then-numerous harbors in the Saintonge region[34] and continued their journey through western France and northern Spain, visiting pilgrimage shrines and churches along the route. Romanesque churches in western France have doorways with richly decorated arches and generally do not have tympana. The absence of tympana is also characteristic of Romanesque doorways in Ireland, with rare exceptions such as Kilmalkedar and Cormac's Chapel, Cashel. The popularity in Irish Romanesque of arches with human and animal heads may also have been inspired by examples seen in the Saintonge region.[35]

The decoration of the church doorway at Dysert O'Dea in county Clare probably reflects influence from the pilgrimage to Santiago (see figs. 9a, 9b, and 9c).[36] The outer order of the arch is decorated with a series of human and animal heads, while the second order has a scalloped design. The scalloped decoration is virtually unique in Ireland, but similar scalloped ornament is found on the south transept facade at Santiago de Compostela (see figs. 10a and 10b) and on other churches along the pilgrimage route in France and northern Spain.[37] Artistic influence from the pilgrimage to Santiago appears to have chiefly involved the use of decorative motifs of this kind and does not appear to have resulted in the adoption of figurative imagery. Although Irish pilgrims traveling through western France and northern Spain to Santiago would have seen churches with extensive figurative sculpture, this imagery does not appear to have had any significant influence on Irish Romanesque sculpture. On most Romanesque churches in Ireland the decoration remained nonfigurative and was dominated instead by animal interlace and geometric ornament inspired by Insular and Viking traditions. This characteristic is evident on the jambs of the doorway at Dysert O'Dea, where the predominant form of decoration consists of zoomorphic or foliage interlace carved in shallow relief (see fig. 9c). Even the chevron ornament, influenced by Anglo-Norman models, is transformed into zoomorphic moldings,

Fig. 9a. Dysert O'Dea (Clare), south doorway. Image by the author

Fig. 9b. Dysert O'Dea, south doorway, detail of arch. Image by the author

Fig. 9c. Dysert O'Dea, south doorway, detail of jamb.
Image by the author

similar to earlier examples in Insular manuscript illumination and metalwork.[38] This emphasis on traditional Insular and Viking artistic traditions is also found in the decoration of the eleventh- and twelfth-century reliquaries, which would have been a focus of veneration for pilgrims to the holy places in Ireland.[39]

Fig. 10a. Santiago de Compostela, Spain, south transept facade. Image by the author

Fig. 10b. (below) Santiago de Compostela, south transept facade, detail of window. Image by the author

Romanesque Pilgrimage Sites and Monuments in County Clare

The focus of the pilgrimage at Dysert O'Dea was the relics of St. Tola, the eighth-century founder of the monastery. His crosier is encased in a splendid metalwork shrine of c. 1100, decorated with geometric ornament and a crest of biting beasts (see fig. 11 below).[40] It is similar in design to some other crosier reliquaries, such as the crosier of the abbots of Clonmacnoise (see fig. 4 above) and the Lismore crosier. The latter is dated by an inscription naming an abbot of Lismore who died in 1113.[41]

The high cross at Dysert O'Dea (see figs. 12a and 12b), like many of the earlier crosses, may also commemorate the local saint; the mitered bishop or abbot with a crosier standing below the crucified Christ is not specifically identified but may represent St. Tola. The cross represents a new type, decorated with large-scale figures of the crucified Christ and a cleric with a crosier, which became popular in the eleventh and twelfth centuries. The crucified Christ at Dysert O'Dea is wearing a long robe, as on the high crosses at Cashel, Roscrea, and Monaincha.[42] The figure of the saint or cleric has a hole that must have served as a socket for the right arm, perhaps with the hand raised in blessing. Harbison has suggested that this might have been a detachable bronze arm, which could have been removed for uses such as healing the sick or swearing oaths.[43] Arm reliquaries appear to have been used liturgically as dispensers of power.[44] One of the earliest surviving examples in western Europe is the Shrine of St. Lachtin's Arm from Donaghmore, county Cork, dating from c. 1120 and richly decorated with dense patterns of animal interlace.[45] It is, however, hard to imagine that a valuable metalwork reliquary containing sacred relics would have been left in such an unprotected situation.

While the main face of the Dysert cross is dominated by large-scale figures in high relief, the other faces (see fig. 12b below) are decorated with animal interlace and geometric ornament in the Insular tradition, similar to the sculpture on the church doorway. This abstract and animal ornament closely resembles the decoration of contemporary metalwork, such as the shrine of St. Lachtin's arm, the bell shrine of St. Patrick (see fig. 3 above), and the crosier reliquaries from Dysert O'Dea and Clonmacnoise (see figs. 11 and 4, respectively).

Dysert O'Dea may have been one of a series of shrines along a pilgrimage route in north county Clare. Harbison has proposed the existence of an ancient "relic-road" focused on sites at Rath Blathmaic, Dysert O'Dea, Killinaboy, Temple Cronan, and Kilfenora, all within a radius of about ten miles (see fig. 1a above).[46] He suggests that the forms of a series of arm, crosier, bell, and house-shaped reliquaries located along the route were referenced in stone carvings on crosses, tomb slabs, and churches. In addition to the crosier-shrine found at Dysert O'Dea, a

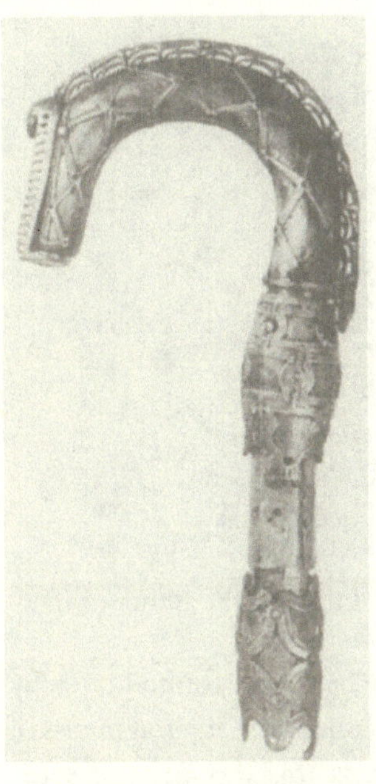

Fig. 11. (left) Dysert O'Dea crosier. Courtesy of the National Museum of Ireland, Dublin

Fig. 12a. (below left) Dysert O'Dea, high cross, from southeast. Image by the author

Fig. 12b. (below right) Dysert O'Dea, high cross, from southwest. Image by the author

Fig. 12c. Dysert O'Dea, high cross, detail of base. Image by the author

similar crosier-shrine made in c. 1100 and two bronze bells were found at nearby Rath Blathmaic,[47] where the ruined medieval church contains many fragments of richly decorated Romanesque sculpture, suggesting that this was a site of some importance in the twelfth century.[48] The church was dedicated to St. Blathmaic, the father of a saint named Onchu, who is recorded in a ninth-century martyrology as one of Ireland's most avid collectors of relics.[49]

Crosiers were important symbols of Irish saints and feature prominently as attributes of clerics depicted on twelfth-century high crosses. Three different types of crosier appear on the crosses at Dysert O'Dea and Kilfenora. The figure on the shaft of the Dysert cross carries a volute crosier (see fig. 12a), while a relief on the base shows two central figures holding a T-shaped staff and a figure on the left holding a drop-headed crosier (see fig. 12c).[50] On the Doorty cross at Kilfenora, a bishop at the top holds a volute crosier, while two figures below hold a drop-headed and a T-shaped crosier, respectively (see fig. 13a).[51] Harbison suggests that these and other images of T-shaped crosiers or crosses along the proposed "relic-road" may reflect the existence of a bronze, T-shaped reliquary that was venerated in North Clare. Only one example of a Tau-crosier of this kind survives in Ireland; it probably dates from the early twelfth century and is decorated with two beast heads on the terminals of the crossbar and a knop with zoomorphic interlace.[52]

The other face of the Doorty cross may include an image of a tomb-shrine at the base of the shaft (see fig. 13b). A rider on horseback stands on top of a gabled roof that is similar in shape to early Irish tomb-shaped reliquaries such as the eighth-century Emly shrine (see fig. 14).[53] Harbison has proposed that the image may represent the shrine or tomb of the saint being visited by a pilgrim on horseback.[54] Similar house-shaped terminals on the tops of some of the ninth- to tenth-century high crosses, such as the cross of Muiredach at Monasterboice (see

Fig. 13a (left) Kilfenora (Clare), Doorty cross, east face. Image by the author

Fig. 13b. (right) Kilfenora, Doorty cross, detail of west face. Image by the author

Fig. 14. Reliquary shrine (Emly Shrine). Museum of Fine Arts, Boston. Theodora Wilbour Fund in memory of Charlotte Beebe Wilbour. Photograph © 2007 Museum of Fine Arts, Boston

fig. 15) or the Cross of the Scriptures at Clonmacnoise, may also represent reliquaries or tomb-shrines. These images of reliquaries may have been used to indicate the presence of relics at the site.[55]

A second cross at Kilfenora, in the field to the west of the cathedral, may actually have incorporated a gabled tomb-shrine at the base of the cross (see fig. 16). Fergus O'Farrell has suggested that the unworked gable-shaped area at the bottom of the shaft was originally concealed by an attached stone tomb of the sort found at Clones and Temple Cronan (see fig. 2 above).[56]

Crosses are not the only structures whose decorations may imitate reliquaries. A depiction of another shrine on this "relic-road" may have been incorporated into the design of the west facade of the church at Killinaboy, between Kilfenora and Dysert O'Dea. The facade, dating from c. 1200, has a double-armed cross built into the masonry, which Harbison has suggested may reflect the veneration

Fig. 15. (left) Monasterboice (Louth), cross of Muiredach. Image by the author

Fig. 16. (right) Kilfenora, "Cross in the Field." Image by the author of a relic of the True Cross in the church.[57] The presence of such relics in twelfth-century Ireland is demonstrated by the reliquary Cross of Cong, which was made in c. 1123 to enshrine a relic of the True Cross acquired by Turlough O'Conor, King of Connaght (see fig. 17).[58] The reliquary cross is decorated with animal interlace, inspired by Insular and Viking traditions. The decoration is similar to that of a monumental stone cross in Tuam set up by Turlough O'Conor between 1126 and 1156 (see fig. 18).[59] The stone cross was no doubt painted to resemble precious metals, thus enhancing the value of the monumental stone sculpture by echoing the characteristics of sacred reliquaries in more valuable materials.

Clonfert Cathedral and the Shrine of St. Manchan

If sacred relics were enshrined and embellished with abstract and decorative ornament, and if crosses indicating pilgrimage routes reflected such decoration, it would seem appropriate to express the sacred contents of a church with a similar design in the doorway. There appears to be a specific relationship of this kind between the doorway of the cathedral at Clonfert, burial place of St. Brendan the

Fig. 17. (left) Cross of Cong. Courtesy of the National Museum of Ireland, Dublin

Fig. 18. Tuam (Galway), high cross, detail of shaft. Image by the author

Fig. 19a. Clonfert Cathedral (Galway), west doorway. Image by the author

Fig. 19b. Clonfert Cathedral, west doorway, detail of arch. Image by the author

Fig. 19c. Clonfert Cathedral, west doorway, south jamb. Image by the author

Navigator (see figs. 19a, 19b, and 19c), and the Shrine of St. Manchan (see figs. 20a, 20b). The similarities involve not only details of decoration but also the overall doorway design.

The early twelfth-century shrine comes from Lemanaghan, county Offaly, some twelve miles east of Clonfert, and contains the relics of Manchan, a local seventh-century saint.[60] It is the only large tomb-shaped reliquary surviving in Ireland and is similar in shape to the gabled tomb-shrine at Temple Cronan (see fig. 2 above).[61] The wooden panels of the shrine were originally fully covered with metal decoration, with a cross on each rectangular face, and bosses, panels, and borders filled with zoomorphic ornament. A series of cast bronze figures remains on the lower part of one face of the shrine and appears to have once filled the spaces surrounding both crosses.[62] The shrine was clearly designed to be carried in procession and is provided with rings for carrying poles.[63] The relics must have been an important focus of veneration and were no doubt visited by pilgrims traveling to the shrine of St. Brendan at Clonfert. It is also possible that the relics of St. Brendan may have been enshrined at Clonfert in a similar reliquary, perhaps even made by the same artist or workshop.

Some of the decorative motifs found on the shrine are incorporated in the decoration of the exuberant late Romanesque west portal at Clonfert (see fig. 19a above). Delicate Urnes-style interlace, similar to that on the bosses and border strips of the shrine, decorates the outer order of the arch and jambs, as well as some of the bosses on the archivolt of the sixth order (see figs. 19b and 19c above). These ornamental bosses are strikingly similar to those on the shrine (see fig. 20b below). The biting beast heads on the impost blocks and on the arch of the second order are similar to those above the carrying rings of the shrine.[64] The human

Fig. 20a. (left) St. Manchan's Shrine, Lemanaghan (Boher, Offaly). Courtesy of the National Museum of Ireland, Dublin

Fig. 20b. (below) St. Manchan's Shrine, detail of boss. Courtesy of the National Museum of Ireland, Dublin

heads set under arcades in the gable, which may originally have had painted bodies, can also be compared to the figures on St. Manchan's shrine.[65]

In addition to these similarities in decorative details between the shrine and the portal, the gabled design of the doorway appears to echo the overall form of the tomb-shaped shrine. The tangent gable over the doorway has generally been interpreted as a late imitation of the gabled north portal of Cormac's Chapel, Cashel, continuing a form found in a series of Irish Romanesque doorways at Roscrea, Donaghmore, Freshford, and Killeshin.[66] O'Keeffe has proposed that the portal was intended to represent the architectural structure of an antechurch, although he also recognized that it might have "reflected the architectural character of a shrine inside the building."[67] The representation of a shrine would have been more recognizable and significant to most twelfth-century Irish viewers than a reference to an unfamiliar architectural model, and the exuberant richness of the decoration on the doorway suggests the fine detail of precious metals rather than the structural qualities of stone architecture. The association of the gabled form with that of tomb-shrines might even have contributed to the popularity of gabled doorways as means of marking entrances to shrines of saints. The tangent gable at Clonfert serves no practical or architectural function and is merely a decorative addition inserted to enhance the facade of an earlier, probably tenth-century, church; it would have served an important function in advertising on the exterior of the church the presence of sacred relics in the interior.

The interpretation of the doorway as an imitation of a metalwork shrine is supported by the structural analysis of the doorway conducted during recent conservation work by Jason Ellis. Based on the variety in the width of the masonry joints and some apparent miscalculations, Ellis argues that the twelfth-century sculptors were imitating the aesthetic effects of metalwork and disregarding practical and structural aspects of the design and decoration of the doorway. In particular, he points out the impracticality of decorating the hood mold of the gable with a cable molding, which allows water to run onto the face of the portal instead of effectively diverting it away from the carved surfaces. A similar cable molding borders the band of enameled geometric ornament at the base of St. Manchan's Shrine. Ellis concludes that "if they were striving to emulate the designs of earlier metalwork," the sculptors "perhaps overlooked the weathering capabilities of their design."[68] Ellis's conclusions, reached independently and based on technical analysis, reinforce my argument that the church facade duplicates and thus advertises the shrine within.

Although the Irish emphasis on holy wells, mountains, and remote locations did not lend itself to elaborate art forms, the tombs and associative relics of saints were considered important. During the eleventh and twelfth centuries many Irish saints' relics were housed in splendid new shrines, often coinciding with the construction of a richly decorated Romanesque church.[69] The sculptural decoration on the twelfth-century churches and high crosses, instead of illustrating biblical or narrative scenes connected with the saints, appears rather to have reflected the abstract traditions of Insular and Viking art used in the decoration of precious shrines containing their relics.

Notes

1. Kathleen Hughes, "The Changing Theory and Practice of Irish Pilgrimage," *Journal of Ecclesiastical History* 10 (1959–60): 143–51, at 143.

2. Mary Lee Nolan, "Irish Pilgrimage: The Different Tradition," *Annals of the Association of American Geographers* 73 (1983): 421–38. See also Peter Harbison, *Pilgrimage in Ireland: The Monuments and the People* (Syracuse, N.Y.: Syracuse University Press, 1992).

3. Lisa M. Bitel, *Isle of the Saints: Monastic Settlement and Christian Community in Early Ireland* (Ithaca, N.Y.: Cornell University Press, 1990), 70; Fergus O'Farrell, "The 'Cross in the Field,' Kilfenora—Part of a 'Founder's Tomb'?" *North Munster Antiquarian Journal* (hereafter *NMAJ*) 26 (1984): 8–13, at 9. A similar example also survives at Killabuonia, county Kerry, with a circular opening in the gable. A shrine of this kind is recorded at Duleek, where St. Adomnan inserted his crosier and mixed up the bones. For the Clones sarcophagus, see Peter Harbison, "The Clones Sarcophagus—a Unique Romanesque-style Monument," *Archaeology Ireland* 49 (vol. 13, no. 3) (1999): 12–16.

4. Raghnall Ó Floinn, *Irish Shrines and Reliquaries of the Middle Ages* (Dublin: National Museum of Ireland, 1994), 33.

5. Gerald of Wales, *The History and Topography of Ireland*, trans. John O'Meara (1951; repr., London: Penguin Books, 1982), 116.

6. Harbison, *Pilgrimage in Ireland*, 196–97, 217–22, figs. 93 and 94. He points out that "in the old Irish annals, the expression used of someone who went on pilgrimage was that 'he took the staff (*bachall*)'" (217).

7. Ó Floinn, *Irish Shrines*, 7; Françoise Henry, *Irish Art in the Romanesque Period (1120–1170 A.D.)* (Ithaca, N.Y.: Cornell University Press, 1970), 74–122. Many of these reliquaries are well documented, with inscriptions giving the names of patrons and craftsmen.

8. Metropolitan Museum of Art, *Treasures of Early Irish Art, 1500 B.C. to 1500 A.D.* (New York: Metropolitan Museum of Art, 1977), cat. nos. 45 and 61; Henry, *Irish Art*, 94–97.

9. Henry, *Irish Art*, 101–2.

10. The story is recounted by Tirechan in the Book of Armagh (ninth century): "And Patrick proceeded to Mons Aigli [Croagh Patrick] intending to fast here for forty days and forty nights, following the example of Moses, Elias and Christ. . . . And Patrick proceeded to the summit of the mountain, climbing Cruachan Aigli and stayed there forty days and forty nights and the birds were troublesome to him and he could not see the face of the sky and land and sea" (Croagh Patrick Archaeological Committee, *Croagh Patrick, Ireland's Holy Mountain*, brochure and information guide [n.d.]).

11. Harbison, *Pilgrimage in Ireland,* 67. St. Patrick is said to have thrown the bell at the birds, causing a piece to break off. The damaged bell was still kept by its hereditary keepers, the Geraghty family, and used by pilgrims in 1838. It was sold to Sir William Wilde, whence it passed to the National Museum of Ireland, Dublin.

12. Croagh Patrick Archaeological Committee, *Croagh Patrick.*

13. Harbison, *Pilgrimage in Ireland,* 53, 69 (recorded in the Annals of Loch Cé).

14. Croagh Patrick Archaeological Committee, *Croagh Patrick.*

15. Peter Harbison and J. O'Brien, *Ancient Ireland: From Prehistory to the Middle Ages* (London: Weidenfeld & Nicholson, 1996), 58. The excavations were conducted by Gerry Walsh.

16. Harbison, *Pilgrimage in Ireland,* 72–74, 80.

17. Ibid., 75, 84, 191, fig. 23 on p. 75. The inscription "ANM COLMAN AILITHIR" was translated by Macalister as "Name of Colman the pilgrim." R. A. S. Macalister, "The Ogham Inscription at Maumanorig, Co. Kerry," *Proceedings of the Royal Irish Academy* (hereafter *PRIA*) 44 C (1938): 241–47. Harbison suggests an alternative reading as a prayer for the soul of Colman the pilgrim. Based on the use of the formula ANM, generally regarded as late in the series of Irish ogham inscriptions, and the appearance of this formula on a dated stone at Ratass, county Kerry, he proposes a date for the cross-inscribed boulder at Kilcolman as "not too far removed from" the eighth or early ninth century. Next to the boulder is a "bullaun" stone (a boulder with a man-made depression, traditionally explained as the mark of a saint's pillow or knees).

18. J. Cuppage, *Archaeological Survey of the Dingle Peninsula* (Ballyferriter: Oidhreacht Chorca Dhuibhne, 1986), 263, #818. The site is listed as Ballinknockane/Ballybrack/Faha. The dressed and carved stones were found when some temporary altars were being constructed.

19. Cuppage, *Archaeological Survey,* 308–18, #855. Malkedar was the son of King Ronan, and his death was recorded in the *Martyrology of Donegal* in 636.

20. Harbison, *Pilgrimage in Ireland,* 65–67, 80.

21. Ibid., 83. The inscription may date from as early as the sixth century.

22. This is known as St. Brendan's House or the "Chancellor's House" and may have served as the priest's house. See Harbison, *Pilgrimage in Ireland,* 183–84.

23. Over 400 beehive huts (*clochain*) were recorded in the area in the nineteenth century by Macalister, and some 150–200 remain in the higher valleys up toward Mount Brandon (Harbison, *Pilgrimage in Ireland,* 76–77, 182, fig. 21).

24. At least one within an Iron Age promontory fort at Dunbeg has provided a radiocarbon date within the ninth to tenth centuries (Harbison, *Pilgrimage in Ireland,* 76).

25. Harbison, *Pilgrimage in Ireland,* 79–80, 84, 188; Tom Fanning, "Excavation of an Early Christian Cemetery and Settlement at Reask, County Kerry," *PRIA* 81 C (1981): 3–172.

26. Harbison, *Pilgrimage in Ireland,* 84, 191–92.

27. Ibid., 83–84, 191–92; R. A. S. Macalister, *Corpus Inscriptionum Insularum Celticarum,* vol. 1 (Dublin: Irish Manuscripts Commission, 1945), 140, no. 145. The stone, now lying on the ground, is approximately six feet high.

28. Dorothy H. Verkerk, "Pilgrimage *ad Limina Apostolorum* in Rome: Irish Crosses and Early Christian Sarcophagi," in *From Ireland Coming: Irish Art from the Early Christian to the Late Gothic Period and Its European Context,* ed. Colum Hourihane, 9–26 (Princeton, N.J.: Princeton University Press, 2001), 21–22. The sources do not specify carved stone crosses.

29. Peter Harbison, *The High Crosses of Ireland: An Iconographical and Photographic Survey* (Bonn: Rudolf Habelt, 1992), 4, cat. 127. Roger Stalley has suggested that the inscription on the Tower Cross may reflect the authority of Abbot Mael Brigte mac Tornain (891–927), who was simultaneously abbot of both Kells and Armagh. Roger Stalley, "The Tower Cross at Kells," in *The Insular Tradition,* ed. Catherine Karkov, Robert Farrell, and Michael Ryan, 115–41 (Albany: State University of New York Press, 1997).

30. Maire De Paor and Liam De Paor, *Early Christian Ireland* (1958; repr., London: Thames & Hudson, 1967), 124; Roger Stalley, *Irish High Crosses* (Dublin: Eason & Son Ltd, 1991), 7–8.

31. Verkerk, "Pilgrimage *ad Limina Apostolorum,*" 23.

32. Diana Webb, *Medieval European Pilgrimage, c. 700–c. 1500* (New York: Palgrave, 2002), 15, 24–32; Richard Hayes, "Ireland's Links with Compostela," *Studies* 37 (1948): 326–27; Roger Stalley, "Sailing to Santiago: The Medieval Pilgrimage to Santiago de Compostela and Its Artistic Influence in Ireland," in *Settlement and Society in Medieval Ireland: Studies Presented to F. X. Martin,* ed. John Bradley, 397–420 (Kilkenny: Boethius Press, 1988), 398.

33. Hayes, "Ireland's Links with Compostela," 326–27; Stalley, "Sailing to Santiago," 398. This was also the route of the wine trade, and it may be that trading contacts were as significant as pilgrimage in the transmission of artistic influences.

34. The coast was not yet silted up (Henry, *Irish Art,* 155).

35. Françoise Henry and George Zarnecki, "Romanesque Arches Decorated with Human and Animal Heads," *Journal of the British Archaeological Association* 20–21 (1957–58): 1–34; Henry, *Irish Art,* 155, 163.

36. The doorway, in the south wall of the church, has been incorrectly rebuilt. See Henry, *Irish Art,* 163; Harbison and O'Brien, *Ancient Ireland,* 120; Tessa Garton, "Dysert O'Dea," in *Corpus of Romanesque Sculpture in Britain and Ireland,* http://www.crsbi.ac.uk (accessed August 3, 2006).

37. The only other examples in Ireland are at Wicklow and on the jambs of the south doorway at Killaloe. See Henry, *Irish Art,* 163; Tessa Garton, "A Romanesque Doorway at Killaloe," *Journal of the British Archaeological Association* 134 (1981): 31–57, at 52.

38. Tessa Garton, "Masks and Monsters: Some Recurring Themes in Irish Romanesque Sculpture," in Hourihane, *From Ireland Coming,* 121–40, at 131, fig. 9.

39. Although some reliquaries, such as the Cross of Cong (see fig. 17), were made for relics acquired from overseas, most were made to enshrine relics connected with Irish saints.

40. Now in the National Museum, Dublin. The crosiers from Dysert O'Dea and Rath Blathmaic were described and illustrated by Thomas Johnson Westropp in "Churches with Round Towers in Northern Clare: Appendix: The Croziers of Rath and Dysert,"

Journal of the Royal Society of Antiquaries of Ireland 24 (1894): 337–40. See also Raghnall Ó Floinn, "Ecclesiastical Objects of the Early Medieval Period from Co. Clare," *The Other Clare* 15 (1991): 12–14.

41. Henry, *Irish Art,* 97, 101, plates 20, 25, 26.

42. This iconography may have been influenced by the famous Volto Santo at Lucca. See Henry, *Irish Art,* 127–28.

43. Peter Harbison, "An Ancient Pilgrimage 'Relic-Road' in North Clare?" *The Other Clare* 24 (2000): 55–59, at 55. A stone forearm was originally suggested by Séan O Murchadha, "Diseart Tola and Its Environs," pt. 2, *The Other Clare* 17 (1993): 36–42.

44. Cynthia Hahn, "The Voices of the Saints: Speaking Reliquaries," *Gesta* 36, no. 1 (1997): 20–31.

45. Henry, *Irish Art,* 103–6, plate 38; J. Huband Smith, "The Shrine of St. Patrick's Hand with Notices of Some Similar Reliquaries," *Ulster Journal of Archaeology* (1854): 207ff. Other arm reliquaries are recorded at Lorrha, Tipperary, and Clonmacnoise (O Floinn, *Irish Shrines,* 16).

46. Harbison, "Ancient Pilgrimage 'Relic-Road.'"

47. Westropp, "Churches with Round Towers," 337–40; Ó Floinn, "Ecclesiastical Objects," 12–14.

48. Peter Harbison, "The Church of Rath Blathmach—a Photo-essay," *The Other Clare* 24 (2000): 23–31.

49. Harbison, "Ancient Pilgrimage 'Relic-Road,'" 55.

50. There is a fourth figure on the right, but the right side of the stone is too damaged to identify any attributes (Harbison, "Ancient Pilgrimage 'Relic-Road,'" 56).

51. Harbison, *High Crosses of Ireland,* 114; Rhoda Cronin, "Late High Crosses in Munster: Tradition and Novelty in Twelfth-Century Irish Art," in *Early Medieval Munster: Archaeology, History and Society,* ed. M. Monk and J. Sheehan, 138–46 (Cork: Cork University Press, 1998).

52. The crosier is preserved in the National Museum, Dublin. The zoomorphic decoration on the knop is similar to that on the Lismore crosier, suggesting a date of c. 1100. See Henry, *Irish Art,* 99–100, plate 19.

53. Preserved in the Museum of Fine Arts, Boston. I would like to thank the Museum of Fine Arts, Boston, for permission to reproduce the Irish reliquary shrine ("Emly Shrine"), described as follows: "Irish, Early medieval, late seventh to early eighth century. Place of manufacture: Ireland. Maker unidentified. Champlevé enamel on bronze over yew wood, gilt bronze moldings, inlay of lead-tin alloy. 9.2 × 4.1 × 10.5 cm (3⅝ × 1⅝ × 4⅛ in.). Museum of Fine Arts, Boston. Theodora Wilbour fund in memory of Charlotte Beebe Wilbour, 52.1396." Photograph copyright (2006) Museum of Fine Arts, Boston. Metropolitan Museum of Art, *Treasures,* 137, cat. no. 31. See also Susan Youngs, ed., *The Work of Angels: Masterpieces of Celtic Metalwork, 6th to 9th Centuries A.D.* (London: British Museum; Austin: University of Texas Press, 1990), 134–40. These reliquaries have commonly been referred to as "house-shaped shrines" but appear to be based on the forms of Late Antique sarcophagi. See Ó Floinn, *Irish Shrines,* 14.

54. Harbison, "Ancient Pilgrimage 'Relic-Road,'" 58.

55. Harbison, *Pilgrimage in Ireland,* 165–67; O'Farrell, "Cross in the Field." O'Farrell (12) suggests that the shrine-shaped tops of the high crosses may have represented the tombs of the founders of the associated churches. It has also been suggested that these are models of buildings rather than of shrines and may represent the heavenly Jerusalem. See Hilary Richardson and John Scarry, *An Introduction to Irish High Crosses* (Cork: Mercier Press, 1990), 25; Tadgh O'Keeffe, *Romanesque Ireland: Architecture and Ideology in the Twelfth Century* (Dublin: Four Courts Press, 2003), 276.

56. O'Farrell, "Cross in the Field," 13. This is shown in a reconstruction drawing (illus. 7).

57. Peter Harbison, "The Double-Armed Cross on the Church Gable at Killinaboy, Co. Clare," *NMAJ* 18 (1976): 3–12.

58. Henry, *Irish Art,* 106–10.

59. There is an inscription on the plinth: *"Pray for Turlough O'Conor, for the . . . of Iarlath by whom was made."* This gives a date of 1126–56.

60. T. D. Kendrick and E. Senior, "St. Manchan's Shrine," *Archaeologia* 86 (1937): 105–18; J. Corkery, *Saint Manchan and His Shrine* (Maynooth: St. Patrick's College, 1970); Henry, *Irish Art,* 110–13. Henry ascribed the shrine to the same workshop as the Cross of Cong and suggested a date of c. 1128–36. It was still in Lemanaghan in the seventeenth century and was moved to the nearby church at Boher, county Offaly, around 1838. The shrine still contains some human bones.

61. Some fragments survive of a similar triangular wooden reliquary, originally covered with copper alloy, from Gwytherin, North Wales. See Nancy Edwards and Tristan Gray Hulse, "A Fragment of a Reliquary Casket from Gwytherin, North Wales," *Antiquaries Journal* 72 (1992): 91–101; "Gwytherin," *Archaeology in Wales* 37 (1997): 87–88.

62. Henry, *Irish Art,* 113. There are nail marks on the wooden panels, suggesting the placement of additional figures.

63. It measures twenty-four inches in length.

64. The arch with biting beast heads is closely related to that on the west portal of the Nuns' Church, Clonmacnoise (dated 1167), and the biting beast heads, like those at Dysert O'Dea, are ultimately of western French origin. See Henry and Zarnecki, "Romanesque Arches," 17–19.

65. They have been compared to the figures with raised heads and flat enameled bodies on the predilla of St. Dominic of Silos in Spain. See Henry, *Irish Art,* 161; Tadgh O'Keeffe, "The Romanesque Portal at Clonfert Cathedral and Its Iconography," in *From the Isles of the North: Early Medieval Art in Britain and Ireland,* ed. Cormac Bourke, 261–69 (Belfast: HMSO, 1995), at 264.

66. Liam De Paor, "Cormac's Chapel: The Beginnings of Irish Romanesque," in *North Munster Studies, Essays in Commemoration of Mons. Michael Moloney,* ed. E. Rynne, 133–45 (Limerick: Thomond Archaeological Society, 1967).

67. O'Keeffe, "Romanesque Portal," 268. In a more recent discussion of the portal, O'Keeffe omits the reference to similarities with a shrine and concludes that the portal is a two-dimensional version of a larger facade structure probably based on western French

models, perhaps representing the heavenly Jerusalem (Tadgh O'Keeffe, *Romanesque Ireland: Architecture and Ideology in the Twelfth Century* [Dublin: Four Courts Press, 2003], 268–78).

68. Jason Ellis, "Conservation at Clonfert: Discoveries Made during Work on the Romanesque Portal," *Archaeology Ireland* 17, no. 4 (Winter 2003): 8–12. I was not aware until after writing this essay that Ellis had come to similar conclusions about the relationship between the doorway and St. Manchan's shrine. He states, "Echoes of both the shape and the decoration of the shrine are very evident in the portal and it is tempting to see this type of object as a source of inspiration for the sculptors" (9).

69. O Floinn, *Irish Shrines,* 7–8, 13–14, citing the examples of Roscrea and Killaloe.

St. Winefride's Well

The Significance and Survival of a Welsh Catholic Shrine from the Early Middle Ages to the Present Day

Robert E. Scully, S.J.

It is a remarkable fact, and one that is unique in the history of Wales and Britain, that from the seventh to the twenty-first centuries it has been possible for pilgrims to travel to a particular shrine—a holy well—to venerate its saint, pray for her intercession, and bathe in her well. This site, St. Winefride's well or Holywell (Tre Ffynnon), is fed by a great flow of water that has its source at the head of the narrow Greenfield Valley in northeastern Wales. The supposedly miraculous reason for its upsurge at the shrine will be discussed below; suffice it to say that the large confluence of water at this site far exceeds that of a typical well. The water rises up through an opening in the crypt of the well chapel and then flows out into a large swimming-pool-sized area. St. Winefride's well is so capacious that many individuals can bathe in its clear but chilly waters, as innumerable pilgrims and visitors have done over the centuries.

History, Historiography, and Hagiography

The true story of the life and sanctity of Winefride (Gwenfrewi) of Wales (Cymru) is deeply shrouded in the mists of legend and hagiography from the early Middle Ages. Aside from the well itself, the physical remains of Winefride's cult comprise three fragments of a finger bone[1] and fragments of a reliquary, which was the focus of her veneration at Gwytherin (Denbighshire). The reliquary from the church at Gwytherin had been lost by the mid–nineteenth century, but two fragments have recently been found: one in 1991 in the Catholic presbytery adjacent to St. Winefride's well; and a second, smaller piece in 1997 in Cheadle, Stoke-on-Trent.[2] Although it is not certain what this reliquary originally contained, based on its diminutive size as well as literary evidence, it was probably not the saint's corporeal remains. More likely it held secondary relics that devotees believed were intimately connected with the saint and her cult.[3] Both the fragments and drawings made in the late seventeenth century support the contention that the reliquary dates to the period from the mid–eighth century to the early ninth century. Triangular in form, like St. Manchan's shrine (see

Garton's essay in this volume, fig. 20a, p. 194), it was either manufactured in or imported into Wales and was probably influenced by Anglo-Saxon or Irish models.[4] Catherine Hamaker considers it to be "the oldest surviving physical evidence of a Welsh saint's formal cult."[5]

Written evidence describes accounts of struggles for control of Holywell by the monasteries at Basingwerk (Flintshire) and Chester (Cheshire), as well as Winefride's shrine at Shrewsbury. The two earliest *Lives* of St. Winefride date from the twelfth century.[6] Robert Pennant (d. 1168), prior of the Benedictine Abbey of Saints Peter and Paul in Shrewsbury, wrote *The Life and Translation of St. Winefride* (hereafter "Robert's *Life*") c. 1140.[7] Another account from the same period, incorrectly ascribed to St. Elerius, is called *The Anonymous Life of St. Winefride.* Traditionally known as the *Vita Prima,* it is much the shorter of the two, being only about one-sixth the length of Prior Robert's *Life.*[8] Based on an exhaustive study, Fiona Winward has concluded that the anonymous author was probably a monk of Basingwerk Abbey and, like Robert of Shrewsbury, a twelfth-century Norman. Winward argues, moreover, that although the dating of the anonymous account is still uncertain, its primacy should no longer be taken for granted. It also seems clear that both authors, to varied extents, recast their saint in accordance with contemporary hagiographical and historical concerns. Although the two *Lives* agree on most major points, there are a few differences, such as the story of Winefride's supposed journey to Rome, which appears only in the anonymous *Life* and is rather doubtful. Still, considering the many parallels between the two accounts, they may well have drawn on a common Cambro-Latin written source, quite possibly a subsequently lost *Life* of St. Beuno, in which Winefride would have been a subsidiary figure.[9]

Beuno played a transformative role in the life of Winefride and, at least in the early traditions of North Wales, was almost certainly the more famous of the two saints. T. Charles-Edwards powerfully sums up Beuno's stature: "Monk, and master of monks, patriot, challenger of tyrants, a principal founding father of his nation, he is one of the greatest of the saints of Wales."[10] How and why Winefride, over time, surpassed her beloved mentor in fame are among the many mysteries related to her cult, but almost assuredly a significant part of the answer lies in the growing reputation of Winefride's well.

The "Historical" Winefride and the Origins of Her Cult

Assuming, as we have good reason to do, that Winefride's cult is based on an actual person, rather than being a figment of the collective medieval Welsh imagination, it is still an almost insurmountable problem to try to separate fact from fiction in order to re-create the historical Winefride and the origins of her well and cult. In his prologue, Robert of Shrewsbury tries to assure the reader as to the veracity of his *Life* of the saint: "I assembled it partly through documents in the churches of the country in which she is known to have lived, and partly I learned it from the reports of certain priests whom venerable antiquity commended and whose words their habit of religious life compelled us to trust."[11] Yet, despite the omission of some supposedly untrustworthy stories, Robert's account includes many descriptions that appear to be hopelessly hagiographical rather than historical.[12] With this in mind, what is the portrait that emerges from the two *Lives*?

Winefride was the daughter of a local magnate named Teuyth in North Wales in the seventh century. At first the father and then even more profoundly the daughter came under the benevolent influence of Beuno, a monk of considerable character and holiness and, purportedly, Winefride's uncle. Winefride decided to dedicate herself wholly—body and soul—to God. Her "martyrdom" resulted when a local chieftain, Caradoc, found her home alone one day and tried to seduce her. By stealth she fled from the house and ran to the nearby church. Caradoc, enraged by Winefride's refusal, caught her near the church door and cut off her head. Beuno emerged from the church, placed Winefride's head back on her body, and, praying over her, brought her back to life. Equally miraculous was the origin of the famous well: "As soon as the head of the maiden fell to the ground, a most clear spring burst forth in that very spot and spread itself copiously, offering health to many sick people through the merits of the holy maiden, which even today has not ceased to flow."[13]

Caradoc was smitten by the words of Beuno and sank into the earth.[14] As for Winefride, for the remainder of her days a slender white scar encircled her neck as a witness to her martyrdom and the miracle of her resurrection. Another supposed prodigy and proof of Winefride's sacrifice was that many of the stones in the stream "are stained as if by [her] congealed blood, nor are they wiped clean by the mold of time nor by the constant washing of the water flowing past."[15] Thus, what might be explained geologically as mineral deposits was interpreted as yet another sign of divine favor connected with Winefride and her well. This would be manifested most clearly through healings. As Beuno promised Winefride, "because your memory will be renowned in this world, and as much as you will have merit with God, many people will bear witness that they have obtained cures for their infirmities through you."[16]

The story of a well of a beheaded saint who is sometimes restored to life is not unique to Winefride. It is something of a commonplace in Celtic hagiography and appears in the lives of several saints, for example, St. Lludd of Brecknock.[17]

In fact, several aspects of the life and legend of St. Winefride are consistent with early medieval Welsh notions of sanctity, particularly female sanctity. In that context, a central aspect of a claim to holiness was chastity, especially for a woman. In Winefride's case, her steadfast determination to retain her chastity resulted in her decapitation and the springing up of a well. This is typical of pre-Christian Celtic beliefs, which included a reverence for the human head, and resulted in an association of decapitated saints with wells. This linked a saint with a specific locale and forged a special bond of sanctity and place. At the same time, the whole landscape through which the saint moved was treated as sacred; it usually contained several foci of veneration for pilgrims, which culminated at the central site of the cult, such as a holy well.[18] Thus, many of the motifs of Winefride's holiness place her squarely within the context of local sanctity in sixth- and seventh-century Wales. The major difference was that she went on to achieve not just local but also national and even international fame and drawing power.

As we have seen, oral legends of Winefride's life were not written down until the twelfth century, some five hundred years after her death, and it is not surprising that they were embellished with the passage of time. It is believed that Winefride became a nun and eventually joined a community at Gwytherin, some nine miles from Holywell. Due to her sanctity and rank, she became the next abbess. It was there that Winefride died, c. 650, and she was buried in the local churchyard.[19]

Her fame continued to spread, and her cult had clearly come into its own by the early twelfth century, by which time Norman influences began to have an impact on various Welsh traditions. Of particular relevance here is the fact that corporeal remains were not held to be an important part of saints' cults in early medieval Wales, any more than in Brittany or Ireland (see Garton's essay in this volume, p. 174). In Wales, the translation of remains was rare due to a native reluctance to disturb a saint's body. Perhaps it was believed that if the corpus was not central to the cult, there was little justification in violating the original burial site. Under the impact of the Normans, however, things began to change. The latter placed great stress on a saint's corporeal remains, and Wales was seen as a land blessed with the bodies of many saints, including saints whose cults could bring both spiritual prestige and financial assistance to new monastic communities.[20]

One such community was the Benedictine Abbey of Saints Peter and Paul at Shrewsbury, which was founded in 1083. According to Prior Robert, the monks searched for such a patron, especially in Wales, for about fifty years; for several years they specifically attempted to acquire St. Winefride's relics. When one of their seriously ill members was restored to health, as they believed, through Winefride's intercession, the monks increased their efforts, which included a visit to the bishop of Bangor. Then in 1137–38 Robert went to Gwytherin and arranged for the transfer of the saint's body to the church of St. Giles in Shrewsbury. Desiring an even closer association with the cult of St. Winefride, probably for both spiritual and financial reasons, in 1138 the monks transferred her relics with much ceremony to their own abbey church. In the fourteenth century, when

Winefride's cult had achieved even greater renown, a new shrine was constructed to display her relics, and the (pilfered) relics of Winefride's mentor, St. Beuno, were placed nearby.[21]

In terms of their relationship, Beuno began as the senior spiritual partner (so to speak), and yet Winefride clearly grew in stature over time. This is hinted at in the anonymous *Life,* which says concerning Beuno's departure from Winefride, "after a mutual blessing, they separated."[22] Traditionally, of course, it would have been Beuno, as a priest, who would have given a blessing to Winefride, but the mention of a "mutual blessing" suggests something of a spiritual parity.[23] Perhaps this is not the sort of thing a Benedictine prior would approve of, and for this reason the passage does not appear in Robert's *Life.* Then again, the writer(s) of the anonymous *Life* may have wanted to emphasize Winefride's status in this way.

It is not certain why Winefride's cult eventually surpassed that of Beuno's in fame, but it appears to have done so, at least by the later Middle Ages. Nor is it certain why Winefride's well came to be seen as far more efficacious for the devout and the desperate than her shrine at Shrewsbury. According to Prior Robert of the shrine abbey, although "divine power works wondrously in both places," more miracles occurred at the well than at the shrine. "I think this has happened for this reason, that [St. Winefride] always held that place [Holywell] as her own special one in which the beginnings of her monastic life first shone forth and she was initiated into the divine mysteries, and in which the signs of her martyrdom remain fresh for all time."[24]

In any event, the spring located at the spot where Winefride was supposedly beheaded became a major object of veneration and pilgrimage, initially in Wales but eventually also from many other parts of Britain. Of course, the notion of and devotion to a "holy well" was not unique to St. Winefride. In fact, holy wells have been important loci of beliefs and rituals in many cultures.[25] There are, for example, more than seven thousand sacred springs and wells located throughout the British Isles; at the present time they are most heavily concentrated in traditionally Celtic areas, especially Ireland and Wales. There is a great deal of speculation as to the origin of devotion at these sites. In some locales it may go back to pre-Christian times and various pagan rituals, which were later adapted and assimilated into Christian worship.[26] The Druids, for example, had exerted their power and performed many of their sacred rituals at "natural" sites, such as sacred stands of trees and holy wells, which served as settings for their cultic functions.[27] As Keith Thomas argues, in a classic work, the "ancient worship of wells, trees and stones was not so much abolished as modified, by turning pagan sites into Christian ones and associating them with a saint rather than a heathen divinity."[28]

In Wales literally hundreds of wells became places of devotion, dedicated to various saints and other sacred associations, and they were connected with various purposes—such as holy wells, healing wells, and wishing wells—that not infrequently overlapped. For example, about 370 wells that did not have saints' names were, nevertheless, primarily reputed to be healing wells. An additional 437 wells bore the names of saints, and nearly all of these were also said to have healing powers. With regard to patronage, many wells were dedicated to non-Celtic saints or other objects of veneration, including approximately 76 wells dedicated to Our Lady, 17 to St. Peter, and 10 to the Holy Trinity.[29]

By way of contrast, only one well and chapel—Holywell—was dedicated to St. Winefride. Francis Jones, one of the leading scholars on Welsh holy wells, comments on this paradox. As he notes, Holywell was "perhaps the most famous well-shrine in medieval Britain. The prestige of St. Winefride was very high, yet it is a remarkable fact that no other single well or church in Wales was dedicated to her."[30] Perhaps the fact that Holywell was linked with two great saints—primarily St. Winefride but also St. Beuno—made this a uniquely holy site.

St. Winefride's Well in the Middle Ages

The origins of pilgrimages to St. Winefride's well, like so much else in early medieval history, are obscure, but Holywell clearly had become an important spiritual destination by the twelfth century. It is possible, of course, that the gradual emergence of writings concerning pilgrimages from that period onward may be a manifestation of the "renaissance" of the twelfth century and somewhat greater degrees of literacy, at least among the upper classes, rather than a lack of pilgrimages in the preceding centuries. In any event, we have a report that in 1115 an ardent pilgrim, Earl Richard of Chester, desired "to visit Saint Winefride" and, therefore, went "devoutly to Holywell in pilgrimage for his great merit and [spiritual] advantage."[31]

Later in that century Holywell received a far more important visitor, a royal pilgrim: Richard I. Although the Lionheart spent less than a year of his ten-year reign (1189–99) in England, he went on a pilgrimage to St. Winefride's well in 1189, a precursor of sorts to his military "pilgrimage" the following year, namely, the Third Crusade.[32] This raises an intriguing and complex question: was St. Winefride's fame so great that it attracted such royal attention and patronage, or was it the visits of several royal supplicants over the centuries that brought fame to an otherwise relatively obscure local saint? In all likelihood, these two factors interacted and proved to be mutually beneficial to the saint and the monarchy. Yet, although devotion to St. Winefride spread after this first royal pilgrimage to Holywell, it appears to have been concentrated primarily in North Wales and its marches, and in parts of South Wales, at least until the late fourteenth century.

With regard to the physical and spiritual maintenance of Holywell, from 1240 until 1537, when they were engulfed by the dissolution of the monasteries, the Cistercian monks of Basingwerk Abbey served as the primary caretakers of the well and church.[33]

The fame of St. Winefride and her well gained major impetus in England in 1398 when Roger Walden, the archbishop of Canterbury (1397–99), mandated that her feast should be observed throughout his ecclesiastical province.[34] Although it is not entirely clear why the primate of England and Wales took such a step at that point, his mandate was reaffirmed and expanded by one of his successors, Henry Chichele (1414–43). The latter had served as a canon in Wales and later as bishop of St. David's, which was located in South Wales and was the largest of the four Welsh dioceses. Chichele was, therefore, sympathetic to Welsh sensibilities. As archbishop, he ordered that the feasts of three Welsh saints—David, Chad, and Winefride—should be solemnly observed throughout the province of Canterbury.[35] According to the minutes of the convocation of January 4, 1416, "To these things we decree by the authority of the said provincial council and we also appoint through these letters that the feasts of Saints David and Chad, bishops, and Winefride, virgin, henceforth are to be celebrated at all future times throughout our province at their proper times . . . with rule of choir and with nine readings."[36]

This elevation of Winefride (along with her two Welsh counterparts) in the liturgical calendar was part of the boom of her cult, which appears to have reached its zenith in the fifteenth and early sixteenth centuries. A brief *Life of St. Winefride* was published in 1401,[37] and in the ensuing century at least two kings visited Holywell, during a period in which the medieval zeal to go on pilgrimage was most widespread.[38] This manifestation of religious fervor sometimes combined with personal, political, and other factors as part of the complex mixture of motivations that often affect human psychology and actions, including those of kings.

We can see this in particular in the life and reign of King Henry V (1413–22), probably England's most famous warrior king. Although his hankering for both religious pilgrimages and military campaigns might seem to be a paradox to the modern mind, it almost certainly was not viewed as such by Henry or, for that matter, most of his contemporaries. During a reign that is most remembered for the conquest of large areas of France, Henry went on pilgrimages and made numerous visits to shrines, including the two most famous ones in England, those of St. Thomas Becket at Canterbury and Our Lady of Walsingham. As for St. Winefride, Henry may have visited her holy well in his youth as Prince of Wales, during a period in which he helped to suppress a protracted Welsh rebellion. It is certain, however, that he made a dramatic visit to Holywell in 1416, initially riding some 160 miles from London to Winefride's shrine at Shrewsbury.[39] From there, according to the chronicler Adam of Usk, the king "with great reverence went on foot in pilgrimage from Shrewsbury to St. Winefride's Well in North Wales."[40] The king evidently went both to give thanks for his great victory at Agincourt the previous year and to pray for the saint's continued intercession for his second, upcoming campaign in France in 1417.[41]

It is not certain why Henry had such a special devotion to this seventh-century Welsh saint, or at least wished to advertise his patronage of her in so public a manner. One of the king's biographers, Harold Hutchison, maintains that this was "an astonishing example of a religious devotion which was now characteristic of this soldier king."[42] Others suggest more secular motivations for the king's visit to Holywell. M. J. C. Lowry, for example, while not denying the sincerity of Henry's (much less other pilgrims') religious convictions, suggests that this ostentatious royal visit was part of a strategy of rendering the Welsh more benevolent and, therefore, more responsive to his economic and military needs. In other words, "Winifred offered a means of wooing Celtic sensibilities,"[43] and Henry, like several subsequent rulers, viewed patronage of Holywell as working to the benefit of both God and man.[44] Although Lowry perhaps overstates the case, Henry V was not atypical among English monarchs in believing that spiritual and secular objectives could be mutually reinforcing. In fact, according to Jeremy Catto, Henry hoped, by various means, "to place the monarchy at the spiritual center" of English and Welsh life.[45]

King Edward IV (1461–83) is an especially intriguing example of a monarch whose life was a blend of seemingly disparate elements. Despite his various amorous activities, he went on several pilgrimages during his reign, including ones to Bury St. Edmunds and Walsingham. Edward also made a pilgrimage to St. Winefride's well, most likely in the summer of 1473. This was probably undertaken from the nearby Yorkist stronghold of Shrewsbury and may have been done both to give thanks and to shore up support for the Yorkist cause. According to the bard Tudur Aled, the king, after showing veneration, placed some soil from the shrine on his crown. Through this "calculated" visit and gesture, the king humbly invoked the saint's spiritual intercession and, in turn, offered his royal patronage.[46] The last of the Yorkist kings, Richard III (1483–85), although he did not visit Holywell, gave an annuity of ten marks to the abbot of Basingwerk for the "yearly sustenance and salary of a priest at the Chapel of St. Winefride."[47]

Holywell's Changing Fortunes under the Tudors

The saint's fame and earthly fortunes gained a major boost with the accession to the throne of Henry VII (1485–1509), the first Welsh king of England and the founder of the Tudor dynasty. Henry had a statue of St. Winefride made for his new chapel in Westminster Abbey, especially famous for its magnificent fan-vaulted ceiling. Far more significant for the Welsh saint's cult was the commencement of desperately needed reconstructive work at Holywell, which had, materially at least, fallen on hard times.[48] As far back as 1427 Pope Martin V (1417–31), whose election to the papacy ended the great western schism, had offered indulgences for the benefit of those who "should visit and give alms to the Chapel of St. Winefride called Holywell in the diocese of St. Asaph, the buildings of which are now collapsed."[49] Subsequently, at the beginning of the sixteenth century, Henry VII's mother, Lady Margaret Beaufort, assisted by some members of the Welsh nobility, paid for the construction of an elaborate well chapel, which was built directly over the well. It is considered an impressive example of late perpendicular Gothic architecture and is probably the finest well chapel ever built in Wales or anywhere in Britain.[50]

Just as Henry VII and the Tudors consciously strengthened their ties to Wales by associating themselves with and patronizing one of its greatest saints, some of their subjects attempted to ingratiate themselves with the Tudors by promoting the cult and well of St. Winefride. Probably the most famous example was the printer and publisher William Caxton (c. 1420–91), who issued a *Life of St. Winefride* early in Henry's reign. Thus, a wide range of people, for a variety of motives, continued to publicly promote Winefride's life and the benefits of her holy well in early Tudor England and Wales.[51]

The Cistercian monks of Basingwerk continued to care for the shrine and the new chapel. They celebrated Mass there and preached to large crowds of pilgrims, especially on St. Winefride's Day, November 3. But their almost three centuries of service at the shrine came to a rather sudden end with the dissolution of the monasteries and the widespread destruction of shrines in the 1530s under Henry VIII (1509–47) and his vicegerent, Thomas Cromwell. Holywell, however, continued to function. It probably helped that it was somewhat inaccessible and yet, at the same time, perhaps too notable for destruction; such a step might have caused a backlash, especially in Wales. Moreover, the continuous donations of pilgrims were a tempting prize for the Henrician regime. In fact, the income from offerings of at least ten pounds a year, if not a great deal more, made St. Winefride's well by far the most lucrative Welsh pilgrimage site in the early sixteenth century.[52]

Some of the local ex-monks, however, were at least as clever and determined as the royal agents and tried to keep the faithful's gifts for the shrine. As an example, it was reported that one year on St. Winefride's Day they "brought boxes into the Chapel crying 'such money as you offer into the common stock shall never be a remedy for your souls for there stands one of the King's servants who will soon take it forth.' And, inviting them to put their oblations in their boxes," they received the pilgrims' offerings of money, as well as an ox.[53]

There is little further evidence about Holywell until the reign of Mary (1553–58), who tried to reverse the "reforming" religious policies inaugurated during the reigns of her father and, even more so, her brother, Edward VI (1547–53), by officially restoring Catholicism and ties to the papacy. Thomas Goldwell, who had served under Cardinal Pole on the Continent, was appointed bishop of St. Asaph in Wales. He obtained a renewal of papal indulgences for pilgrims, and this encouraged a resurgence of pilgrimages to St. Winefride's well.[54] This resurgence may also have been assisted by the spread of reports of the healing of a crippled teenager named Harry, who, in "memory of this so miraculous cure," was thereafter called Harry St. Winefride.[55]

Although the official restoration of Catholicism in England and Wales did not long survive the death of Queen Mary, Holywell evidently continued to function relatively unencumbered in the early years of the Elizabethan regime (1558–1603). During a period of transition, many traditional religious practices continued under a de facto governmental policy of "benign" neglect, especially in more remote areas of the kingdom such as Wales.

Still, as the Elizabethan religious settlement began to take hold through the advantages of time and resources that the government had on its side, there was increasingly less tolerance, especially among the "godly," for beliefs and practices that smacked of "popery." Thus, in 1567 the bishop of Bangor decried what he perceived to be manifestations of ignorance and superstition in Wales: "I have found since I came to this country images and altars standing in churches undefaced, lewd and indecent vigils and watches observed, much pilgrimage going, many candles set up to the honor of saints, some relics yet carried about," and myriad other "abuses."[56] It is not clear what steps the distressed bishop took to stamp out these "abuses," but a common pattern was that pressure from above merely drove traditional religious beliefs and practices underground, rather than eradicating them.

In spite of her personal inclination for liturgical ritual (see Beasley's essay in this volume, p. 153), by the middle years of her reign, Queen Elizabeth and her government were increasingly in agreement that greater efforts were needed to put an end to the vestiges of Catholicism, which refused to die a natural death, especially at places such as Holywell. Therefore, on June 13, 1579, the queen instructed the Council of the Marches "To discover all Papist activities and recommend measures for suppressing them . . . to pay particular attention to the pilgrimages to St. Winefride's Well and in view of the claim that the water is medicinal to appoint two men to test its properties; if not medicinal the Well should be destroyed."[57] Once again, it is not certain what action, if any, the royal servants took, but Holywell survived relatively unscathed and continued to welcome large numbers of pilgrims. In fact, the well of St. Winefride continued to be "one of the most magnetic foci of Catholic worshippers anywhere"[58] in North Wales, if not over a far greater area.

Shortly after the start of their mission to England and Wales in 1580, the Jesuits developed their own long and often fruitful connection to Holywell, as both pilgrims and curators. The indefatigable Jesuit missionary John Gerard wrote one of the more extensive accounts of the spiritual and physical benefits awaiting pilgrims "to St. Winefride's well, a famous shrine and, as it were, a standing miracle." With regard to St. Winefride, he wrote that she "was a saintly and very beautiful girl in North Wales, and her faith and love of chastity made her more beautiful still."[59] He went on to describe his own experiences at the shrine in 1593:

> Once I was there on the 3rd of November, St. Winefride's feast, and saw the change that takes place in the well that day. (The water rises a good foot above its ordinary level, and turns red as it rises, but the next day it is clearer than ever.) I myself watched the water moving and turning a reddish color, water (mind you) that on any other day is so remarkably clear that you can pick out a pin lying on the bottom. It was winter. . . . But frost or no frost, I went down into the well like a good pilgrim. For a quarter of an hour I lay down in the water and prayed. When I came out my shirt was dripping. But I kept it on and I pulled all my clothes over it, and I was none the worse for my bath.
>
> These are true facts. Also, there are frequently great and manifest miracles at the well. For instance, there is the story of the Protestant visitor who was watching some Catholics bathe and stood mocking their devotion. "What are they up to, washing here in the water? I'll show them. I'll clean my boots in it." So in he jumped, boots, sword and all. Scarcely had he touched the water than he felt its supernatural powers which he had refused to believe in. Then and there he was struck with paralysis. . . . For several years afterwards he was wheeled around in a pushcart like a cripple.
>
> Thus he was punished, and others confirmed in their belief.
>
> I have myself spoken to a number of people who saw the lame man and heard the story both from his own lips and from men who knew him. It was they who told me the sequel: how the man repented and recovered the use of his limbs in the very well where he had been struck down. This is just one of many stories of the kind.[60]

This account, which had evidently circulated widely, referred to William Shone (Owen) of Denbighshire, who in 1574 had mockingly jumped into the well and supposedly suffered major paralysis. After some time living as a cripple, others convinced him to repent and return to the site where he was struck down. At the well he prayed and also asked others "to intercede for him to God and St. Winefride for pardon and recovery of his health."[61] He soon recovered a good deal of his former strength, became a Roman Catholic, and lived in his newfound faith until his death some seven years later.

Gerard's description of the miraculous change in the level and color of the well water on the saint's feast day is intriguing, but this phenomenon is not highlighted in most other reports on the well, which tend to focus primarily on the healings of individuals. In that vein, Gerard goes on to record the remarkable experiences of his friend and fellow Jesuit Edward Oldcorne, who had developed anemia and cancer of the tongue. Oldcorne set out on a pilgrimage to the shrine in 1601 and underwent a healing that involved one of the stone relics from the well:

> Father Oldcorne had his heart set on visiting the holy well; but St. Winefride forestalled him. On his way he stopped at the dwelling of two maiden sisters. They were poor people, but rich in other ways, for they feared God, living and serving him together, and keeping in their house a priest whom they looked up to as their father. This good priest had taken from the stream one of those stones sprinkled with [the blood of St. Winefride]. At the time of Mass he used to place it on the altar with the other relics. When Father Oldcorne noticed it he took it in his hands and kissed it very reverently. Then going aside by himself, he went down on his knees and began to lick the stone and hold part of it to his mouth. He prayed silently all the time. After an hour he got up: all his pain was gone and the cancer cured. But he finished his pilgrimage to the well—not to beg a cure from St. Winefride, but to make his thanksgiving for it. While he was there he recovered also from that anemia which was thought to be the cause of his cancer, and he came back stronger and healthier than he had been for many years.
>
> I have told the story in the words that Father Oldcorne told it to me. The priest, in whose house Father Oldcorne found the stone, confirmed the facts when I met him at St. Omers. He told me, too, of the wonderful things that had occurred after Father Oldcorne's death.[62]

While many of these claims might be met nowadays with sizable doses of skepticism, Elizabeth's instructions for investigating the well, cited above, indicate that many contemporaries were willing to accept the "fact" of a cure while differing on their explanations of its causation. As a result, St. Winefride's well continued to attract many pilgrims seeking cures of their physical and/or spiritual maladies, and this often involved bathing at the shrine and invoking the intercession of the saint. To dissuade any pilgrims' concerns that the temperature or substance of the water might be harmful, Gerard was encouraging and forthright:

"The water from the spring is extremely cold, but no one ever came to any harm by drinking it or bathing in it. I took several gulps of it myself on an empty stomach and nothing happened to me."[63]

According to a report in 1586, a sick man was cured at the well after he had repented of his sins, prayed for forgiveness, and then bathed in its waters. Another visitor washed three times in the well and completed his ritual by praying in the church. Yet another pilgrim, Sir George Peckham, who was a very sick man, had himself immersed in the healing waters of the well. While there he prayed the "Our Father" and invoked the intercession of St. Winefride.[64] In Peckham's case it is not clear whether or not he was physically cured of his malady. It is important to note, however, that some of the accounts of supplicants at Holywell were probably recorded to convey the message that although pilgrims might not receive physical cures, they would receive spiritual benefits. This, implicitly, was a more important reason to visit this sacred stream: to be spiritually fortified for the remainder of one's lifelong pilgrimage, the journey of faith. This outlook was probably a manifestation of post-Tridentine Catholic spirituality, which was beginning to take hold in many areas by the late sixteenth century.

Transformations during the Stuart Era

A large group of pilgrims to St. Winefride's well in 1605 included the following: Henry Garnet, the Jesuit superior in England and Wales; Nicholas Owen, the Jesuit brother who constructed many of the ingenious priest hiding holes of the period; several other Jesuits; and many laypeople. As they made their way through the midlands toward North Wales, they picked up additional spiritual travelers, including men and women, gentry and commoners. As a result, by "the time Holywell was reached the pilgrimage numbered thirty, not counting the servants. On the last stages the ladies walked barefoot to the shrine."[65] It is not clear whether the men also walked barefoot, either for some or all of the journey.

This peaceful pilgrimage scene is somewhat misleading, suggesting as it does the absence of religious persecution during the early years of the reign of James VI and I (1603–25), the first monarch to unite the crowns, if not the kingdoms, of "Great Britain." Hopes that this son of the Catholic Mary Queen of Scots would allow official toleration of Catholicism were shattered only a few months after this large pilgrimage to Holywell by the devastating "explosion" of the Gunpowder Plot. It not only ensnared Garnet, Owen, Oldcorne, and many others, often unjustly, in 1605–6, but also permanently impaired the Catholic cause.[66]

The dedicated but harried ministrations of a Welsh missionary priest, Edward Hughes—who concentrated his efforts in his native diocese of St. Asaph—provide a good illustration of the tense realities facing the Catholic clergy and laity. At one point he was arrested, according to the Elizabethan spymaster Richard

Topcliffe, for doing "much mischief in Wales" over a period of many years. Hughes was exiled in 1603, but he tenaciously returned the same year and continued his itinerant ministry.[67] Among the many people he assisted were members of the Edwards family of Denbighshire, including a period as their "Chief Sayer of Mass."[68] This recusant family did much to uphold Catholicism in North Wales, in part through their devotion to St. Winefride and her well. Especially devout was Anne Edwards, who "was accustomed to travel by night to Holywell to hear Mass on every feast of St. Winefride."[69]

John Bennet (c. 1550–1625) provides a particularly telling example of the importance of and devotion to St. Winefride's well. His ministry as a seminary priest, and later as a Jesuit, spanned much of the Elizabethan and Jacobean period. He worked in various areas but expended most of his efforts in Wales, especially at Holywell in his native Flintshire. A leading historian of the Jesuit mission, Henry Foley, has called Bennet "the Apostle of North Wales in the times of Queen Elizabeth and James I," due to the longevity and intensity of his devoted service.[70] In 1582 he was captured, and his trial evidently took place at Holywell, in the chapel built over the well. It is not clear whether he escaped condemnation or was condemned and later spared. In any event, he suffered imprisonment and torture at Ludlow Castle and was exiled in 1585. During this period on the Continent, he entered the Society of Jesus at Verdun (in 1586). He was granted permission to return to the English-Welsh mission in 1590 and spent the next thirty-five years working in Wales, especially at Holywell, using a variety of aliases.[71] Christopher David is undoubtedly correct in his assessment of how Bennet survived for so long on so dangerous a mission: "Nothing other than his popularity with the people can have saved him from betrayal and death."[72]

It is probably also true that St. Winefride's well was saved from destruction due to *its* popularity with the people. Thus, in spite of intermittent directives from the government, efforts to ban pilgrimages and other religious activities at Holywell were "sporadic and curiously half-hearted" throughout most of the Elizabethan and Stuart periods.[73] Clearly, large numbers of people, including many non-Catholics, found the well to be a source of physical and/or spiritual solace and rejuvenation. Sion Dafydd Rhys, a Welsh grammarian and physician, for example, promoted the well's "medicinal" benefits and advised some of his patients, regardless of their religion, to go there and bathe in its healing waters.[74]

The purported medicinal benefits of Winefride's well—alongside what many believed to be its even greater spiritual benefits—probably provide part of the explanation as to why it continued to thrive despite a great deal of talk and some sporadic action by governmental and ecclesiastical authorities to shut it down. As we have seen, many other holy wells were also believed to be healing wells, that is, to have natural healing properties. Therefore, the authorities and various skeptics could maintain (or at least rationalize) that much of the activity at Holywell was not superstitious papist nonsense but, rather, the legitimate use of a healing well or spring, similar to the one at Bath in Somerset, famous at least since Roman times for its supposed medicinal effects. Believers could counter such arguments with examples of individuals who attempted the "cure" at Bath to no avail but were later healed of their infirmities after they prayed and bathed at Holywell.[75]

In fact, throughout the early modern period, "St. Winefride's remained queen among Welsh wells. Visited by Catholic and Protestant alike, both in search of health, the former alone carried out the ritual with any appreciation of the religious association."[76] There are numerous accounts of a wide array of healings at the well during the seventeenth century, in particular.[77] All the while, the Stuart regime, as well as various segments of the Protestant population, continued their schizophrenic relationship with St. Winefride and her well, with many arguing that it should be shut down but taking relatively little action to do so.

After premature reports of success in suppressing pilgrimages to the well in 1617, a report from 1624 expressed dismay at Winefride's continuing fame: "Every year about midsummer many superstitious Papists of Lancashire and other more remote places go in pilgrimage. . . . [Let] me add that they were so bold about midsummer last year that they intruded themselves several times into the Church or public chapel at Holywell and there said Mass without contradiction."[78] The following year the bishop of Bangor informed the House of Lords: "There is a great concourse of people to St. Winefride's Well. In an old chapel near, a public Mass is said continually."[79]

The cycle of attempted suppression by the authorities and renewed determination by the faithful continued. The mayor of Poole tried to justify his efforts at suppression to the Privy Council in 1626: "I have taken the best course I could for restraint of the resort of persons ill-affected in religion to St. Winefride's Well in Flintshire, both by binding the lodgers of strangers there to discover the names of their guests to the next Justices of the peace, and by a watch there kept."[80] Yet, only a few years later, on St. Winefride's Day in 1629, large crowds of pilgrims descended on her well, including "knights, ladies, gentlemen and gentlewomen of divers countries to the number of fourteen or fifteen hundred; and the general estimation about a hundred and fifty or more priests, the most of them well known what they were."[81]

The Privy Council tried to enforce its will once again in the mid-1630s and ordered Sir John Bridgeman, the chief justice of Chester, to stop all pilgrimages to Holywell. In 1637 Bridgeman went there himself and ordered the churchwardens to "take away the iron posts around the fountain . . . and disfigure the image of the Saint," which, quite remarkably, was still there.[82] Winefride's staying power was undoubtedly buoyed by reports of the powerful effects that many visitors to her well, both devotees and detractors, experienced. As a dramatic example of the latter, "When a man was found dead at the well in 1630 after having made scoffing remarks about its supposed powers a local jury brought in a verdict of death by divine judgment."[83] In any event, in 1642 the Jesuits tried, though unsuccessfully, to build a large house for pilgrims, who continued to risk varying degrees of religious persecution for the perceived benefits of a visit to Holywell.[84] Even stronger winds of change, however, were soon to sweep across the country. These were the manifestation and outcome of the political and religious struggles between those who supported and those who opposed the "divine right" policies of Charles I (1625–49).

Many Catholic (and Laudian) religious sites and images were decimated by waves of iconoclasm during the resulting civil wars and interregnum of the 1640s and 1650s, and this time Holywell did not escape its enemies' malevolence. Both the chapel and the well crypt were heavily damaged, and the statue of St. Winefride was finally destroyed. There was also a human toll due to heightened persecution. Despite greater circumspection, Catholics—and priests in particular—were probably more vulnerable than they had been since the tragic days of the Gunpowder Plot. One victim was Humphrey Evans, a Jesuit ministering at Holywell, who was imprisoned and severely beaten in 1656.[85]

The situation improved somewhat during the early to middle years of the restoration under Charles II (1660–85). The Jesuits played a major role in maintaining the shrine and ministering to the faithful who continued to come in spite of danger or widespread spiritual indifference. In fact, Holywell became a center for Jesuit missionary activity over a wide area. In 1667 the Jesuits formed the North Wales District, which included all the northern shires of Wales as well as Shropshire. It was also known as the Residence of St. Winefride because it was under her patronage. This mission included several chaplaincies, especially at Holywell, where the Star Inn became the official residence of the Jesuits. In addition, some of the fathers, numbering an average of about six each year, went on periodical missionary circuits through the district.[86]

The importance of Holywell is highlighted by the fact that the secular clergy also had a residence there, at the Cross Keys Inn. Similar to that of the Jesuits, the inn served as both an apostolic center and a base for the priests' "long and arduous circuits amongst the remote towns and villages in North Wales."[87] Through it all, St. Winefride's well maintained its reputation as a source of healing. In 1674 many people attested to the healing of a crippled youth from Cardiganshire, who, having made the ninety-mile journey to Holywell "full of the hope" of a cure, recovered "his former health and strength."[88] The religious climate, however, deteriorated once again for Catholics, and especially for Jesuits, during the manufactured Popish Plot of Titus Oates in 1678–79, which sent some innocent people to their deaths.[89]

There was a brief respite for the "old faith" with the accession of a Catholic monarch, James II, in 1685. With his Protestant first wife, Anne Hyde, James had two daughters who were brought up as Protestants. He strongly desired, however, to have an heir who was both male and Catholic. After Anne's death, James married the Catholic Mary of Modena, but she suffered a series of miscarriages. To assist in improving her poor state of health, Mary had gone to Bath and taken the waters there. On a journey through parts of his kingdom in 1686, James visited St. Winefride's well. There is conflicting evidence as to Mary's travels, with one account suggesting that the queen returned to Bath, while another indicates that she accompanied the king on his journey into Wales. According to the latter, on August 29, 1686, the royal pilgrims arrived at Holywell "to crave the prayers of Winefride that they might be blessed with a son. The king presented the chapel with part of a dress worn by Mary Queen of Scots at her execution, and the queen gave 30 pounds towards the chapel fabric."[90]

If the visit caused a local sensation, the news of the birth of the prince in June 1688 had far wider repercussions. According to some reports, "When the Prince of Wales was born it was thought St. Winefride's prayers had done it."[91] Whether the royal birth came about due to the queen's visit to Bath, the king's (and queen's?) prayers at Holywell, or serendipity is ultimately unanswerable. There is little doubt, however, as to the convictions of the royals. The queen promoted plans for the repair of the well chapel, and she favored the Jesuits to minister there. Some restoration work at the well was begun, but hopes for a Catholic revival were swept away in the tidal wave of the Glorious Revolution of 1688–89, which sent James and Mary into exile and established William and Mary on the throne as cosovereigns of a Protestant monarchy that became entrenched in law as well as in popular will.[92]

Nonetheless, pilgrims, travelers, and curiosity seekers came in a seemingly steady stream to Holywell from near and far. Concerning her journeys of 1698, Celia Fiennes remarked: "I saw [an] abundance of devout papists on their knees all round the well. . . . [They] tell of many lamenesses and aches and distempers which are cured by it. . . . They come also to drink the water which they take up where the spring rises."[93] A Jesuit, Philip Metcalf, gave his impression of the scene in 1712: "In the travelling season the town of Holywell appears populous, crowded with zealous pilgrims from all parts of Britain. The well itself receives a succession of visitants from sunrise till late at night."[94]

Metcalf's description was part of his biography, *The Life of St. Winefride,* published in 1712.[95] That this work was clearly not just a case of sectarian exaggeration is shown by the fact that William Fleetwood, the bishop of St. Asaph, felt compelled to respond to it. The result was *The Life and Miracles of St. Wenefrede,* which reproduced Metcalf's English text but added an introduction and footnotes that were both scholarly and scathing.[96] Fleetwood argued that Winefride's cult was a postconquest fabrication foisted on a gullible populace by dastardly monks. Undoubtedly, the reason for his strong condemnation was the fact, which he grudgingly admitted, that "Great resort is had to Holywell by pilgrims (as they call them) from all the different quarters of the Kingdom and even from Ireland."[97]

From the Georgian to the Modern Era: Decline and Revitalization

In the early Georgian period, local authorities took a drastic step to curtail "popish" activities at the shrine. In 1723 the chapel over the well was closed to Catholic worship and converted into a schoolroom. It was remarkable, in fact, that so public a Catholic chapel had functioned for so long, a circumstance that was undoubtedly both a tribute to the cult of St. Winefride and a testimonial to the popularity of her well. As it turned out, once again the Catholic faithful were not so easily deterred. As one observer wrote after the closing of the well chapel, "to supply the loss the Roman Catholics have chapels erected in almost every inn for the devotion of the pilgrims that flock hither from all the popish parts of England."[98] Perhaps it was at this time that other "St. Winifred's Wells" arose, named for what was then the most famous Catholic shrine in England and Wales.[99]

The well continued to attract many visitors, as is clear from comments by the well-known writer Daniel Defoe, who stopped in Holywell on his tour of England and Wales in 1724. He noted that "numbers of pilgrims resort to it with no less devotion than ignorance; under the chapel the water gushes out in a great stream, and the place where it breaks out is formed like a cistern, in which they bathe." He added that "the priests that attend here are very numerous and appear in 'disguise.'"[100]

The eighteenth century witnessed the eclipse of Catholicism throughout much of England and Wales. Over the course of the century, the economic as well as the religious climate changed. Proto-industrialization was but a harbinger of the dawning and dramatically transforming Industrial Revolution. Northeastern Wales—and the area around Holywell in particular—was at the heart of this process of change. Coal mining, metal works, and cotton mills reconfigured the formerly sylvan landscape. In fact, when the renowned scholar and eccentric Dr. Johnson visited Holywell in 1774, it was largely a market town, which had almost twenty metal works within two miles of St. Winefride's well, in tandem with perhaps the richest lead mine in Britain.[101] Yet, Holywell never lost its hold on the imagination, or in the devotions, of some segments of the population. Dr. Johnson commented that "the bath is completely and indecently open: a woman bathed while we all looked on."[102] Near the end of the century, in 1795, another writer commented that, although the number of pilgrims "has considerably decreased, . . . still a few are to be seen in water in deep devotion up to their chins for hours, sending up their prayers."[103]

Among the visitors to St. Winefride's well, besides the devout, were those who came solely for its medicinal effects, as well as antiquarians, travelers, and even revelers. Spiritual pilgrimages to the well probably reached their nadir in the early nineteenth century, amidst a general atmosphere of religious indifference. In what may have been a manifestation of such attitudes, the sexton of the church at Gwytherin resorted to sawing pieces off of Winefride's shrine and selling them to visitors for a shilling each.[104] On the other hand, some of the people who bought fragments of the shrine may well have been pious Catholics who valued them as relics. In any event, a nascent Catholic revival from about the middle of the century onward redounded to the benefit of Holywell. The trickle of pilgrims gradually increased to a fairly steady stream. The Sisters of Charity established a residence in 1859, and a hospice for pilgrims opened in 1870. By the turn of the century, Holywell was once again a vital spiritual center, and in the summer months in particular, it was crowded with pilgrims and visitors from throughout Britain.[105]

The Bards Sing St. Winefride's Praises

Although St. Winefride's well owes its fame largely to the throngs of pilgrims who traveled there from the Middle Ages onward, a brief word should be added about the artists and writers who extolled the saint and her well over the centuries. Many paintings and engravings have memorialized this shrine, but the efforts of the poets are especially worthy of mention. Poems (*cywyddau*) have played an important role in Welsh culture, and bards have long sung the praises of Welsh and other saints, often deriving their inspiration from earlier prose *vitae.* These poems often lauded shrines devoted to individual saints; two of the most popular of these shrines were those of the Blessed Virgin Mary at Penrhys and St. Winefride at Holywell. Winefride was extolled in the verses of poets from at least the fourteenth century onward.[106] As one example, in the fifteenth century a bard, Ieuan Brydydd Hir, emphasized the spiritual significance of the well, and not just for Wales: "Here is a fountain of the Faith, / A baptismal font for the World."[107]

Even after the Reformation, and perhaps with even more determination, poets continued to venerate St. Winefride through their verse. Among them was Gwilym Pugh, a seventeenth-century Welsh Benedictine, who composed numerous dogmatic religious poems throughout his life. Then, in his old age, evidently as a sign of his devotion, he wrote a "Life of Saint Winefride" in popular folk metrical form.[108]

Yet, it was the great Victorian Jesuit poet Gerard Manley Hopkins who composed what was probably the most famous series of poems on St. Winefride and Holywell. He visited the saint's well frequently in the 1870s and was clearly moved by bathing there and contemplating its history of so many centuries. Among his writings was his brief tribute "On St. Winefred":

As wishing all about us sweet,
She brims her bath in cold or heat;
She lends, in aid of work and will,
Her hand from heaven to turn a mill—
Sweet soul! not scorning honest sweat
And favouring virgin freshness yet.[109]

He also wrote "The Leaden Echo and the Golden Echo (Maidens' Song from St. Winefred's Well)" and a short piece in Latin, "In S. Winefridam."[110] However, his longest and most important paean to the beloved medieval Welsh saint was his spiritual saga "St. Winefred's Well." After a description of some important people and events related to Winefride's life and martyrdom, Hopkins focuses his gaze on the well and its ongoing lure to so many pilgrims across time and place:

Here to this holy well shall pilgrims be,
And not from purple Wales only nor from elmy England,
But from beyond seas, Erin, France and Flanders, everywhere,
Pilgrims, still pilgrims, more pilgrims, still more poor pilgrims. . . .
What sights shall be when some that swung, wretches, on crutches
Their crutches shall cast from them, on heels of air departing,
Or they go rich as roseleaves hence that loathsome came hither!

The poem concludes with a ringing affirmation and optimism as to the continuing vitality of St. Winefride and her well:

As sure as what is most sure, sure as that spring primroses
Shall new-dapple next year, sure as to-morrow morning,
Amongst come-back-again things, things with a revival, things with a recovery,
Thy name [Winefride will live].[111]

Conclusion

Although the currents of modernization and secularization have affected Holywell, as elsewhere, during the course of the twentieth and early twenty-first centuries, the well is still there and continues to attract, among others, the sick, the devout, and the curious. As one historian of Holywell has written concerning its extraordinary longevity and staying power: "Alone of all the pilgrimages in Wales it has continued with unbroken, if at times fluctuating, vigor down to the present day. Nothing was able to stop it. It links modern Wales through her medieval past with the Age of the Saints and the founding of the Welsh nation."[112]

Its unique status and seeming indestructibility are difficult to explain, but paramount among the probable factors has been the great respect and devotion afforded a young Welsh woman who was gifted with exceptional courage and sanctity. Concerning the latter quality, Christopher David sums up the sentiments of centuries of devotees of Winefride and her cult: "Her sanctity is unquestioned, her reputation too deeply embedded in the local traditions of Holywell and Gwytherin" to be dismissed as fictive, despite the historical embroidering that clearly occurred, especially during the Middle Ages.[113]

Since then the pilgrimages have continued, whether somewhat covertly in the later Tudor, Stuart, and Georgian periods or more openly in modern times. In our own day there is an annual national Catholic pilgrimage to the well in late June, which commemorates the ancient summer feast of St. Winefride on June 22. Upward of two thousand Catholics walk in procession to the well, join in the celebration of Mass, and have the opportunity to venerate the saint's relic, pray for healing, and be sprinkled with water from the well.[114]

Whether praying for themselves or others, seeking spiritual solace or historical enrichment, or for a combination of motives, these pilgrims and visitors are confronted—and some are fortified—with the belief that Winefride has lovingly and successfully interceded for innumerable supplicants from throughout Wales, Britain, and the wider world over a remarkable span of more than thirteen hundred years. Not only pilgrims but also a host of other travelers continue to come to St. Winefride's well. Some are drawn primarily by its spiritual and therapeutic allure, others by its historical and cultural attractions. Yet, through all the variations of time, place, and culture, and although the numbers and the motives continue to fluctuate, the flow of visitors to this ancient but continually intriguing site shows no signs of abating.

Notes

1. Fragments are said to have existed in Rome, at Holywell, and at Shrewsbury in the mid–nineteenth century; see *Two Mediaeval Lives of Saint Winefride,* trans. Ronald Pepin and Hugh Feiss, O.S.B. (Toronto: Peregrina, 2000), 7–12 (hereafter referred to as *Lives of Saint Winefride*). One of them is used in the pilgrimage Mass to this day; see Janet Bord (with assistance from Tristan Gray Hulse), "St Winefride's Well, Holywell, Clwyd," *Folklore* 105 (1994): 99–100, at 99.

2. Lawrence Butler and James Graham-Campbell, "A Lost Reliquary Casket from Gwytherin, North Wales," *Antiquaries Journal* 70, no. 1 (1990): 40–48; Nancy Edwards, F.S.A., and Tristan Gray Hulse, "A Fragment of a Reliquary Casket from Gwytherin,

North Wales," *Antiquaries Journal* 72 (1992): 91–101; Nancy Edwards, F.S.A., and Tristan Gray Hulse, "Gwytherin," *Archaeology in Wales* 37 (1997): 87–88.

3. Nancy Edwards, "Celtic Saints and Early Medieval Archeology," in *Local Saints and Local Churches in the Early Medieval West,* ed. Alan Thacker and Richard Sharpe, 225–65 (Oxford: Oxford University Press, 2002), esp. 249–50; Edwards and Hulse, "Fragment of a Reliquary Casket," 97.

4. Butler and Graham-Campbell, "Lost Reliquary Casket," 40–48; Edwards and Hulse, "Fragment of a Reliquary Casket," 97.

5. Catherine Hamaker, "Winefride's Well-Cult," in *Lives of Saint Winefride,* 117–26, at 121.

6. Fiona Winward, "The Lives of St. Wenefred," *Analecta Bollandiana* 117 (1999): 89–132, at 95, 98–100. The "Lives" are published in the *Acta Sanctorum,* Nov. 1 (Paris, 1887), 702–31. Translations cited in this article are from *Lives of Saint Winefride* (see n. 1). See also *Lectiones de Sancta Wenefreda* and the appendix in *Acta Sanctorum,* 732–59.

7. Robert, Prior of Shrewsbury, *The Life and Translation of Saint Winefride,* in *Lives of Saint Winefride,* 25–93; *Acta Sanctorum,* 708–31, where it is referred to as the "*Vita Secunda Sanctae Wenefredae.*"

8. *The Anonymous Life of St. Winefride,* in *Lives of Saint Winefride,* 97–113 (the running header for this part of the book, however, labels the text "The Second Life of Winefride of Holywell"); *Acta Sanctorum,* 702–8, where it is referred to as the "*Vita Prima Sanctae Wenefredae.*"

9. *Lives of Saint Winefride,* 12–20; *Acta Sanctorum,* 702–31; Winward, "Lives of St. Wenefred," 89–132.

10. T. Charles-Edwards, *Saint Winefride and Her Well: The Historical Background* (London: W. Williams & Son, 1964), 13.

11. Robert's *Life,* 26; *Acta Sanctorum,* 708–9.

12. Robert's *Life,* 23–93, esp. 25–26; *Acta Sanctorum,* 708–9. For an in-depth discussion on "Early Welsh Saints and History," see G. H. Doble, *Lives of the Welsh Saints,* ed. D. Simon Evans, 1–55 (Cardiff: University of Wales Press, 1971), esp. 12–17.

13. Robert's *Life,* 35; *Acta Sanctorum,* 709–14.

14. *Acta Sanctorum,* 713. For this motif in Celtic hagiography, see Winward, "Lives of St. Wenefred," 113–14.

15. Robert's *Life,* 39; *Acta Sanctorum,* 714.

16. Robert's *Life,* 42; *Acta Sanctorum,* 715. See also Christopher David, *St. Winefride's Well: A History & Guide* (Llandysul, Wales: Gomer Press, 2002), [2].

17. Francis Jones, *The Holy Wells of Wales* (Cardiff: University of Wales Press, 1992), 38; Winward, "Lives of St. Wenefred," 109–12.

18. Winward, "Lives of St. Wenefred," 105–6, 109–12; Alan Thacker, "*Loca Sanctorum:* The Significance of Place in the Study of the Saints," in Thacker and Sharpe, *Local Saints and Local Churches,* 1–43; Edwards, "Celtic Saints," 225–27; Anne Ross, "Severed-Heads in Wells: An Aspect of the Well Cult," *Scottish Studies* 6 (1962): 13–48. It is important to mention that, according to several of these sources, some of these motifs may have

been a continuation of pre-Christian religious beliefs and practices, and some traditions were not exclusively Celtic; see, in particular, Winward, "Lives of St. Wenefred," 109–11. Another motif that is common in the legends of female saints is their rejection of pagan suitors because they have devoted their virginity to Christ.

19. Robert's *Life,* 42–68; *Acta Sanctorum,* 715–24; *Lives of Saint Winefride,* 8–10.

20. *Acta Sanctorum,* 727; O. J. Padel, "Local Saints and Place-Names in Cornwall," in Thacker and Sharpe, *Local Saints and Local Churches,* 303–60, esp. 345–46; Thacker, "*Loca Sanctorum,*" 42; Edwards, "Celtic Saints," 236–38, 243.

21. Robert's *Life,* 77–93; *Acta Sanctorum,* 726–31; *Lives of Saint Winefride,* 10–11; Winward, "Lives of St. Wenefred," 89, 96–97.

22. *Anonymous Life of St. Winefride,* in *Lives of Saint Winefride,* 101.

23. Ibid.

24. Robert's *Life,* 75–76; *Acta Sanctorum,* 726.

25. Hamaker, "Winefride's Well-Cult," 119.

26. Ibid., 117–19.

27. For a fuller discussion on these and related matters concerning the Druids and other "pagan" religions in the pre-Roman and pre-Christian British Isles, see Ronald Hutton, *The Pagan Religions of the Ancient British Isles: Their Nature and Legacy* (Oxford, U.K.: Blackwell, 1991), 165–76; and Geoffrey Ashe, *Mythology of the British Isles* (London: Methuen, 1990), 121–26.

28. Keith Thomas, *Religion and the Decline of Magic* (New York: Charles Scribner's Sons, 1971), 47–48. Cf. James Rattue, *The Living Stream: Holy Wells in Historical Context* (Woodbridge, Suffolk: Boydell Press, 1995), 17. Rattue's work is iconoclastic and questions many of the traditional ideas concerning saints and wells in Britain. See also Michael P. Carroll, *Irish Pilgrimage: Holy Wells and Popular Catholic Devotion* (Baltimore: Johns Hopkins University Press, 1999). Carroll argues that the Irish tradition of holy wells, rather than being a remnant of ancient Celtic culture, emerged after the Council of Trent in the sixteenth century. This is a debatable contention, but it demonstrates the importance of holy wells in Celtic areas in the early modern period, a major focus of this essay.

29. Francis Jones, *Holy Wells of Wales,* 10, 45–49, 97, 140.

30. Ibid., 49.

31. Cited in David, *St. Winefride's Well,* [1]. Note: The spellings of quotations throughout the article have been modernized.

32. Hamaker, "Winefride's Well-Cult," 122; Francis Jones, *Holy Wells of Wales,* 49–50.

33. David, *St. Winefride's Well,* [5]; Charles-Edwards, *Saint Winefride and Her Well,* 2.

34. Charles-Edwards, *Saint Winefride and Her Well,* 3.

35. Ibid.; Jeremy Catto, "Religious Change under Henry V," in *Henry V: The Practice of Kingship,* ed. G. L. Harriss (Dover, N.H.: Alan Sutton, 1993), 107–8. See also Barrie Dobson, "The Monks of Canterbury in the Later Middle Ages, 1220–1540," in *A History of Canterbury Cathedral,* ed. Patrick Collinson, Nigel Ramsay, and Margaret Sparks, 69–153 (Oxford: Oxford University Press, 1995), esp. regarding aspects of the long archbishopric of Henry Chichele.

36. E. F. Jacob, ed., *Register of Henry Chichele* (Oxford, U.K.: Clarendon Press, 1943), 8.

37. See C. de Smedt, S.J., *Documenta de S. Wenefreda,* in *Analecta Bollandiana,* vol. 6 (Paris and Brussels, 1887), 306–10 (hereafter *Documenta Wenefreda*).

38. For a description of the popularity of pilgrimages in medieval England, as well as the major pilgrimage sites, see Compton Reeves, *Pleasures and Pastimes in Medieval England* (New York: Oxford University Press, 1998), 174–82. Also see, of course, Geoffrey Chaucer's *Canterbury Tales* (written mostly after 1387). Additional scholarly treatments of pilgrimages include Colin Morris and Peter Roberts, eds., *Pilgrimage: The English Experience from Becket to Bunyan* (Cambridge: Cambridge University Press, 2002); Ronald Finucane, *Miracles and Pilgrims: Popular Beliefs in Medieval England* (New York: St. Martin's Press, 1995); and Jonathan Sumption, *Pilgrimage: An Image of Mediaeval Religion* (Totowa, N.J.: Rowman and Littlefield, 1975).

39. Christopher Allmand, *Henry V* (Berkeley: University of California Press, 1992), 27, 158, 160, 416–17.

40. Adam of Usk, *The Chronicle of Adam Usk (1377–1430),* ed. and trans. C. Given-Wilson (Oxford: Oxford University Press, 1997), 263.

41. David, *St. Winefride's Well,* [5].

42. Harold F. Hutchison, *King Henry V: A Biography* (New York: John Day Company, 1967), 101–2.

43. M. J. C. Lowry, "Caxton, St. Winifred and the Lady Margaret Beaufort," *The Library,* 6th ser., 5, no. 2 (June 1983): 101–17, at 111.

44. Ibid., esp. 110–13; Charles-Edwards, *Saint Winefride and Her Well,* 6–7.

45. Catto, "Religious Change," 97–115, esp. 110. Catto goes even further and concludes, "In all but name, more than a century before the title could be used, Henry V had begun to act as the supreme governor of the Church of England" (115).

46. Charles Ross, *Edward IV* (Berkeley: University of California Press, 1974), 128; David, *St. Winefride's Well,* [5]; Charles-Edwards, *Saint Winefride and Her Well,* 7. According to Lowry, in "Caxton, St. Winifred and the Lady Margaret Beaufort," if Edward's visit to Holywell took place, "it was as calculated a gesture as Henry V's in 1416" (113).

47. Harleian MS 433F37B, cited in David, *St. Winefride's Well,* [5].

48. David, *St. Winefride's Well,* [5–6]; Charles-Edwards, *Saint Winefride and Her Well,* 7.

49. *Papal Registers Concerning Great Britain,* 7:504, in David, *St. Winefride's Well,* [6]. The reference to a papal indulgence for pilgrims visiting Holywell highlights the complex interaction in the later medieval period between the papacy, on the one hand, and the English (and Welsh) monarchy and church, on the other. For a discussion of these and related issues, see Denys Hay, "The Church of England in the Later Middle Ages," *History* 53 (1968): 35–50.

50. David, *St. Winefride's Well,* [6]. Henry VII's promotion of the cult of St. Winefride, in addition to its Welsh connection, may well have been connected to this monarch's overall religious goals and policies; see Anthony Goodman, "Henry VII and Christian Renewal," in *Religion and Humanism,* ed. Keith Robbins, 115–25 (Oxford, U.K.: Basil Blackwell, 1981). According to Goodman, Henry envisaged "his mission as being closely bound up with a renewal of the religious authority of kingship" (122).

51. Lowry, "Caxton, St. Winifred and the Lady Margaret Beaufort," 113–17.

52. Hamaker, "Winefride's Well-Cult," 123; Francis Jones, *Holy Wells of Wales,* 59. For a discussion of the reasons behind and the consequences of the destruction of many shrines under Henry VIII, especially the famous one of St. Thomas Becket at Canterbury, see Robert Scully, S.J., "The Unmaking of a Saint: Thomas Becket and the English Reformation," *Catholic Historical Review* 86, no. 4 (October 2000): 579–602. A factor that may have militated against actions to close, much less destroy, a shrine such as Holywell was the contemporary large-scale uprising in northern England, provoked at least in part by the government's malevolent religious policy regarding the monasteries and many shrines; see R. W. Hoyle, *The Pilgrimage of Grace and the Politics of the 1530s* (Oxford: Oxford University Press, 2001).

53. *Records of the Court of Augmentations Relating to Wales,* 1538–39, cited in David, *St. Winefride's Well,* [6].

54. J. Gwynfor Jones, *Early Modern Wales, c. 1525–1640* (New York: St. Martin's Press, 1994), 140; David, *St. Winefride's Well,* [6].

55. *Documenta Wenefreda,* 310–11.

56. Dr. Robinson, bishop of Bangor, to Sir William Cecil, October 7, 1567, in Joan Abse, ed., *Letters from Wales* (Bridgend, Wales: Seren, 2000), 51–52.

57. P.R.O. Patent Rolls 21. Eliz. Part 7, cited in David, *St. Winefride's Well,* [9].

58. Glanmor Williams, *Wales and the Reformation* (Cardiff: University of Wales Press, 1997), 278.

59. John Gerard, *The Autobiography of a Hunted Priest,* trans. Philip Caraman (Chicago: Thomas More Press, 1952), 66.

60. Gerard, *Autobiography,* 67–69.

61. *Documenta Wenefreda,* 311.

62. Gerard, *Autobiography,* 66, 69; see a parallel account in *Documenta Wenefreda,* 312–15.

63. Gerard, *Autobiography,* 67.

64. Francis Jones, *Holy Wells of Wales,* 102. Evidently the custom of bathing three times in the well derived from the ancient Celtic rite of baptism by triple immersion; see David, *St. Winefride's Well,* [13].

65. Philip Caraman, *Henry Garnet (1555–1606) and the Gunpowder Plot* (New York: Farrar, Straus, 1964), 325; see also David, *St. Winefride's Well,* [9].

66. See Antonia Fraser, *Faith and Treason: The Story of the Gunpowder Plot* (New York: Doubleday, 1996). Yet, in spite of ongoing persecution, the Jesuit mission and the broader Catholic mission continued; see, for example, "*De missione Soc. Jesu apud Holywell et Residentia S. Wenefredae usque ad hodiernum diem,*" in *Acta Sanctorum,* 736–40.

67. Godfrey Anstruther, O.P., *The Seminary Priests: A Dictionary of the Secular Clergy of England and Wales, 1558–1850,* vol. 1 (Durham: Ushaw, [1968]), 178. For more on Topcliffe and the extensive spy network, see Alan Haynes, *Invisible Power: The Elizabethan Secret Services, 1570–1603* (New York: St. Martin's Press, 1992).

68. Charles-Edwards, *Saint Winefride and Her Well,* 8–9.

69. D. Aneurin Thomas, ed., *The Welsh Elizabethan Catholic Martyrs* (Cardiff: University of Wales Press, 1971), 41–44.

70. Henry Foley, S.J., *Records of the English Province of the Society of Jesus,* 7 vols. (London: Burns and Oates, 1878), 4:497.

71. Ibid., 4:497–516; Anstruther, *Seminary Priests,* 31.

72. David, *St. Winefride's Well,* [9].

73. Ibid.

74. Geraint Bowen, *Welsh Recusant Writings* (Cardiff: University of Wales Press, 1999), 52–56.

75. *Documenta Wenefreda,* 337, 339–40, 341, 350–51.

76. Francis Jones, *Holy Wells of Wales,* 64.

77. There is a good collection of seventeenth-century reports of healing at the well in *Documenta Wenefreda,* 312–52. For a catalog of Jesuits ministering at Holywell from the mid–seventeenth century until Catholic emancipation in 1829, see Geoffrey Holt, S.J., *The English Jesuits, 1650–1829: A Biographical Dictionary* (London: Catholic Record Society, 1984), 281.

78. *"Foot out of Ye Snare"* in *Somer's Collection of Tracts,* 3:64, in David, *St. Winefride's Well,* [9].

79. Cited in David, *St. Winefride's Well,* [9–10].

80. *State Papers Domestic Charles I,* vol. 38, no. 73, in Foley, *Records,* 4:534. See also David, *St. Winefride's Well,* [11].

81. *State Papers Domestic Charles I,* vol. 151, no. 13, in Foley, *Records,* 4:534–35. See also David, *St. Winefride's Well,* [14].

82. David, *St. Winefride's Well,* [14].

83. Keith Thomas, *Religion and the Decline of Magic,* 70.

84. Francis Jones, *Holy Wells of Wales,* 64.

85. David, *St. Winefride's Well,* [14–15]; Francis Jones, *Holy Wells of Wales,* 64–65. See also Rattue, *Living Stream,* 107, 110.

86. Foley, *Records,* 4:491; Bowen, *Welsh Recusant Writings,* 62; David, *St. Winefride's Well,* [14].

87. "The Catholic Registers of Holywell, Flintshire," in *Miscellanea III* (London: Catholic Record Society, 1906), 105. For an account of the registers of the Secular and Jesuit missions, intermittent from 1698 until Catholic emancipation, see ibid., 105–34.

88. Foley, *Records,* 4:536–37.

89. See John Kenyon, *The Popish Plot* (London: Heinemann, 1972).

90. Francis Jones, *Holy Wells of Wales,* 65; cf. Maurice Ashley, *James II* (London: J. M. Dent & Sons, 1977), 208. See also David, *St. Winefride's Well,* [15]; and John Miller, *James II* (New Haven, Conn.: Yale University Press, 2000), 180–81.

91. Cited in David, *St. Winefride's Well,* [15].

92. Francis Jones, *Holy Wells of Wales,* 65; Ashley, *James II,* 218–19.

93. *Journeys of Celia Fiennes 1698,* ed. Christopher Morris (1947), 180, in David, *St. Winefride's Well,* [20].

94. Cited in David, *St. Winefride's Well,* [20].

95. P. Metcalf, *Life of St. Winefride,* ed. H. Thurston (London, 1917). Metcalf largely based his biography on a paraphrase by John Falconer of Robert of Shrewsbury's *Life;* see J. Falconer, *The Admirable Life of Saint Wenefride* (St. Omer, 1635).

96. W. Fleetwood, *The Life and Miracles of St. Wenefrede,* 2nd ed. (London, 1713).

97. Cited in David, *St. Winefride's Well,* [20]. See also Winward, "Lives of St. Wenefred," 92; John Bossy, *The English Catholic Community, 1570–1850* (London: Darton, Longman & Todd, 1975), 98, 270; and Francis Jones, *Holy Wells of Wales,* 65.

98. Cited in David, *St. Winefride's Well,* [21].

99. Roy Fry and Tristan Gray Hulse, "The Other St. Winifred's Wells," *Source,* new ser., 1 (Autumn 1994), on line at http://www.bath.ac.uk/lispring/sourcearchive/ns1/ns1tgh4.htm (accessed October 6, 2006). It should be emphasized that these wells were not of medieval origin.

100. Daniel Defoe, *Tour thro' England & Wales,* 2:66, cited in David, *St. Winefride's Well,* [21]. See also Francis Jones, *Holy Wells of Wales,* 70.

101. John Davies, *A History of Wales* (London: Penguin Press, 1993), 325, 353. See also Glanmor Williams, *Renewal and Reformation: Wales, c. 1415–1642* (Oxford: Oxford University Press, 1993), 397.

102. *Dr. Johnson and Mrs. Thrale,* 233 (Broadley), cited in David, *St. Winefride's Well,* [22].

103. Robert Pennant, *History of Whitford & Holywell,* 230, cited in David, *St. Winefride's Well,* [22].

104. Edwards and Hulse, "Fragment of a Reliquary Casket," 92.

105. Francis Jones, *Holy Wells of Wales,* 67–70, 76–81; Edwards, "Celtic Saints," 245; Edwards and Hulse, "Fragment of a Reliquary Casket," 91–101; David, *St. Winefride's Well,* [22].

106. Charles-Edwards, *Saint Winefride and Her Well,* 19–23; Francis Jones, *Holy Wells of Wales,* 77; Williams, *Renewal and Reformation,* 127–28.

107. Cited in Charles-Edwards, *Saint Winefride and Her Well,* 20.

108. Bowen, *Welsh Recusant Writings,* 74–83.

109. Gerard Manley Hopkins, *The Poems of Gerard Manley Hopkins,* ed. W. H. Gardner and N. H. MacKenzie, 4th ed. (Oxford: Oxford University Press, 1970), 178, 310–11.

110. Ibid., 91–93, 218, 282–83, 333–35.

111. Ibid., 187–93 (esp. 192–93), 314–15. See also David, *St. Winefride's Well,* [26].

112. Charles-Edwards, *Saint Winefride and Her Well,* 1.

113. David, *St. Winefride's Well,* [3].

114. Bord, "St. Winefride's Well," 99. As to the water in St. Winefride's well, the original flow of water was disrupted by mining operations in the early twentieth century, and the well is now fed from the town's municipal water supply; see http://www.welshdragon.net/resources/sacred/stwinifred.shtml (accessed October 6, 2006); and David, *St. Winefride's Well,* [23].

Holy Wells and National Identity in Iceland

MARGARET CORMACK

A VOLCANIC ISLAND IN THE NORTH ATLANTIC, Iceland was long an uninhabited, religiously neutral landscape. Discovered by Scandinavians in the late ninth century, it was soon settled by their descendants, many of whom had acquired female companions in the British Isles.[1] Both Scandinavia and Britain abound in "holy" springs or wells, so it is hardly surprising to meet the phenomenon in Iceland. We even have accounts of an Icelandic bishop, Guðmundur Arason, who traveled through the country blessing, and thus sanctifying, natural water sources. His action could be explained in several ways; it could, for example, be argued that it was a means of formally incorporating locally recognized "holy" sites into the ideology and geography of the established church. To determine whether this is likely, or whether he was indeed engaging on an original exercise in sanctification, it is necessary to examine the evidence for religious belief before the formal adoption of Christianity in Iceland in the year 1000.

The most concrete evidence for the deities worshiped in Iceland in the tenth century is found in place-names: for example, Þórshöfn (Thor's Harbor), Freysnes (Frey's Peninsula), and Goðafjall (Mountain of the Gods) provide tantalizing references to places associated with heathen gods, as may the ambiguous Helgafell (Holy Mountain), a location that eventually became the site of a monastery.[2] There was evidently no perceived inconsistency that a monastery should be located on Þórsnes (Thor's Peninsula). Some twenty-four places called "Hof" may have been the sites of heathen temples or simply of large farms. The name Kristnes (Christ's Peninsula) is said to have been given by a settler who had been brought up in Ireland and whose faith was "very much mixed; he believed in Christ but invoked Thor for sea-voyages and emergencies."[3] Unfortunately there is no way of being sure whether Kristnes and other names such as Vestmannaeyjar (Islands of the Westmen, that is, inhabitants of Ireland or the British Isles) were given at the time of settlement or during subsequent centuries. The earliest history of Iceland, the "Book of the Icelanders," even mentions Christian hermits —apparently Irish—who departed when the heathen Scandinavians arrived.[4]

However, with the exception of a few names and vocabulary items, speakers of Celtic had little effect on Icelandic culture and none on the church that developed after Christianity was officially accepted. A certain amount of contact can be deduced from folklore, which traveled between Celtic-speaking territories and Iceland; however, the time and place of its transmission is still a subject of controversy. The existing evidence of both archaeology and written texts reflects a culture that was overwhelmingly Scandinavian.[5]

By 1200 Iceland had more than three hundred churches, as well as numerous small chapels.[6] The cult of saints was practiced much as it was elsewhere in Europe, and Iceland had just acquired two saints of its own, one from each of the two dioceses: Þorlákur Þórhallsson, bishop of Skálholt from 1178 to 1193; and Jón Ögmundarson, bishop of Hólar from 1106 to 1121. In spite of the time period separating the lives of these men, their relics were translated within a few years of each other, in 1198 and 1200, respectively.[7] Closely involved in the sanctification process was a priest, Guðmundur Arason, who was bishop of Hólar from 1203 to 1237. Icelandic sagas relating the lives and miracles of these three men provide insight into the beliefs and practices of clergy and laity in the early thirteenth century.

In the minds of educated Icelanders at this time, the pagan gods had either been euhemerized or identified as demons.[8] For the average Icelander, however, the "land-spirits" (*landvættir*) may have been more important than the gods of the pantheon had been. A purported quotation from a pre-Christian law code mentions the necessity of removing animal heads from ships when approaching the country, lest the *landvættir* be scared away.[9] These beings appear to have been guardian spirits of the land, which they inhabited quite literally; a fourteenth-century source tells us of a supernatural being who lived in a cliff and provided guidance to the local farmer, while another recounts the departure of such beings when Christianity arrived.[10]

The reason for believing that these late sources present a more or less accurate account of a pre-Christian mind-set concerning *landvættir* is that the belief in such beings still existed at the time of writing. In fact, the belief continues to the present day, the *landvættir* having been replaced by, or transformed into, the beneficent and humanlike elves of post-Reformation folklore.[11] Creatures inhabiting waterfalls were of some concern to medieval legislators in Norway[12] and also appear in Icelandic sagas and folklore. Postmedieval folklore occasionally populates lakes, rivers, and larger bodies of water with Loch Ness–type monsters or water-horses;[13] however, the elves, or "hidden people" as they were also called, generally inhabited rocks or hills. Mountains and the more remote parts of the Icelandic landscape were thought to be populated by trolls, who were unambiguously hostile to human beings. There do not appear to have been spirits of any sort associated with springs or other sources of drinking water.

I have emphasized the chthonic as opposed to aqueous habitation of the trolls and most *landvættir* because the saint whose memory is still preserved in the Icelandic landscape—Guðmundur Arason (1160–1237)—was famous for his consecration of springs and wells.[14] Given the situation I have described, his aim cannot have been to exorcise them of evil spirits or replace pagan associations with Christian ones. Nor is there any evidence that springs were already considered sacred. One would expect any form of "competition" with other supernatural powers to be explicitly mentioned, as it is in the case of trolls (see below).[15]

Early in his career Guðmundur received the appellation "the Good," a term that was to acquire a technical meaning of semisanctity corresponding to Latin *beatus,* that is, one who has taken the first step toward canonization. It is not known whether this association would have been made by those who initially applied the term to Guðmundur, and in fact Guðmundur was never formally beatified. He was a charismatic priest and was portrayed in his sagas as beloved by the poor, whom he was always ready to aid, but abominated by the local aristocracy.[16] I do not intend to discuss the power struggles that marred his episcopate but rather to emphasize two forms of Christian piety that he appears to have popularized in Iceland: the consecration of springs and the veneration of portable relics. I do not claim that he was the first Icelander to adopt such practices, but he appears to have carried them to new levels of popularity—as well as, literally, carrying them around the country. One version of his saga states that Guðmundur "adopted many religious practices not known by anyone to have been observed hitherto in Iceland,"[17] and this observation would appear to be accurate.

Relics must have existed in Iceland before Guðmundur's time, at the very least in altars and also in reliquaries in major churches. One of the miracles attributed to St. Jón concerns the miraculous splitting of the cathedral's relic of St. Martin so that a priest could have a relic for his own church.[18] Jón is presented as reluctant to divide the relic himself, and this may reflect a common attitude (it will be recalled that Gregory the Great was reluctant to divide the bodies of the saints, even for the benefit of the empress of Byzantium). Guðmundur, however, seems to have had no trouble acquiring relics. According to his saga, when he was a young priest about twenty-six years of age:

> Wherever he went, he now began to collect such sacred relics as he could manage to get. He carried them with him on all his journeys and used to hold them over the sick, and this was an indication that he had greater faith

> in their sanctity than in his own merits. Yet all thought it was evident, from these and many other things, that God was better pleased with Guðmundur's conduct than with that of others. The stories we have just told, and many others like them, were carried throughout Iceland, and the people began to show deep devotion to Guðmundur in their faith. Many invited him to their homes so that he might bless the water on their land and hear their confessions.[19]

There were skeptics, both within the church and without: "On holidays and festivals it was Guðmundur's custom to let people kiss the holy relics, but Þorsteinn asserted that he did not know whether these were the bones of holy men or of horses."[20] Guðmundur formally charged Þorsteinn with blasphemy.

The skepticism of Þorsteinn may have been justified. Quite possibly such relics as had arrived in Iceland during the early centuries of Christianity were still considered too rare or too holy to be taken out of churches. The stories about Guðmundur are the first to make reference to private possession of relics in Iceland. The question as to where he could have obtained them remains unanswered. It must be recalled that contact relics (dirt from a grave, water in which a relic had been washed, cloths or anything else that had been in contact with the saint or his tomb) were just as potent as any other kind. However, the saga specifically mentions bones; here (as also for the contact relics) the possibilities arising from the creation of the two new saints immediately spring to mind. One such relic is the object of another story, in which a priest is skeptical not so much about the authenticity of the object (a bone of Jón Ögmundarson, recently declared a saint) as about the question of Jón's sanctity.[21]

Guðmundur also made generous use of holy water, which had long been a staple sacramental for blessing and purifying within the church and should, in theory, have been effective independent of the priest who blessed it. However, Guðmundur apparently produced a higher-quality product than did other priests, as attested by none other than the Virgin Mary, who appeared in a vision and gave the following advice for the cure of a madwoman: "Send for some water blessed by my friend, Guðmundur the Good, for I believe his benediction to be the best, and this will cure her."[22] At a more mundane level, when Guðmundur was at Skálholt to assist in the translation of St. Þorlákur, we are told that "Bishop Páll requested Guðmundur to consecrate a large cask full of water for curing the sick, for wherever Guðmundur had blessed water throughout the land miracles had taken place affecting both men and beasts, as necessity arose."[23] Not only does water blessed by Guðmundur have curative powers but so does that in which he washes his hands, the latter said to be particularly efficacious against eye diseases.[24] None of this, however, is particularly unusual in a medieval saint's life, and there is in fact a long tradition according to which special waters can be used to cure eye ailments.[25] Water blessed by Guðmundur could stop fires where buckets of ordinary water had had no effect.[26] Using relics to turn aside a fire is another extremely common hagiographic motif; indeed, water blessed by Guðmundur functions as a sort of "relic" said to have been used even during his lifetime.

What was more unusual—and controversial—was his habit of blessing natural sources of water. This practice is the one invoked in his sagas as characteristic and indicative of his sanctity: "Moreover, many signs were immediately manifest when he blessed springs and performed blessings, and men attached deep significance to these. They strengthened his own faith and that of his friends and kinsmen, and were an indication that God was well pleased with his conduct. The common people showed their opinion of him by the nickname they gave him of 'Guðmundur the Good.'"[27] Once again his activities raised some eyebrows among Guðmundur's contemporaries: "At Reykhólar he consecrated a well into which people afterwards urinated in derision of him, but the well retained its powers of healing none the less."[28] This contrasts, by the way, with the story of a holy spring that bubbled forth on the spot where a potential Norwegian saint had been slain; when desecrated by having "broth made from a dog" poured into it, the spring lost its power.[29]

As noted above, there is no evidence that springs were thought to be inhabited by evil beings who might need to be exorcised, nor is there any indication that they were associated with spirits or deities, or credited with powers of healing, before being blessed by Guðmundur. A source probably written during Guðmundur's lifetime does mention a missionary bishop, Bernard the Saxon, active in the middle of the eleventh century, who is said to have blessed "churches and bells, bridges and springs, fords and lakes, cliffs and bells, which were the cause of notable things which were thought to manifest his true nobility and grace."[30] It is striking, however, that the objects are arranged in alliterative pairs, suggesting that poetic effect may have been of greater interest to the author than accurate documentation. At best, this shows that the idea of blessing springs and other items that could then serve as indicators of the sanctity of the person responsible was "in the air" in Guðmundur's day. It may even have developed in Iceland as a result of Guðmundur's own practice.

It is in fact difficult to assess the attitude of Guðmundur's contemporaries since the earliest sagas about him date from the early fourteenth century, a hundred years after his death.[31] While their treatment of the period of his life before he became bishop is based on a source probably written by a contemporary, that author's aim was clearly to praise Guðmundur, and a certain amount of exaggeration on his part—and on the part of the later redactors—should be allowed for. When one of these redactors complains of the way enthusiasm for Guðmundur's springs has fallen off,[32] we should consider whether, outside of Guðmundur's immediate circle, it was ever as great as the author claims. The same saga tells of actual opposition to the wells; in the late thirteenth or early fourteenth century Bishop Árni of Skálholt is said to have had one of them blocked up.[33] Again, the lack of independent evidence leaves open the possibility that the well had simply been filled up or forgotten from lack of use and had to be "discovered" at a later date. It is also possible that Bishop Árni *did* give such orders. Disapproval of holy wells was not limited to Iceland; they were also condemned by English bishops in the thirteenth century.[34] In the fourteenth century, when the existing sagas about Guðmundur were written, a justification for the blessing of running water was considered necessary, and one author put into Guðmundur's mouth a theological defense of his practice that is said to have convinced no less a personage than the archbishop of Nidaros.[35]

The average Icelander, however, would not have been interested in such theological subtleties. The sagas relate numerous stories illustrating the power of water from wells blessed by Guðmundur to benefit humans and animals. It was even possible to transport this water under adverse circumstances: "While he was in Sauðlauksdalur he blessed some water, and a woman there took it home in her cap, for she had no vessel to put it in, and the outside of the cap kept dry and the water remained inside. A certain man was crossing a steep mountain carrying the water in a bucket; he put the bucket down beside him while he was fastening his shoe, and it rolled down the mountain, bumping from stone to stone until it reached the level. The man grieved for the loss of the water and went down the mountain to the place where his bucket had come to rest. He found it undamaged, and not a drop of the water was spilt."[36] Guðmundur's water could be burned instead of oil.[37] The idea is carried a bit further with the claim that some people in Hornafjörður actually used it to light a fire.[38] It could also make food go farther than expected.[39]

Guðmundur's blessings were not confined to water; he also blessed dangerous cliffs, from which both rocks and humans could fall.[40] Here the presence of evil beings that must be exorcised is quite clear. Sagas about Guðmundur contain episodes in which he defeats trolls[41] (exceptionally, there is also one case in which he does not);[42] there are no comparable miracles for the other native saints, Jón and Þorlákur. A nineteenth-century folktale makes explicit the implications of his activities: "All the ancient [that is, heathen] *landvættir* depart from places that are blessed."[43] Water, however, appears to have contained only natural hazards, which could normally be avoided by, for example, crossing oneself before drinking.[44] Indeed, one of the saga episodes makes it explicit that the farmer in question wishes Guðmundur to sanctify, rather than to exorcise, his well. When the consecration was completed, the narrator informs us that "the water was so *holy* that it was carried across Steingrímsfjörður in a linen hat."[45]

His sagas are adamant that Guðmundur visited—and thus, by implication, sanctified—all of Iceland. One of them puts the following words into his mouth: "It may truly be said, that there is no desert or remote skerry in Iceland that is so forbidding that I have not come there, together with the miserable ones who wanted to be with me in my outlawry."[46] The Icelandic term used is that of secular outlawry, but it is easily adaptable to the Christian concept of pilgrimage and exile from one's spiritual homeland.

Guðmundur had been such a controversial figure during his lifetime that both ecclesiastical and secular authorities probably breathed sighs of relief when he died. Possibly his troubled episcopate caused the archbishop and chapter of Nidaros to reject the next Icelandic candidates for both Icelandic dioceses and to appoint Norwegians instead.[47] Although there had been Icelandic bishops at the see of Hólar in the intervening period, it was a Norwegian bishop who began to promote Guðmundur's cult in the fourteenth century. We are told that the king of Norway had the original idea, perhaps thinking that it would help gain support for the bishop from the Icelanders over whom he was appointed.[48] At any rate, the idea took off; four sagas about Guðmundur appeared during the first half of the fourteenth century. They promote Guðmundur as the holiest bishop Iceland has had. In a vision set just before he is chosen bishop, the visionary is rescued from the grasp of demons by St. Olaf, St. Magnus, and St. Hallvard, patron saints of Norway and the Orkney Islands, that is, the saints whose "territories" were closest to Iceland.[49] The visionary is shown the mansions of the blessed:

> Here you see the dwellings assigned to righteous men, both the living and the deceased, but these are not all equally fair. Here do your bishops dwell, for they have all been saintly men, yet the most saintly are Bishop Jón and Bishop Þorlákur the Younger [that is, St. Þorlákur], and next to them Bishop Björn, Bishop Ísleifur and Bishop Þorlákur the Elder. Likewise those bishops now living are holy men, on account of the trials they undergo and their patience with the disobedience of their flock, for each man is holier, the more he endures in God's name . . . beside [the house of a hermit] stands another dwelling, lofty and magnificent, from which you can hear fair song and loud and glorious music, and that is the abode of Guðmundur Arason, for his prayers keep this land from destruction even as ours uphold Norway and the Orkney Islands, and he will become the greatest upholder of this land and take a place no lower than that of Archbishop Thomas of England.[50]

Two points about this passage are worth noting. The first is the emphasis on suffering the opposition of laypeople as a virtue; if we use the accounts in their sagas to rank the degree of opposition suffered by the three saintly bishops, Guðmundur certainly comes out highest.[51] This particular theme is one that would have been easier to emphasize under the sponsorship of a Norwegian bishop than an Icelandic one who would almost inevitably have been related to several of the chieftains who had been Guðmundur's opponents. The sagas' emphasis on Guðmundur's sympathy for the poor and displaced, as he and they are persecuted by powerful chieftains, likewise fits well into a context where foreign bishops may have been trying to court popularity with farmers when they themselves suffered opposition from the local aristocracy. The second point to be noted is that Guðmundur is represented as the patron saint not just of Hólar but of all Iceland. It is he, rather than the popular Þorlákur, who is comparable to St. Olaf of Norway or St. Thomas Becket. The saga's emphasis on his travels and the benefits received thanks to his blessing of springs throughout Iceland is well designed to support such a claim.

In fact, Guðmundur was never formally recognized as a saint, although he was treated like one in Iceland: his feast day was entered in calendars, and vows were made in his name under the sponsorship of bishops of Hólar. Statues of Guðmundur are recorded at several churches. Attempts to obtain formal canonization from Rome were ended by the Protestant Reformation in 1550.

At this time Iceland was a colony of Denmark, and the Reformation took place by order of the Danish king, who, like Henry VIII in England, acquired extensive lands as a result. In contrast to England and Denmark, there was no major display of iconoclasm in Iceland at that time. Images that attracted pilgrims were removed, and as early as 1547 Bishop Gissur Einarsson had sent a letter through his bishopric warning against idolatry and representing veneration of relics as a financial swindle on the part of priests. While objects of veneration such as the wonder-working crucifix at Kaldaðarnes were removed or destroyed, some churches still recorded statues in their inventories up to the arrival of pietism in the eighteenth century.[52]

Certain traditions and beliefs continued in modified form. Poems about saints continued to be copied, even though they were not printed until scholarly editions were produced in the twentieth century. Although St. Margaret appears to have been forgotten, copies of her saga (a translation of the Latin *vita*) were used as charms for women giving birth.[53] It is claimed that memory of the original patron saint of the church at Oddi (St. Nicholas) survived in oral tradition until the nineteenth century, along with the idea that the saint would not let his church suffer lack.[54] Baptismal water retained some of the powers ascribed to holy water.[55] In addition, although it was no longer possible to make vows to a saint or crucifix, the practice of making vows is still associated with some churches at the present day. The church itself became the recipient of vows; contemporary oral tradition has it that vows to Strandarkirkja, on the southern coast of Iceland, account for one-third to one-half of the income of the Icelandic Lutheran Church.[56]

What of the three native saints? Stories about Jón Ögmundarson appear to reflect learned tradition.[57] Some stories credit Þorlákur with blessing the cliff Látrabjarg, and he is commemorated in place-names, including a spring (*Þorláksbrunnur*) and a hot spring (*Þorlákshver*) on land belonging to his former see, Skálholt.[58]

It is Guðmundur, however, who was remembered by a farmer, also named Guðmundur, who lived in Hornstrandir and looked on the bishop as his patron saint (and that in the nineteenth century, when patron saints were no longer part of the official creed). He used to circumambulate his farm while reciting prayers on the morning of Guðmundur's day (which still had its place in the calendar), and he drove away a young farmhand for referring to the bishop by the familiar form of his name, "Gvendur," instead of "Guðmundur."[59] ("Gvendur" is the shortened form that is incorporated in place-names associated with the bishop.) Within living memory another careless boy was upbraided by local farmers near Reykholt in Borgarfjörður for urinating in the river that flowed out of one of the springs said to have been consecrated by Guðmundur.[60]

In fact, Guðmundur appears much more widely than the other two saints, both in the published corpus of folklore and in place-names, which include dozens of *Gvendarbrunnar*, "Guðmundur's springs" (sg. *Gvendarbrunnur*), as well as other localities associated with him. Furthermore, some of the springs and wells consecrated by him have retained a reputation for healing properties. One at Keldur in Rangárvellir (named for the Virgin Mary) is identified with the one consecrated by Guðmundur and blocked up by Bishop Árni. An article published in 1939 notes that "belief in its power has re-awakened," that its water was considered good for curing eye ailments, and that people were said to have come from great distances to collect it in bottles.[61] The water from a *Gvendarbrunnur* at Mýrar in Dýrafjörður is also said to have been good for eye ailments,[62] while that from the well Brynhildur in Grímsey was sought to ease childbirth.[63] *Gvendarbrunnar* at Gvendarnes and Lönd in Stöðvarfjörður, Foss in Mýrdalur, and Snartastaðir in Lundarreykjardalur were thought to have healing power,[64] as was the source of a natural sauna at Jarðbaðshólar, Mývatnssveit.[65]

Ólafur Lárusson, author of the only published study of Guðmundur's springs, notes that in addition to those specifically attributed to Guðmundur, there are many springs said to have special power because they had been blessed, although the person responsible was not remembered.[66] Conversely, an attribution to Guðmundur may survive even when the place-name does not support it, for example, the *Maríubrunnur* at Keldur mentioned above. Guðmundur was credited with an especially close relationship to the Virgin Mary, which might account for the name. (The patron saint of the church at Keldur was not the Virgin but St. Paul; however, given the Virgin's extreme popularity in Iceland, it is possible that she was associated with water sources in her own right.)

Guðmundur is known to have spent time in Grímsey. The sagas about him do not specifically mention the consecration of springs there, but at this point the sources used by their authors are secular rather than ecclesiastical, and the originals they copied from may not have shown interest in such matters. In addition to Brynhildur, *Gvendarbrunnar* exist in two other places in Grímsey, neither of which is any longer a significant source of water.[67] The well blessed by Guðmundur at Reykhólar is called *Biskupsbrunnur* (bishop's spring), recognizing Guðmundur's subsequent rank even though he would have been only a priest when he visited the spot. At Hvammur in Fáskrúðsfjörður a well is called variously *Gvendarbrunnur* or *Vígðibrunnur* (blessed spring),[68] and a *Vígðá* (blessed river) attributed to Guðmundur exists in Ísafjörður.[69]

Like the sagas, folktales tell how Guðmundur overcame trolls. Sea birds and their eggs are an important source of food in Iceland: to obtain them it is necessary to be lowered from the edge of the cliff on a rope. This procedure is dangerous, fatal if the rope should break. The explanation given in the folktales has nothing to do with the age of the rope or jagged rocks in the cliff; rather, the beings living in the cliffs resent the intrusion of humans and cut their ropes. Guðmundur is said to have blessed the cliffs and so driven out the monsters, or else we are told that the rope from which a man hung included a strand blessed by Guðmundur—the only one that could not be cut.[70]

There are, in some cases, alternative accounts associated with other saints; St. Þorlákur, as well as Guðmundur, is said to have blessed Látrabjarg, while in some tales two Finnar (Saami) sorcerers, rather than Guðmundur, is given credit for dealing with the sea serpent in Lagarfljót.[71] However, stories about Guðmundur predominate. He is said to have blessed fords, waterfalls, and mountain paths; in such places, no matter how dangerous they looked, a traveler could pass safely.[72] There is a converse to this; there are also cliffs and other areas that are studiously avoided because Guðmundur did *not* bless them. He is said to have gone along the cliff, blessing and sprinkling holy water to drive out the evil beings, until a voice emerging from the cliff begged him to stop because "even the evil have to be *somewhere*."[73] The Guðmundur of the sagas would never have made such a concession, but the Guðmundur of folklore apparently found the request reasonable and refrained from blessing certain areas, to which the cliff dwellers are now confined. This justifies the existence of tabu areas where no one will go, often referred to as "heathen" spots. Comparable tabu areas, not necessarily associated with Guðmundur, exist throughout Iceland; they include enchanted/cursed spots called *álagablettir,* small patches of fields that must not be disturbed, especially by cutting hay from them; the tabu is defied at one's peril.

Modern folklore would thus appear to support the medieval claim that Guðmundur visited—and blessed—virtually all of Iceland. Of course, it is not possible to prove or disprove any given claim, but it is clear that Guðmundur's popularity must have led to the multiplication of stories about him in the same way that urban legends spread today. One must also be wary of the influence of increased literacy and education on the traditions. As seen in some of the examples mentioned, place-name and story do not always coincide, but it is characteristic that Ólafur Lárusson collected references to "blessed" springs not specifically named for Guðmundur, apparently on the assumption that the original association had been lost. A *Gvendarbrunnur* is what one expects a curative spring—or perhaps any spring with particularly good water—to be called.

A *Gvendarbrunnur* thus becomes part of the natural landscape with a (purported) direct link to the Golden Age of the medieval past, its name incorporating the Icelandic language, which has changed little since that time and comprised an important part of the nineteenth- and early twentieth-century argument for independence and nationhood. It thus embodies the three main features of "land, nation, and language" that characterize the Icelandic nationalism with which most Icelanders over the age of fifty have grown up.[74]

This can be seen in a recent controversy regarding a spring traditionally associated with Guðmundur. A resident of Snæfellsnes issued a map of his land on which a *Gvendarbrunnur* appears as *Maríulind* (Mary's spring). The rationale behind this is unknown but could possibly be hype for tourists, who would have heard of the Virgin Mary but not of Guðmundur and would possibly feel that Guðmundur was not, after all, a saint. Even Lutheran Icelanders take quite seriously the papacy's claim to define who is a saint and who is not, and the Vatican has, so far, recognized that status only for Þorlákur (in 1984). The plaque by the well claims a vision of the Virgin on the site, which is consistent with current Catholic doctrine and piety focused on the Virgin.[75] It is, however, doubtful that this tradition is much older than the plaque.

Of special interest is the reaction of a former resident of the district, who in the year 2000 sent a letter to the Place-name Institute of Iceland protesting the change and demanding that the original name of the spring appear on all official maps—a request that has been favorably received. The letter does not call the vision itself into question but states that it was completely unknown to former residents, including the author of the letter, whose family had lived in the district for five generations. The recent changes in the district (which include promotion of the mountain Snæfell as a source of "pyramid power") are attributed to new residents who are also New Agers, and whose promotion of their ideology brings them financial benefit. The author represents himself as an environmentalist with an interest in folk traditions and considers it "the duty of all of us to hold unbroken faith with all old place-names; they are a part of the national heritage which must not be torn asunder"; changing place-names is "an insult to our history, culture, and past generations."[76] It is no longer the well itself but its name that is sacred. Since the independence movement of the nineteenth century,[77] certainly during the youth of the middle-aged letter-writer, the Icelandic language and folk traditions have retained symbolic value as the core of Icelandic identity. For such individuals, Guðmundur's name still has power as a valued part of their cultural heritage that is firmly located in the landscape.

The sheer number of *Gvendarbrunnar* and other places associated with Guðmundur is astounding, and it is undoubtedly they, rather than anything else, that have kept his memory alive. It is, of course, much more difficult to destroy a spring than an image—and easier to rationalize its purported healing qualities, which can be seen as being genuine and having nothing to do with the saint. However, the very fact that Guðmundur was *not* officially recognized as a saint by the Catholic Church may have worked in his favor in Lutheran times. The sanctity of Þorlákur and Jón was focused at their shrines in Skálholt and Hólar; when these were deprived of supernatural authority at the Reformation, memory of the saints, for the most part, died out. Guðmundur, never canonized, had no shrine—or rather, all of Iceland was his shrine. Memory of places he had blessed could not be eradicated because it had no single locus but was inscribed on the landscape itself.

Notes

Abbreviations used in the notes include the following:

BS *Biskupa sögur*, ed. Guðbrandur Vigfússon and Jón Sigurðsson, 2 vols. (Copenhagen: Hið íslenzka bókmentafélag, 1858, 1878).

Bisk. *Biskupa sögur I*, ed. Sigurgeir Steingrímsson, Ólafur Halldórsson, and Peter Foote, Íslenzk fornrit 15, 1 vol., 2 pts. (Reykjavík: Hið íslenzka fornritafélag, 2003).

JÁ Jón Árnason, *Íslenzkar þjóðsögur og ævintýri*, ed. Árni Böðvarsson and Bjarni Vilhjálmsson, 6 vols. (Reykjavík: Bókaútgáfan Þjóðsaga, 1954–61).

LGG *The Life of Gudmund the Good, Bishop of Holar*, trans. G[abriel] Turville-Petre and E. S. Olszewska (London: Viking Society for Northern Research, 1942).

ÓL Ólafur Lárusson, "Guðmundur góði í þjóðtrú Íslendinga," in *Byggð og saga*, 244–79 (Reykjavík: Ísafoldarprentsmiðja, 1944); repr. from *Skírnir* 116 (1942): 113–39.

In the following, I use modern Icelandic spelling and alphabetization conventions. The "þ" is pronounced "th" as in "thin," and "ð" is pronounced "th" as in "this"; "æ" is pronounced like long "i", "ö" as in German; "ð" follows "d"; the other letters are found at the end of the alphabet.

1. Recent DNA research shows that, of the original settlers, around 60 percent of the women and 20 percent of the men came from Ireland or the Northern Isles. See Agnar Helgason, "Uppruni Íslendinga: Vitnisburður erfðafræðinnar," in *Hlutavelta tímans* (Reykjavík: Þjóðminjasafn Íslands, 2004), 49–55; Agnar Helgason, E. Hickey, S. Goodacre, E. Vega, V. Bosnes, K. Stefánsson, R. Ward, and B. Sykes, "mtDNA and the Islands of the North Atlantic: Estimating the Proportions of Norse and Gaelic Ancestry," *American Journal of Human Genetics* 68 (2001): 723–37; Agnar Helgason, S. Sigurðardóttir, J. Nicholson, B. Sykes, E. Hill, D. G. Bradley, V. Bosnes, J. R. Gulcher, R. Ward, and K. Stefánsson, "Estimating Scandinavian and Gaelic Ancestry in the Male Settlers of Iceland," *American Journal of Human Genetics* 67 (2000): 697–717.

2. The most recent survey of work on pagan place-names in Iceland is Svavar Sigmundsson, "Átrúnaður og örnefni," in *Snorrastefna*, ed. Úlfar Bragason, Rit Stofnunar Sigurðar Nordals 1, 241–54 (Reykjavík: Stofnun Sigurðar Nordals, 1992). The assumption that these place-names do, in fact, date from the pagan period is one that cannot be tested, though it seems likely. For Helgafell, see *The Book of Settlements,* trans. Hermann Pálsson and Paul Edwards, University of Manitoba Icelandic Studies 1 (Winnipeg: University of Manitoba Press, 1972), 45; or *The Saga of the People of Eyri,* trans. Judy Quinn, in *Gisli Surssons Saga and the Saga of the People of Eyri,* with an introduction and notes by Vésteinn Ólason (London and New York: Penguin, 2003), 77 (two related versions of the same tale).

3. *Íslendingabók,* in *Íslendingabók—Landnámabók,* ed. Jakob Benediktsson, Íslenzk fornrit 1 (Reykjavík: Hið íslenzka fornritafélag, 1968), 250–53. This book was composed in the years 1122–33.

4. Ibid., 5.

5. As reflected in artifacts, burial practices, building style, language, legal system, poetic form, and mythology. It is possible that current archaeological work in Iceland will change the picture, but at the time of writing there are no unambiguously Christian remains that can be dated to a period significantly before the year 1000.

6. Margaret Cormack, *The Saints in Iceland: Their Veneration from the Conversion to 1400,* Subsidia Hagiographica 78 (Brussels: Société des Bollandistes, 1994). For the early history of Christianity in Iceland, see Orri Vésteinsson, *The Christianization of Iceland: Priests, Power, and Social Change, 1000–1300* (Oxford: Oxford University Press, 2000).

7. Here the Icelandic bishops followed the tradition of canonization by the local bishop. While canonization by the papacy was customary in the second half of the twelfth century (this fact may account for Bishop Páll's initial reluctance to act in the case of his uncle Þorlákur), it was not fully incorporated into canon law until 1234; see Eric Waldram Kemp, *Canonization and Authority in the Western Church* (London: Oxford University Press, 1948), 107.

8. Sagas about the missionary kings of Norway sometimes feature the Scandinavian gods as demons. The Icelander Snorri Sturluson (d. 1241) was largely responsible for

redefining the pagan gods as a human aristocracy of Asian origin who made claims of divinity after settling in Scandinavia, although there is also evidence of euhemerization in Ari Þorgilsson's *Íslendingabók*, 27–28. Snorri's rationalization may have been a reaction to conservative churchmen who still tended to identify the gods with demons; see Margaret Cormack, "Poetry, Paganism, and the Sagas of Icelandic Bishops," in *Til heiðurs og hugbótar: Greinar um trúarkveðskap fyrri alda,* ed. Svanhildur Óskarsdóttir and Anna Guðmundsdóttir, 33–51 (Reykholt: Snorrastofa, 2003).

9. *Íslendingabók—Landnámabók,* 313.

10. In "Af Þiðranda ok dísunum," set just before the advent of Christianity, the seer Þórhallur says to Síðu-Hallur (who will be one of the first Christian converts) that he sees "many a hill open, and all the creatures, great and small, are packing their bags and moving house" (margr hóll opnask ok hvert kykvendi býr sinn bagga, bæði smá ok stór, ok gera fardaga); see *Bisk.,* 2:125. Valdimar Hafstein has recently argued that the motif of such beings departing from their homes appears to be associated with times of cultural change; see his "Groaning Dwarfs at Granite Doors: Fieldwork in Völuspá," *Arkiv för nordisk filologi* 118 (2003): 29–45.

11. Elves (*álfar*) were part of the pre-Christian belief system, but are not prominent in medieval literature. It is quite possible that the idea of elves overlaps with that of *landvættir.* No one really knows what *landvættir* are supposed to have looked like; most of the extant passages suggest they are human-looking. The main exception is the description of four guardian spirits of the country which, however, appears to have been modeled on the traditional symbols of the four evangelists. See Jón Hnefill Aðalsteinsson, "Þjóðtrú," in *Íslensk þjóðmenning V. Trúarhættir,* ed. Frosti F. Jóhannsson, 341–400 (Reykjavík: Bókaútgáfan Þjóðsaga, 1988), esp. 349–54, and the references cited there. Post-Reformation elves (*álfar, huldufólk*) form a society parallel to that of human beings, inhabiting cliffs or hills. In appearance they are often indistinguishable from humans, with whom they often interact. They are also Christian, and in Icelandic tradition they are less likely to be hostile to humans than in Scandinavia, Ireland, or the Scottish Isles (Bo Almqvist, lecture and discussion "Álfkona í barnsnauð," held at the fifth Celtic-Nordic-Baltic Folklore Symposium on Folk Legends, Reykjavík, June 15, 2005). In "Groaning Dwarfs at Granite Doors," Valdimar Hafstein argues that in the stories of departure of such beings, it is their function that is important, and that their precise nature is irrelevant.

12. The Christian Laws' Section of the Younger Law of the Gulaþing mentions the heathen belief "in *landvættir,* that they are in groves or mounds or waterfalls" (*at trua a landvættir at se j lundum æda haugum æda forsom*); see *Norges gamle love indtil 1387,* ed. R. Keyser and P. A. Munch (Oslo/Christiania, 1848), 2:308.

13. Terry Gunnell, "The Coming of the Christmas Visitors: Folk Legends Concerning the Attacks on Icelandic Farmhouses Made by Spirits at Christmas," *Northern Studies* 38 (2004): 51–75, at 51, notes as an exception to the rule some isolated instances in which elves or spirits vanish into lakes or ponds (but not springs or wells).

14. The water sources under discussion in this article are for the most part natural, although in some cases they have been improved by human activity. In modern Icelandic, *brunnur* is generally translated as "well," with the implication that some human activity

has taken part in its formation. Initially, however, it applied to any water source. *Kelda* originally meant "spring." *Lind* is a postmedieval term for "spring."

15. Such accounts do occur in the narratives about the conversion period, in which missionaries compete with sorcerers or berserks. The relevant passages have been collected into a single volume in *Bisk.*, part 2. Sagas of the Norwegian missionary kings, Olaf Tryggvason (d. 999) and St. Olaf (d. 1029), feature conflicts with the pagan gods.

16. For information on Guðmundur, see Magnús Már Lárusson, "Guðmundr inn góði Arason," in *Kulturhistorisk leksikon for nordisk middelalder fra vikingetid til reformationstid* (Copenhagen, Helsingfors, Reykjavík, Oslo, and Malmö, 1960), vol. 5, cols. 538–42; and *LGG.*

17. *LGG,* 18; *BS,* 1:431. Where *LGG* is quoted, that translation is used, with occasional corrections and emendations to preserve consistency in the spelling of personal and place-names. All other translations are my own.

18. *BS,* 1:169; *Bisk.*, 2:222–23.

19. *LGG,* 24; *BS,* 1:440.

20. *LGG,* 31; *BS,* 1:449.

21. *LGG,* 44; *BS,* 1:468–69; *Bisk.*, 2:297.

22. *LGG,* 23; *BS,* 1:438. For a historical discussion of the use of various types of consecrated or otherwise sanctified water, see Adolph Franz, *Die Kirchlichen Benediktionen im Mittelalter* (Freiburg im Breisgau: Herdersche Verlagshandlung, 1909), 1:79–109.

23. *LGG,* 35; *BS,* 1:455.

24. *LGG,* 32; *BS,* 1:451.

25. For pre- and early-Christian Europe, see Aline Rouselle, "From Sanctuary to Miracle-Worker: Healing in Fourth-Century Gaul," in *Ritual, Religion, and the Sacred: Selections from "Annales, Economies, Sociétés, Civilisations,"* ed. Robert Forster and Orest Ranum, trans. Elborg Forster and Patricia M. Ranum, 7:95–127 (Baltimore and London: Johns Hopkins University Press, 1982); this was originally published in *Annales, Economies, Sociétés, Civilisations* 31 (November–December 1976): 1085–1107. Wells believed to have curative powers thanks to the presence of a deity, often replaced by a Christian saint, were common throughout Europe. Ólafur Lárusson counted 618 in Denmark; see his "Guðmundur góði í þjóðtrú Íslendinga," in ÓL, 244–79, at 250 (repr. from *Skírnir* 116 [1942]: 113–39). In present-day Iceland the water used for baptism is thought to be good for curing eye ailments, and after a home christening I have noticed older women casually dip their fingers in the water and rub it over arthritic joints. For this and other uses of baptismal water, see Hjalti Hugason, "Kristnir trúarhættir," in *Íslensk þjóðmenning V. Trúarhættir,* ed. Frosti F. Jóhannsson, 76–339 (Reykjavík: Bókaútgáfan Þjóðsaga, 1988), at 318.

26. *LGG,* 29; *BS,* 1:445–46.

27. *LGG,* 18; *BS,* 1:431. The word here translated "blessings" is *yfirsöngur,* literally "singing over," a term that seems to have been used for a variety of types of prayers and curses (including non-Christian spells). Turville-Petre's overly specific translation, "exorcism," is supported by none of the examples cited in the dictionaries nor by other examples of medieval usage that I have come across.

28. *LGG,* 36; *BS,* 1:457.

29. Snorri Sturluson, *Heimskringla,* trans. Lee M. Hollander (Austin: University of Texas Press, 1964), 767.

30. "Kirkjur ok klukkur, brúr ok brunna, vöð ok vötn, björg ok bjöllur, ok þikja þessir hlutir hafa birt sanna tign hans gæzku" (*Hungrvaka, BS,* 1:65). *Hungrvaka* hints at miraculous blessings by Bishop Bernharður and also Bishop Ísleifur. The work serves as a prelude to the saga of St. Þorlákur, and the aim of the author is to paint a picture of the diocese of Skálholt as the seat of noble and possibly even holy bishops, without overshadowing the reputation of the recognized saint. Crediting their blessings with supernatural power could be a way of claiming such virtue for them without making specific claims that could be called into question by readers who had never heard of the events.

31. For discussion of the sagas about Guðmundur, see Stefán Karlsson, "Guðmundar sögur biskups," in *Medieval Scandinavia: An Encyclopedia,* ed. Phillip Pulsiano et al., 245–46 (New York and London: Garland, 1993).

32. *BS,* 1:595–96.

33. Ibid., 612. There were two successive bishops of Skálholt named Árni who ruled the diocese of Skálholt from 1269 to 1320.

34. F. M. Powicke and C. R. Cheney, eds., *Councils and Synods with Other Documents Relating to the English Church* (Oxford, U.K.: Clarendon Press, 1964), vol. 2, pt. 1, 303, 622, 722.

35. *BS,* 1:575–78; *BS,* 2:95–103.

36. *LGG,* 38–39; *BS,* 1:461. Gregory the Great, *Dialogues,* trans. Odo John Zimmerman, Fathers of the Church, vol. 39 (Washington, D.C.: Catholic University Press, 1977), Dialogue 2, chap. 28, 97, tells of a glass vessel full of oil that does not shatter when thrown out the window, reminiscent of the bucket that rolls down the mountain. The *Dialogues* appear to have been much read in Iceland, and numerous parallels with their contents can be found in the Icelandic miracle corpus. Régis Boyer has collected examples in *La vie religieuse en Islande* (Paris: Fondation Singer-Polignac, 1979), 170–76.

37. *BS,* 1:596.

38. *BS,* 1:616; *BS,* 2:176.

39. *BS,* 1:597; *BS,* 2:134–35.

40. *BS,* 1:598–99.

41. *BS,* 1:464, 561, 598. Here he may be taking over the role of the god Thor, although Guðmundur uses Christian prayers and ritual objects rather than a magic hammer and physical strength. It should be noted that the trolls are not Christianized versions of the pre-Christian gods but rather the enemies of the gods in the pre-Christian worldview. In Norwegian folklore, it was St. Olaf who took on the function of dealing with such beings.

42. *BS,* 2:140.

43. "Allar fornar landvættir leggjast frá þeim stöðum sem vígðir eru" (JÁ, 3:217). (It should be noted that older scholarship sometimes refers to the two-volume version of this work, published in Leipzig in 1863–64.) It would be interesting to know whether this informant included elves in the category of "ancient *landvættir*" and whether the adjective

"ancient" is explicitly intended to distinguish pre-Christian supernatural beings from those that might still exist at the time of writing. Generally speaking, "heathen" refers to individuals who are not members of the human Christian community, that is, supernaturals or unbaptized humans, including newborn infants.

44. *BS,* 2:171–74, in which someone accidentally swallows a worm.

45. *BS,* 1:606.

46. "Svá má sannliga frá segja, at engi öræfi eða útsker sé svá ill á Íslandi, at ek hafa eigi í komit eða í verit, ok þeir vesalíngar, er með mér vildu vera í útlegðum" (*BS,* 1:580). At this time Guðmundur had been driven away from his cathedral and was roaming around Iceland accompanied by a band of impoverished followers.

47. Sigvarður Þéttmarsson to Skálholt and Bótólfur to Hólar, both appointed in 1238.

48. *Lárentíus saga biskups,* in *Biskupa sögur III,* ed. Guðrún Ása Grímsdóttir, Íslenzk fornrit 17 (Reykjavík: Hið íslenzka fornritafélag, 1998), 325.

49. Cormack, *The Saints in Iceland,* 60–61.

50. *LGG,* 34–35; *BS,* 1:454.

51. This theme is anticipated in *Hungrvaka,* a brief history of the bishops of Skálholt before the time of St. Þorlákur, as pointed out by Jørgen Jørgensen, "Hagiography and the Icelandic Bishop Sagas," *Peritia* 1 (1982): 1–16, at 12.

52. Statues of the Virgin survived in some churches. The shrine of St. Þorlákur—presumably a man-sized reliquary—was removed from the place of honor over the altar but stood in the choir until 1800. Reliquaries from the churches at Keldur and Valþjófsstaður are now preserved at the national museums of Denmark and Iceland, respectively. The former was apparently still in the choir of the church when acquired by the National Museum of Denmark in 1820. See Hjalti Hugason, "Kristnir trúarhættir," 132, 135–38; Loftur Guttormsson, *Frá siðaskiptum til upplýsingar,* vol. 3 of *Kristni á Íslandi,* gen. ed. Hjalti Hugason (Reykjavík: Alþingi, 2000), 105–6.

53. Jón Steffensen, "Margrétar Saga and Its History in Iceland," *Saga-book of the Viking Society* 16 (1965): 273–82.

54. Hjalti Hugason, "Kristnir trúarhættir," 325.

55. Ibid., 318.

56. While vows are clearly still made to Strandarkirkja, the extent to which payment of these vows keeps the established church in funds has clearly become a topos. I argued at the fifth Celtic-Nordic-Baltic Folklore Symposium on Folk Legends, Reykjavík, June 15, 2005, that vows were originally made to the patron saint of the church, Thomas Becket. There is evidence from Sweden of vows to churches after the Reformation; see Monica Weikert, *I sjukdom och nöd: Offerkyrkoseden i Sverige från 1600-tal till 1800-tal* (Göteborg: [Historiska institutionen, Göteborgs universitet], 2004).

57. ÓL, 244.

58. Sigurður Skúlason, "Örnefni um Skálholtsland í Biskupstungum," *Árbók hins íslenzka fornleifafélags,* 1927, 60–65, cited in ÓL, 245. The article cited also mentions in the same area a *Þorlákssæti* (Þorlákur's seat) in a cliff, a *Þorláksbúð* (Þorlákur's booth) commemorating a small building that is now represented only by ruins, and several other names incorporating the words for "church," "bishop," and "Mass." Of course, there is no

way of knowing how old these place-names actually are. The possibility of identifying place-names reflecting a memory of Jón Ögmundarson is complicated by the fact that *Jón* (English "John") is one of the most popular given names in Iceland, so that it would be almost impossible to determine whether the saint or some other individual were being commemorated.

59. Þorleifur Bjarnason, *Hornstrendingabók* (Akureyri: Þorsteinn M. Jónsson, 1943), 69, cited in ÓL, 245–46.

60. Rev. Geir Waage, personal communication. He recollects that this event took place in 1981 or 1982.

61. "Nú í seinni tíð hefur trúin á mátt hans vaknað aftur, og þykir vatn hans einkum gott til augnlækninga (þó ekki fái blindir sýn). Kona ein, sem lengi var búin að þjást af augnveiki, varð alheil með því að drepa fingri sínum í augun, vættum úr Maríubrunni, og dæmi eru til, að menn hafa fengið vatn á flöskur langar leiðir að. (Hefði það eflaust haft sama mátt, þótt það væri úr öðrum lindum; allt vatn er hjer afburða-gott og heilnæmt)" (Helga Skúladóttir, "Örnefni á Keldum á Rangárvöllum," *Árbók hins íslenzka fornleifafélags,* 1939, 113–39, quotation from 117–18, cited in ÓL, 264–65); cf. *BS,* 1:612, which does not, however, involve an eye disease. The author's main informant was her father, Skúli Guðmundsson of Keldur.

62. ÓL, 265.

63. Jón Þorkelsson, *Þjóðsögur og munnmæli: Nýtt safn* (Reykjavík: Sigfús Eymundsson, 1899), 200, cited in ÓL, 264. The original publication from the end of the nineteenth century notes that water was "formerly" sought for this purpose.

64. ÓL, 265. JÁ, 2:30, notes that *Gvendarbrunnar* never freeze in the winter nor dry up in the summer, and that their water is especially healthy. Some of them have maintained this reputation through the twentieth century. A thorough study of *Gvendarbrunnar* and other "special" water sources, and the folklore associated with them, is a desideratum.

65. Þorvaldur Thoroddsen, *Ferðabók: Skýrslur um rannsóknir á Íslandi 1882–1898* (Copenhagen: Hið Íslenska fræðafélag, 1942), 294–95, cited in ÓL, 266. In the reprinting of this work by Snæbjörn Jónsson & Co. (Reykjavík, 1958) the relevant passage is on 299–300. Thoroddsen quotes an account by a local official (*sýslumaður*) named Jón Benediktsson from 1747, according to which the sauna is most effective for improving health between the feast of John the Baptist and that of the Visitation (June 24–July 2); according to Jón Benediktsson, many people came there at that time. However, a traveler in 1820 reported that the site was little used and blamed the small size and awkwardness of the bath chamber. The precise date of this traveler's visit is not mentioned. Guðmundur is not associated with this sort of natural phenomenon in the medieval sagas nor, as far as I have been able to ascertain, in recent memory.

66. ÓL, 266, mentions such wells or springs at Kálfanes in Borgarfjörður, Fremri-Þröm in Blöndudalur (Húnavatnssýsla), Bakki in Haukagilshólar in Vatnsdalur, and Ásar in Vatnsnes. ÓL, 259, mentions one at Kirkjuból in Stöðvarfjörður.

67. Jón Þorkelsson, *Þjóðsögur og munnmæli,* 200, cited in ÓL, 258.

68. ÓL, 259.

69. Sigurjón Sigurðsson, personal communication.

70. The oldest version of the story is in a saga about Guðmundur written in the fourteenth century (*BS,* 1:599). In modern folklore, similar stories are told about Þorlákur, and some cliffs are associated with elves or *landvættir* rather than trolls. A rationalized version of the rope story is attributed to a Lutheran priest who died in 1881 and is said to have ordered his parishioners to sing hymns so that they would not hear him sawing away the sharp projecting rocks (JÁ, 1:137–38). Jón Þorkelsson, *Þjóðsögur og munnmæli,* 199, notes the existence of alternative descriptions of how much of the cliff Guðmundur consecrated and why he was interrupted (by an attack instead of a voice from the cliffs); in one case traditions are combined, and the Lutheran priest consecrates the area that Guðmundur did not.

71. JÁ, 1:138, 635–36; ÓL, 270–71. Historically, both Látrabjarg and Lagarfljót belonged to the diocese of Skálholt and thus would have fallen under St. Þorlákur's jurisdiction. Folklore associates Guðmundur especially with the western fjords (where Látrabjarg is located); the residents' hospitality to him during his wanderings is said to have had the result that the Black Death never reached that area.

72. For example, a ford in Hvítá, near Fróðastaðir, blessed by Guðmundur after one of his men drowned there. No one has drowned since. See JÁ, 2:30.

73. JÁ, 1:138; JÁ, 3:217.

74. Gísli Sigurðsson, "Icelandic National Identity: From Romanticism to Tourism," in *Making Europe in Nordic Contexts,* ed. Pertti J. Anttonen, NIF publication no. 35, 41–75 (Turku: Nordic Institute of Folklore, 1996), esp. 41–46.

75. See essays by Westerfelhaus and Pasquier in this volume.

76. Letter from the file for Hellnar at the Place-name Institute of Iceland.

77. For a discussion of the historical relation of folklore collecting and the independence movement in Iceland, see Hallfreður Örn Eiríksson, "Þjóðsagnasöfnun og þjóðfrelsishreyfing," in *Gripla,* ed. Jónas Kristjánsson, Stofnun Árna Magnússonar á Íslandi rit 19, 4:186–97 (Reykjavík: Stofnun Árna Magnússonar, 1980). Probably the slow development of interest in folklore as an expression of nationalism reflects the fact that the sagas and Eddic poetry already provided a recognized, and ancient, focus of national identity.

The Fountain of Youth

History of an Errant Shrine

Ryan K. Smith

For four days one college summer, I served out waters from the Fountain of Youth. Every hour or so I led groups of visitors to the Spring House, where I introduced the bubbling exhibit and recited a short history. After each talk, I filled a plastic pitcher from a spigot set within the exhibit's stone base. As visitors approached, I poured the sulphur-smelling liquid into little cups and handed out samples for them to drink. And then I watched.

The varied reactions that followed point to a surprising depth beneath the surface of Ponce de Leon's Fountain of Youth National Archaeological Park. Founded in the 1910s just north of downtown St. Augustine, Florida, this attraction is one trolley stop amidst dozens of related tourist curiosities. Although it might be dismissed as an antiquated theme park or folklore holdover, few destinations feature such a dramatic blend of history and desire. The park's private owners promote it as Juan Ponce de León's original 1513 landing site on the continent, and they suggest that the well now sheltered by the Spring House was the very object of the Castilian's mythical search. Historians may dismiss these claims, but the Fountain of Youth has succeeded in localizing one of the country's founding tales and has inspired a steady stream of visitors to seek and taste its waters. In other words, the site has become an active shrine.

No church or government sanctions the park's role as a shrine. Its background is murky, ranging from colonial reports and rumors to modern marketing and hucksterism. Yet, in its steady, stubborn popularity, the park presents several challenges for academic history and traditional religion. For example, is the water-drinking ritual, with its lines of visitors daydreaming about life-restoring sips, a cheap echo of honored religious practices or a novel expression of persistent human needs? Either way, the site demonstrates that a ritual typical of Christianity can thrive outside the bounds of a church. Why do so many tourists to this historical attraction seem untouched by eighty years of strident revisionist scholarship on Juan Ponce de León? The park's durable presence highlights the limits of professional history's ability to shape our view of the past. Clearly, visitors are

Fig. 1. Roadside billboard advertising "Ponce de Leon's Fountain of Youth National Archaeological Park," St. Augustine, Florida. Photo by Ryan K. Smith, 2003

seeking something other than accuracy and legitimacy. The Fountain of Youth's popular alchemy raises the possibility that an invention might be as meaningful a monument as any other. So how did this unlikely invention arise?

Building the Fountain

No one knows exactly what prompted Juan Ponce de León to seek out new lands in 1513. Most likely, he shared the same motivations as other explorers from the era, including a desire for power, fame, and riches; allegiance to his king; and belief in his church's mission. Juan Ponce, a seasoned warrior, was quite familiar with the West Indies—he led important campaigns on Hispaniola and San Juan (Puerto Rico) and became the first governor of the latter island in 1510. His Florida expedition in 1513 marked an extension of these activities as it followed the loss of his post on San Juan to a family of higher rank. Early historians added another reason for his voyage, describing it as a quest to find a magical spring spoken of by island Indians.[1]

This attribution is not entirely far-fetched. Medieval Europeans held varied beliefs in magic, and the idea of a *fons aeternae juventutis* was a traditional concept dating back to ancient Greece. Tales of Alexander the Great's conquests included a story about the explorer's discovery of a healing "river of paradise." Variations of this story celebrating wonderful springs in Asia circulated throughout the Middle Ages, such as the *Letter of Prester John,* which described a spring near paradise whose waters granted eternal health and perpetual youth to all who drank it. Indeed, tales of miraculous, restorative waters were common in cultures throughout the world, including examples from Polynesia, Japan, and the Canary Islands.[2] Since descriptions of the New World relayed the rumor of such a fountain only twenty-two years after initial contact, it seems likely that the Taino Indians around Hispaniola told the Europeans about a rejuvenating river to the north. Further, during these early years of contact, Indian and Spanish beliefs often intersected, bolstering their respective legends. For example, local Mexican tales of wealthy hinterland cities fueled the Spaniards' search for the fabled Seven Cities of Gold, while the initial appearance of Hernán Cortés's forces mimicked Aztec prophecies of a white god's return.[3]

Still, there is no contemporary evidence suggesting that Juan Ponce de León was aware of the tale. In his correspondence with King Ferdinand, Juan Ponce may have claimed knowledge of the "secrets" held by nearby Caribbean islands, but the royal contracts for his expeditions to Florida made no mention of any fountain or fantasy. Juan Ponce's summary reports to the Castilian court do not survive. We do know that he navigated the coast of the peninsula for some months in 1513, landed at several spots, engaged the local Indians, and found little silver or gold. After leaving Florida, he skirted the Bahama Islands and then decided to return to San Juan, ordering one ship to stay behind and continue exploring. With that last ship's safe arrival in February 1514, Juan Ponce then presented his findings in person to the king. He would not return to Florida until 1521, when he launched a colonizing expedition to the southwestern tip of the peninsula. The effort failed; Juan Ponce received a mortal wound while battling area Indians and died in Cuba shortly thereafter.[4]

The first recorded links between Juan Ponce and the fountain were made by the Spanish historian Gonzalo Fernández de Oviedo in 1535. In his officially commissioned account of the West Indies, Gonzalo Fernández de Oviedo suggested that Juan Ponce had wasted time during his exploration searching for the rejuvenating waters spoken of by Indians. This was a slap at Juan Ponce's sexual vigor as much as at his gullibility. Medieval fountain myths commonly emphasized links to sensual, erotic love and restored performance, and the historian directly accused Juan Ponce of searching for the fountain to cure "*el enflaquecimiento del sexo,*" or impotence.[5] The charges seem baseless and politically driven, for Juan Ponce was only thirty-nine years old at the time of his first voyage and had recently fathered several children. But years later, in 1575, another author affirmed Juan Ponce's interest in the fountain. Hernando de Escalante de Fontaneda, a shipwreck survivor who had lived among Florida's Indians for years, exaggerated the quest by treating it as the primary objective for Juan Ponce's expedition. The most exhaustive and authoritative account of the voyage appeared in 1601, when Antonio de Herrera y Tordesillas, King Philip II's "Chief Historian of the Indies," discussed Juan Ponce's first expedition in detail. Working from the earlier histories as well as documents now lost, Herrera reviewed Juan Ponce's course nearly day by day. He mentioned the fountain at the voyage's end as he explained why Juan Ponce sent out the solitary ship to search among the Bahamas for the island of Bimini: "He had an account of the wealth of this island and especially that singular *Fuente* [fountain or spring] that the Indians spoke of, that turned men from old men to boys." When that lone ship finally returned to port, its crew "reported that Bimini had been found, but not the Fountain."[6] Elsewhere in his *Historia,* Herrera made references to "the spring of Bimini and a river in Florida, the Indians of Cuba and Hispaniola affirming that old people bathing themselves in them, became young again."[7] These works established Juan Ponce as a wistful hero whose dramatic role overshadowed his remarkable accomplishments.

The United States cared little for Juan Ponce until the annexation of Florida as a territory in 1819. By then the nation had established its own founding mythology, from Pocahontas to the Pilgrims. Juan Ponce joined the fold after the sexual impotency themes surrounding the tale had been scrubbed out. Serious historians of the day, such as George Bancroft, relayed the basics of Herrera's interpretation, and Washington Irving's colorful account, published in 1831, captured the public's imagination. Poets and painters considered the tale from several angles, lingering over its philosophical themes of immortality, age, and hope. By the mid–nineteenth century the story had become ingrained in history and metaphor, and Americans venerated Juan Ponce as a romantic cavalier.[8]

Shortly thereafter, the locus of this literary institution gradually became fixed in northeast Florida. Although Herrera's 1601 account could not pinpoint Juan Ponce's original landing sites precisely and the supposed location of the magical spring or fountain had always been a mystery, St. Augustine now emerged as the preferred harbor for both. Ironically, northern tourists helped drive the identification. For the waves of travelers that visited Florida after the Civil War in search of a healthier winter climate, Juan Ponce's legend meshed nicely with the area's exotic tropical landscape and historic Spanish presence. In 1870 a St. Augustine real-estate developer, playing on the story's guidebook popularity, promoted his property by transforming a nearby stream into "the Ponce de Leon Spring and Fountain of Youth." He built a small shelter for the waters, and two years later a new stagecoach ride carrying visitors from town to the spring "was found too small to accommodate all who wanted to go," according to a local newspaper.[9] At the same time, local gossip began to spread word of another possible fountain of youth just north of the city gates. This "Ponce de Leon Spring" seemed to be a well on the overgrown estate of the horticulturist Henry H. Williams. In 1875 *Harper's Magazine* correspondent Constance Fenimore Woolson narrated a trip to the "spring" in which her party drank the tepid water, discussed its history, observed its ramshackle surroundings, and stretched their hotel-weary legs.[10] The curbed well they gazed on would serve as the foundation for today's park.

As real-estate values and tourist numbers rose, the links between St. Augustine and the Ponce de León expedition became more formalized. In 1886 the railroad baron Henry Flagler raised his magnificent Hotel Ponce de Leon in the center of St. Augustine, where it became one of the state's premier resorts. He then decorated it with the artist Thomas Moran's similarly oversized painting of Juan Ponce's landing party. Also during the 1880s, the city began celebrating an annual Ponce de León Day, commemorating the explorer's first landing with elaborate reenactments and ceremonies every April. Eventually residents placed an honorary statue of the explorer in the city's central plaza. Other sites around the state, such as a Fountain of Youth in St. Petersburg and De Leon Springs in Volusia County, competed for a portion of Juan Ponce's historical aura, but none was as successful as "the oldest city."[11]

The modern Fountain of Youth park emerged after an adventurous couple purchased the Williams estate and its popular well around 1900. Fresh from the gold rush in Canada's Yukon Territory, Luella Day and Edward McConnell charmed St. Augustine society, boasting of personal riches, aristocratic lineage, and medical expertise. The feisty, theatrical Luella Day McConnell took charge of the estate.[12] By 1909 she had produced a series of surprising finds, including a small silver container and a cross of stones, both of which had been allegedly unearthed next to the curbed "spring." The fourteen-by-ten-foot Latin cross consisted of twenty-seven pieces of local coquina stone, arranged so that fifteen stones could be counted down the staff and thirteen across the beam. The decorated silver container, apparently an old saltcellar, was said by McConnell to have held a bit of old parchment with writing in Spanish from Juan Ponce de León's party testifying to their laying of the cross in 1513.[13]

In April 1909 the *St. Augustine Evening Record* applauded the discoveries, reporting that "Mrs. MacConnell [*sic*] recently discovered a coquina cross, placed by Ponce de León to mark the spot where he found a spring of fresh water."[14] A curator of the St. Augustine Historical Society and Institute of Science visited the excavations and took photographs of the cross, which eventually became a common postcard subject. The manuscript and the saltcellar soon disappeared, but not before an exact replica of the saltcellar had been made for display. The cross remained on the ground as part of the attraction. McConnell then moved the old Williams house away from the prized well, raised an archway over the entrance to the grounds, began charging admission, and sold water from the well by the glass. Her park became popular; the *Record* estimated that with the exception of the old Spanish fort, more people came to St. Augustine to see the Fountain of Youth

Fig. 2. This postcard shows the Williams well just after Luella Day McConnell opened her attraction to the public. Differing reports suggest that this well was dug for the Williams estate in about 1875 or that it was a centuries-old spring later lined with stone. Its domestic setting would be entirely changed several decades later with the construction of the Spring House over this site and the refashioning of the well's base. *Fountain of Youth 1513, Saint Augustine, Florida,* 1907, image PC3406, Florida Photographic Collection, Florida State Archives, Tallahassee, Florida

than to see any other area attraction.[15] In addition, McConnell's efforts settled the location of Juan Ponce's landing for the general public.

In 1927 the politician and local businessman Walter B. Fraser bought the property and upgraded the park. He pledged to make it "a credit to the city of which it is an important historical part, and make it another of the quaint attractions which are yearly increasing St. Augustine's popularity as a resort."[16] However, he faced new criticism from the St. Augustine Historical Society and other academic voices that began to challenge McConnell's original claims by highlighting the colonial records. In response, Fraser aggressively promoted and defended the park's claims, filing libel lawsuits against skeptical publications, producing supportive affidavits, and publishing his own historical findings. He expanded the attraction, building new exploration-related exhibits, employing historically costumed guides, and, most significantly, uncovering a series of skeletons that proved to be some of the earliest Christian Indian burials in North America. The Smithsonian Institution conducted tests and excavations, and the University of Florida launched a follow-up project in 1950. Thus, the Fountain of Youth had become "a National Archaeological Park" as well as a quaint staple of the local trolley circuit.[17]

Fig. 3. This postcard shows the cross and remodeled well inside the Spring House during Walter B. Fraser's early ownership of the property. *The Fountain of Youth, St. Augustine, Florida,* 1948

The park remains remarkably unchanged to this day. It is still owned by the Fraser family, and the stone cross, the saltcellar replica, and the exploration exhibits are still on display. At some point the upper structure of the well's curbing was fashioned into its current state, with a bubbling stream of water spurting from a short coquina wall down into a narrow, bulb-lit well shaft. In addition, the Spring House's backdrop of flowers and greenery was replaced with a full-size diorama showing Juan Ponce and other Spanish soldiers greeting Indians at the coast. Guides, though no longer in period costume, still hand out cups of fountain water, and visitors exit through the gift shop. The Florida Museum of Natural History continues excavations on the grounds, now focusing on the newfound remains of Pedro Menendez's earliest (1565) Spanish camp. Recent figures suggest that seventy-five thousand to one hundred thousand people visit the Fountain of Youth annually, and my return trip in 2003 found it humming with patrons.[18] Somewhere, Juan Ponce must be amused.

The Park as Shrine

In 1896, four years before Luella McConnell moved onto the Williams estate, Roman Catholic priests in Indiana built an elaborate new shrine on the campus of the University of Notre Dame. Their tribute to the grotto at Lourdes, France, where a young woman had reported miraculous visions of the Virgin Mary in

1858, replicated the main features of the original European shrine. It was built with rocks and boulders arranged over a small spring, and the site quickly developed a reputation for supernatural healings, related to those at Lourdes. Prior to the erection of the tributary shrine, university priests had been importing "official" Lourdes water from France and mailing bottled samples to eager Catholics all over the country, producing testimonies to its wonderful cures. The new Indiana grotto became a popular pilgrimage site and helped expand Americans' appreciation for the healing waters associated with Lourdes.[19]

Lourdes's popularity grew amidst a broadening interest in healing waters. For decades natural springs in western Virginia, upstate New York, and western Arkansas had hosted busy resorts for the healthy and sick alike. A related, pseudoscientific industry emerged at midcentury touting the restorative qualities of certain waters, and customers across the country bought bottled water cures from a variety of sources, such as Buffalo Lithia Springs in Virginia and Poland Spring in Maine.[20] Interestingly, springs were suddenly "discovered" at Gettysburg, Pennsylvania, in 1865 after the Civil War, and local promoters advertised the battlefield-area waters as capable of producing miracle cures. In 1868 a New York company began bottling and selling these waters, and that same year an enthusiast in the *New York Times* even hinted that the waters might "possess the power of imparting perpetual youth."[21] The multiplication of medicinal springs into the twentieth century reinforced the Lourdes phenomenon and illustrated the prevalence of the idea.[22]

Such themes surely fed St. Augustine's appetite for a Fountain of Youth, but McConnell does not seem to have consciously drawn from Lourdes or any other operation for her attraction. However, her park did demonstrate connections to shrine culture. Outside McConnell's window and across a small creek, the Roman Catholic Shrine of Our Lady of La Leche stood adjacent to the Fountain of Youth park. This shrine was a notable institution; tradition held that on its grounds Father Mendoza Grajales had offered the first Mass after the Menendez expedition landed in 1565. Fifty-five years later mission priests constructed a sanctuary there, dedicated it to *Nuestra Señora de La Leche y Buen Parto* (Our Lady of the Milk and Happy Delivery), and enshrined a small statue of the nursing Virgin and child. Eventually the shrine fell into ruin, but it underwent a celebrated rededication at the hands of St. Augustine's bishop, Augustin Verot, in 1875. After a destructive hurricane, it was restored yet again in 1915, at the time of McConnell's series of enterprises next door. As a historical entrepreneur, McConnell must have observed its pilgrim activity. She made direct reference to the shrine through a short-lived, rival claim that the actual Shrine of Our Lady of La Leche chapel stood on her own Fountain of Youth property. Pointing to a humble wooden structure, she erected a coquina-stone chapel over the site and exhibited it as a replica of the earliest shrine, which had been destroyed in 1728.[23] It is unclear when this replica was removed. Today the neighboring Shrine of Our Lady of La Leche remains active and welcomes approximately one hundred thousand annual visitors, many of whom maintain the tradition of asking the Holy Mother's intercession for a healthy motherhood or for other blessings.[24] Thus, the Fountain of Youth shares with religious shrines not only conceptual space but physical space as well.

Scholars define shrines as locations of sacred power.[25] In medieval Europe, Christian shrines inspired deep traditions; they typically commemorated a holy person or event in the life of the church, and they could be sites of miracles, healings, and revelations. As destinations, they hosted pilgrims who made offerings of prayer and devotion and who sometimes sought divine intervention in personal crises.[26] The Lourdes grotto and Our Lady of La Leche in St. Augustine illustrate how aspects of these traditions have continued into the present.[27] Modern society has expanded the concept of a shrine to include secular types, such as popular shrines and civic shrines. These destinations memorialize people or events, localizing national or cultural ideals rather than religious beliefs. Examples range from war memorials to sports facilities and include the battlefield at Gettysburg, the Lincoln Memorial in Washington, D.C., the Alamo in San Antonio, Elvis Presley's Graceland in Memphis, and the Baseball Hall of Fame in Cooperstown. Such sites may evoke a general sense of divine providence, but their references to the supernatural are tightly restricted.[28]

The Fountain of Youth blurs these boundaries. It might be described as a civic shrine—as a tribute to Juan Ponce's European "discovery" of Florida—yet its mythology regularly widens into the realm of pilgrimage and supernatural healing. Other civic shrines occasionally host candlelight vigils and solemn ceremonies, but the Fountain of Youth, despite its playful character, mimics the overall form and contents of regular Christian shrines. These ecclesiastical parallels may help explain its longevity. Though the park does not fit into a structured religious system, its success may draw from a similar psychological well.

First, the park centers around a stylized "saint," Juan Ponce de León. In legend and at the park, Juan Ponce is portrayed as a founding martyr: an impassioned explorer, a key figure of the American errand, and one who died in pursuit of his mystic beliefs. Some versions of the legend also ridicule Juan Ponce for his gullibility, but the park generally lauds his quest. It invokes his name at every opportunity and consistently represents him in sturdy military attire. On billboards he points to a stream, and in the Spring House diorama he converses with an Indian at the water's edge. Further, like official Catholic saints, he is an intercessory figure—it is not through his authority that the waters have any special power; rather, he merely reveals their source.

In keeping with Juan Ponce's role as saint, the park contains an odd collection of related relics. Two—the stone cross and the saltcellar—are shown as direct evidence of his hand. Their correspondence to traditional Christian symbols, such as the Latin cross and, perhaps, the tabernacle, enhances their resonance. Apocryphal stories have arisen to support their validity; for example, owner Walter Fraser argued that previous owner Henry H. Williams "discovered a coquina cross near the Fountain of Youth spring and covered it up" in 1868, prior to McConnell's later "discovery" of the same item.[29] In addition, though the original saltcellar and its contents supposedly disappeared just after a metal replica was cast, a treasured, unmarked scrap of parchment survives. These relics carry a heavier ideological burden than the more common, museum-type exhibits distributed throughout the grounds. They are all found in the Spring House, an airy coquina structure that is fashioned after Florida's early missions. Inside, the objects are arranged below the life-sized mannequin of Juan Ponce and next to the celebrated well, where their presence bolsters the claims for the waters and helps form something of a sanctuary.

The park also features notable tombs, as was the custom at medieval shrines. However, these do not contain the explorer's mortal remains. Nor do they reflect the intentions of the shrine's designers. Rather, these colonial-era Timucua Indian graves were uncovered accidentally by park workers in the 1930s and then incorporated into the exhibit after study. At first the archaeologists left the graves exposed, with scores of half-embedded skeletons facing up from their shallow mounds. The park's owners soon enclosed these skeletons in a large "log structure" to protect them and exemplify Indian building traditions.[30] Only in 1991 were they reinterred. Throughout this time the park gradually highlighted the site's Indian-related resources. Archaeologists found evidence of a long-standing Timucua village on the grounds, including hut foundations and artifacts that now have their own displays. Yet almost all of these, including the reburials, are at the far end of the park, removed from the primary attractions such as the Spring House and related "Discovery" programs. The graves added another layer of mortality and spirituality to the park, but Indians, allegedly the original advocates of the waters, appear inside the Spring House only as mannequins greeting Juan Ponce's landing party.

Above all, it is the well and the water-drinking ritual that transform this otherwise dated biographical museum. The interaction between the visitors and the water drives the entire operation, from its layout to its marketing. The visitors' curiosity to see and taste the water, their fascination with a magical means to eternal youth, resonates back in time, connecting them with the imaginations of nineteenth-century poets, sixteenth-century court historians, medieval minstrels, ancient Greek choruses, and others who have explored this very human yearning.

Fig. 4. These are among the dozens of skeletons unearthed by archaeologists during the 1930s, pictured as they were displayed, within a log shelter. "Section of Indian Burial Ground," from Carita Doggett Corse, *The Fountain of Youth and Ancient Indian Village and Burial Ground* (St. Augustine, Florida, 1934), 35

Fig. 5. A view of the water-drinking ritual in 1949. "Tourists receiving water at the Fountain of Youth: Saint Augustine, Florida," 1949, image c011991, Florida Photographic Collection, Florida State Archives, Tallahassee, Florida

It is a mark of the park's success that it has embodied such a common, complex belief with any sense of authenticity at all. Visitors come to partake in this global myth themselves, by the cupful.

Yet, can we classify the park's visitors as pilgrims? Surely their bemused, half-hearted, ironic faith in the enterprise falls far short of that of traditional religious pilgrims. Earlier tourists did travel to St. Augustine seeking to improve their health, but they were not expecting miracles. Today's visitor rides in comfort from park to park, stopping at the Fountain of Youth as another attraction, not as a destination in itself. Perhaps the same could be said for the city's "official" shrines —the chapel of Our Lady of La Leche and the nearby Greek Orthodox shrine of St. Photios on St. George Street. One recent study of Roman Catholic pilgrimage practices in the United States reported that pilgrims nearly always combine social and recreational motives with religious motives for their travel and that Roman Catholic shrines are commonly found in the vicinity of tourist attractions.[31] Thus, it seems customary for modern religious pilgrims to have fun on the side. Since visitors travel to St. Augustine for relaxation and edification, the Fountain of Youth attraction provides a focus for the larger forces drawing tourists to the area. At a minimum, Fountain of Youth patrons are travelers open to wonder.[32]

The park's venerable water-drinking ritual, like other rituals, consists of a prescribed ceremony that works to remove participants from their everyday experiences. At set times and in groups visitors enter the Spring House, where their guide begins by explaining the meaning and importance of the waters before them. This rote speech, which is usually delivered from a small, railed stand, reviews the legend's history, describes the feats of Juan Ponce, and tells how the cross and the saltcellar were later found.[33] The guide takes questions and then invites the group to follow him or her down several steps to the sputtering well, where the cups are filled by pitcher and then handed out one by one. Visitors drink their samples, reflect on the experience or make small comments, and then file back outside into the sunlight. The ritual's pacing, therefore, offers a preparatory beginning, a pivotal encounter, and a meditative postlude before returning participants to the outside world.

I have observed a variety of responses to the ritual and the water. Humor usually diffused the accompanying awkwardness of the scene. Guides and visitors joked about the promise of magical water, without addressing issues of faith directly. Frequently visitors appeared disappointed by the spectacle in the end. They often stood around the low well, grumbling into their plastic cups about the sour taste of the flat water. Given the park's aggressive advertising, plus the weight of its cultural background, the grumblers may have expected something more impressive in presentation and taste. Occasionally visitors appeared angry and complained of being cheated by a sham. Yet, I have also seen visitors treat the

Fig. 6. The modern spring exhibit. A small stream of water flows out from a narrow tube set within the coquina-rock base. The diorama and mannequins stand just to the right of this well. The exposed stone cross, not pictured here, also lies to the right. Photo by Ryan K. Smith, 2003

Fig. 7. Bottles of fountain water for sale in the gift shop. Such gifts have been sold for decades, and the bottles can occasionally be found for sale at online auctions such as eBay.com. Photo by Ryan K. Smith, 2003

water with reverence. Some savored their sips silently, and some earnestly requested that extra water be poured into their own bottles to carry away with them.[34]

Enthusiastic visitors can also purchase bottles of Fountain of Youth water in the park's gift shop. This gift shop is so elaborate that it highlights a final characteristic of the park as shrine—namely, the customary link between pilgrimages and commerce. For centuries shrines have nurtured a host of related industries, from lodgings to refreshments to works of art.[35] However, unlike religious shrines, the Fountain of Youth achieved this blending of the sacred and the profane from the opposite starting point. There had been a demand for a "fountain of youth" in St. Augustine prior to Luella McConnell's activities in the early 1900s, but McConnell opened her park as a decidedly entrepreneurial attraction, and it was her marketing that solidified the park's status as a landmark. Gradually her business achieved a more sacrosanct aura. Today the moneymaking aspect of the park's character remains prominent, but its gift-shop offerings still recall the format of sacred-water-bottling operations at Lourdes and elsewhere. Aside from T-shirts, postcards, and jewelry, the Fountain of Youth gift shop also features a bottle-your-own version of the Spring House well spigot, plus labeled, sealed bottles of Fountain of Youth water in various sizes. The shelves of such kitsch objects are the last things visitors see before exiting—reflections of the park's imaginative power, relics for the taking.

Errant and Unrepentant

Critics have presented evidence to debunk the Fountain of Youth on nearly all of its original claims. From the park's earliest days, waves of scholars have attacked its alleged connections with Juan Ponce de León's expedition. In the 1920s St. Augustine Historical Society research associate Emily Wilson called the park "silly and quacky" and questioned founder Luella McConnell's sanity.[36] Wilson made a research trip to the Library of Congress and returned with copies of Spanish-era colonial documents that enabled her to dismiss any claims of links among Juan Ponce de León, the St. Augustine area, and a "Fountain of Youth." In 1935 the *Florida Historical Quarterly* published much of the original source material on Juan Ponce's voyages with commentary that ignored McConnell's claims and concluded that romantic writers had wrongly emphasized the role of the fountain legend in the voyages.[37] In 1937 a vocal member of the Florida Historical Society recounted the history of the Williams "spring," confirming its origins as a domestic well dug about 1875.[38] The legend and the park maintained their popularity, however, spurring a crop of revisionist biographies in the second half of the twentieth century. These grew increasingly insistent, with the latest by Robert H. Fuson in 2000 contending that King Ferdinand mentioned the fountain to Juan Ponce as an afterthought and that the explorer's crew never got farther north than the

Daytona Beach area.[39] The St. Augustine Historical Society has continued to hack away at the local curiosities; for example, in 1981 it acquired the personal testimony of a resident who remembered the laying of McConnell's coquina cross.[40] In addition, the fountain waters themselves do not help the cause since Juan Ponce died without any apparent change in condition, and there is no modern testimony to its positive effects.

All of these critiques focus on the issue of authenticity. However, even among religious shrines the question of authenticity is not always foremost. It is true that Lourdes water gained popularity in America by being bottled at a celebrated site and by public testimonials among the Catholic community. Still, many shrines arose imitating the Lourdes grotto but without any material connection to the original. An example is the 1896 grotto built at the University of Notre Dame, whose waters inspired related healings and whose alcoves also sheltered praying pilgrims. These secondary shrines were able to access the same spiritual power as the original, "authentic" sites. Likewise, the Shrine of Our Lady of La Leche across from St. Augustine's Fountain of Youth park presents a living, sacred space attended by thousands of pilgrims annually, notwithstanding the fact that the chapel and its statue have been lost and remade several times. Such places demonstrate that pilgrims do not require "authenticity"—ties with an accurate original—for their faith and tributes. Rather, they frequent sites that, whatever their specific history, are able to continually renew their connections with a larger, more intangible source.

In the same way, the ongoing attraction of the Fountain of Youth park may lie in its ability to conjure the spirit of the explorer's quest. It presents the first meeting of Spaniard, Indian, and continent as a mystical one, distant yet accessible through the spring water and relics. In its suggestion of restored youth, it compounds the power of this historic encounter with a recurrent human fantasy of rejuvenation. More than an official historical record and more than a recognized sacrament, the park becomes an open font inviting visitors to test the depths for themselves. Skeptical attacks do not sway this ability. Whatever its inaccuracies or blasphemies, the Fountain of Youth flows with something vital.

Notes

I'd like to thank Lyn Causey, Charles Tingley, Eric Johnson, and Margaret Cormack for their comments on this essay.

1. For background on Juan Ponce de León and the controversies surrounding his life, see Robert Henderson Fuson, *Juan Ponce de León and the Spanish Discovery of Puerto Rico and Florida* (Blacksburg, Va.: McDonald & Woodward, 2000); Anthony Q. Devereux, *Juan Ponce de León, King Ferdinand, and the Fountain of Youth* (Spartanburg, S.C.: Published in association with Waccamaw Press by the Reprint Co., 1993); Vicente Murga

Sanz, *Juan Ponce de León: Fundador y primer gobernador del Pueblo Puertorriqueño, descubridor de la Florida y del Estrecho de las Bahamas* (San Juan: Ediciones de la Universidad de Puerto Rico, 1959); and Luis Rafael Arana, "The Exploration of Florida and Sources on the Founding of St. Augustine," *Florida Historical Quarterly* 44 (August 1965): 1–16.

2. Leonardo Olschki, "Ponce de León's Fountain of Youth: History of a Geographic Myth," *Hispanic American Historical Review* 21 (August 1941): 361–385; Constantine B. Lerner, "The 'River of Paradaise' and the Legend about the City of Tbilisi: A Literary Source of the Legend," *Folklore* 16 (November 2001): 72–77; Devereux, *Juan Ponce de León,* 87–104; Fuson, *Juan Ponce de León,* 119. See also Alev Lytle Croutier, *Taking the Waters: Spirit, Art, Sensuality* (New York: Abbeville Press, 1992).

3. George E. Buker, "The Search for the Seven Cities and Early American Exploration," *Florida Historical Quarterly* 71 (October 1992): 155–68. For Taino traditions, see Antonio M. Stevens-Arroyo, *Cave of the Jaguar: The Mythical World of the Tainos* (Albuquerque: University of New Mexico Press, 1988).

4. Devereux, *Juan Ponce de León,* 88. For translations of the relevant documents, see Fuson, *Juan Ponce de León,* 92–95, 103–14, 129–31, 160–66 and T. Frederick Davis, "Juan Ponce de Leon's Voyages to Florida," *Florida Historical Quarterly* 14 (July 1935): 8–63.

5. Samuel Eliot Morison, *The European Discovery of America: The Southern Voyages* (New York: Oxford University Press, 1974), 503; Douglas T. Peck, "Misconceptions and Myths Related to the 'Fountain of Youth' and Juan Ponce de Leon's 1513 Exploration Voyage," http://www.newworldexplorersinc.org (accessed January 7, 2005); Arana, "Exploration of Florida," 4–5.

6. Herrera, quoted in Fuson, *Juan Ponce de León,* 114. Antonio de Herrera y Tordesillas's work is titled *Historia general de los hechos los castellanos en las islas i tierra firme del mar océano,* 8 vols. (Madrid: Emplenta Real [by Juan Flamenco & Juan de la Questa], 1601–15). See also Davis, "Juan Ponce de Leon's Voyages"; Devereux, *Juan Ponce de León,* 87–141; Fuson, *Juan Ponce de León,* 99–115.

7. Herrera, quoted in Olschki, "Ponce de León's Fountain of Youth," 366.

8. Ann Uhry Abrams, *The Pilgrims and Pocahontas: Rival Myths of American Origin* (Boulder, Colo.: Westview Press, 1999); George Bancroft, *History of the United States from the Discovery of the American Continent,* 15th ed. (Boston: Little, Brown & Co., 1856), 1:31–35; Washington Irving, *The Life and Voyages of Christopher Columbus: To Which Are Added Those of His Companions* (New York: G. P. Putnam, 1861), 3:278–84. For artistic works inspired by the tale, see Robert Wilson Torchia, *A Florida Legacy: Ponce de León in Florida* (Jacksonville, Fla.: Cummer Museum of Art & Gardens, 1998), 15–19.

9. "Ponce de Leon Spring," *Florida Press,* March 9, 1872, quoted in Torchia, *Florida Legacy,* 8–11. The real-estate developer was John Francis Whitney, and his tract, Ravenswood, sat just northwest of town. Whitney also published a pamphlet entitled *A Brief Account of St. Augustine and Its Environs: Its Advantages as a Winter Residence; Climate, Productions, Resources, & c., & c.,* 2nd ed. (St. Augustine, Fla., 1873). For an example of an early St. Augustine guidebook that included the legend of Juan Ponce de León, see Thérèse Yelverton, *St. Augustine, Florida: Sketches of Its History, Objects of Interest, and*

Advantages as a Resort for Health and Recreation (New York: G. P. Putnam & Son, 1871).

10. See Constance Fenimore Woolson, "The Ancient City," *Harper's New Monthly Magazine* 50 (January 1875): 165–86. Describing this scene, she wrote:

> At last we came to the place, and filed in through a broken-down fence. We found a deserted house, an overgrown field, a gully, a pool, and an old curb of coquina surrounding the magic spring. . . . "The Fountain of Youth," declaimed John, ladling out the water. "Who will drink?". . . We all drank; and then there was a great silence. "Well," said the poet, deliberately, looking around from his seat on the curb, "take it altogether, that shanty, those bushes, the pig-sty, the hopeless sandy field, the oozing pool, and this horrible tepid water, drawn from, to say the least, a dubious source—a very dubious source—it is, all in all, *about* the ugliest place I ever saw!" There was a general shout. "We have suspected it in our hearts all winter," said the "other young lady;" "but not one of us dared put the thought into words, as it was our only walk."

Woolson's story demonstrates that demand for such an attraction arose as early as or earlier than the groomed site itself.

Williams's estate was known as the Paradise Grove and Rose Garden (Torchia, *Florida Legacy*, 9–10). In 1937 one sleuth claimed that this well was "dug about 1875 by Philip Gomez and Philip Capo of St. Augustine" (Charles B. Reynolds, *Fact versus Fiction for the New Historical St. Augustine* [Mountain Lakes, N.J.: published by the author, 1937], 28).

11. Thomas Graham, *Flagler's Magnificent Hotel Ponce de Leon* (St. Augustine, Fla.: St. Augustine Historical Society, 1990); Torchia, *Florida Legacy*, 6, 19. See also Fuson, *Juan Ponce de León*, 228–31.

12. Karen Harvey, *Daring Daughters: St. Augustine's Feisty Females, 1565–2000* (Virginia Beach, Va.: Donning Company, 2002), 77–84. For McConnell's early autobiography, see Luella Day, *The Tragedy of the Klondike: This Book of Travels Gives the True Facts of What Took Place in the Gold-fields under British Rule* (New York: N.p., 1906).

13. *The First Landing Place of Juan Ponce de Leon on the North American Continent in the Year 1513* (St. Augustine, Fla.: Walter B. Fraser, 1956), 10–15, 26. McConnell visited Spain in 1908, where she claimed to have researched her St. Augustine finds. One 1912 city guidebook reprinted a portion of an old document McConnell supposedly received from the "Archivo General de Indias" and Columbus Library in Sevilla, Spain. Written from Juan Ponce's perspective, it stated: "I went ashore with the Indian. We landed near a spring that they called the Fountain of Youth; there they had a temple built where they worshipped the sun, and there I built a cross out of coquina. . . . In the heart of the cross I placed a descriptive 'image' of myself and took possession in the name of our beloved Catholic king" (*Post Card Guide and History of Old St. Augustine* [St. Augustine, Fla.: H. J. Usina, 1912], 28). There is no mention of this suspect document in the historical literature.

Yet, the story of Juan Ponce planting a cross does have a basis within the historical record. Herrera explained that after the party's initial landing on Florida's coast, the expedition sailed south for about two weeks. Then the explorers went ashore a second time, where they encountered a group of Indians, found a stream to fill their water casks, and marked the stream with "a cross hewn from stone, with an inscription." Afterward, they continued sailing down the coast. See Davis, "Juan Ponce de Leon's Voyages," 18; and Arana, "Exploration of Florida," 3. In 1981 St. Augustine resident Hubert W. Carcaba told the St. Augustine Historical Society that Benjy Pacetti laid the coquina cross before World War I (personal communication dated December 9, 1981, in the Fountain of Youth vertical files, St. Augustine Historical Society, St. Augustine, Fla.).

14. *St. Augustine Evening Record,* quoted in *First Landing Place,* 14.

15. James C. Clark, "Fountain of Myths," *Florida Magazine* (December 8, 1991): 17–18; Reynolds, *Fact versus Fiction,* 28–30.

16. Walter B. Fraser, quoted in M. B. Prout, "Title Cleared, Fountain Park Being Groomed," *St. Augustine Record,* September 4, 1927; *First Landing Place.*

17. See Carita Doggett Corse, *The Fountain of Youth and Ancient Indian Village and Burial Ground* (St. Augustine, Fla., 1934), 31–36; and the Florida Museum of Natural History's collections at http://www.flmnh.ufl.edu/histarch/sasites.htm (accessed October 6, 2006).

18. Walter Putnam, "Fountain of Youth Attracts 75,000 to 100,000 Yearly," *St. Augustine Record,* November 10, 1983. The attendance figure came from owner John R. Fraser. See also http://www.fountainofyouthflorida.com (accessed October 6, 2006). In 2003 St. Johns County reported approximately three million overnight visitors to St. Augustine annually (personal communication from Nicole Spruill, St. Johns County Visitors and Convention Bureau, September 5, 2003).

19. Colleen McDannell, *Material Christianity: Religion and Popular Culture in America* (New Haven, Conn.: Yale University Press, 1995), 132–62; Mary Pat Dowling Beal, "The Praying Cave at 100," *Notre Dame Magazine* 25 (Summer 1996).

20. Thomas A. Chambers, *Drinking the Waters: Creating an American Leisure Class at Nineteenth-Century Mineral Springs* (Washington, D.C.: Smithsonian Institution Press, 2002); Susan E. Cayleff, *Wash and Be Healed: The Water-Cure Movement and Women's Health* (Philadelphia: Temple University Press, 1987); McDannell, *Material Christianity,* 144–48.

21. The *New York Times* quoted in James Powell Weeks, *Gettysburg: Memory, Market, and an American Shrine* (Ph.D. diss., Pennsylvania State University, 2001), 55–56.

22. In September 2003 the online auction house Ebay.com featured a 1929 photograph showing a roadside "Fountain of Youth" stand in New Mexico that sold water from an "Old Indian Spanish American Well." This informal, apparently short-lived venture further illustrated the theme's contemporary currency.

23. Reynolds, *Fact versus Fiction,* 34–35.

24. Zsolt Aradi, *Shrines to Our Lady around the World* (New York: Farrar, Straus, and Young, 1954), 167–85; Corse, *Fountain of Youth,* 19–26; personal interview with Eric Johnson, director of the Shrine of Our Lady of La Leche, St. Augustine, Fla., September 18, 2003. See also Matthew J. Geiger, *Mission of Nombre de Dios Shrine of Our Lady of La Leche, St. Augustine, Florida: A Brief History* (St. Augustine, Fla.: Published by the Shrine Gift Shop, 2003); http://www.missionandshrine.org (accessed October 6, 2006).

25. Entries in the *Oxford English Dictionary* trace the gradually widening definition of "shrine," from a box for a saint's relics to a place for the veneration of some person or thing (*Oxford English Dictionary,* 2nd ed. [Oxford, U.K.: Clarendon Press; New York: Oxford University Press, 1989], 15:376–77). See Paul B. Courtright, "Shrines," in *The Encyclopedia of Religion,* ed. Mircea Eliade, 13:299–302 (New York: Macmillan, 1987); and "Shrine," in *The HarperCollins Dictionary of Religion,* ed. Jonathan Z. Smith, William Scott Green, and Jorunn Jacobsen Buckley, 992–94 (San Francisco: HarperSanFrancisco, 1995).

26. For medieval shrines, see Mary Lee Nolan, "The European Roots of Latin American Pilgrimage," in *Pilgrimage in Latin America,* ed. N. Ross Crumrine and Alan Morinis, 19–52 (Westport, Conn.: Greenwood Press, 1991).

27. For modern Roman Catholic shrines, see Gisbert Rinschede, "Catholic Pilgrimage Places in the United States," in *Pilgrimage in the United States,* ed. G. Rinschede and S. M. Bhardwaj, 63–135 (Berlin: Dietrich Reimer Verlag, 1990). Rinschede cites the sanctuary at Chimayo, New Mexico, as one of America's premier shrines for miraculous cures. Today, El Santuario de Chimayo attracts about three hundred thousand visitors per year.

28. For civic shrines, see Ian Reader and Tony Walter, eds., *Pilgrimage in Popular Culture* (Hampshire, U.K.: Macmillan, 1993); John Bodnar, *Remaking America: Public Memory, Commemoration, and Patriotism in the Twentieth Century* (Princeton, N.J.: Princeton University Press, 1992); David Chidester and Edward T. Linenthal, eds., *American Sacred Space* (Bloomington: Indiana University Press, 1995); Harriet F. Senie and Sally Webster, eds., *Critical Issues in Public Art: Content, Context, and Controversy* (Washington, D.C.: Smithsonian Institution Press, 1998); Holly Beachley Brear, *Inherit the Alamo: Myth and Ritual at an American Shrine* (Austin: University of Texas Press, 1995); Gerald Redmond, "A Plethora of Shrines: Sport in the Museum and Hall of Fame," *Quest* 19 (1971): 41–48; Jon Pahl, *Shopping Malls and Other Sacred Spaces: Putting God in Place* (Grand Rapids, Mich.: Brazos Press, 2003); and Jim Weeks, *Gettysburg: Memory, Market, and an American Shrine* (Princeton, N.J.: Princeton University Press, 2003).

29. *First Landing Place,* 26.

30. Corse, *Fountain of Youth,* 31–36. Ironically, these historic burials might recommend the site as a modern Indian shrine, but there has been no public movement in that direction.

31. Rinschede, "Catholic Pilgrimage Places," 68. Scholars define pilgrimage as a round-trip journey undertaken by pilgrims who consider their destination sacred, allowing for a negotiation between the known and the unknown ("Pilgrimage" in *The HarperCollins Dictionary of Religion,* 841–47; Simon Coleman and John Elsner, *Pilgrimage: Past and Present in the World Religions* [Cambridge, Mass.: Harvard University Press, 1995]).

32. For a related consideration of tourist motivations in modern America, see Umberto Eco, *Travels in Hyper Reality: Essays,* trans. William Weaver (New York: Harcourt Brace Jovanovich, 1986).

33. At my return visit in June 2003, our guide repeated essentially the same speech that I had memorized years earlier. The speech contains several questionable assertions, including the statement that Juan Ponce tasted these waters and reported them to be "good

and sweet," which appears nowhere in the historical record except perhaps on McConnell's "lost" parchment. Guides also claim that the park's owners have had the waters tested and found that the spring's readings do not match those of other nearby sources, thereby suggesting a unique, mysterious reservoir.

34. An example of a positive family review of the Fountain of Youth water ritual can be found at http://www.familytravelreviews.com/fountainofyouth.htm (accessed January 7, 2005).

35. For the link between pilgrimages and commerce, see McDannell, *Material Christianity;* and Leigh Eric Schmidt, *Consumer Rites: The Buying and Selling of American Holidays* (Princeton, N.J.: Princeton University Press, 1995).

36. Emily Wilson quoted in Harvey, *Daring Daughters,* 84, from letter in the H. H. Williams / Fountain of Youth vertical file, St. Augustine Historical Society, St. Augustine, Fla.

37. Davis, "Juan Ponce de Leon's Voyages."

38. Reynolds, *Fact versus Fiction,* 28–29.

39. Fuson, *Juan Ponce de León,* 114–19. Contrast with the relatively strong emphasis on the fountain of youth legend presented in Devereux, *Juan Ponce de León.*

40. Personal communication, December 9, 1981, by Hubert W. Carcaba in the Fountain of Youth vertical files, St. Augustine Historical Society, St. Augustine, Fla. See also Thomas Graham, "St. Augustine Historical Society, 1883–1983," *Florida Historical Quarterly* 64 (July 1985): 1–31.

Contributors

Nicholas M. Beasley is a doctoral candidate in history at Vanderbilt University. He previously earned an M.Div. at Yale Divinity School, a diploma in Anglican studies from Berkeley Divinity School, and a B.A. from the University of the South (Sewanee). He won the Ellen Davies Rodgers Prize in History at Sewanee and is a Fellow of the Episcopal Church Foundation. His dissertation, "Christian Liturgy and Social Power in British Plantation Colonies, 1640–1760," is supported by a dissertation fellowship from Vanderbilt's Center for the Americas.

Margaret Cormack is associate professor of religious studies at the College of Charleston. She has published *The Saints in Iceland: Their Veneration from the Conversion to 1400* and edited a collection of essays entitled *Sacrificing the Self: Perspectives on Martyrdom and Religion.* She is currently extending her study of the cult of saints in Iceland through the Reformation and creating an online database that will make the data accessible. See http://www/tasc.mpg.de/iceland (accessed August 3, 2006).

John Corrigan is Edwin Scott Gaustad Professor of Religion, professor of history, and director of the Institute for the Study of Emotion at Florida State University. He is coeditor of *Church History* and has published widely in the field of American religious history. His recent publications include *Religion and Emotion: Approaches and Interpretations* and *Business of the Heart: Religion and Emotion in the Nineteenth Century.* He is a coauthor of a Web site of French and Spanish missions in colonial America, http://www.ecai.org/na-missions/index/html (accessed August 3, 2006).

Giovanna Fiume is professor of modern history in the Faculty of Political Science at the University of Palermo, Sicily. Untill 2005 she was the editor in chief of *Genesis,* the magazine of the Società Italiana delle Storiche (Italian Society of Women Historians), and she is on the editorial boards of the journals *Quaderni storici* and *Incontri Mediterranei.* She has edited "Il santo e la città: Devozioni, culti, strategie di età moderna; La schiavitù nel Mediterraneo," a special issue of *Quaderni storici* 107 (2001), and is the author of *La crisi sociale del 1848 in Sicilia; Bande armate in Sicilia: Violenza e organizzazione del potere (1818–1849);*

La vecchia dell'aceto: Un processo per veneficio nella Palermo di fine Settecento; and *Il santo Moro: I processi di canonizzazione di Benedetto da Palermo (1595–1807).*

Tessa Garton is professor of art history at the College of Charleston. She received a B.A. Honours in art history in 1969 from the University of East Anglia, Norwich, U.K., and a Ph.D. in art history from the Courtauld Institute, University of London, in 1974. She has taught at Trinity College, Dublin, at the University of Aberdeen, Scotland, and since 1988 at the College of Charleston. Her main area of interest is in Romanesque art, particularly sculpture, and she has studied regional styles and developments in southern Italy, Britain, and Ireland. She has published articles on Romanesque sculpture in Italy, Scotland, and Ireland. Since 1987 she has been researching and preparing catalog entries for the "Corpus of Romanesque Sculpture in Britain and Ireland," online at http://www.crsbi.ac.uk (accessed August 3, 2006) and on CD-ROM.

Patrick J. Hayes is assistant professor of theology at St. John's University, Staten Island Campus. After completing his doctorate on Catholic intellectual life at the Catholic University of America in 2003, he has turned his attention to more popular expressions of Catholic identity and is presently at work on a book on nineteenth-century American Catholic miracle stories. He is the author of several essays, articles, and book reviews in the fields of Catholic studies, ecclesiology, and ethics.

Michael Pasquier graduated from Louisiana State University in 2002. He is currently a doctoral candidate in the Department of Religion at Florida State University. His paper in this volume is based on his 2001 undergraduate honors thesis.

Rodger Payne is chairman of the Department of Philosophy and Religious Studies at Louisiana State University. His current research involves popular Catholic devotionalism in southern Louisiana, and he serves as editor of the online *Journal of Southern Religion* (http://jsh.rice.edu [accessed August 3, 2006]). He has published *The Self and the Sacred: Conversion and Autobiography in Early American Protestantism.*

Juan Javier Pescador is assistant professor in the Department of History at Michigan State University. He has published *The New World inside a Basque Village: The Oiartzun Valley and Its Atlantic Immigrants, 1550–1800* and is a coauthor of *The Early History of Greater Mexico.*

Robert E. Scully, S.J., is associate professor of history and law at Le Moyne College in Syracuse, New York. He received a licentiate in sacred theology from the Jesuit School of Theology at Berkeley and the University of California at Berkeley (1996) and also holds the degree of J.D. in legal and constitutional history from Seton Hall University School of Law. His major publications include "In the Confident Hope of a Miracle: The Spanish Armada and Religious Mentalities in the Late Sixteenth Century," *Catholic Historical Review* 89 (2003): 643–70; and "The Unmaking of a Saint: Thomas Becket and the English Reformation," *Catholic Historical Review* 86 (2000): 579–602. He is currently working on a monograph entitled "Into the Lion's Den: The Jesuit Mission in Elizabethan England and Wales, 1580–1603."

Ryan K. Smith is assistant professor of history at Virginia Commonwealth University. He earned his undergraduate degree at Stetson University at the time that he worked for the Fountain of Youth. He then earned M.A. and Ph.D. degrees in American history at the College of William and Mary and the University of Delaware, respectively. His articles have appeared in *Church History* and *El Escribano,* and his book *Gothic Arches, Latin Crosses: Anti-Catholicism and American Church Designs in the Nineteenth Century* was published in 2006.

Robert Westerfelhaus is assistant professor in the Department of Communication of the College of Charleston. He received his B.A. from Ohio Dominican University and his M.A. and Ph.D. degrees from Ohio University. Professor Westerfelhaus applies rhetorical and semiotic theories to communication issues related to culture, ethics, religion, and human sexuality. He has published articles in *Critical Studies in Media Communication, Communication Quarterly,* and the *Journal of Communication Inquiry* and has contributed chapters to textbooks including *Critical Approaches to Television* (2nd ed.) and *Communicating Ethnic and Cultural Identity.*

Index

The Icelandic letter ð is alphabetized after d *and* Þ *after* z.

www.ingramcontent.com/pod-product-compliance
Lightning Source LLC
LaVergne TN
LVHW050149080826
844660LV00002B/134

* 9 7 8 1 5 7 0 0 3 6 3 0 9 *